GERMAN TODAY 1

GERMAN TODAY 1

FOURTH EDITION

Jack Moeller
Helmut Liedloff
Clifford J. Kent

HOUGHTON MIFFLIN COMPANY **Boston**

Atlanta   Dallas   Geneva, Illinois   Palo Alto   Princeton   Toronto

About the Authors

Jack Moeller, senior author of the series, is Professor of German at Oakland University in Rochester, Michigan. Professor Moeller has taught at both private and public high schools in the United States and Germany. He is a co-author of *Deutsch heute: Grundstufe, Blickpunkt Deutschland, Kaleidoskop, Ohne Mühe!, Noch dazu!* (Houghton Mifflin), and of several other texts.

Helmut Liedloff is Professor of German at Southern Illinois University in Carbondale, Illinois. A native of Bremen, Germany, he has taught at the secondary school and university levels in Germany and at a number of colleges in the United States. He is a co-author of *Deutsch heute: Grundstufe, Kaleidoskop,* and *Ohne Mühe!* (Houghton Mifflin) and is a contributor to numerous professional journals.

Clifford J. Kent is Supervisor of Foreign Languages for the Beverly Public Schools in Massachusetts, where he has helped develop exchange programs between Beverly High School and schools in Cologne and Nuremberg. He has taught German at the junior high, high school, and college levels, as well as to adults, and he participated in an NDEA summer institute at Hofstra University.

WORKBOOK/LAB MANUAL: Sonia Schweid Reizes was formerly Assistant Program Administrator and taught German, French, and Spanish in the Bedford Public Schools, Bedford, Massachusetts. She currently teaches German at Middlesex Community College.

CASSETTE PROGRAM
LISTENING COMPREHENSION EXERCISES: Sonia Schweid Reizes

TESTING PROGRAM: Clifford J. Kent, Constance E. Putnam
Constance E. Putnam taught German and Latin at John Marshall High School and at The Catlin Gabel School in Portland, Oregon. She also lived in Germany for several years and taught at the *Gymnasium* in Duderstadt and the *Pädagogische Hochschule* in Hildesheim.

Cover photograph copyright © J. Messerschmidt from Bruce Coleman, Inc.

Art credits follow the Index.

Printed in the U.S.A.
Student's Edition ISBN: 0-395-47122-2
Teacher's Edition ISBN: 0-395-47146-X

ABCDEFGHIJ-D-9543210-898

Contents

ix

German Around You

As you begin to learn German, you will discover that you know more about the language than you think you do.

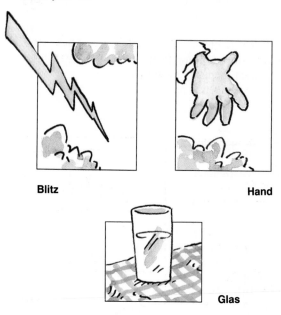

Blitz

Hand

Glas

You can probably guess the meanings of the German words illustrated on this page, because they resemble English words. Words that are related in spelling and meaning and are derived from the same source language are called **cognates.** There are hundreds of German-English cognates.

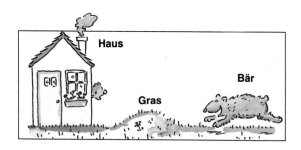

Haus

Bär

Gras

The German language and culture have been present in the United States since the colonial days. German settlers fought in the Revolutionary War, and they continued to play an important role as their adopted country grew and prospered. The names of many towns and cities reflect the German

Kaufmann

Koch

Schuhmacher

origin of their founders. Towns like Berlin, Hamburg, Bremen, and Vienna all have counterparts in one of the German-speaking countries. You probably know many families with German names. As in English, the name often refers to the occupation of the person's ancestors.

Over the years, German immigrants have contributed to several areas of American life.

City

Kindergarten

Look around you and you'll find that cognates, borrowed words, and German names have given you a head start in learning German.

The exchange in culture and language has gone the other way, too. Speakers of German have borrowed many English words that are now part of the German language.

Oh Tannenbaum

Rucksack

Make-up   **Computer**

Harmonika

Gesundheit!

Fan

Bretzel

Maus

Acknowledgments

The authors and publisher would like to thank the following foreign language educators for their observations and suggestions during the development of this text. Their input has proved valuable in the creation of the Fourth Edition of *German Today.*

Petra Bailey, Westwood High School, Mesa, Arizona
Robert Bordwell, Mountain View High School, Mesa, Arizona
James Brandenburg, John Marshall High School, San Antonio, Texas
Jan Bungarz, Southwest High School, Fort Worth, Texas
Gayle Cope, W. T. White High School, Dallas, Texas
Idy Fischler, Penncrest High School, Media, Pennsylvania
Judith Fullerton, Corona Del Sol High School and Tempe High School, Tempe, Arizona
Peter Glaser, Dunbar High School, Fort Worth, Texas
Elsbeth Glocker, Marcos De Niza High School, Tempe, Arizona
Georgiana Graf, Sentinel High School, Missoula, Montana
Walter Graf, Big Sky High School, Missoula, Montana
Rosalind Hudgens, Hellgate High School, Missoula, Montana
Carol June, Newburyport, Massachusetts
Ann Layton, Chandler Junior High School and Willis Junior High School, Chandler, Arizona
Rosalie Maher, Chandler Senior High School, Chandler, Arizona
Elisabeth Mroczek-Pruett, Indianapolis, Indiana
Ursula Schuster, Upper Merion High School, Norristown, Pennsylvania
Betty Schiele, Dobson High School, Mesa, Arizona
Georg F. Steinmeyer, Amherst Regional Junior and Senior High School, Amherst, Massachusetts
Marlies Stueart, Wellesley High School, Wellesley, Massachusetts
Kendall Weeks, Chippewa Valley High School, Mount Clemens, Michigan
Keith Williams, Skyline High School, Dallas, Texas

Europa

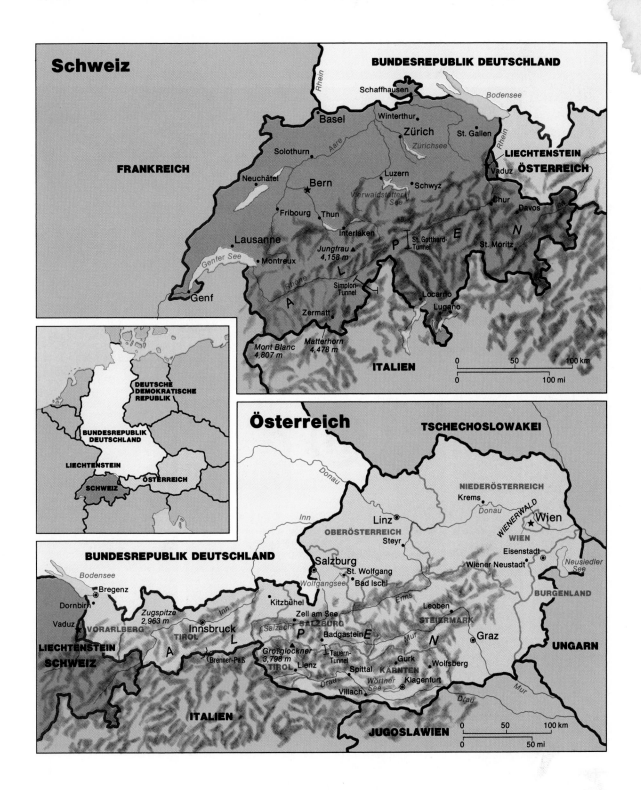

Schweiz

FRANKREICH

BUNDESREPUBLIK DEUTSCHLAND

Schaffhausen
Bodensee
Basel
Winterthur
Zürich
St. Gallen
Zürichsee
Solothurn
LIECHTENSTEIN
Vaduz
ÖSTERREICH
Neuchâtel
Bern
Luzern
Schwyz
Chur
Vierwaldstätter See
Davos
Fribourg
Thun
Interlaken
St. Gotthard-Tunnel
N
Lausanne
E
P
St. Moritz
Jungfrau
4,158 m
L
Montreux
Simplon-Tunnel
Locarno
Genfer See
Rhone
A
Lugano
Genf
Zermatt
Mont Blanc
4,807 m
Matterhorn
4,478 m
ITALIEN

Rhein
Aare

0   50   100 km
0   100 mi

DEUTSCHE
DEMOKRATISCHE
REPUBLIK

BUNDESREPUBLIK
DEUTSCHLAND

LIECHTENSTEIN

ÖSTERREICH

SCHWEIZ

Österreich

TSCHECHOSLOWAKEI

Donau
NIEDERÖSTERREICH
Krems
Donau
WIENERWALD
Wien
Inn
Linz
WIEN
OBERÖSTERREICH
Steyr
Eisenstadt

BUNDESREPUBLIK DEUTSCHLAND
Salzburg
St. Wolfgang
Wolfgangsee
Bad Ischl
Wiener Neustadt
Neusiedler See
Bodensee
Bregenz
Ems
Leoben
BURGENLAND
Dornbirn
Zugspitze
2,963 m
Inn
Kitzbühel
Zell am See
STEIERMARK
Vaduz
VORARLBERG
Salzach
SALZBURG
Graz
Innsbruck
L
Badgastein
E
Mur
UNGARN
LIECHTENSTEIN
TIROL
A
P
N
Großglockner
3,796 m
Tauern-Tunnel
Gurk
Wolfsberg
SCHWEIZ
Brenner-Paß
Lienz
Spittal
KÄRNTEN
Klagenfurt
TIROL
Drau
Wörther See
Mur
Villach
ITALIEN
Drau
JUGOSLAWIEN

0   50   100 km
0   50 mi

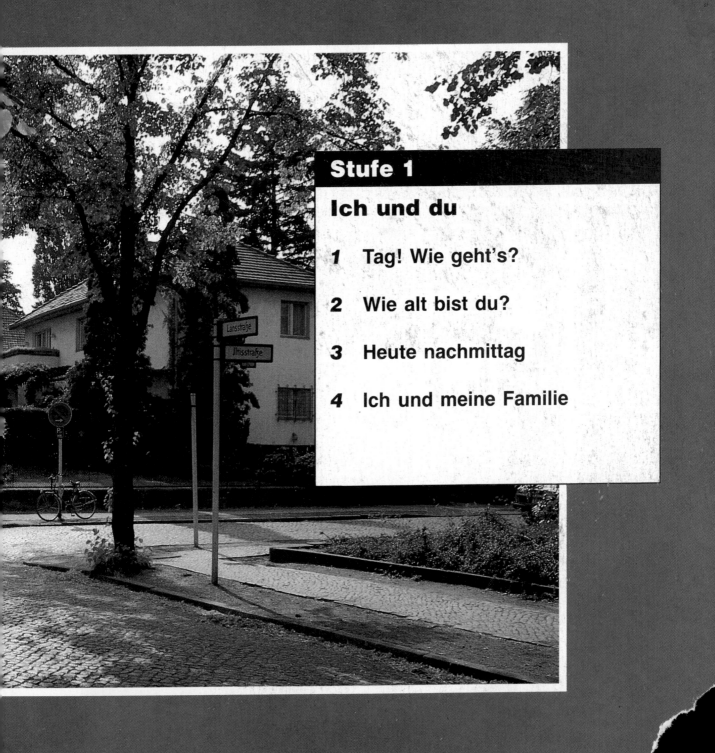

Stufe 1

Ich und du

Kapitel 1

Tag! Wie geht's?

A fountain in Ulm, a meeting place for young people

Wie heißt du?

Ute Braun lives in Bonn. She meets a new girl at school and discovers they have something in common.

UTE BRAUN	Wie heißt du?
UTE SCHMIDT	Ute.
UTE BRAUN	Toll! Ich heiße auch Ute.
UTE SCHMIDT	Wirklich?

Du hast das Wort

The material in this section gives you the opportunity to talk about your personal feelings and experiences. Substitute your own words for those in brackets. New vocabulary is indicated by a raised degree mark (°). You will find a complete vocabulary list at the end of each chapter.

1. **Wie heißt du?** Choose a German name for yourself from the list in the Appendix. Walk around the class asking your classmates their names, following the model:

   Getting acquainted

DU (YOU)	GESPRÄCHSPARTNER/IN (CONVERSATION PARTNER)
Wie heißt du?	[Monika].
Ich heiße [Barbara].	

2. **Ja oder nein?** (Yes or no?) It is difficult to remember the names of many new people in a class or at a party. See how well you do with the German names (or real names) of your classmates. If you're wrong, your classmates will correct you.

DU	GESPRÄCHSPARTNER/IN
Heißt du [Mark]?	Ja°.
Du heißt [Gerd], nicht°?	Nein°, ich heiße [Martin].

„Hallo, Franz! Ich heiße Beta 1 und bin der Neue."

„Deine elegante Technik hat mir spontan gefallen."

Grundig Beta 1. Der Luxus Akku-Netz-Rasierer mit der patentierten Scherkopf-Form. Nur im Fachgeschäft, wo Beratung und Service stimmen.

GRUNDIG
Es lebe die Leistung

Tag! Wie geht's?

Ingrid runs into some friends and asks them how they are.

INGRID	Tag, Gisela. Wie geht's?
GISELA	Hallo, Ingrid.
INGRID	Tag, Dieter. Wie geht's?
DIETER	Schlecht.
INGRID	Was ist denn los?
DIETER	Ich bin krank.
INGRID	Das tut mir leid.

Du hast das Wort

1. **Wie geht's?** A classmate asks how you are. How would you respond?   **Asking how people are**

GESPRÄCHSPARTNER/IN

Hallo, [Tanja]. Wie geht's?

DU

Danke°, gut°.
Prima°!
Sehr° gut.
Nicht° schlecht.
Ganz° gut.
Danke, es geht°.

2. **Was ist los?** At the beginning of class you ask several classmates how they are. They respond that they are not doing well. Ask them what is wrong.

DU

Hallo, [Dieter]. Wie geht's?
Was ist los?

GESPRÄCHSPARTNER/IN

Schlecht.
Ich bin sehr müde°.
Ich bin kaputt°.
Ich bin krank.

3. **Wie geht's?** Pretend you haven't seen several classmates or your teacher for a few days. Get up, greet them, and ask how they are.

Tag, Peter.
Tag, Frau° [Weiß]. | Wie geht's?
    Herr° [Braun] |

Sind Sie wieder gesund?

Ute sees Frau Weiß and wants to know whether she is feeling better.

UTE   Guten Tag, Frau Weiß. Wie geht's?
FRAU WEISS   Guten Tag, Ute. Es geht wieder.
UTE   Sind Sie wieder gesund?
FRAU WEISS   Ja, ich bin nur sehr müde.

Land und Leute

An important characteristic of German is the use of "flavoring" words like **denn** to express the speaker's attitude about an utterance. These flavoring words relate the utterance to something the speaker or the listener has already said or thought. Depending on the choice of the word and sometimes on the tone of voice, the speaker may express interest, surprise, impatience, and so on.

Denn, for example, is often used in questions. It gives a little extra emphasis to the question and implies that one is interested in the answer.

Was ist los?   What's the matter?
Was ist **denn**   Well, what *is* the
    los?   matter?

Was ist denn los? Ist er krank?

The meaning of flavoring words varies, depending on the context. With experience, you will gain a feeling for the meaning and use of these words in German.

Du hast das Wort

Sind Sie müde? Ask your teacher whether she/he is tired.

Asking how people are

Sind Sie müde, [Frau] Braun?
          [Herr] Braun

Bist du zufrieden?

Monika and Volker are discussing the results of their last test.

VOLKER   So, Monika, bist du zufrieden?
MONIKA   Ja, sehr. Du auch?
VOLKER   Nein, ich bin wirklich sauer.

Du hast das Wort

You are taking a poll to find out how many of your classmates are satisfied with their grades. Walk around, asking everyone and making a note of their answers.

Expressing satisfaction

DU

Bist du zufrieden?

GESPRÄCHSPARTNER/IN

Ja, sehr zufrieden.
Ja, ich bin glücklich°.
Nein, ich bin sauer.
Nein, gar nicht°.

Land und Leute

Frau is the official term of address for all women over 18 years of age. **Frau** can be used as the equivalent for Ms. Whereas **Frau** was once used only for married women and **Fräulein** for all unmarried women, **Fräulein** is used today mostly for girls under 18.

How would you address these women in German?

Warum ist Volker so sauer?

Frank asks Monika why Volker looks so gloomy.

FRANK   Wie geht es Volker?
MONIKA   Schlecht.
FRANK   Warum ist er so sauer?
MONIKA   Keine Ahnung°.

Du hast das Wort

1. A classmate asks you about one of your friends. Respond with one of the following sentences or make up your own.

   Asking about others

GESPRÄCHSPARTNER/IN	DU
Ist [Dieter] heute° faul°?	Ja, er ist sehr faul.
	Nein, er ist heute krank.
	Nein, er ist heute müde.
Ist [Gerda] zufrieden?	Ja, sie° ist sehr zufrieden.
	Ja, sie ist wirklich glücklich.
	Nein, sie ist nicht zufrieden.

2. Ask your teacher what her/his mood is today.
   Sind Sie [zufrieden, sauer, glücklich]?

Land und Leute

The 100 million speakers of German live in a number of countries, located mostly in Central Europe. The Federal Republic of Germany, or **Bundesrepublik Deutschland,** is the largest of the German-speaking countries. It is about the size of Oregon and has a population of 60 million. Its capital is Bonn. The GDR (German Democratic Republic, or **Deutsche Demokratische Republik**) is a little larger than Ohio and has a population of 17 million. Its capital is the eastern part of Berlin, which is called **Ost-Berlin** by the West but simply **Berlin** by the GDR. Both the Federal Republic and the GDR are modern, industrialized countries, with a high level of production in agriculture as well.

The landmark Brandenburger Tor in Berlin (East) and a view of Bonn and the Rhine River

Greetings and farewells

Hallo!
Guten Morgen!
Guten Tag!
Guten Abend!

Auf Wiedersehen!
Tschüß!
Bis später.
Guten Abend!
Gute Nacht!

Hallo is used to say hi or hello to an acquaintance.

Guten Morgen is used to say hello in the morning.

Guten Tag is used to say hello at any time during the day. **Tag** is an informal version of **Guten Tag.**

Guten Abend is used to say both hello and good-by during the evening.

Gute Nacht is used as a farewell late in the evening and at bedtime.

Auf Wiedersehen is used at any time of the day or night as an expression of farewell.

Tschüß is an informal farewell and is equivalent to *so long.*

Bis später is equivalent to *see you later.*

A. Hallo! Respond to each of the following greetings and farewells.

▶ Tag, [Ingrid]! *Tag, [Frank]!*

1. Guten Morgen!
2. Auf Wiedersehen!
3. Tschüß!
4. Bis später!
5. Guten Abend!
6. Gute Nacht!

B. Guten Tag! How would you greet a person at the following times?

1. 8:00 A.M.
2. 7:00 P.M.
3. 4:00 P.M.
4. 10:00 A.M.
5. 2:00 A.M.
6. 7:00 A.M.

Greetings and farewells may vary in the different German-speaking countries and even within one country. For instance, in southern Germany or in Austria one might hear **Grüß Gott**, **Grüß dich**, or **Servus**. In Switzerland one often hears **Grüetzi** or **Salut** (pronounced **Sálü**).

Auf Wiedersehen can be shortened to simply **Wiedersehen**. In some areas **Auf Wiederschauen**, **Adieu**, or **Ade** (pronounced **Adé**) are used to say good-by.

The resort town Wengen (near Bern, Switzerland) welcomes guests and visitors with *Grüss Gott.*

Du hast das Wort

Hallo, Ingrid! You and your classmates should stand in two concentric circles, facing each other.

Meeting and greeting people

1. Do you remember the German name of the person facing you? When your circle moves, ask the next person.

Du heißt Gerd, nicht?
                                Ja.
                                Nein, ich heiße Martin.

2. When you return to your original partner, greet her/him. When your circle moves again, greet the next person.

Morgen, [Ingrid]!   Tag, [Tanja]!
Wie geht's?   Gut, danke.
                                Schlecht.

3. Greet your original partner again. Ask her/him how she/he is. You get a grouchy answer. Shake hands, say good-by, and move on to your next partner.

Hallo, [Martin]. Wie geht's?   Schlecht.
Was ist los?   Ich bin sauer.
Tschüß, [Martin].   Bis später.

Descriptive adjectives

Gerda ist **gesund.**

Paul ist **krank.**

Jürgen ist **sauer.**

Heike ist **fleißig.**

Georg ist **faul.**

Martin ist **müde.**

Marco ist **glücklich.**

Petra ist **unglücklich.**

Isabel ist **zufrieden.**

C. Ich bin glücklich. Which adjective on page 11 describes best how you feel today? Your partner will try to find out which adjective you have chosen. Ask five more people.

GESPRÄCHSPARTNER/IN

Bist du heute [faul]?

DU

Nein, ich bin nicht [faul].
Ja, [sehr faul].
Nein, ich bin [nur müde].
Nein, [krank].
Unsinn°, ich bin [fleißig]!

D. Sie/er ist glücklich. You haven't asked everyone in the class how she/he is. Try to make a complete list of how everyone else is feeling without asking the person you are interested in directly.

DU

[Stefan], wie geht es [Ingrid]?

GESPRÄCHSPARTNER/IN

[Sie] ist [krank].

When you are finished, your teacher will ask you as a group to report on your findings.

LEHRER/IN (TEACHER)

Wie geht es [Stefan]?

KLASSE (CLASS)

Er ist [glücklich].

Aussprache

In the pronunciation sections of this text, special symbols in brackets are used to represent various German sounds. Each symbol represents only one sound. In written German, different letters or letter combinations may represent the same sound. Vowels are classified as long or short.

long vowel [i] prima, wie
short vowel [I] bin, nicht, Unsinn

A. Practice vertically in columns and horizontally in pairs.

[i]	[I]
Lied	litt
bieten	bitten
Ihnen	innen
Bienen	binnen
Kiepe	Kippe

Stille Wasser sind tief.

B. Practice the sounds [i] and [I]. Read the sentences aloud.

1. Ingrid ist wieder krank.
2. Unsinn. Sie ist nur müde.
3. Wie geht es Ilse?
4. Dieter ist müde.
5. Ich bin zufrieden.

Übungen

1. The subject pronouns **ich, du, Sie, er,** and **sie**

ich	I
du	you (familiar)
Sie	you (formal)
er	he
sie	she

The subject pronouns **ich, du, Sie, er,** and **sie** are equivalent to the English pronouns *I, you* (familiar), *you* (formal), *he,* and *she.*

The subject pronouns **du** and **Sie**

The German subject pronouns **du** and **Sie** are both equivalent to the English pronoun *you.*

Bist **du** müde, Inge?

Du is a familiar form of address and is used in addressing a relative, a close friend, and any person under about fifteen. Unlike the English word *you,* **du** can refer to only one person.

Sind **Sie** müde, Frau Braun?

Sie is a more formal form of address and is used in addressing strangers or adults whom the speaker does not know as close friends. Like the English word *you,* **Sie** can refer to one or more persons.

A.   Was sagt man? (What does one say?)   Give the subject pronouns you would use in the following situations.

▶   You're talking about your mother.   *sie*

1. You're talking to a male friend.
2. You're talking to your teacher.
3. You're talking about a female teacher.
4. You're talking about a male student.
5. You're talking about yourself.
6. You're talking to a female friend.
7. You're talking to a clerk in a store.
8. You're talking to your father.
9. You're talking to your brother.

2. Present tense of **sein**: singular forms

ich **bin**
du **bist**
Sie **sind**
er **ist**
sie **ist**

The forms of the verb **sein** *(to be)* vary according to the subject used.

Hans! **Bist du** müde?   Hans, *are you* tired?
Ja, **ich bin** müde.   Yes, *I'm* tired.

B. Was ist los? Your friends are trying to find out what's wrong with you. Answer their questions in the affirmative.

▶ Bist du müde?   *Ja, ich bin sehr müde.*

1. Bist du sauer?
2. Bist du faul?
3. Bist du zufrieden?

4. Bist du unglücklich?
5. Bist du kaputt?

C. Warum? Your friends tell you how they're feeling. Ask them why they're feeling that way.

▶ Ich bin glücklich.   *Warum bist du denn glücklich?*

1. Ich bin kaputt.
2. Ich bin müde.
3. Ich bin sauer.

4. Ich bin unglücklich.
5. Ich bin zufrieden.

Sie ist zufrieden.

Frau Braun, **sind Sie** zufrieden?
Ja, **ich bin** sehr zufrieden.

Ms. Braun, *are you* satisfied?
Yes, *I am* very satisfied.

D. Warum? Your teacher describes how she/he feels. Ask why she/he feels that way.

▶ Ich bin unglücklich.   *Warum sind Sie denn unglücklich?*

1. Ich bin sauer.
2. Ich bin müde.
3. Ich bin kaputt.

4. Ich bin krank.
5. Ich bin zufrieden.
6. Ich bin glücklich.

Sabine ist unglücklich. **Sie
ist** krank.
Robert ist unglücklich. **Er
ist** krank.

Sabine is unhappy. *She's* ill.

Robert is unhappy. *He's* ill.

E. Wieder gesund. There's been a flu epidemic at school, but it's over now. When Christa asks about various people, say they're well again.

▶ Wie geht es Stefan?   *Er ist wieder gesund.*

▶ Wie geht es Inge?   *Sie ist wieder gesund.*

1. Wie geht es Andrea?
2. Wie geht es Kurt?
3. Wie geht es Nicole?
4. Wie geht es Ilse?

5. Wie geht es Hans?
6. Wie geht es Georg?
7. Wie geht es Frau Braun?

F. Er ist fleißig. Form sentences using the cued subject pronouns and adjectives.

▶ er / fleißig   *Er ist fleißig.*

1. du / müde
2. ich / unglücklich
3. er / sauer
4. sie / krank
5. ich / glücklich
6. Sie / müde

7. du / faul
8. er / gesund
9. sie / glücklich
10. ich / zufrieden
11. Sie / fleißig

3. The negative word **nicht**

Ich bin **nicht** müde.   I'm *not* tired.
Ilse ist **nicht** faul.   Ilse is*n't* lazy.

Nicht is equivalent to English *not*.

G.   Wie geht's? Tanja wants to know how your friends and your teacher are feeling. Answer her questions in the negative.

▶ Wie geht es Udo? Ist er wieder müde?   *Nein, er ist nicht müde.*

1. Wie geht es Frank? Ist er wieder krank?
2. Wie geht es Inge? Ist sie wieder glücklich?
3. Wie geht es Barbara? Ist sie wieder sauer?
4. Wie geht es Walter? Ist er wieder müde?
5. Wie geht es Jens? Ist er wieder glücklich?
6. Wie geht es Heidi? Ist sie wieder sauer?
7. Wie geht es Ingrid? Ist sie wieder zufrieden?
8. Wie geht es Frau Braun? Ist sie wieder zufrieden?

Hallo, wie geht's?

The letters in parentheses following grammatical headings refer to the corresponding exercises in the **Übungen.**

The subject pronouns **ich, du, Sie, er, and sie** (A)

ich	I
du	you (familiar)
Sie	you (formal)
er	he
sie	she

The pronouns **ich, du, Sie, er,** and **sie** are equivalent to the English pronouns *I, you* (familiar), *you* (formal), *he,* and *she.* They are used as the subject of a sentence.

The subject pronouns **du** and **Sie**

Bist **du** glücklich, Frank?
Sind **Sie** müde, Herr Lange?

The pronouns **du** and **Sie** are both equivalent to the English *you.* The familiar form **du** is used to address a relative, a close friend, or a person under about fifteen. **Du** is also used frequently among members of a group such as students, athletes, workers, or soldiers. **Du** is used to address a single individual.

Sie is a more formal term of address. It is used in addressing strangers or adults whom the speaker does not consider close friends. **Sie** is used to address one or more individuals.

Often people agree to use **du** with each other once a relationship has become more familiar.

The subject pronouns **er** and **sie**

Ist **Stefan** krank?   Nein, **er** ist nur faul.
Ist **Ingrid** unglücklich?   Nein, **sie** ist glücklich.

When talking about people, the pronoun **er** is used to refer to a male; the pronoun **sie** is used to refer to a female.

An old wall is a nice place to chat with a friend.

The meanings and uses of **sie** and **Sie**

Ist **sie** krank?   Is *she* sick?
Sind **Sie** krank?   Are *you* sick?

In spoken German, the meanings of **sie** (*she*) and **Sie** (*you*) can be distinguished with the help of the corresponding verb form and the context.

sie + **ist** = she
Sie + **sind** = you

In written German, **Sie** (*you*) is always capitalized.

Present tense of **sein**: singular forms (B–F)

ich **bin**	I **am**
du **bist**	you **are**
Sie **sind**	you **are**
er **ist**	he **is**
sie **ist**	she **is**

Subjects and their verb forms must agree. The German verb **sein,** like the English verb *to be,* has different singular forms in the present tense.

The negative word **nicht** (G)

Ich bin **nicht** krank.
Christa ist **nicht** faul.

Nicht is equivalent to English *not.* The position of **nicht** in a sentence can vary. One common position is just before the element that is being negated (for example, **nicht krank**).

Notes about written German

1. All nouns are capitalized: **Morgen, Tag, Abend.**

2. The pronoun **ich** is not capitalized, unlike its English equivalent, *I.*

3. An apostrophe indicates the omission of the letter **e: Wie geht's? = Wie geht es?**

4. The letter **ß** is called an **Ess-tset** and replaces **ss:**
   a. at the end of a word: **Tschüß**
   b. before a consonant: **du mußt** = you must
   c. after a long vowel: **fleißig**

5. In addition to **ß,** the German alphabet has three other letters that the English alphabet doesn't have: **ä, ö,** and **ü,** called **Umlaut a, o,** and **u.** The symbol (¨) indicates that a vowel is umlauted.

Wiederholung

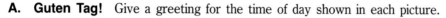

A. Guten Tag! Give a greeting for the time of day shown in each picture.

▶ *Guten Morgen!*

B. Was sagt man? Complete the sentences with the correct subject pronoun.

▶ _____ bin müde. *Ich*

1. _____ bin glücklich.
2. Bist _____ zufrieden?
3. Wie geht es Peter? Ist _____ krank?
4. Wie geht es Monika? Ist _____ wieder gesund?
5. Sind _____ unglücklich, Herr Braun?

C. Kurze Gespräche. (Short conversations.) Answer the questions after each dialogue.

INGRID Wie geht es Frank?
DIETER Er ist glücklich.
INGRID Warum?
DIETER Er ist wieder gesund.

MONIKA Wie geht es Gerda?
JÜRGEN Ganz gut.
MONIKA Ist sie nicht wieder krank?
JÜRGEN Nein. Sie ist nur faul.

1. Wie geht es Frank?
2. Warum ist er glücklich?

1. Wie geht es Gerda?
2. Ist sie krank?

D. Wie sagt man das? (How does one say that?) Express the following in German.

1. Hi, how are you?
   I'm exhausted.
2. What's the matter?
   Why are you unhappy?
3. I'm sick again.
   You're not sick, you're just lazy.
4. So long!
   See you later!

E. Wie sagt man das? Mr. Schmidt, a teacher, has a chat with his colleague, Ms. Meier. Express it in German.

HERR S. Good morning, how are you?
FRAU M. Not good.
HERR S. Why? What's the matter? Are you sick? Are you annoyed?
FRAU M. No, I'm just very tired. I'm completely exhausted.

F. Schreib es auf! (Write it down.)

1. Write your neighbor, asking how she/he is doing today. Pass the note.
2. Answer the note you receive. Say whether you are having a good day.
3. When you get the answer back, if your neighbor is having a bad day ask her/him why or what's wrong. If she/he is having a good day, ask why. Then send the note back.

G. Land und Leute.

1. How many people speak German? Do all of those people live in the Federal Republic of Germany? What is the population of the Federal Republic? What is the German name for the German Democratic Republic? What is its population?
2. You are an American meeting a German for the first time. How are your ways of greeting each other likely to be different?

Vokabeln

Be sure you can recognize and use actively the following words and expressions before going on to Chapter 2.

Substantive (Nouns)

Der, das, *and* **die** *all mean* the. *The use of these articles will be practiced in Chapter 5.*
(die) Frau,-en   Mrs., Ms.; woman; wife
(der) Herr,-en   Mr.; gentleman

Verben (Verbs)

sein   to be
  ich bin   I am
  du bist   you are
  Sie sind   you are
  er/sie ist   he/she is

Andere Wörter (Other Words)

auch   also, too
danke   thanks, thank you
denn   *flavoring word often used in questions*
du   you *(familiar singular)*
er   he
es   it
faul   lazy
fleißig   industrious, diligent
ganz   quite; complete(ly)
gesund   healthy, well
glücklich   happy
gut   good
hallo   hello
heute   today
ich   I
ja   yes
kaputt   exhausted; broken, out of order
krank   ill, sick
müde   tired
nein   no
nicht   not
nur   only, just
prima   excellent, fine, great

Andere Wörter (cont.)

sauer   cross, annoyed; sour
schlecht   bad
sehr   very
sie   she
Sie   you *(formal)*
so   so
toll!   great, fantastic
und   and
unglücklich   unhappy
warum   why
was   what
wie   how
wieder   again
wirklich   really
zufrieden   content

Besondere Ausdrücke (Special Expressions)

wie heißt du?   what's your name?
ich heiße . . .   my name is . . .
was ist (denn) los?   (well,) what's the matter?
das tut mir leid   I'm sorry
wie geht's?   how are you (doing)?
es geht   OK, can't complain
ganz gut   OK, pretty well
keine Ahnung   (I have) no idea
Unsinn!   nonsense!
gar nicht   not at all
guten Abend!   good evening!
guten Morgen!   good morning!
gute Nacht!   good night!
guten Tag!   hello!, hi!; **Tag** hi!
auf Wiedersehen   good-by
tschüß!   so long!
bis später   till later, see you later
nicht?   isn't that so? *(at the end of a sentence)*

Kapitel 2

Wie alt bist du?

Zum Geburtstag gibt es viele Geschenke.

Jung oder alt?

Michael and his friends live in Vienna. Michael's birthday party prompts Heike and Dirk to compare ages.

HEIKE   Wie alt ist Michael?
DIRK   Sechzehn.
HEIKE   Und du?
DIRK   Auch sechzehn. Wir sind beide sechzehn.
HEIKE   Seid ihr *wirklich* sechzehn?
DIRK   Ja. Warum?
HEIKE   Ihr seid so jung.
DIRK   Wie alt bist *du* denn?
HEIKE   Schon siebzehn.
DIRK   Das ist aber sehr alt.

Fragen

1. Wie alt ist Michael?
2. Wie alt ist Dirk?
3. Wer° ist siebzehn?
4. Ist Heike alt oder jung?

Du hast das Wort

1. **Wie alt bist du?**   You want to find out who in the class is already 15, 16, or 17 years old.

DU
Bist du schon [fünfzehn]?

GESPRÄCHSPARTNER/IN
Ja.
Ja, du auch, nicht?
Nein.
[Fünfzehn]? Ich bin schon [sechzehn].

2. **Ja oder nein?**   Find someone in the class whose age you know. Other pairs will try to guess your ages.

GESPRÄCHSPARTNER/IN
Ihr seid beide sechzehn, nicht?

DU
Ja.
Nein. Wir sind beide [fünfzehn].
Nein. [Petra] ist erst° fünfzehn und ich bin sechzehn.
Ich bin sechzehn. [Mark] ist schon siebzehn.

Wann hast du Geburtstag?

Petra finds she was mistaken about her friends' birthdays.

PETRA   Ich habe im März Geburtstag. Du auch, oder?
DIRK   Nein.
PETRA   Wann hast du denn Geburtstag?
DIRK   Im April.
PETRA   Ach so. Hat Gerd nicht auch im April Geburtstag?
DIRK   Nein, erst im Mai.
PETRA   Ach ja, richtig.

Richtig oder falsch?

1. Petra hat im März Geburtstag.
2. Dirk hat auch im März Geburtstag.
3. Petra und Gerd haben im April Geburtstag.

Viel Spaß und Freude am Geburtstag...

Land und Leute

In German-speaking countries birthdays are celebrated in different ways. The "birthday child" **(Geburtstagskind)** may have an afternoon coffee party **(Geburtstagskaffee)** with family members and friends or a more extensive birthday party in the evening. At the **Geburtstagskaffee** candles are placed around the edge of a birthday cake **(Geburtstagskuchen)** and blown out by the person who has the birthday. Although the **Geburtstagskind** is often taken out by family members or friends, he or she usually invites friends to a party or brings a cake to work. Besides giving presents **(Geburtstagsgeschenke)** it is common to send a birthday card. Common greetings are: **Herzlichen Glückwunsch zum Geburtstag!** (Happy birthday!) or **Alles Gute zum Geburtstag!** (All the best on your birthday!)

Have a good time on your birthday . . .

Land und Leute

Austria **(Republik Österreich)**, with 7.5 million people, is the third largest of the German-speaking countries. It has interesting cities — **Wien** (Vienna) and **Salzburg** — as well as dramatic landscapes — the Alps, lakes, and forests.

Vienna, the capital, offers a great variety of cultural events and historical sights. Its theaters and philharmonic orchestra are world-class. Famous composers who lived in Vienna include **Wolfgang Amadeus Mozart, Ludwig van Beethoven, Franz Schubert,** and **Johann Strauß.** Two well-loved pastimes in Vienna are going to the **Prater** (an amusement park) and to coffeehouses **(Kaffeehäuser),** where one can read a newspaper, play chess, and drink a **Mélange** (special Viennese coffee made with hot milk) or a **Kaffee mit Schlag** (coffee with whipped cream).

Many visitors see Vienna from a carriage *(Fiaker).*

Wortschatzerweiterung

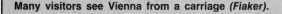

Zahlen: 0–19

0 null	5 fünf	10 zehn	15 fünfzehn
1 eins	6 sechs	11 elf	16 sechzehn
2 zwei	7 sieben	12 zwölf	17 siebzehn
3 drei	8 acht	13 dreizehn	18 achtzehn
4 vier	9 neun	14 vierzehn	19 neunzehn

Sechzehn loses the final **-s** of **sechs. Siebzehn** loses the final **-en** of **sieben.**

A. Wie alt bist du? Ask a classmate how old she/he is.

B. Deine Telefonnummer. (Your telephone number.) Give your telephone number to a classmate.

Wieviel° ist eins und zwei?
Eins und zwei ist drei.

Wieviel ist sieben weniger zwei?
Sieben weniger zwei ist fünf.

Wieviel ist sechs mal drei?
Sechs mal drei ist achtzehn.

Wieviel ist zwölf durch vier?
Zwölf durch vier ist drei.

C. Wieviel? Do the following arithmetic problems with a classmate.

▶ 1 + 3 = ?   *Wieviel ist eins und drei?*
                   Eins und drei ist vier.

1. 3 + 7 = ?   3. 4 + 13 = ?
2. 2 + 9 = ?   4. 1 + 18 = ?

▶ 10 − 7 = ?   *Wieviel ist zehn weniger sieben?*
                   Zehn weniger sieben ist drei.

5. 18 − 12 = ?   7. 17 − 13 = ?
6. 12 − 5 = ?   8. 18 − 1 = ?

▶ 5 × 3 = ?   *Wieviel ist fünf mal drei?*
                   Fünf mal drei ist fünfzehn.

9. 4 × 3 = ?   11. 6 × 3 = ?
10. 8 × 2 = ?   12. 5 × 2 = ?

▶ 10 ÷ 2 = ?   *Wieviel ist zehn durch zwei?*
                   Zehn durch zwei ist fünf.

13. 15 ÷ 3 = ?   15. 9 ÷ 3 = ?
14. 18 ÷ 6 = ?   16. 14 ÷ 7 = ?

Monate

Januar	April	Juli	Oktober
Februar	Mai	August	November
März	Juni	September	Dezember

Wie alt sind sie?

D. Wann hast du Geburtstag? Ask a classmate when her/his birthday is.

▶ Wann hast du Geburtstag?   *Im [Mai].*

E. Geburtstage. Take a poll of your classmates to find out how many birthdays there are in each month. Write the total on the board.

▶ Wer hat im [Januar] Geburtstag?

Aussprache

long vowel [e]   Eva, See, geht
short vowel [ɛ]   es, denn, Männer

A. Practice vertically in columns and horizontally in pairs.

[e]	[ɛ]
Beet	Bett
den	denn
wen	wenn
stehlen	stellen
fehlen	fällen

Reden ist Silber,
Schweigen ist Gold.

B. Practice the following words horizontally in pairs.

[i]	[I]	[e]	[ɛ]
bieten	bitten	beten	Betten
stiehlt	stillt	stehlt	stellt
Wiesen	Wissen	Wesen	wessen
vieler	Filter	fehle	Felle
wiegen	wickeln	Wege	wecken

C. Practice the sounds [e] and [ɛ]. Read the sentences aloud.

1. Was ist denn los, Eva?
2. Petra hat im Dezember Geburtstag.
3. Detlev Keller ist sechzehn.

Übungen

1. The subject pronouns **wir, ihr, Sie,** and **sie**

wir	we
ihr	you (familiar)
Sie	you (formal)
sie	they

The subject pronouns **wir, ihr, Sie,** and **sie** are equivalent to the English pronouns *we, you* (familiar plural), *you* (formal, singular and plural), and *they.*

The familiar form **ihr** is plural. It is used to address more than one relative, close friend, or person under about fifteen.

The formal form **Sie** can refer to one or more persons.

A. Was sagt man? (What does one say?) Give the subject pronouns you would use in the following situations.

1. You're talking to two friends.
2. You're talking about your teachers.
3. You're talking about yourself and a friend.
4. You're talking about Erik and Ingrid.
5. You're talking to your parents.
6. You're talking to Mr. and Mrs. Weiß.
7. You're talking to two adults.

Schüler sagen immer „du". (*Students always say* du.) (*München*)

2. Present tense of sein: plural forms

wir sind
ihr seid
Sie sind
sie sind

Hans und Inge, **seid ihr** müde?	Hans and Inge, *are you* tired?
Ja, **wir sind** sehr müde.	Yes, *we're* very tired.

B. Ja, wirklich. Beate expresses doubt about how you and your friend feel. Tell her you really feel that way.

▶ Seid ihr wirklich glücklich? *Ja, wir sind sehr glücklich.*

1. Seid ihr wirklich müde?
2. Seid ihr wirklich kaputt?

3. Seid ihr wirklich zufrieden?
4. Seid ihr wirklich sauer?

C. Wirklich? Ask whether Dieter and Gisela really mean what they say.

▶ Wir sind müde. *Seid ihr wirklich müde?*

1. Wir sind sauer.
2. Wir sind krank.

3. Wir sind zufrieden.
4. Wir sind kaputt.

Herr Schmidt, **sind Sie** müde?	Mr. Schmidt, *are you* tired?
Nein, **ich bin** nicht müde.	No, *I am* not tired.

D. Wirklich? Your teacher doesn't seem to feel well. Ask whether she/he really feels the way she/he says.

▶ Ich bin krank. *Sind Sie wirklich krank?*

1. Ich bin müde.
2. Ich bin unglücklich.

3. Ich bin kaputt.
4. Ich bin sauer.

Alex und Tanja sind sauer.	*Alex and Tanja are* in a bad mood.
Sie sind sehr müde.	*They're* very tired.

E. Nicht so alt. Jan always thinks people are a year older than they really are. Correct him, as in the model.

▶ Andrea und Erik sind siebzehn, nicht? *Nein, sie sind erst sechzehn.*

1. Hans and Ursel sind vierzehn, nicht?
2. Eva und Monika sind sechzehn, nicht?
3. Helmut und Uwe sind achtzehn, nicht?
4. Silke und Lutz sind fünfzehn, nicht?

3. The pronouns **sie** (singular) and **sie** (plural)

Ist **Birgit** müde? Ja, **sie** ist sehr müde.
Sind **Eva und Jan** glücklich? Ja, **sie** sind sehr glücklich.

F. Ja, sehr. You and Gabi are discussing mutual acquaintances. Confirm what Gabi asks. Use either **sie** *(sg.)* or **sie** *(pl.)* as required by the question.

▶ Brigitte ist krank, nicht? *Ja, sie ist sehr krank.*

▶ Trudi und Otto sind glücklich, nicht? *Ja, sie sind sehr glücklich.*

1. Ursel ist sauer, nicht?
2. Marianne ist zufrieden, nicht?
3. Inge und Thomas sind unglücklich, nicht?
4. Michael und Wolf sind fleißig, nicht?
5. Heidi ist krank, nicht?

G. Sag das! (Say that.) Form sentences using the cued subjects and adjectives.

▶ wir / müde   *Wir sind müde.*

1. ich / krank
2. Thomas und Ilse / sauer
3. ihr / fleißig
4. sie *(pl.)* / unglücklich
5. wir / glücklich
6. Sie / toll
7. Frank / alt
8. du / faul
9. sie *(sg.)* / jung
10. Sie / gesund

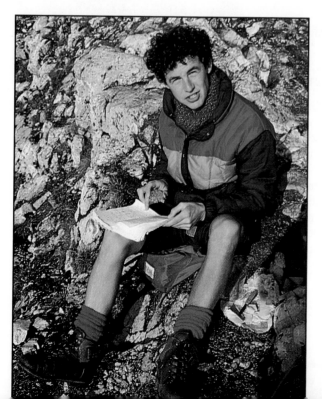

This hiker in the Austrian Alps records the day's events in a log.

4. Present tense of **haben**

ich **habe**		wir **haben**
du **hast**	Sie **haben**	ihr **habt**
er/sie **hat**		sie **haben**

H. Geburtstage. Frank and his friends are comparing birthdays. Say that the people mentioned were born in the same month as their friends.

▶ Du hast im März Geburts- *Jens hat auch im März Geburtstag.*
  tag. (Jens)

1. Petra hat im Juni Geburtstag. (ich)
2. Wir haben im Februar Geburtstag. (Karin und Urs)
3. Jürgen hat im Mai Geburtstag. (ihr)
4. Ulrike und Thomas haben im September Geburtstag. (wir)
5. Anke hat im März Geburtstag. (du)
6. Ich habe im November Geburtstag. (Ellen)
7. Ich habe im Januar Geburtstag. (Sie)

I. Wann haben sie Geburtstag? Kathrin and her hockey team are talking about their birthdays. Complete their conversation with the correct form of **haben.**

▶ Gabi *hat* im Februar Geburtstag.

1. Wann _____ du Geburtstag, Conny?
2. Ich _____ im Januar Geburtstag.
3. Stefanie und Karola, wann _____ ihr Geburtstag?
4. Wir _____ im Mai Geburtstag.
5. Wer _____ im Dezember Geburtstag?
6. Kathrin und Evelyn _____ im Dezember Geburtstag.
7. Wann _____ Sie Geburtstag, Herr Meyer?

5. Specific questions

Wie alt bist du? ↘	Sechzehn.
Wann hast du Geburtstag? ↘	Im Dezember.
Warum bist du so faul? ↘	Ich bin müde.
Wer hat im Mai Geburtstag? ↘	Christine.
Wieviel ist sechs und sieben? ↘	Dreizehn.

Specific questions begin with interrogatives such as **wie, wann, warum, wer,** or **wieviel,** and require specific answers to supply the desired information. The voice normally falls at the end of a specific question.

Eine Geburtstagsparty. —
Wie alt ist das
Geburtstagskind?

J. Wie bitte? (I beg your pardon?) At a crowded party, you can't hear everything Udo is saying. Ask questions to get the desired information.

▶ Jan ist *vierzehn*.   *Wie alt ist Jan?*

▶ Das ist *Ingrid Schmidt*.   *Wer ist das?*

1. Das ist *Jens Wagner*.
2. *Frank* hat im Mai Geburtstag.
3. Christa ist *siebzehn*.
4. Monika ist erst *zwölf*.
5. Es geht Inge *gut*.
6. Es geht Ralf *schlecht*.
7. Thomas hat *im Januar* Geburtstag.
8. Paula hat auch *im Januar* Geburtstag.

6. General questions

Bist du fünfzehn? ↗   **Ja.**
Ist Gerda auch fünfzehn? ↗   **Nein,** Gerda ist vierzehn.

General questions begin with a verb and require a **ja/nein**-answer. The voice
normally rises at the end of a general question.

K. Wirklich? Ask whether the statements are really true.

▶ Frank ist vierzehn. *Ist Frank wirklich vierzehn?*

1. Ich bin fünfzehn.
2. Ursel ist elf.
3. Jens ist krank.

4. Gerda ist zufrieden.
5. Udo hat im Juni Geburtstag.
6. Anke ist fleißig.

Grammatische Übersicht

Subject pronouns (A)

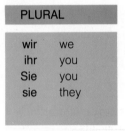

SINGULAR		PLURAL	
ich	I	wir	we
du	you	ihr	you
Sie	you	Sie	you
er	he	sie	they
sie	she		

The plural subject pronouns **wir, ihr, Sie,** and **sie** function like the English pronouns *we, you* (familiar plural), *you* (formal), and *they.*

The familiar form **ihr** (you) is used to address relatives, close friends, or persons under about fifteen.

The meanings and uses of sie and Sie (F–G)

Ist **sie** müde?	Is *she* tired?
Sind **sie** müde?	Are *they* tired?
Sind **Sie** müde?	Are *you* tired?

In spoken German, the meanings of **sie** (she), **sie** (they), and **Sie** (you) can be distinguished with the help of the corresponding verb form and the context.

sie + **ist** = she
sie + **sind** = they
Sie + **sind** = you

Historically speaking, **sie sind** (they are) and **Sie sind** (you are) are the same form. It was considered polite to address someone as **sie** (they) and to capitalize the pronoun in writing.

Present tense of **sein** (B–E)

SINGULAR			PLURAL		
ich **bin**	I am		wir **sind**	we are	
du **bist**	you are		ihr **seid**	you are	
Sie **sind**	you are		Sie **sind**	you are	
er/sie **ist**	he/she is		sie **sind**	they are	

Like the English verb *to be,* the German verb **sein** has several forms in the present tense. The verb forms agree with their subject pronouns.

Present tense of **haben** (H–I)

ich **habe**	I have		wir **haben**	we have	
du **hast**	you have		ihr **habt**	you have	
Sie **haben**	you have		Sie **haben**	you have	
er/sie **hat**	he/she has		sie **haben**	they have	

Like the English verb *to have,* the German verb **haben** has several forms in the present tense. The forms must agree with their subject pronouns.

Sie sind glücklich.

Specific questions and general questions (J–K)

Wie alt bist du? ↘   *How* old are you?
Wann hast du Geburtstag? ↘   *When* is your birthday?

A specific question asks for a particular bit of information and begins with an interrogative such as **wie, wann, warum, wer,** or **wieviel.** The voice normally falls at the end of a specific question.

Ist Gerda schon 15? ↗   *Is* Gerda 15 already?
Hat sie im Mai Geburtstag? ↗   *Is* her birthday in May?

A general question can be answered with **ja** or **nein** and begins with a verb. The voice normally rises at the end of a general question.

Wiederholung

A. Kurzes Gespräch. (Short conversation.) Answer the questions after the dialogue.

INGRID   Tag, Peter! Wie geht's?
PETER   Sehr schlecht.
INGRID   Was ist denn los? Bist du krank?
PETER   Nein, nur kaputt.

1. Wie geht es Peter?
2. Ist Peter sehr müde?

Er ist kaputt.

B. Was bedeutet das? (What does that mean?) Give the English equivalents.

1. Wie alt bist du denn?
2. Wann hast du denn Geburtstag?
3. Wie geht's denn?
4. Bist du denn wieder krank?
5. Was ist denn los?
6. Norbert ist sauer. Warum denn?

C. Sag das! Form complete sentences from the cues below.

▶ Peter / sein / wirklich / sehr fleißig   *Peter ist wirklich sehr fleißig.*

▶ wie / alt / sein / Dieter und Meike /?   *Wie alt sind Dieter und Meike?*

1. wann / haben / du / Geburtstag /?
2. ich / haben / im Juli / Geburtstag
3. wie / alt / sein / du /?
4. sein / Ute / wirklich / unglücklich /?
5. ich / sein / sauer
6. wir / sein / beide / kaputt
7. haben / Sie / im März / Geburtstag /?

D. Wer? Was? Wie? Complete the questions with the appropriate interrogative (using **wer, was,** and **wie**).

1. _____ hat im April Geburtstag? — Jürgen.
2. Jürgen, _____ alt bist du? — Ich bin sechzehn.
3. _____ ist sauer? — Ulla. — Warum denn?
4. _____ ist los? Ist sie unglücklich?
5. Tag, Ulla. _____ geht's? — Danke, schlecht. Ich bin unglücklich.

E. Wie sagt man das? Express the following in German.

1. See you later!
2. That's correct.
3. I'm only fifteen.
4. I am very lazy.
5. Anja is sick again.

F. Was sagst du? (What do you say?) Answer according to your mood and situation.

1. Wie geht's?
2. Wann hast du Geburtstag?
3. Bist du schon fünfzehn?
4. Wie alt bist du?
5. Bist du alt oder jung?
6. Bist du faul oder fleißig?

In many German schools, two students share a desk.

G. Welches Wort? (Which word?) Complete each sentence with an appropriate word from the list below.

aber   denn   los   nicht   nur   wie

1. Du bist auch sechzehn, _____?
2. Das ist _____ sehr alt.
3. Wie alt bist du _____?
4. _____ geht's?
5. Was ist denn _____?
6. Wir sind nicht sauer, _____ sehr müde.

H. Logische Antworten. (Logical answers.) Choose a logical response or combination of responses from column B for each of the questions in column A.

▶ Du bist schon 17, nicht?   *Nein. Ich bin erst 15.*

A	B
Du bist erst dreizehn, nicht?	Ja. / Nein.
Du bist sehr jung, nicht?	Richtig. / Du auch, nicht?
Du hast im Juli Geburtstag, nicht?	Ich bin schon [vierzehn].
	Ich bin erst [fünfzehn].
Du bist zufrieden, nicht?	Ich bin nur müde.
Was ist los?	Ja, sehr.
Bist du denn krank?	Ich bin krank. / Ich bin sauer.

I. Geburtstage. You have been assigned to notify the class when each member has a birthday. Ask six classmates their age and the month they were born. Prepare a list.

NAME   GEBURTSTAG/MONAT   WIE ALT?

NAME	GEBURTSTAG/ MONAT	WIE ALT?

J. Land und Leute.

1. How are birthdays celebrated in Germany? Are there any differences between these and American celebrations?
2. Why do you think Vienna is considered a special city?

Vokabeln

Substantive

der Geburstag, *pl.* **Geburstage** birthday
der Monat, *pl.* **Monate** month

die Zahl, *pl.* **Zahlen** number

Verben

haben to have
sein: wir sind we are
      ihr seid you are *(familiar pl.)*
      sie sind they are
      Sie sind you are *(formal)*

Andere Wörter

aber *flavoring word, implies surprise:* **Du bist aber sehr jung!** You're really very young!
ach oh
alt old
beide both
erst only; first; **ich bin erst fünfzehn** I'm only fifteen

Andere Wörter (cont.)

falsch wrong
ihr you *(familiar pl.)*
jung young
mal times
oder or; isn't that right? *(at end of sentence)*
richtig correct, right
schon already
sie *(pl.)* they
wann when
weniger minus, less
wer who
wieviel how much
wir we

Besondere Ausdrücke

ach so! oh, I see!
wie alt bist du? how old are you?
ich habe Geburtstag it's my birthday
im [März] in [March]
[sechs] durch [drei] [six] divided by [three]

Heute nachmittag

Heute nachmittag machen sie Hausaufgaben.

Wo wohnst du?

Erik and Sabine live in Bern. School is out. Erik catches up with Sabine as she leaves for home.

ERIK   Gehst du jetzt nach Hause?
SABINE   Ja.
ERIK   Wo wohnst du?
SABINE   In der Gartenstraße.
ERIK   Ist das weit von hier?
SABINE   Nein, nur zehn Minuten.

Fragen

1. Wer geht nach Hause?
2. Wohnt Sabine weit von hier?

Du hast das Wort

Wo wohnst du?   At a party you meet several people. Ask each one on what street or in what town she/he lives.

Getting information

DU
Wo wohnst du?

Ist das weit von hier?

GESPRÄCHSPARTNER/IN
In der [Garten]straße.
In [Bergdorf].

Nein, nicht sehr weit.
Nein, nur fünf Minuten.
Ja, zehn Kilometer°.
Ja, ziemlich° weit.

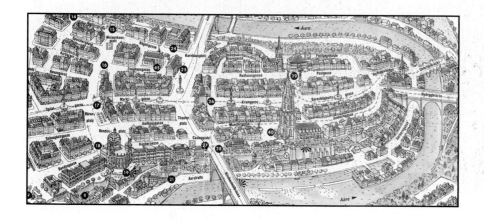

Marks Fotoalbum

Petra spielt sehr gut Volleyball.

Ilse wandert viel.

Andreas und Gerd spielen gern Basketball.

Ute und Bettina gehen oft spazieren.

Herbert schwimmt gern.

Stefan spielt gern Tennis.

Er spielt auch gern Fußball.

Land und Leute

Hiking and walking are favorite pastimes in all of the German-speaking countries. There are well-maintained trails all over the country. Some are no more than paths through local scenic spots or city parks, while others belong to a network of trails stretching from the **Ostsee** (Baltic Sea) to the **Alpen** (Alps). Some parks also feature **Trimm-dich-Pfade** (marked jogging paths with exercise stops).

Bonn: within minutes of the center of the German capital are trails used by Germans of all ages.

Fragen

1. Was macht° Herbert gern?
2. Wer spielt Tennis? Basketball?
3. Was machen Ute und Bettina?

Du hast das Wort

Was machst du gern?   You are looking for some people to share leisure activities with. Ask four classmates whether they like to engage in a particular sport or outdoor activity. You will report back to your teacher about your classmates.

Expressing likes and dislikes

DU	GESPRÄCHSPARTNER/IN
Spielst du gern [Tennis]?	Ja, ich spiele gern [Tennis].
	Ja, aber° ich spiele nicht gut.
	Nein, ich spiele nicht gern [Tennis].
Gehst du gern [spazieren]?	Ja, sehr gern.
	Ja, natürlich°.
	Nein, ich gehe nicht gern [spazieren].
[Wanderst] du gern?	Ja, du nicht?
	Nein, ich [wandere] nicht gern.

[Christa] spielt gern Tennis. [Ute] . . .

Was machst du?

Jan and Gisela are walking home from school together.

JAN   Bleibst du heute nachmittag zu Hause?
GISELA   Ja.
JAN   Was machst du denn?
GISELA   Hausaufgaben. Was sonst?

Du hast das Wort

Wann machst du Hausaufgaben? You think you know when your classmates do their homework, but ask four of them anyway. Report on their answers.

Having your assumptions confirmed or denied

DU   GESPRÄCHSPARTNER/IN

Machst du	heute nachmittag	Hausaufgaben?
	heute abend°	
	heute morgen°	

Ja, natürlich.
Ja, du nicht?
Nein, natürlich nicht.
Nein, ich bin zu° müde.

[Frank] macht heute abend Hausaufgaben. [Petra] . . .

Land und Leute

Whether the Swiss call it "**Schweiz,**" "**Suisse,**" or "**Svizzera,**" they mean one and the same country: Switzerland. There are four national languages, each spoken in a separate region. About 70% of the population of 6.5 million speaks a form of German called **Schwyzerdütsch.** The rest speak French, Italian, and Romansh, which is close to Latin. The Latin name for Switzerland, "Helvetia," is used on stamps and coins.

Switzerland is known for manufacturing precision products, especially watches. Tourism is also a major industry. The Alps attract skiers in winter and hikers in summer.

The capital of Switzerland is Bern.

In Bern, a well-known street is the Kramgasse.

Musikinstrumente

Klavier

Geige

Schlagzeug

Klarinette

Flöte

Gitarre

A. Spielst du ein Musikinstrument? You are trying to form a small band. Ask three classmates whether they play a particular instrument. They will ask you the same questions.

Asking about personal interests

DU

Spielst du [Klavier]?

GESPRÄCHSPARTNER/IN

Ja, natürlich.
Nein, aber [Geige].
Nein, ich spiele nicht [Klavier].

B. Spielst du gut? If the classmate above plays an instrument, ask how well.

DU

Spielst du gut?

GESPRÄCHSPARTNER/IN

Ja, sehr gut.
Ja, nicht schlecht.
Ja, ganz gut.
Nein, nicht sehr gut.

Aussprache

long vowel [y]   müde, Schüler, Stühle
short vowel [Y]   fünf, Günter, Flüsse

A. Practice vertically in columns and horizontally in pairs.

[y]	[Y]
Füßen	Füssen
büßte	Büste
Düne	dünne
Mühle	Müll
fühlen	füllen

In der Kürze liegt die Würze.

B. Practice the following words horizontally in pairs.

[i]	[y]
Biene	Bühne
diene	Düne
Kiel	kühl
liegen	lügen

[I]	[Y]
Binde	Bünde
bitte	Bütte
Kissen	küssen
Lifte	Lüfte

C. Practice the sounds [y] and [Y]. Read the sentences aloud.

1. Günter, wieviel ist fünf und fünfzehn?
2. Warum seid ihr so müde?
3. Rüdiger ist unglücklich.

Glottal Stop

Say aloud *a nice man* and then say *an ice man*. The second phrase sounds different from the first because you break the stream of air between *an* and *ice*. This process of stopping and starting the air stream in the back of the throat is called a *glottal stop*. Both English and German use the glottal stop before vowels as a device to keep words and parts of words from running together. The glottal stop occurs more frequently in German than in English.

D. Read the following sentences aloud. An asterisk (*) indicates a glottal stop.

1. Wo *ist *Erik heute *abend?
2. Wie geht *es *Eva?
3. Wie *alt *ist *Otto?

E. Now try reading a few sentences without an asterisk.

1. Guten Abend!
2. Was ist das, Astrid?
3. Ist Udo wieder krank?
4. Wo ist Anna?

1. Present tense of regular verbs

ich/du

ich geh**e**   du geh**st**
ich spiel**e**   du spiel**st**

The endings of regular verbs change according to a pattern. The **ich**-form ends in **-e,** the **du**-form ends in **-st.**

A.   Was machst du?   Sabine is trying to find out more about you and your plans. Answer her questions affirmatively.

▶   Gehst du jetzt nach Hause?   *Ja, ich gehe jetzt nach Hause.*

1. Wohnst du weit von hier?
2. Spielst du heute nachmittag Tennis?
3. Bleibst du heute abend zu Hause?
4. Machst du heute abend Hausaufgaben?

B.   Wie bitte? (Pardon?)   You didn't hear when Petra intends to do certain things. Ask her when it's going to be.

▶   Ich spiele heute morgen Fußball.   *Wann spielst du Fußball?*

1. Ich gehe heute nachmittag schwimmen.
2. Ich spiele heute nachmittag Tennis.
3. Ich gehe heute abend spazieren.
4. Ich mache heute abend Hausaufgaben.

Sie

Spiel**en** Sie gut Tennis, Frau Schmidt?
Tag, Herr Braun, Tag, Frau Schmidt. Bleib**en** Sie heute zu Hause?

The **Sie**-form of regular verbs ends in **-en.**

C.   Machen Sie das oft?   Your teacher says what she/he is doing today. Ask whether she/he does those things often.

▶   Ich gehe heute schwimmen.   *Gehen Sie oft schwimmen?*

1. Ich spiele heute Fußball.   3. Ich bleibe heute nachmittag zu Hause.
2. Ich gehe heute spazieren.   4. Ich spiele heute abend Geige.

Sie spielen gern Geige.

wir/ihr

wir geh**en**	ihr geh**t**
wir spiel**en**	ihr spiel**t**

The **wir**-form ends in **-en,** the **ihr**-form ends in **-t.**

D. Nein, das nicht. Bruno is curious and wants to know what your plans are. Keep him guessing by answering all of his questions in the negative.

▶ Geht ihr nach Hause? *Nein. Wir gehen nicht nach Hause.*

1. Bleibt ihr hier?
2. Geht ihr spazieren?
3. Spielt ihr Tennis?
4. Geht ihr schwimmen?
5. Spielt ihr Volleyball?

E. Macht ihr das oft? Your friends tell you what they're doing today. Ask whether they do these things often.

▶ Wir spielen heute Tennis. *Spielt ihr oft Tennis?*

1. Wir spielen heute Fußball.
2. Wir spielen heute Basketball.
3. Wir gehen heute schwimmen.
4. Wir gehen heute spazieren.
5. Wir bleiben heute zu Hause.

er/sie (singular) /sie (plural)

er/sie geht   sie gehen
er/sie spielt   sie spielen

The **er/sie**-form ends in **-t**, the **sie**-*(plural)* form ends in **-en**.

F. Spielen sie gut? Marta asks how well several classmates play their instruments. Answer in each instance that they play either very well or very badly.

▶ Spielt Karin gut Klavier?   *Ja, sie spielt sehr gut.*
                                Nein, sie spielt sehr schlecht.

1. Spielt Bernhard gut Gitarre?
2. Spielt Astrid gut Klarinette?
3. Spielen Detlev und Erik gut Schlagzeug?
4. Spielt Detlev gut Flöte?
5. Spielen Rita und Christl gut Geige?

G. Sie spielen gut. Say that the persons indicated play their instruments well.

▶ Frank   *Frank spielt gut Klavier.*

1. du   2. ihr   3. wir   4. ich

H. Sag das! Karin is asking you and your friend about your and other friends' activities today. Complete the sentences using the correct verb forms.

▶ Erik *geht* heute schwimmen. (gehen)

1. Was _____ ihr heute? (machen)
2. Wir _____ heute zu Hause. (bleiben)
3. Sabrina _____ heute nachmittag Basketball. (spielen)
4. Peter und Ute _____ spazieren. (gehen)
5. Und du? Was _____ du? (machen)
6. Hm, ich? Ich _____ nichts. Ich _____ Klavier. (machen/spielen)
7. Ich _____ oft. (wandern)
8. Und Anke? Was _____ sie? (machen)
9. Sie _____ zu Hause. (bleiben)

2. Present tense to express future time

Ich mache heute abend Hausaufgaben.   *I'm going to do* homework tonight.
Spielst du heute nachmittag Tennis?   *Are you playing* tennis this afternoon?

German, like English, may use the present tense to express action intended or planned for the future. The time reference (for example, **heute abend**) indicates whether a sentence refers to the present or the future.

I. Heute nachmittag? The following people often engage in sports or outdoor activities. Ask whether they plan to do them this afternoon.

▶ Paul spielt oft Fußball.   *Spielt er heute nachmittag?*

1. Gerd und Rita spielen oft Tennis.
2. Gustav und Lutz spielen oft Basketball.
3. Gabi spielt oft Volleyball.
4. Tanja und Birgit spielen oft Volleyball.
5. Kai wandert oft.
6. Ute und Christl schwimmen viel.

3. Using **gern** with verbs

Ich **spiele gern** Basketball.   I *like to play* basketball.
Ich **spiele nicht gern** Tennis.   I *don't like to play* tennis.

The most common way of saying in German that you like or dislike doing something is to use **gern** or **nicht gern** with the appropriate verb.

J. Nicht oft, aber gern. Sometimes the things you enjoy most are those you don't do very often. Say that you enjoy the activities asked about below.

▶ Spielst du viel Tennis? *Nein, aber ich spiele gern Tennis.*

1. Schwimmst du viel?
2. Spielst du viel Klavier?
3. Spielst du viel Gitarre?
4. Wanderst du viel?
5. Gehst du viel spazieren?

K. Nicht oft und nicht gern. When Lutz asks whether various classmates are involved in certain sports and activities, respond in the negative. Say that they don't like to do those things.

▶ Schwimmt Frank viel? *Nein. Er schwimmt nicht gern.*

1. Spielt Wolf oft Tennis?
2. Spielen Luise und Gerda oft Volleyball?
3. Wandert Michael viel?
4. Geht Klaus viel spazieren?
5. Spielt Cornelia oft Geige?

L. Was machen Sie? Your teacher says what she/he likes to do. Choose an appropriate personal response.

▶ Ich spiele gern Tennis. *Spielen Sie* | *viel?*
                                               | *oft*
                                               | *gut*

1. Ich wandere gern.
2. Ich spiele gern Klavier.
3. Ich schwimme gern.
4. Ich spiele gern Volleyball.
5. Ich gehe gern spazieren.
6. Ich bleibe auch gern zu Hause.

4. Using gern with haben

Jens **hat** Kirstin **gern**. Jens *likes* Kirstin.
Kirstin **hat** Jens **nicht gern**. Kirstin *doesn't like* Jens.

To express fondness for someone, German uses **gern** with the verb **haben**. **Nicht gern** is used to express a dislike.

M. Wir haben sie gern. Jochen and his friends are discussing which classmates they like. Form sentences with **haben** and **gern,** using the cues provided.

▶ wir / Martina *Wir haben Martina gern.*

1. ich / Rolf
2. du / Ingrid / ?
3. Susanne / Rudi
4. ihr / Petra / ?
5. wir / Thomas

5. The phrases **zu Hause** and **nach Hause**

Gerd bleibt **zu Hause.**   Gerd is staying *home.*
Inge geht **nach Hause.**   Inge is going *home.*

When the verb expresses location, **zu Hause** is used.
When the verb expresses direction or movement, **nach Hause** is used.

N.   Zu Hause oder nach Hause?   Complete the sentences with **zu Hause** or **nach Hause,** as appropriate.

▶   Ich gehe heute nachmittag _____.   *Ich gehe heute nachmittag nach Hause.*

▶   Ich bleibe heute abend _____.   *Ich bleibe heute abend zu Hause.*

1. Wir bleiben heute morgen _____.
2. Petra und Erik gehen _____.
3. Dieter ist _____.
4. Gehst du _____?
5. Meike spielt _____.
6. Wann geht ihr _____?
7. Wann bist du _____?
8. Wann gehen Sie _____?

Sie bleibt zu Hause und macht Hausaufgaben.

O. Sag das! Form sentences by using an appropriate verb.

bleiben   gehen   sein   spielen

▶   er / zu Hause   *Er ist zu Hause. / Er bleibt zu Hause.*

1. wir / zu Hause
2. wann / du / nach Hause / ?
3. Marta / zu Hause
4. ich / nach Hause

5. ihr / nach Hause / ?
6. wann / du / zu Hause / ?
7. wann / Sie / nach Hause / ?

Grammatische Übersicht

Present tense of regular verbs   (A–H)

Infinitive and infinitive stem

INFINITIVE =	STEM + ENDING
bleiben	bleib en
wandern	wander n

The basic form of a German verb is the infinitive. Most German infinitives end in **-en**; a few end in **-n**. In vocabularies and dictionaries, verbs are listed under the infinitive form. The infinitive stem is the infinitive minus the **-(e)n** ending.

Present-tense endings of regular verbs

INFINITIVE	SINGULAR		PLURAL	
spielen	ich spiel **e**		wir spiel **en**	
	du spiel **st** Sie spiel **en**		ihr spiel **t**	
	er/sie spiel **t**		sie spiel **en**	

German verb endings change, depending on what the subject of the verb is. The verb endings are added to the infinitive stem. In the present tense most verbs have four different endings: **-e, -st, -t, -en.**

Sie spielen gut Fußball.

Present-tense meanings

Detlev **spielt** gut.	Detlev *plays* well. Detlev *is playing* well.
Spielt er gut?	*Is* he *playing* well? *Does* he *play* well?

Notice that German uses one present-tense form to express ideas that require several different present-tense forms in English.

Present tense to express future time (I)

Spielt Jutta heute nachmittag?	*Is* Jutta *going to play* this afternoon?
Wann **gehst** du nach Hause?	When *are* you *going to go* home?

In German, as in English, the present tense may be used to express action intended or planned for the future. The time reference indicates whether a sentence refers to the present or the future.

Using **gern** with verbs (J–L)

Ich schwimme **gern.**	I *like* to swim.
Ich spiele **nicht gern** Fußball.	I *don't like* to play soccer.

The most common way of saying in German that you like doing something is to use **gern** with a verb. To say that you dislike doing something, use **nicht gern** with a verb.

Using **gern** with **haben** (M)

Jens **hat** Kirstin **gern.**   Jens *likes* Kirstin.
Sie **hat** aber Jens **nicht gern.**   But she *doesn't like* Jens.

One way of expressing fondness for someone in German is to use **gern** with the verb **haben.** One way of saying that you *don't* like someone is to use **nicht gern** with **haben.**

The phrases **zu Hause** and **nach Hause** (N–O)

Erika ist **zu Hause.**   Erika is *at home.*
Beate geht **nach Hause.**   Beate is going *home.*

The phrases **zu Hause** and **nach Hause** both mean *home,* but they are used in somewhat different ways. **Zu Hause** is used to talk about being *at home.* **Nach Hause** is used to talk about *going home.*

Wiederholung

A. Kurzes Gespräch. (Short conversation.) Answer the questions based on the following dialogue.

UTE   Tag, Karsten! Was ist denn los? Bist du sauer?
KARSTEN   Ja, sehr. Gisela ist nicht zu Hause.
UTE   Wo ist sie denn?
KARSTEN   Sie spielt wieder Basketball, und ich mache Hausaufgaben.

1. Was macht Gisela?
2. Warum ist Karsten sauer?

B. Wieviel? Ask a classmate the following arithmetic problems, beginning each question with **Wieviel ist . . . .**

1. $10 + 6 = ?$
2. $19 - 1 = ?$
3. $3 \times 4 = ?$
4. $15 - 2 = ?$
5. $2 \times 7 = ?$

6. $8 + 9 = ?$
7. $18 \div 3 = ?$
8. $16 \div 4 = ?$
9. $3 + 8 = ?$
10. $4 \times 5 = ?$

C. Viele Fragen. (Many questions.) Begin each question with the appropriate interrogative.

1. _____ ist denn los?
2. _____ bist du so unglücklich?
3. _____ geht es?
4. _____ wohnst du?
5. _____ hast du Geburtstag?

D. Wie sagt man das? You and a friend are discussing your plans for the afternoon. Express the following dialogue in German.

A Hi, [. . .]! What are you doing this afternoon?
B I'm going to play soccer. You, too?
A No, I'm going home.
B But why?
A I'm going to do homework.

E. Nein, das nicht. You are having a bad day. Answer everyone's questions in the negative, and then reinforce what you have to say by using an antonym in your second sentence.

▶ Bist du krank?   *Nein, ich bin nicht krank. Ich bin gesund.*

1. Schwimmt Peter gut?
2. Ist Peter alt?
3. Ist Inge faul?
4. Bist du unglücklich?
5. Seid ihr glücklich?

F. Wer bist du? A new student is trying to find out more about you. How would you answer her/his questions?

1. Wo wohnst du?
2. Wie alt bist du?
3. Wann hast du Geburtstag?
4. Schwimmst du gern?
5. Spielst du gern Basketball? Spielst du oft?
6. Spielst du Gitarre? Spielst du gut?
7. Was machst du heute abend?

G. Spielst du gut Tennis? List the sports your school offers. Ask your partner or your other classmates who in your school participates in these sports. Then ask whether these people play them well or not so well. Your teacher will ask you for the names of these athletes and your opinion of them.

H. Wer spielt Klavier? First make a list of activities mentioned in this chapter. Leave blank spaces for names.

_____ spielt Klavier.
_____ schwimmt gut.
_____ ist heute müde.

Then, going down the list, ask your classmates whether they do the activities listed. If you receive a yes answer, fill in the name. If the answer is no, try another classmate. Include ideas from previous chapters.

DU

Andrea, spielst du Klavier?

GESPRÄCHSPARTNER/IN

Ja, ich spiele Klavier.

Andrea spielt Klavier.

I. Machst du das auch? With a partner, try to find three things you have in common and three things you don't have in common. Report back to the class. Listen well to the other reports. Your teacher will ask you to either write down or tell what you remember about each person.

J. Land und Leute. With a partner review the cultural notes you have read about the **Bundesrepublik,** the **DDR, Österreich** and **die Schweiz.** Together write notes on what you know about the geography of these countries. How does the geography influence free-time activities? What are some of the differences between these countries? What are their capitals and populations?

Vokabeln

Substantive

der Basketball   basketball
der Fußball   soccer
der Kilometer   kilometer (= .062 miles)
der Volleyball   volleyball

das Fotoalbum   photo album
das Klavier   piano
das Musikinstrument   musical instrument
das Schlagzeug   drums
das Tennis   tennis

Substantive (cont.)

die Flöte   flute
die Geige   violin
die Gitarre   guitar
die Klarinette   clarinet
die Minute   minute
die Straße   street

die Hausaufgaben *(pl.)*   homework

Verben

bleiben   to remain, to stay
gehen   to go
machen   to do; to make
schwimmen   to swim
spazieren   to walk, to stroll; **spazieren
  gehen**   to go for a walk
spielen   to play
wandern   to hike, to go hiking
wohnen   to live

Andere Wörter

aber   however, but
gern   gladly, with pleasure
hier   here
in   in(to)
jetzt   now
natürlich   naturally, of course
oft   often

Andere Wörter (cont.)

viel   much, many, a lot
von   from
weit   far (away)
wo   where
ziemlich   quite
zu   to; too

Besondere Ausdrücke

heute morgen   this morning
heute nachmittag   this afternoon
heute abend   tonight; this evening
was sonst?   what else?
nach Hause   home *(direction)*
zu Hause   at home
in der Gartenstraße   on Garden Street
gern haben   to like, to be fond of

Kapitel 4

Ich und meine Familie

Ein Familienbild

Der Brieffreund

Barbara lives in Wisconsin, a state with a large German-speaking population. She has just started to correspond with a pen pal in the Federal Republic of Germany. In her first letter she introduces herself and her family.

Milwaukee, den 12. Dezember

Lieber Michael!

Ich heiße Barbara Braun. Ich bin fünfzehn Jahre alt. Ich bin Schülerin und lerne schon zwei Jahre Deutsch. Mein Hobby ist Musik. Ich spiele gern Klavier, aber nur klassische Musik.

Mein Bruder heißt Bill. Er ist achtzehn Jahre alt. Er ist groß und schlank. Er spielt Gitarre und singt nicht schlecht. Er spielt oft Rockmusik.

Meine Schwester heißt Susan. Sie ist elf Jahre alt. Sie ist klein und dünn. Sie spielt sehr gut Geige. Oft ist sie doof. Sie ist aber noch ein Kind.

Meine Mutter ist Apothekerin. Sie arbeitet von Montag bis Donnerstag. Am Freitag, Samstag und Sonntag ist sie zu Hause. Das ist natürlich schön. Sie ist sehr musikalisch. Sie spielt Klavier und Geige.

Mein Vater ist Elektriker. Er arbeitet viel und kommt oft spät nach Hause. Abends hört er gern Musik, und er kocht (er kocht gern und gut! Toll, nicht?). Er spielt Klarinette. Am Wochenende machen wir oft Musik, meine Mutter, mein Vater, meine Schwester, mein Bruder und ich. Das macht natürlich Spaß.

Was machst Du abends gern? Spielst Du ein Instrument? Spielst Du Klavier oder Gitarre? Hörst Du gern Musik? Wie findest Du klassische Musik? Treibst Du gern Sport? Tanzt Du gern? Hoffentlich schreibst Du bald.

Herzliche Grüße

Barbara

P.S. Das Bild ist von mir.

Du hast das Wort

1. **Barbaras Familie.** Summarize the information about Barbara's family. Use the following questions as guidelines.

Wie heißt Barbaras Bruder? Wie alt ist er? Ist er klein oder groß? Ist er musikalisch?

Wie heißt Barbaras Schwester? Wie alt ist sie? Ist sie klein oder groß? Was spielt sie? Warum ist sie oft doof?

Was ist Barbaras Mutter? Von wann bis wann arbeitet sie? Wann ist sie zu Hause? Was spielt sie?

Was ist Barbaras Vater? Was macht er abends? Was spielt er?

Was macht die Familie oft am Wochenende?

Summarizing information

In the Federal Republic of Germany more than half of the women work outside the home, even though they usually take care of the household as well. In some cases the man takes care of the house and children. The woman is a **Hausfrau,** he is a **Hausmann.**

Because it is not as common for German parents to hire babysitters as it is for American parents, they spend much of their free time with their young children. On Sunday afternoons families like to be together, whether for a walk, a party in the garden, or some other outdoor activity. While teenagers often prefer to spend their time with friends, they still take part in family events and usually join the family on vacation.

Ist der Vater auch Hausmann?

2. **Michaels Familie.** When Michael gets Barbara's letter, he starts to think of how he would describe his family to her. Make up a family for Michael and describe it.

Describing a family

Meine Mutter heißt . . . Sie ist . . . Sie . . .
Mein Vater . . .
Meine Schwester [Claudia] . . .
Mein Bruder [Thomas] . . .

3. **Deine Familie.** Draw your own family tree. Your partner wants to know the names of your family members.

Describing your family

GESPRÄCHSPARTNER/IN		DU
Wie heißt	dein° Vater?	Er heißt . . .
	dein Bruder?	Er heißt . . .
	deine Mutter?	Sie heißt . . .
	deine Schwester?	Sie heißt . . .

4. **Am Wochenende.**   Think of three things you will be doing this weekend. A friend asks you what you're going to do this Saturday and Sunday. How would you respond?

Planning your weekend

GESPRÄCHSPARTNER/IN   DU

Was machst du	am Samstag?	Ich mache meine Hausaufgaben.
	am Sonntag?	Ich spiele Tennis.
	am Wochenende?	Ich spiele Karten°.
		Ich gehe schwimmen.
		Ich gehe tanzen°.
		Ich arbeite.

5. **Du bist Michael.**   Have one of your classmates pretend to be Michael. Ask her/him the questions Barbara asked in her letter.

Was machst du gern abends?
Spielst du Klavier oder Gitarre?
   etc.

Land und Leute

In the United States, family names, names of towns, and certain customs recall the many Germans who have immigrated to this country. In cities like New York and Detroit there are still many families who speak German at home. They shop in German stores and keep up with news through German radio programs and newspapers. Many German-speaking communities have clubs that foster social and cultural activities, such as choral singing and dramatics.

Harvestfest parade in Leavenworth, Washington passing by a German-style *Fachwerkhaus* (half-timbered house)

Berufe

Herr Schwarz ist **Geschäftsmann.**
Frau Schwarz ist **Geschäftsfrau.**

Herr Stein ist **Friseur.**
Frau Kneip ist **Friseurin.**

Herr Schmidt ist **Arbeiter.**
Frau Meier ist **Arbeiterin.**

Herr Weiß ist **Verkäufer.**
Frau Klein ist **Verkäuferin.**

Herr Wagner ist **Lehrer.**
Frau Wagner ist **Lehrerin.**

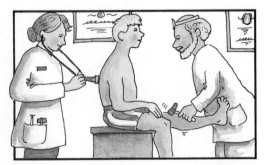

Herr Müller ist **Arzt.**
Frau Müller ist **Ärztin.**

In German there are usually different forms of a noun to indicate a man and a woman in the same profession. Often the feminine equivalent simply adds **-in** to the masculine form. Occasionally, an umlaut must also be added to the feminine form.

Note that in German the article **ein** *(a, an)* is not used when stating what a person's profession is.

Sie ist **Ärztin**.   She's *a doctor.*

A. Berufe. Say what the following people's parents do for a living. (Both parents have the same occupation.)

▶ Ritas Mutter ist Friseurin.   *Er ist Friseur.*
     Was ist Ritas Vater?

1. Utes Mutter ist Lehrerin. Was ist Utes Vater?
2. Peters Mutter ist Arbeiterin. Was ist Peters Vater?
3. Ottos Vater ist Arzt. Was ist Ottos Mutter?
4. Georgs Mutter ist Geschäftsfrau. Was ist Georgs Vater?
5. Inges Vater ist Apotheker. Was ist Inges Mutter?
6. Sabines Mutter ist Verkäuferin. Was ist Sabines Vater?
7. Franks Vater ist Friseur. Was ist Franks Mutter?

Inges Vater ist Apotheker in Berlin.

Zahlen: 20–1.000

20 zwanzig	50 fünfzig	80 achtzig	200 zweihundert
30 dreißig	60 sechzig	90 neunzig	500 fünfhundert
40 vierzig	70 siebzig	100 hundert	1.000 tausend

Dreißig ends in **-ßig** instead of **-zig**.

Sechzig loses the final **-s** of **sechs**.

Siebzig loses the final **-en** of **sieben**.

Hundert and **tausend** are generally used instead of **einhundert** and **eintausend**.

B. Zahlen. You're at an auction. Each time a bid is made you raise it by 10.

▶ 40 (vierzig)   *(50) fünfzig*

1. 90
2. 30
3. 70
4. 20
5. 60
6. 80

21 einundzwanzig	79	neunundsiebzig
22 zweiundzwanzig	101	hunderteins
34 vierunddreißig	121	hunderteinundzwanzig
57 siebenundfünfzig	265	zweihundertfünfundsechzig

The German numbers within the twenties, thirties, and so on follow the number pattern used in the English nursery rhyme "four-and-twenty blackbirds."

In compound numbers with **eins,** the **-s** of **eins** is dropped:

eins > **einundzwanzig**

C. Das ist falsch. Your friends are trying to guess the numbers you're thinking of. Each time their guess is one short. Correct them.

▶ 24 (vierundzwanzig)?   *Nein, fünfundzwanzig.*

1. 75?
2. 98?
3. 37?
4. 68?
5. 120?
6. 782?
7. 998?
8. 1.206?
9. 1.300?

Zentimetermaß

1 Meter (1 m) = 39,37 in.
1 Zentimeter (1 cm) = 0,39 in.
2,54 Zentimeter (2,54 cm) = 1,0 in.

In German, a comma is used to write decimals.

Wie groß bist du?	1,62 m	Ein Meter zweiundsechzig.
		Eins zweiundsechzig.

There are several ways to express height in German.

m/cm	ft/in
1,95	6'5"
1,90	6'3"
1,85	6'1"
1,80	5'11"
1,75	5'9"
1,70	5'7"
1,65	5'5"
1,60	5'3"
1,55	5'1"
1,50	4'11"
1,45	4'9"
1,40	4'7"
1,35	4'5"
1,30	4'3"

D. Wie groß bist du? Ask your classmates how tall they are and make a list.

Asking for personal information

DU	GESPRÄCHSPARTNER/IN
Wie groß bist du?	[Ein Meter fünfundvierzig].

Das sind fünfundfünzig Zentimeter.

E. Wie groß sind sie? Now find out from a classmate how tall members of her/his family are.

> DU
>
> Wie groß ist dein [Vater, Bruder]?
> Wie groß ist deine [Mutter, Schwester]?

F. Wie groß? Use a centimeter ruler to measure the following things. Give your measurements in German.

1. the length of your pencil (pen)
2. the width of this book
3. the length of your thumb
4. the length of a blackboard eraser
5. the width of your hand

Use a meterstick to measure larger items.

6. the circumference of your desk
7. the width of a blackboard
8. the length of the classroom
9. the length of a yardstick

Aussprache

long vowel [ø]   schön, Flöte
short vowel [œ]   zwölf, Wörter

A. Practice vertically in columns and horizontally in pairs.

[ø]	[œ]
Höhle	Hölle
Öfen	öffnen
fröhlich	Frösche
König	können
lösen	löschen

B. Practice the following words horizontally in pairs.

[e]	[ø]	[ɛ]	[œ]
lesen	lösen	kennt	könnt
hehlen	Höhlen	helle	Hölle
bete	böte	stecke	Stöcke
flehe	Flöhe	fällig	völlig

Viele Köche verderben den Brei.

C. Practice the sounds [ø] and [œ]. Read the sentences aloud.

1. Jörg hört gern klassische Musik.
2. Petra spielt das Flötensolo sehr schön.
3. Sie wohnt in der Goethestraße.

Übungen

1. Verbs with stem ending in -d or -t

finden		
ich finde		wir finden
du **findest**	Sie finden	ihr **findet**
er/sie **findet**		sie finden

arbeiten		
ich arbeite		wir arbeiten
du **arbeitest**	Sie arbeiten	ihr **arbeitet**
er/sie **arbeitet**		sie arbeiten

Verbs with stem ending in **-d** or **-t** have an **-e** before the **-st** and **-t** endings in the present tense.

A. Sie arbeiten abends. Inform Gabi that all of the people she mentions work in the evenings.

▶ Was macht Inge abends? *Sie arbeitet.*

1. Was macht Herr Klein abends?
2. Was machst du abends?
3. Was macht Frau Kluge abends?
4. Was macht ihr abends?

B. Rockmusik ist toll! Hans-Jürgen asks what you and others think of rock music. Say that everyone finds it great.

▶ Wie findet Claudia Rockmusik? *Sie findet Rockmusik toll.*

1. Und Dieter?
2. Frau Lenz?
3. Und du?
4. Margit?
5. Ihr?
6. Und Sie?

2. Verbs with stem ending in a sibilant

heißen
ich heiße
du heißt
er/sie heißt

tanzen
ich tanze
du tanzt
er/sie tanzt

The **-st** of the **du**-form ending contracts to **-t** when the verb stem ends in any sibilant (**-s, -ss, -ß, -z,** or **-tz**).

C. Wer tanzt gern? Ask whether each of the following persons likes to dance.

▶ Petras Bruder *Tanzt Petras Bruder gern?*

1. Inges Schwester
2. Dieters Bruder
3. du
4. ihr
5. Ritas Schwester
6. Sie

3. Position of the verb in statements

1	2	3	4
Wir	arbeiten	abends	nicht.
Abends	arbeiten	wir	nicht.
Heute abend	arbeiten	wir	nicht.

In a German statement, the verb is always in second position, even when an element other than the subject is in the first position. When words other than the subject begin a sentence, the subject follows the verb.

Spielt sie klassische Musik oder Rock?

D. Natürlich! Günther asks you what your interests are. Say that of course you do each of the things he asks about.

▶ Spielst du Klavier?   *Natürlich spiele ich Klavier!*

1. Spielst du Tennis?
2. Hörst du gern Musik?
3. Arbeitest du viel?
4. Tanzt du gut?
5. Gehst du oft spazieren?
6. Kochst du gern?

E. Nein, das nicht. Say that you don't do any of the following things. Begin each sentence with **Nein** and the emphasized word or phrase.

▶ Gehst du *abends* spazieren?   *Nein, abends gehe ich nicht spazieren.*

1. Arbeitest du *heute abend?*
2. Arbeitest du *am Samstag?*
3. Spielst du *Tennis?*
4. Singst du *gut?*
5. Bist du *musikalisch?*
6. Spielst du *klassische Musik?*

4. Possession with proper names

Ist das **Inges** Gitarre? Is that *Inge's* guitar?
Wie alt ist **Utes** Bruder? How old is *Ute's* brother?

In German, an **-s** is usually added to a proper name to show possession or other close relationship.

Ist das **Thomas'** Mutter? Is that *Thomas's* mother?

If the name already ends in an **s**-sound, no **-s** is added. In written German, an apostrophe is used after a name ending in an **s**-sound.

F. Ihre Brüder auch. (Their brothers too.) The students mentioned below each have a brother who plays the same instrument. Point that out to a friend.

▶ Gerda spielt Klavier. *Gerdas Bruder spielt auch Klavier.*

1. Bernd spielt Geige.
2. Petra spielt Klarinette.
3. Hans spielt Gitarre.
4. Thomas spielt Schlagzeug.
5. Inge spielt Flöte.
6. Karin spielt Klavier.

5. Possessive adjectives

mein/dein

Mein Vater arbeitet viel. **Dein** Vater auch?
Meine Mutter arbeitet viel. **Deine** Mutter auch?

The possessive adjectives **mein** and **dein** are equivalent to *my* and *your (sg.)*. Possessive adjectives end in **-e** when they modify feminine nouns.

G. Wie bitte? Gisela tells you about the activities in which various friends and relatives participate. Ask to make sure you heard the right person.

▶ Mein Freund schwimmt gern. *Wer? Dein Freund?*

1. Meine Freundin schwimmt gut.
2. Mein Vater wandert gern.
3. Mein Bruder spielt Fußball.
4. Meine Schwester spielt Basketball.
5. Meine Mutter spielt Tennis.
6. Mein Freund spielt Volleyball.
7. Meine Mutter spielt gut Tennis.

H. Ist das richtig? Ute asks you questions about various people. Check to make sure you know which person she's asking about, and then confirm her judgment.

▶ Ist deine Mutter jung?　　*Meine Mutter? Ja, sehr jung.*

1. Ist dein Vater jung?
2. Ist dein Bruder faul?
3. Ist deine Schwester fleißig?
4. Ist dein Freund Hans-Dieter groß?
5. Ist deine Freundin Inge glücklich?

sein/ihr

Seine Mutter ist Apothekerin.　　*His* mother is a pharmacist.
Ihr Vater ist Geschäftsmann.　　*Her* father is a businessman.

I. Wer ist das? At a school event Ilse is trying to identify a number of spectators. Confirm Ilse's identifications.

▶ Das ist Jochens Mutter, nicht?　　*Ja, das ist seine Mutter.*

1. Das ist Volkers Vater, nicht?
2. Das ist Utes Schwester, nicht?
3. Das ist Giselas Bruder, nicht?
4. Das ist Walters Freund, nicht?
5. Das ist Heidis Freundin, nicht?

J. Das ist falsch! Rolf asks about the occupation of a number of acquaintances. Say that his guesses are wrong.

▶ Ist Martas Mutter Lehrerin?　　*Ihre Mutter Lehrerin? Nein.*

▶ Ist Martas Vater Lehrer?　　*Ihr Vater Lehrer? Nein.*

1. Ist Ritas Freund Verkäufer?
2. Ist Ritas Freundin Geschäftsfrau?
3. Ist Rudis Mutter Ärztin?
4. Ist Rudis Vater Arzt?
5. Ist Franks Bruder Apotheker?

unser/euer

Unser Arzt ist gut.
Unsere Ärztin ist gut.　　*Our* doctor is good.

Ist **euer** Arzt auch gut?
Ist **eure** Ärztin auch gut?　　Is *your* doctor good, too?

When **euer** has an ending, the **-e** before the **-r** is usually omitted.

Unser Elektriker ist gut.

K. Wie sind sie? You've just moved to a new town, and your relatives are curious about the professional people you've found there. Answer that they're good.

▶ Wie ist eure Ärztin? *Unsere Ärztin ist gut.*

1. Wie ist euer Apotheker?
2. Wie ist euer Lehrer?
3. Wie ist eure Friseurin?
4. Wie ist euer Elektriker?

L. Warum? You are talking to a pair of twins. Inquire why their friends and relatives feel or act as they do.

▶ Bruder / müde   *Warum ist euer Bruder so müde?*

1. Schwester / faul
2. Vater / sauer
3. Mutter / glücklich
4. Freund / doof
5. Freundin / unglücklich

ihr (singular) and ihr (plural)

Hier ist **Gerda.** Und das ist **ihre** Mutter.	Here's *Gerda.* And that's *her* mother.
Hier sind **Trudi und Jens.** Und das ist **ihre** Mutter.	Here are *Trudi and Jens.* And that's *their* mother.

Ihr can mean *their* as well as *her*. Context usually makes the meaning clear.

M. Wer ist das? You and Heike are at a band concert. Heike asks about the identity of a number of people in the audience. Say that she has guessed correctly.

▶ Ist das Elkes Schwester?   *Ja, das ist ihre Schwester.*

1. Ist das Juttas Bruder?
2. Ist das Ottos und Pauls Lehrer?
3. Ist das Helgas und Eriks Lehrerin?
4. Ist das Evas Vater?
5. Ist das Günters und Tanjas Mutter?

Ihr (formal, singular and plural)

Ist **Ihr** Bruder Arzt, Herr Schmidt?	Is *your* brother a doctor, Mr. Schmidt?
Ist **Ihre** Schwester Ärztin, Frau Schneider?	Is *your* sister a doctor, Ms. Schneider?

The word **Ihr** is the formal form for *your,* both singular and plural. In writing **Ihr** *(your)* is always capitalized.

N. Ihre Familie. Ask your teachers and other adults about their families and friends.

▶ Bruder / Arzt   *Ist Ihr Bruder Arzt?*

1. Vater / Kaufmann
2. Schwester / Lehrerin
3. Freund / Apotheker
4. Mutter / Ärztin
5. Freundin / Geschäftsfrau

Ist eure Ärztin gut?

O. Freunde und Familie. Gerd asks you a number of questions about your friends and relatives. Answer him in the negative.

▶ Tanzt Gerds Bruder gut? *Sein Bruder? Nein.*

1. Spielt Tanjas Schwester Tennis?
2. Kocht dein Bruder gut?
3. Spielt deine Schwester Geige?
4. Ist Stefans Vater Arzt?
5. Ist Volkers Mutter Geschäftsfrau?
6. Ist euer Arzt jung?
7. Ist eure Lehrerin alt?

P. Wir machen Musik. Your class is going to meet at your teacher's house next weekend, where everyone is going to play some music. You are discussing this with a friend. Answer the questions using German equivalents of the possessive adjectives in parentheses.

▶ Wo wohnt _____ Lehrer? *Wo wohnt euer Lehrer?*
   (your, familiar pl.)

1. Hey, wo ist _____ Flöte? *(my)*
2. Ist _____ Lehrer musikalisch? *(your, familiar pl.)*
3. Was spielt _____ Freundin Christine? *(your, familiar pl.)*
4. Kommt _____ Freund auch? *(her)*
5. Spielt _____ Freund Oliver nur Rockmusik? *(your, familiar sg.)*
6. Spielen Stefan, Paul und _____ Schwester Geige? *(their)*
7. _____ Musik ist wirklich gut. *(our)*

Sie finden klassische Musik schön.

Verbs with stem ending in -d or -t (A–B)

finden		
ich finde		wir finden
du **findest**	Sie finden	ihr **findet**
er/sie **findet**		sie finden

arbeiten		
ich arbeite		wir arbeiten
du **arbeitest**	Sie arbeiten	ihr **arbeitet**
er/sie **arbeitet**		sie arbeiten

Verbs with stem ending in **-d** or **-t** require an **-e** before the present-tense endings **-st** or **-t.**

Verbs with stem ending in a sibilant (C)

heißen		
ich heiße		wir heißen
du **heißt**	Sie heißen	ihr **heißt**
er/sie **heißt**		sie heißen

tanzen		
ich tanze		wir tanzen
du **tanzt**	Sie tanzen	ihr **tanzt**
er/sie **tanzt**		sie tanzen

The sounds represented by the letters **s, ss, ß, z,** and **tz** are called sibilants. When a verb stem ends in a sibilant, the **-st** of the **du**-form ending contracts to **-t,** making the **du-** and **er/sie**-forms identical.

Position of the verb in statements (D–E)

1	2	3	4
Brigitte	arbeitet	am Samstag	zu Hause.
Am Samstag	arbeitet	Brigitte	zu Hause.

In a German statement the verb is always in second position, even when an element other than the subject (for example, an adverb or a prepositional phrase) is in first position. When a word or phrase other than the subject begins the sentence, the subject follows the verb.

Position of **nicht**

Frau Wagner arbeitet **nicht.**   Ms. Wagner does *not* work.

Mark spielt heute **nicht.**   Mark is *not* playing today.

Er spielt **nicht** gut und auch **nicht** oft.   He does *not* play well and also *not* often.

In German, **nicht** always follows the verb (for example, **arbeitet, spielt**). **Nicht** follows specific adverbs of time (for example, **heute**). **Nicht** precedes most other adverbs (for example, **gut**) and adverbs expressing general time (for example, **oft**).

Possession with proper names (F)

Das ist **Bettinas** Gitarre.   That's *Bettina's* guitar.

Wie alt ist **Peters** Schwester?   How old is *Peter's* sister?

A proper name is a word that designates a specific individual or place, for example: Bettina. In German, as in English, possession and other close relationships are expressed by adding **-s** to proper names. In written German, no apostrophe is used before the **-s.**

Ist das **Jens'** Vater?   Is that *Jens's* father?

Wie alt ist **Franz'** Bruder?   How old is *Franz's* brother?

German does not add an **-s** if a name already ends in an **s**-sound. In written German, an apostrophe is used after a name ending in an **s**-sound.

Bettinas Vater ist jung.

Possessive adjectives (G–P)

SUBJECT PRONOUN	POSSESSIVE ADJECTIVE	
ich	mein/meine	my
du	dein/deine	your
er	sein/seine	his
sie	ihr/ihre	her
wir	unser/unsere	our
ihr	euer/eure	your
sie	ihr/ihre	their
Sie	Ihr/Ihre	your

Mein Bruder arbeitet viel.
Meine Schwester arbeitet auch viel.

Possessive adjectives add no special ending when they modify masculine nouns. They end in **-e** when they modify feminine nouns.

Hier ist **Rita.** Und das ist **ihr** Vater.	Here's *Rita.* And that's *her* father.
Hier sind **Inge und Jens.** Und das ist **ihr** Vater.	Here are *Inge and Jens.* And that's *their* father.
Guten Tag, Frau Meier. Ist das **Ihr** Vater?	Hello, Ms. Meier. Is that *your* father?

Context usually makes clear whether one is speaking about **ihr/e** (her), **ihr/e** (their), or **Ihr/e** (your). In writing, **Ihr/e** (your) is always capitalized.

Wie alt ist **euer** Vater?
Wie alt ist **eure** Mutter?

When **euer** has an ending, the **-e** before the **-r** is usually omitted: **euere** > **eure**.

Capitalization of **du** and **dein** / **ihr** and **euer** in letters

Lieber Michael!
. . . Was machst **Du** am Samstag? Was macht **Dein** Bruder Jens? Geht **Ihr** tanzen? . . . Hoffentlich schreibst **Du** bald . . .

In letters or notes the German equivalents for *you* and *your* are capitalized: **Du, Dein/e, Ihr/e,** and **Eu(e)r/e.**

A. Was sind sie von Beruf? (What careers do they have?) Identify the occupations shown in the drawings. Use the German name for each occupation in a brief sentence.

▶ *Meine Mutter ist Ärztin.*
Ist deine Freundin Ärztin?

B. Wer ist das? You're showing some snapshots of people to Kurt, who tries to identify them. Confirm or deny his guesses, as in the model.

▶ Das ist Gerdas Vater, nicht?   *Ja, das ist ihr Vater.*
                                    Nein, das ist nicht ihr Vater.

1. Das ist Brunos Schwester, nicht?
2. Das ist Petras Bruder, nicht?
3. Das ist Andreas' Mutter, nicht?
4. Das ist Lottes Freund, nicht?
5. Das ist deine Freundin Katja, nicht?
6. Das ist dein Freund Stefan, nicht?
7. Das ist Kurts Vater, nicht?
8. Das ist euer Lehrer, nicht?
9. Das ist Jans und Ellens Mutter, nicht?

C. Inges Geburtstag. Choose the phrase that best completes each statement based on the following paragraph.

Meine Schwester Inge hat am Samstag Geburtstag. Am Samstag abend kommen ihr Freund Hans und seine Schwester Gabi. Hans ist Verkäufer, und Gabi ist Friseurin. Sie sind beide sehr musikalisch. Gabi spielt gut Klavier. Hans spielt sehr gut Schlagzeug. Inge spielt nicht schlecht Gitarre. Ich spiele Klarinette — nicht gut, aber gern. Hoffentlich spielen wir am Samstag. Das macht wirklich Spaß.

1. Am Samstag . . .
   a. arbeitet Inge.
   b. kommen Inges Freund und seine Schwester.
   c. geht Inge nach Hause.
2. Gabi . . .
   a. spielt nicht gern Klavier.
   b. spielt Klavier, und Hans spielt Schlagzeug.
   c. ist die Freundin von Hans.
3. Inges Bruder . . .
   a. spielt auch Schlagzeug.
   b. spielt gern Klarinette.
   c. spielt gut Klarinette.

D. Sag das! Form questions, using the cues provided.

▶ warum / du / arbeiten / nicht / ?   *Warum arbeitest du nicht?*

1. dein Vater / arbeiten / abends / ?
2. du / tanzen / gern / ?
3. wie / deine Schwester / heißen / ?
4. wann / wir / gehen / nach Hause / ?
5. wann / Rita / arbeiten / ?

E. Deine Familie und Freunde. Make a list of your friends. Show this and the family tree you have already drawn (p. 62) to your friend. She/he is very interested in the people you know. Tell her/him as much as you can. She/he may use the following questions or make up her/his own.

Ist deine Mutter jung oder alt?
Ist dein Vater jung oder alt?
Ist dein Bruder [Volker] prima oder doof?
Ist deine Schwester [Erika] faul oder fleißig?
Ist dein Freund [Hannes] groß oder klein? Und deine Freundin [Barbara]?
Ist deine Freundin [Cordula] glücklich oder unglücklich? Und dein Freund [Alex]?
Ist deine Freundin [Petra] oft sauer? Und dein Freund [Hans-Dieter]?
Ist dein Freund [Stefan] faul oder fleißig? Und deine Freundin [Angelika]?

F. Wie sagt man das? Say in German that . . .

1. your friend likes to play tennis.
2. in the evening, you play cards.
3. that's fun.
4. Peter's brother is home.
5. he plays the piano well.

G. Eine andere Familie. Write a short paragraph about two members of your friend's family. Show it to your friend to make sure the information is correct.

H. Land und Leute.

1. Compare the ways German and American families spend time together.
2. Compare the ways Sundays are spent in German and American families.
3. What do you think the differences are between the German influence in the United States and the American influence in the German-speaking countries?

Vokabeln

Substantive

der Apotheker/die Apothekerin pharmacist
der Arbeiter/die Arbeiterin worker
der Arzt/die Ärztin doctor, physician
der Brieffreund/die Brieffreundin pen pal
der Elektriker/die Elektrikerin electrician
der Freund/die Freundin friend
der Friseur/die Friseurin hairdresser
der Geschäftsmann/die Geschäftsfrau
  businessman/businesswoman
der Lehrer/die Lehrerin teacher
der Schüler/die Schülerin student
der Verkäufer/die Verkäuferin salesman/
  saleswoman

der Beruf career, profession
der Brief letter
der Bruder brother
der Donnerstag Thursday
der Freitag Friday
der Meter meter
der Montag Monday

Substantive (cont.)

der Name name
(der) Rock rock (music)
der Samstag Saturday
der Sonntag Sunday
der Vater father
der Zentimeter centimeter

das Bild picture; photo
(das) Deutsch German language
das Hobby hobby
das Jahr year
das Kind child
das Wochenende weekend

die Familie family
die Musik music; Musik machen to play
  music; Musik hören to listen to music
die Mutter mother
die Schwester sister

die Karten (playing) cards

Verben

arbeiten to work
finden to find; **wie findest du Rockmusik?** What do you think of rock?
heißen to be named, called
hören to hear; **Musik hören** to listen to music
kochen to cook
kommen to come
lernen to learn; to study
schreiben to write
singen to sing
tanzen to dance; **tanzen gehen** to go dancing

Andere Wörter

abends evenings, in the evening
bald soon
bis till, until
dein your *(sg.)*
doof goofy, dumb, stupid
dünn thin
ein(e) a, an
euer your *(pl.)*
groß big; tall (refers to people)
hoffentlich I hope, let's hope
ihr her; their
Ihr your *(formal)*
klassisch classical
klein small, little; short (refers to people)

Andere Wörter (cont.)

lieber/liebe dear *(opening in letters)*
mein my
mir me
musikalisch musical
noch still, yet
schlank slender, slim
schön nice
sein his
spät late; **zu spät** too late, tardy
unser our
von of; **das Bild ist von mir** the picture is of me

Besondere Ausdrücke

ich lerne schon zwei Jahre Deutsch I've been studying German for two years
ich bin fünfzehn Jahre alt I'm fifteen years old
sie ist aber noch ein Kind she's still a child
wie groß bist du? how tall are you?
treibst du Sport? are you active in sports?
das macht Spaß! that's fun!
herzliche Grüße best wishes, kind regards, sincerely *(closing in letters)*
am Samstag on Saturday

NOCH EINMAL

A

Wer bin ich? Prepare a short autobiography. It may include information about your age, birthday, appearance, address, family members, parents' occupations, work habits, hobbies. The autobiographies are divided between two panels of five members each. First one team of panel members takes turns reading the information provided in the autobiographies, while the other team tries to identify the writer. The panels then switch roles. The team that guesses the identities of the most students wins. The quiz continues with new panels until all students have participated.

B

Deutsche in der Welt. Gather information on the German influence in the United States. Look through a telephone directory and list 25 names of people who might be of German origin. From a state map, see how many names of towns indicate they may have been settled by Germans. Collect magazine pictures that pertain to German-speaking people around the world. Report your findings.

C

Deutsche Teenager. Look at the pictures of the young people in the photographs in this Stage and describe two or three of them in German as completely as you can (name, age, height, personality, hobbies, family); or, select several of the teenagers you have met in the dialogues of Chapters 1–4 and discuss them, based on the dialogue material. In either case you may wish to invent some additional information.

Ein Interview. Interview a classmate in German. During your conversation, fill out a form with the answers to questions such as:

- **Name?**
- **Wie alt?**
- **Wie groß?**
- **Wohnen / wo?**

- **Gern machen?**
- **Vater?**
- **Mutter?**
- **Familie / gern machen?**

Wir sind eine Familie. In groups of three, four, or five, form a family. What are your names? How old are you? Where do you live? How tall are you? What is your relationship to each other? What do you have in common?

Guten Tag! Role-play the following situation. You may use the families developed in activity E.

You have just moved into a new neighborhood where other students live. Visit your neighbors and get to know them!

- **Name?**
- **Familie: Vater? Bruder? Mutter? Schwester?**
- **Wie alt?**
- **Geburtstag?**
- **Wie groß?**
- **Interessen?** (*interests*)
- **Was machst du (nicht) gern?**

Stufe 2

So leben wir

Kapitel 5

Brauchst du neue Sachen?

Der Pullover ist toll!

Das ist zu teuer

Astrid, Gisela, and Erik are window-shopping, looking at clothes.

ASTRID   Wie teuer ist das Kleid da?
GISELA   100 Mark, und das ist zu teuer.
ASTRID   Wie meinst du das?
GISELA   Ich finde, es ist häßlich.

ERIK   Die Jeans da sind echt klasse.
ASTRID   Meinst du? Wieviel kosten sie?
ERIK   60 Mark.
ASTRID   60 Mark! Das ist aber preiswert. Kaufst du sie?
ERIK   Ja.

Fragen

1. Ist das Kleid teuer?
2. Ist es schön?
3. Wie sind die Jeans?
4. Wieviel kosten sie? Ist das teuer?

Toll! Für Mädchen und Jungen!

1. das Hemd
   DM 35,—
2. die Jacke
   DM 75,—
3. die Hose
   DM 70,—
4. die Socken
   DM 8,—
5. die Bluse
   DM 38,—
6. der Gürtel
   DM 25,—
7. die Jeans
   DM 80,—

Schick! Für Damen und Herren!

1. der Pulli
   DM 80,—
2. der Rock
   DM 77,—
3. die Schuhe
   DM 90,—
4. der Anzug
   DM 300,—
5. die Krawatte
   DM 28,—
6. der Mantel
   DM 350,—
7. die Handschuhe
   DM 36,—

Fragen

1. Wieviel kostet das Hemd? die Jacke? der Rock?
2. Wieviel kosten die Jeans? die Schuhe? die Socken?

Du hast das Wort

1. **Teuer oder billig?** What is your reaction to the price of each item of clothing   **Evaluating prices**
   mentioned below?

   GESPRÄCHSPARTNER/IN

   Das Hemd kostet DM 80,— .
   Die Krawatte kostet DM 7,— .
   Der Mantel kostet DM 800,— .
   Die Handschuhe kosten DM 4,— .
   Die Jacke kostet DM 150,— .
   Die Bluse kostet DM 28,— .
   Der Pullover° kostet DM 80,— .
   Der Gürtel kostet DM 25,— .
   Die Hose kostet DM 75,— .
   Der Anzug kostet DM 550,— .

   DU

   Das ist furchtbar° teuer.
   Das ist (sehr) teuer.
   Das ist preiswert.
   Das ist billig°.
   Das ist spottbillig°.

2. **Wie findest du das?** A friend asks you to react to some of the clothes pictured on pages 89–90. How would you respond?

GESPRÄCHSPARTNER/IN		DU
Wie ist	die Jacke?	Toll!
	der Rock?	Klasse!
	das Hemd?	Modisch°.
		Schick°.
		[Sehr] schön.
		[Sehr] hübsch°.
		Gut.
		Nicht schlecht.
		Altmodisch°.
		Häßlich.
		Scheußlich°.

3. **Das ist aber schön!** Compliment your friends. Walk around the room complimenting your classmates on what they are wearing.

Giving compliments

Deine Jacke ist toll!
Der Gürtel ist klasse!
Deine Hose ist nicht schlecht.
Die Bluse ist sehr schön.

Land und Leute

German stores are permitted by law to have a clearance sale **(Ausverkauf)** twice a year: a winter sale **(Winterschlußverkauf)** at the end of January and a summer sale **(Sommerschlußverkauf)** at the end of July. In addition, there may be special offers **(Sonderangebote)** periodically.

Im Winterschlußverkauf ist alles billiger.

KONFEKTIONSGRÖSSEN: EUROPA/USA

Kleidung für Damen						Kleidung für Herren					
Blusen, Röcke, Kleider, Mäntel, Hosen						**Anzüge, Jacken, Mäntel, Hosen**					
Europa	32	34	36	38	40	42	Europa	40	42	44	46	48	50
USA	4	6	8	10	12	14	USA	30	32	34	36	38	40

Pullis						**Hemden**					
Europa	38	40	42	44	46	48	Europa	35	36	37	38	39	40
USA	30	32	34	36	38	40	USA	13½	14	14½	15	15½	16

Schuhe						**Schuhe**					
Europa	36	37	38	39	40	41	Europa	38	39	40	41	42	43
USA	5	6	7	8	9	10	USA	5	6½	7½	8½	9	10

Welche Größe trägst du?

Astrid is helping Erik look for a new coat.

ASTRID   Hier ist ein Mantel in Braun. Schön, nicht?

ERIK   Ja, toll. Er ist auch schön warm.

ASTRID   Paßt er?

ERIK   Leider nicht. Er ist zu groß.

ASTRID   Welche Größe trägst du denn?

ERIK   Größe 40.

ASTRID   Hier ist deine Größe.

ERIK   Das ist aber kein Mantel. Das ist eine Jacke.

ASTRID   Ach ja. Schade.

Du hast das Wort

1. **Welche Größe tragen sie?** Name an article of clothing you'd like to buy for   **Shopping** a friend or relative. Give the size you need according to the chart.

Jacke   Er/sie trägt Größe . . .

2. **Paßt es?** Take the role of a salesperson trying to help a customer in a clothing store.

DU

Paßt [der Mantel]?

GESPRÄCHSPARTNER/IN

Ja.
Ja, [er] paßt sehr gut.
Nein, [er] ist zu groß.
Nein, [er] ist zu klein.
Nein, ich brauche Größe [40].

3. **Die falsche Größe.** Create a dialogue with a partner. You are in a store looking for a sweater for a friend. You both wear the same size. The salesperson shows you one that is too large.

Land und Leute

German fashion magazines for teenagers are filled with terms that people from America or Great Britain would recognize. This **Trend** started many years ago, when **Jeans** conquered the fashion market. After the American brands **Levi's, Wrangler,** and **Lee** had proven popular among teenagers, clothing firms in the Federal Republic began giving their own jeans such labels as **Bronco, Pioneer, Mustang,** and **Explorer.** Stores now sell **T-Shirts, Sweatshirts,** and **Boots** to go with the jeans. Those who find this **Street-Look** too casual can buy **Pumps mit Pep** or a **Blazer mit Schick.** When they go dancing, girls may choose **Make-up im Opera-Look,** including **Styling-Schaum** (styling mousse) and **Color Spray** to give their **Outfit** a nice finish. But who knows? What is **in** this year may be **out** next year.

Sind die beiden in der Bundesrepublik oder in den USA?

Die Farben

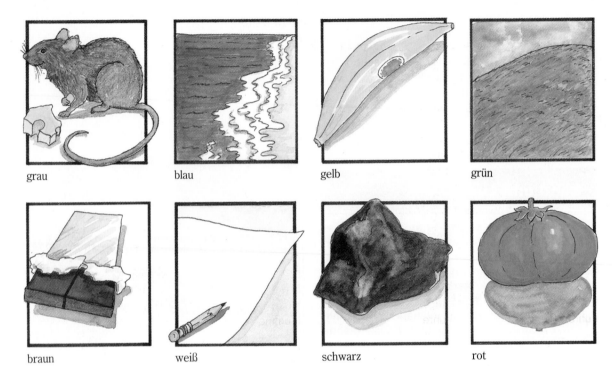

grau

blau

gelb

grün

braun

weiß

schwarz

rot

A. Farben. Use the pictures above to complete these sentences.

1. Die See ist _____.
2. Die Schokolade ist _____.
3. Die Banane ist _____.
4. Die Maus ist _____.

5. Das Gras ist _____.
6. Die Tomate ist _____.
7. Die Kohle ist _____.
8. Das Papier ist _____.

B. Welche Farbe? Ask a classmate about the color of the clothes she/he is wearing.

▶ Welche Farbe hat | dein Pulli?   *Mein Pulli ist [rot].*
                                   | dein Hemd?
                                   | dein Gürtel?
                                   | dein Kleid?
                                   | deine Jacke?
                                   | deine Bluse?
                                   | deine Hose?

Aussprache

long vowel [u] gut, Bluse, Schuh
short vowel [U] und, Pulli

A. Practice vertically in columns and horizontally in pairs.

[u]	[U]
Buße	Busse
Buch	Bucht
Huhne	Hunne
Buhle	Bulle
Mus	muß

B. Practice the following words horizontally in pairs.

[u]	[y]	[U]	[Y]
Fuße	Füße	mußte	müßte
Hute	Hüte	Busche	Büsche
Zuge	Züge	junger	jünger
Fuhre	führe	krummen	krümmen
gute	Güte	dunkel	Dünkel

Ende gut, alles gut.

C. Practice the sounds [u] and [U]. Read the sentences aloud.

1. Wieviel kosten die Bluse und der Pulli?
2. Warum trägt Utes Bruder keine Schuhe?
3. Der Junge spielt gut Fußball.
4. Ritas Mutter mag Musik.

Übungen

1. Verbs with stem-vowel change a > ä

tragen
ich trage
du trägst
er/es/sie trägt

Tragen has a stem-vowel change **a > ä** in the **du-** and **er/es/sie-**forms of the present tense.

A. Sachen für die Party. Find out what your friends are wearing to the party tonight.

▶ Paula *Was trägt Paula heute abend?*

1. Rita
2. Günter
3. Stefan

4. du
5. Birgit und Ute
6. ihr

B. Was trägst du gern? Some friends are talking about clothes. Complete the sentences with the appropriate form of **tragen.**

▶ Ich *trage* gern Röcke.

1. Was ____ Stefanie?
2. Inge und Gerd ____ heute Handschuhe.
3. ____ du gern Jeans?
4. Ja, und ich ____ auch gern T-Shirts.
5. Was ____ ihr am Samstag?
6. Wir ____ natürlich Jeans.

2. The singular definite articles **der, das, die**

der Mann   **das** Mädchen   **die** Frau
der Gürtel   **das** Kleid   **die** Bluse

The definite articles **der, das,** and **die** are used with nouns and are equivalent to the English definite article *the*.

C.   Wieviel kostet . . . ?   Inquire about the price of each article of clothing.

▶   der Pulli   *Wieviel kostet der Pulli?*

1. die Jacke   3. die Bluse   5. die Krawatte
2. das Hemd   4. der Anzug   6. der Gürtel

D.   Meine Meinung. (My opinion.)   Give your opinion of each of the following articles of clothing.

▶   *Der Pulli ist klasse [häßlich, schön, etc.].*

E. Wie heißen sie? You don't recognize a number of people at a school event. Ask a friend to identify them.

▶ die Frau da   *Wie heißt die Frau da?*

1. die Lehrerin da
2. der Lehrer da
3. das Mädchen da

4. der Junge da
5. der Mann da
6. das Kind da

3. Noun plurals

SINGULAR	PLURAL
ein Mantel	zwei **Mäntel**
ein Rock	zwei **Röcke**
ein Kleid	zwei **Kleider**
ein Hemd	zwei **Hemden**

There is no simple way of predicting the plural form of a noun. German noun plurals are formed according to several basic patterns. The patterns are listed in the **Grammatische Übersicht** on page 105.

Schneyer in Karlsruhe hat Sachen für Damen und Herren.

F. Was kosten . . . ? You and a friend are applying basic multiplication patterns to practical situations. Tell what the following purchases would cost.

▶ Ein Kleid kostet 200 Mark.   *Zwei Kleider kosten 400*
    Was kosten zwei Kleider?   *Mark.*

1. Ein Mantel kostet 300 Mark. Was kosten zwei Mäntel?
2. Ein Gürtel kostet 20 Mark. Was kosten vier Gürtel?
3. Ein Hemd kostet 30 Mark. Was kosten drei Hemden?
4. Eine Jacke kostet 100 Mark. Was kosten zwei Jacken?
5. Eine Krawatte kostet 15 Mark. Was kosten drei Krawatten?
6. Ein Anzug kostet 250 Mark. Was kosten zwei Anzüge?

4. The plural definite article **die**

SINGULAR		PLURAL	
Der Pulli		**Die** Pullis	
Das Kleid	ist teuer.	**Die** Kleider	sind teuer.
Die Jacke		**Die** Jacken	

The definite article **die** is used with plural nouns.

G. Meine Meinung. You're shopping in a department store with Mark. Tell him what you think about the following items.

▶ Schuhe / klasse   *Die Schuhe sind klasse.*

1. Jeans / preiswert
2. Socken / schön warm
3. Hemden / häßlich
4. Pullis / toll
5. Gürtel / spottbillig
6. Jacken / scheußlich

5. Noun-pronoun relationship

Singular

Der Junge ist toll. **Der Gürtel** ist toll.	**Er** ist toll.
Das Kind ist hübsch. **Das Kleid** ist hübsch.	**Es** ist hübsch.
Die Frau ist schick. **Die Jacke** ist schick.	**Sie** ist schick.

Kaufhaus in Hamburg

H. Ja, wirklich. Confirm Ute's guesses about the following articles of clothing.

▶ Ist der Pullover teuer? *Ja, er ist wirklich teuer.*

1. Ist der Mantel billig?
2. Ist der Rock häßlich?
3. Ist der Anzug altmodisch?
4. Ist das Hemd alt?
5. Ist das Kleid schön?
6. Ist die Jacke preiswert?
7. Ist die Hose doof?
8. Ist die Bluse schick?

Modisch immer schön locker bleiben.

I. Nein, so ist es nicht. Tanja disagrees with everything Margot says. Take the part of Tanja.

▶ Der Mantel ist billig, nicht? *Der Mantel? Nein, er ist teuer.*

1. Das Hemd ist häßlich, nicht?
2. Die Bluse ist modisch, nicht?
3. Der Pulli ist neu, nicht?
4. Die Hose ist teuer, nicht?
5. Das Kleid ist schön, nicht?

J. Wie spielen sie? Ask whether the following people are good at the things they do.

▶ Mein Bruder spielt Tennis. *Spielt er gut?*

1. Meine Mutter spielt Klavier.
2. Mein Freund spielt Volleyball.
3. Mein Vater spielt Gitarre.
4. Meine Schwester spielt Flöte.
5. Meine Freundin spielt Klarinette.
6. Mein Lehrer spielt Fußball.

Plural

Die Jeans sind klasse.   **Sie** sind wirklich toll.
Die Hemden sind klasse.   Und **sie** sind billig.

K. Ja, ziemlich. You are at a flea market with Katrin. Say that you agree more or less with her opinions.

▶ Die Schuhe da sind teuer, nicht? *Ja, sie sind ziemlich teuer.*

1. Die Handschuhe da sind preiswert, nicht?
2. Die Jeans da sind billig, nicht?
3. Die Hemden da sind gut, nicht?
4. Die Jacken da sind alt, nicht?

5. Die Gürtel da sind neu, nicht?
6. Die Blusen da sind schick, nicht?
7. Die Verkäufer da sind jung, nicht?

L. Sind die Sachen preiswert? Thomas is pointing out various items in a clothing catalogue. Ask him whether they're reasonably priced.

▶ Der Mantel ist schön.   *Ist er preiswert?*

▶ Die Socken sind warm.   *Sind sie preiswert?*

1. Der Rock ist schick.
2. Das Kleid ist klasse.
3. Die Bluse ist hübsch.
4. Das Hemd ist toll.

5. Der Gürtel ist schön.
6. Die Schuhe sind schick.
7. Die Jeans sind klasse.
8. Die Handschuhe sind warm.

M. Wie sind sie? Ask original questions about the following items of clothing.

▶ *Petras Hemd ist schick. Ist es neu?*

Petras	Hemd	ist	schick.	Ist	es	neu?
	Rock		toll.		er	
	Mantel		zu groß.		er	
	Schuhe	sind	schön.	Sind	sie	
	Handschuhe		hübsch.			

Sind diese super Preise wirklich billig?

6. Nominative case of ein

Der Anzug kostet 1500 Mark.	**Ein Anzug** kostet wirklich 1500 Mark?
Das Hemd kostet 150 Mark.	**Ein Hemd** kostet wirklich 150 Mark?
Die Jacke kostet 600 Mark.	**Eine Jacke** kostet wirklich 600 Mark?
Die Schuhe kosten 250 Mark.	**Schuhe** kosten wirklich 250 Mark?

The indefinite articles **ein** and **eine** are equivalent to English *a* or *an*. **Ein** and **eine** have no plural form.

N. Wieviel kosten die Sachen?   You're trying to find out how much clothing costs in the Federal Republic. Ask your teacher about the price of the following things.

▶ Anzug   *Wieviel kostet ein Anzug?*

1. Pulli	4. Hemd	7. Krawatte
2. Bluse	5. Jacke	8. Gürtel
3. Kleid	6. Rock	9. Hose

O. Echt?   Some acquaintances brag about how much their clothes cost. You find the prices ridiculous. Say that the things *can't* be that expensive.

▶ Meine Jacke kostet 200 Mark.   *Echt? Eine Jacke kostet nicht soviel!*

1. Meine Hose kostet 500 Mark.
2. Mein Hemd kostet 300 Mark.
3. Mein Mantel kostet 900 Mark.
4. Petras Bluse kostet 200 Mark.
5. Ellens Kleid kostet 800 Mark.
6. Hugos Jacke kostet 600 Mark.

7. Nominative case of kein

Ist das **ein Pulli?**	Nein, das ist **kein Pulli,** das ist ein Hemd.
Ist das **ein Hemd?**	Nein, das ist **kein Hemd,** das ist ein Pulli.
Ist das **eine Bluse?**	Nein, das ist **keine Bluse,** das ist eine Jacke.
Sind das **Blusen?**	Nein, das sind **keine Blusen,** das sind Hemden.

Kein and **keine** are equivalent to English *not a, not an, not any,* or *no.* **Kein** is used before **der-** and **das-**nouns. **Keine** is used before **die-**nouns and plural nouns.

P. Das ist zu teuer. Andreas is guessing the price of clothes in a catalogue. Disagree with his guesses.

▶ Was kostet der Mantel? 2000 Mark?　　*Nein, kein Mantel kostet 2000 Mark.*

1. Was kostet der Pulli? 900 Mark?
2. Was kostet die Jacke? 3000 Mark?
3. Was kostet das Hemd? 500 Mark?
4. Was kostet die Bluse? 150 Mark?
5. Was kostet die Krawatte? 400 Mark?
6. Was kosten die Handschuhe? 90 Mark?

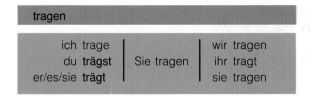

Schön zu kombinieren: **Jacke und Rock, Hemd und Hose**

Verbs with stem-vowel change a > ä (A–B)

tragen		
ich trage		wir tragen
du **trägst**	Sie tragen	ihr tragt
er/es/sie **trägt**		sie tragen

A number of German verbs have a stem-vowel change (for example **a > ä**) in the **du-** and **er/es/sie-**forms of the present tense. In the vocabularies of this text, the stem-vowel change of the **du-** and **er/es/sie-**forms is shown in parentheses directly after the infinitive: **tragen (ä).**

Nominative case

Meine Schwester spielt Klavier.
Spielt **dein Freund** Klarinette?

German nouns show different cases depending on how they are used in a sentence. When a noun is used as the subject of a sentence, it is in the nominative case.

SUBJECT		PREDICATE NOUN
Das Mädchen	ist	meine Schwester.
Der Junge da	ist	der Bruder von Inge.

A predicate noun is a noun that designates a person, concept, or thing that is equated with the subject and follows the verb **sein** or **heißen**. A predicate noun is in the nominative case.

The singular definite articles **der, das, die** (C–E)

der Mann	**das** Mädchen	**die** Frau
der Gürtel	**das** Kleid	**die** Bluse

The singular definite articles **der, das,** and **die** function like the English definite article *the*. They are used with singular nouns in the nominative case.

There are three groups of nouns in German: **der**-nouns, **das**-nouns, and **die**-nouns. Most nouns referring to males are **der**-nouns; most nouns referring to females are **die**-nouns. (**Das Mädchen** is an exception.) Objects may belong to any group, for example **der Gürtel, das Kleid, die Bluse.** Since there is no simple way of predicting which group a noun belongs to, it is very important to learn the definite article when you learn the noun. Learn **der Gürtel,** not just **Gürtel.**

The plural definite article **die** (G)

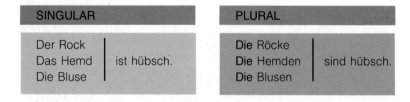

SINGULAR	
Der Rock	
Das Hemd	ist hübsch.
Die Bluse	

PLURAL	
Die Röcke	
Die Hemden	sind hübsch.
Die Blusen	

The definite article used with plural nouns is **die.**

Noun plurals (F)

In German, noun plurals are formed according to five basic patterns. There is no simple way of predicting the plural form of a noun. You will, however, gradually discover that there is a kind of system to these patterns.

This "system" depends partly on whether the noun is a **der-**, **das-**, or **die-** noun, and partly on how many syllables it has. From now on, learn the plural of the noun when you learn the singular form.

PATTERN 1

no change in plural	das Mädchen	die Mädchen
	der Gürtel	die Gürtel
plural adds umlaut	der Vater	die Väter
	der Mantel	die Mäntel

PATTERN 2

plural adds **-e**	der Freund	die Freunde
	der Schuh	die Schuhe
plural adds **-e** and umlaut	der Anzug	die Anzüge
	der Rock	die Röcke

PATTERN 3

plural adds **-er**	das Kind	die Kinder
	das Kleid	die Kleider
plural adds **-er** and umlaut	der Mann	die Männer
	das Buch	die Bücher

PATTERN 4

plural adds **-n**	der Junge	die Jungen
	die Schwester	die Schwestern
plural adds **-en**	das Hemd	die Hemden
plural adds **-nen**	die Lehrerin	die Lehrerinnen
	die Ärztin	die Ärztinnen

PATTERN 5

plural adds **-s**	das Hobby	die Hobbys
	der Pulli	die Pullis

In the vocabularies of this text, the plural of most nouns will be indicated directly after the singular. For example:

der Lehrer, —   indicates that there is no change in the plural form of the noun: **der Lehrer > die Lehrer.**

der Rock, ⸚e   indicates that an **-e** is added in the plural, and an umlaut is added to the appropriate vowel: **der Rock > die Röcke.**

Here are the plurals of some other familiar nouns.

der Apotheker, —   die Apothekerin, —nen
der Arbeiter, —   die Arbeiterin, —nen
der Arzt, ⸚e   die Ärztin, —nen
der Ball, ⸚e   die Elektrikerin, —nen
der Brief, —e   die Familie, —n
der Bruder, ⸚   die Frau, —en
der Elektriker, —   die Freundin, —nen
der Friseur, —e   die Friseurin, —nen
der Lehrer, —   die Geschäftsfrau, —en
der Mann, ⸚er   die Lehrerin, —nen
der Name, —n   die Minute, —n
der Schüler, —   die Mutter, ⸚
der Tag, —e   die Schülerin, —nen
der Verkäufer, —   die Straße, —n
                              die Verkäuferin, —nen

das Jahr, —e

Noun-pronoun relationship (H–M)

SINGULAR	
Der Mann ist alt. Der Anzug ist alt.	Er ist alt.
Das Kind ist schön. Das Kleid ist schön.	Es ist schön.
Die Frau ist hübsch. Die Jacke ist hübsch.	Sie ist hübsch.

PLURAL	
Die Lehrer sind neu. Die Jeans sind neu.	Sie sind neu.

Meloni
JOHANNES-DAUR-STR. 19   7015 KORNTAL
DIE FRISCHE MODE

A pronoun is a word used to replace a noun. The pronouns **er, es, sie** *(sg.)*, and **sie** *(pl.)* may refer to either persons or things.

In the singular, **er** replaces **der**-nouns.
               es replaces **das**-nouns.
               sie replaces **die**-nouns.

In the plural, **sie** replaces all nouns.

Nominative case of **ein** and **kein** (N–P)

Das ist **ein** Hemd.	That's *a* shirt.
Das ist **eine** Bluse.	That's *a* blouse.
Das ist **kein** Pulli.	That's *not a* sweater
Das ist **keine** Jacke.	That's *not a* jacket.

The indefinite articles **ein** and **eine** are equivalent to English *a* or *an*. The negative forms **kein** and **keine** are equivalent to English *not a (not an), not any,* or *no*.

SINGULAR	
der Pulli	Das ist **ein** Pulli.
	kein
das Hemd	Das ist **ein** Hemd.
	kein
die Bluse	Das ist **eine** Bluse.
	keine

ZU JEANS PASST JEDE JACKENFORM

Ein and **kein** are used before **der-** and **das-**nouns in the nominative case. **Eine** and **keine** are used before **die-**nouns in the nominative case.

PLURAL	
die Jeans	Das sind Jeans.
	Das sind **keine** Jeans.

Ein and **eine** have no plural form.
Keine is used before plural nouns in the nominative case.

Kein and nicht

Ist das **ein Hemd?**	Nein, das ist **kein Hemd.**
Trägst du **Jeans?**	Nein, ich trage **keine Jeans.**
Ist das **die Jacke?**	Nein, das ist **nicht die Jacke.**
Ist das **dein Hemd?**	Nein, das ist **nicht mein Hemd.**

Kein is used to negate a noun that would be preceded by **ein** or by no article at all in an affirmative sentence. **Nicht** is used in a negative sentence when the noun is preceded by a definite article or a possessive adjective.

Wiederholung

A. Was trägst du? Jan and Paul are talking about the party on Saturday. Answer the questions, based on the dialogue.

JAN Trägst du am Samstag eine Jacke?
PAUL Nein, ich trage keine Jacke. Ich trage nur ein Hemd.
JAN Warum?
PAUL Ich trage nicht gern Jacken. Und eine Jacke ist auch zu warm.

1. Was trägt Paul am Samstag?
2. Warum trägt er keine Jacke?

B. Sag das! Form sentences, using the cues provided.

1. Petra / treiben / gern / Sport
2. tanzen / du / viel / ?
3. was / tragen / Paula / am Samstag / ?
4. ich / tragen / oft / Jeans
5. wie / heißen / der Junge da / ?

C. Was meinst du? You are in a negative mood, so you find fault with everything Susanne says. Use **er, es,** or **sie** in your answers, as appropriate.

▶ Das Hemd ist schick, nicht?   *Nein, ich finde, es ist häßlich.*
                                 Die Farbe ist furchtbar.
         Ja, aber es ist furchtbar teuer.

1. Die Bluse ist toll, nicht?
2. Claudias Kleid ist schön, nicht?
3. Ihr Rock ist hübsch, nicht?
4. Volkers Schuhe sind klasse, nicht?
5. Sein Pulli ist prima, nicht?

D. Wie findest du sie? Make up at least two sentences about the objects in each picture.

▶   *Hier sind zwei Hemden.*
                                      Sie sind preiswert.
                                      Sie sind ziemlich neu.

E. Antonyme. Complete each sentence with an appropriate antonym.

1. Die Jeans sind nicht zu teuer; sie sind _____.
2. Der Rock ist nicht häßlich; er ist sehr _____.
3. Der Pulli ist nicht zu groß; er ist zu _____.
4. Die Jacken da sind nicht alt; sie sind _____.
5. Die Schuhe sind nicht gut; sie sind sehr _____.
6. Das Kleid ist nicht billig; es ist furchtbar _____.

F. Wie sagt man das? Express the following in German.

1. Is Jörg going home?
2. He's going to play basketball this afternoon.
3. Does he play well?
4. Will you play tennis this afternoon?
5. No, I don't like to play tennis.
6. When are we going to go swimming?
7. Why are they going?

G. Meinungen. Column A consists of questions or comments about clothing. Choose an appropriate response to each one from column B.

A	B
Ist der Rock teuer?	Schade.
Die Mäntel da sind wirklich klasse.	DM 29,50.
Wieviel kostet die Krawatte da?	Nein, er ist ziemlich billig.
Das Hemd hier kostet nur DM 12,—.	Meinst du?
Wie findest du die Jacke?	Das ist ja spottbillig!
Die Jeans passen leider nicht.	Wirklich klasse!

H. Wie sagt man das? Express the following in German.

1. What's the name of that girl (there)?
   Her name is [. . .].
2. What color is her dress?
   It's [. . .].
3. How expensive is the sweater?
   It's a very good buy.
4. How much do the shoes cost?
   They cost [. . .].

I. Du und der Verkäufer. You want to buy a sweater for a friend. With a partner, develop a conversation between you and the salesperson.

J. Land und Leute.

1. What can you say about how teenagers in the German-speaking countries dress? How do German fashion magazines for teenagers often advertise their products?
2. Compare clearance sales in the Federal Republic of Germany and the United States.

Deutsche Mark: Geldscheine und Hartgeld

Geld°

money

Das ist eine Mark.
Eine Mark hat hundert Pfennig.

Das sind zehn Mark (DM 10,—).
Das ist ein Zehnmarkschein°.

10–Mark bill

Das sind auch zehn Mark (DM 10,—).
Das sind aber zwei Fünfmarkstücke°.

5–Mark pieces (coins)

Was bekommt° man für fünfzehn Mark?
Zum Beispiel°:

Zwei Tassen° Kaffee	DM 4,40
Zwei Stück Torte°	DM 7,00
	DM 11,40

get
zum Beispiel: for
example
cups
2 pieces of cake

Kaffee ist teuer in Deutschland. Torte auch.

A. Wieviel Stunden? Say how long the following people have to work in order to earn enough money for the items they want.

1. Ingrid verdient *(earns)* zwölf Mark die Stunde *(an hour)*. Sie kauft eine Jacke für *(for)* DM 120,— . Wieviel Stunden arbeitet sie für die Jacke?
2. Jan verdient zehn Mark die Stunde. Er kauft ein Polohemd für DM 50,— . Wieviel Stunden arbeitet er für das Polohemd?
3. Peter verdient neun Mark die Stunde. Er kauft eine Gitarre für DM 270,— . Wieviel Stunden arbeitet er für die Gitarre?
4. Ulrike verdient elf Mark die Stunde. Sie kauft Handschuhe für DM 22,— . Wieviel Stunden arbeitet sie für die Handschuhe?

Land und Leute

While the German-speaking countries are similar in many ways, they do not share a common currency. The Federal Republic's basic monetary unit is the **Mark.** The German Democratic Republic also uses a **Mark,** although its value is somewhat different from that of the Federal Republic. There are 100 **Pfennig** in a **Mark.**

Switzerland's basic unit is the **Franken,** roughly equal in value to the **Mark** of the Federal Republic. There are 100 **Rappen** in a **Franken.**

Austria's basic unit is the **Schilling.** The **Schilling** is a much smaller unit than the **Mark:** a piece of cake would cost about twenty-five **Schilling** in Austria and about three **Mark** and fifty **Pfennig** in the Federal Republic. There are 100 **Groschen** in a **Schilling.**

Vokabeln

Substantive

der Anzug, -̈e man's suit
der Gürtel, – belt
der Handschuh, -e glove
der Herr, -en gentleman
der Junge, -n boy
der Mann, -̈er man
der Mantel, -̈ coat
der Pulli, -s pullover
der Pullover, – sweater
der Rock, -̈e skirt
der Schuh, -e shoe

(das) Europa Europe
das Hemd, -en shirt
das Kleid, -er dress
das Mädchen, – girl

die Bluse, -n blouse
die Dame, -n lady, woman
die Farbe, -n color
die Größe, -n size
die Hose, -n pants, slacks
die Jacke, -n suit coat, jacket
die Kleidung clothing
die Krawatte, -n tie
die Mark German coin (DM = Deutsche
    Mark = 100 Pfennig)
die Sache, -n thing; (pl.) Sachen clothes
die Socke, -n sock

die Jeans (pl.) jeans

Verben

brauchen to need
kaufen to buy
kosten to cost
meinen to think; to mean
passen to fit; to match
tragen (ä) to wear

Andere Wörter

altmodisch old-fashioned, outdated
billig inexpensive, cheap

Andere Wörter (cont.)

blau blue
braun brown
da here, there
das that, the
echt really (colloquial); genuine
für for
furchtbar terribly
gelb yellow
grau gray
grün green
häßlich ugly
hübsch pretty; nice
kein not a, not any
klasse terrific (colloquial)
leider unfortunately
modisch stylish
neu new
preiswert a good buy
rot red
scheußlich horrible, hideous
schick chic, stylish
schön beautiful
schwarz black
spottbillig dirt-cheap
teuer expensive
warm warm
weiß white
welch (-er, -es, -e) which, what

Besondere Ausdrücke

wieviel kostet der Pulli? how much is the
    sweater?
welche Farbe hat dein Pulli? what color is
    your sweater?
welche Größe trägst du? what size do you
    wear?
ein Mantel in Braun a coat in brown
schade too bad

Kapitel 6

Der Schultag

Haben sie heute einen Klassentest?

Ingrids Stundenplan

Ingrid Wagner				Klasse 10		
Zeit	**Montag**	**Dienstag**	**Mittwoch**	**Donnerstag**	**Freitag**	**Samstag**
8.00 – 8.45	Sport	Physik	—	Deutsch	—	—
8.50 – 9.35	Sport	Mathe	Chemie	Erdkunde	Geschichte	Physik
9.35 – 9.55	1. große Pause					
9.55 – 10.40	Englisch	Englisch	Latein	Chemie	Mathe	Deutsch
10.45 – 11.30	Geschichte	Latein	Deutsch	Geschichte	Mathe	—
11.30 – 11.50	2. große Pause					
11.50 – 12.35	Mathe	Erdkunde	Englisch	Kunst	Latein	—
12.45 – 13.30	Biologie	Musik	Biologie	Kunst	Deutsch	—

Fragen

1. Was hat Ingrid Montag um° acht Uhr? Dienstag um 9.55 Uhr (neun Uhr fünfundfünfzig)? Donnerstag um 11.50 Uhr (elf Uhr fünfzig)?
2. Was hat Ingrid am Samstag?

Du hast das Wort

1. **Welche Fächer?** A classmate asks you which subjects you have today. How would you respond?

   Talking about school

GESPRÄCHSPARTNER/IN	DU
Welche Fächer° hast du heute?	Heute habe ich [Bio, Chemie und Deutsch].

2. **Welche Fächer?**   Ask a classmate which subjects she/he has this year.

DU

Welche Fächer hast du
   dieses° Jahr?

GESPRÄCHSPARTNER/IN

[Deutsch, Mathe, Bio, Englisch
   und Geschichte.]

3. **Dein Stundenplan.**   Using a **Stundenplan** like the one on page 115, draw
up what you think would be the perfect schedule for your school day. Then find
a partner. Ask your partner about her/his schedule and fill in the information on
a new schedule.

DU

Was hast du um 8 Uhr?

GESPRÄCHSPARTNER/IN

Ich habe Physik.

Im Klassenzimmer

Gisela and Dieter are waiting for class to begin.

GISELA   Was haben wir um neun? Chemie?
DIETER   Nein, heute haben wir keine Chemie. Wir haben Mathe.
GISELA   Oh, prima!
DIETER   Mathe und „prima"?
GISELA   Ja, ich finde Mathe interessant. Mathe ist mein Lieblingsfach.

Fragen

1. Was hat Gisela um neun Uhr?
2. Was ist Giselas Lieblingsfach?
3. Findet Dieter Mathe interessant?

Du hast das Wort

1. **Dein Lieblingsfach.** (Favorite subject.)   Ask a classmate which subjects
she/he likes and why.

**Expressing likes
and dislikes**

DU

Was ist dein Lieblingsfach?

Warum?

GESPRÄCHSPARTNER/IN

[Englisch].

Ich finde [Englisch] | toll.
   | interessant.
   | prima.
   | leicht°.

2. **Welches Fach hast du nicht gern?** Ask a classmate which subject she/he does not like and why.

DU	GESPRÄCHSPARTNER/IN
Welches Fach hast du nicht gern?	[Bio].
Warum?	Es ist langweilig°.
	zu schwer°.

3. **Welches Fach hast du gern?** Ask five members of the class which subjects they like and dislike and why. Make a tally. The teacher will ask you for a summary of your findings.

▶ *Sally, Bob, Jim und Sue machen Englisch gern. Es ist interessant.*

Land und Leute

Grades are based on class performance, written tests called **Klassenarbeiten,** and frequent quizzes called **Klassentests.** Pressure to achieve good grades is very strong because admission to a university (and to some jobs) depends primarily on the applicant's secondary school grades.

Extracurricular activities such as clubs, organizations, and sports are limited in German schools. Where such activities do exist, they are not really part of the school day.

Hausaufgaben sind wichtig *(important)*. Viele Schüler und Schülerinnen gehen später auf die Universität.

In der Pause

Karin and Norbert are in the school yard, discussing homework. Norbert is unhappy about the news he hears.

KARIN   Hast du deine Hausaufgaben schon fertig?
NORBERT   Welche? Die Matheaufgaben?
KARIN   Nein, die Chemieaufgaben.
NORBERT   Die mache ich heute abend. Was machst du heute nachmittag?
KARIN   Ich mache Bio.
NORBERT   Mensch! Haben wir morgen auch Bio?
KARIN   Klar!

Fragen

1. Wann macht Norbert Chemie?
2. Was macht Karin am Nachmittag°?
3. Wann haben Norbert und Karin Biologie?

Du hast das Wort

Wann machst du Hausaufgaben?   You're looking for someone to do homework with. Ask a classmate when she/he intends to do homework.

DU		GESPRÄCHSPARTNER/IN
Wann machst du deine	Matheaufgaben?	Heute nachmittag.
	Bioaufgaben?	Heute abend.
	Hausaufgaben für	Jetzt.
	Deutsch?	Später°.
		Morgen.

Jetzt haben sie Bio.

118

Wieviel Uhr ist es?

Dieter is always late for class. Sabine doesn't seem to find that a serious problem.

DIETER   Wie spät ist es?
SABINE   Es ist fünf nach zehn.
DIETER   Mensch! Ich komme wieder zu spät.
SABINE   Ist ja nicht so schlimm. Du bist ja gut in Chemie.

Fragen

1. Ist es schon zehn Uhr?
2. Wie spät ist es?
3. Welches Fach hat Dieter jetzt?
4. Wer ist gut in Chemie?

Wortschatzerweiterung

The flavoring word ja

DIETER	Mensch! Ich komme wieder zu spät!	Oh no! I'm going to be late again!
SABINE	Ist **ja** nicht so schlimm.	That's not so bad.
	Du bist **ja** gut in Chemie.	You're good in chemistry (after all).

In Sabine's statements, the implication is that she and Dieter both know that Dieter is good in chemistry, so there's no need to worry. As a flavoring word, **ja** is often used to point out that both the speaker and the listener are aware of the circumstances to which the utterance refers. **Ja** also often has a reassuring tone.

A. Wie sagt man das? Restate the sentences, inserting the flavoring word **ja** where indicated. Then give the English equivalents.

▶   Was? Der Mantel kostet nur 50 Mark?   *Das ist ja spottbillig!*

1. Natürlich hat sie Mathe gern. Mathe ist _____ ihr Lieblingsfach.
2. Jan geht jetzt schwimmen. Er hat seine Hausaufgaben _____ fertig.
3. Diese Schuhe kaufe ich nicht. Sie sind _____ viel zu klein!
4. Du gehst auch Tennis spielen? Das ist _____ toll!
5. Meine Mutter spielt gut Tennis. Sie spielt _____ auch viel.
6. Mark spielt Geige und Klavier. Er ist _____ musikalisch.

Land und Leute

Most German students go to school from 8 A.M. to around 1 P.M., five days a week, although some have school on Saturday twice a month. Classes in the various subjects meet on alternating days, and students often take ten or more subjects in one term. In the morning there is a five-minute break after each class, and two **große Pausen** of ten to twenty minutes. During these breaks students go into the school yard **(Schulhof)** or to lounges to relax and have a snack. They can bring these snacks from home or buy them at school. Sometimes they have a free period **(Freistunde),** and in the summer students may get time off if the weather is too hot **(hitzefrei).**

In der großen Pause auf dem Schulhof

Schulsachen

1. das Buch
2. das Heft
3. das Papier
4. der Bleistift

5. der Kugelschreiber
   (der Kuli)
6. der Radiergummi
7. die Mappe

Adjectives

Der Kuli ist **kurz.**
Der Bleistift ist **lang.**

Das Buch ist **dick.**
Das Heft ist **dünn.**

Die Mappe ist **schwer.**
Das Papier ist **leicht.**

B. Was ist es? Think of an object in the classroom. Have your classmates ask questions until they guess which object you've picked.

Ist es lang?	Ja.
Ist es alt?	Nein.
Ist es teuer?	Ja.
Ist es dünn?	Ja.
Ist es blau?	Ja.
Ist es ein Kuli?	Ja.

Das Alphabet

The German alphabet has 26 regular letters and 4 special letters.

a	ah	f	eff	k	kah	p	peh	u	uh	z	tsett
b	beh	g	geh	l	ell	q	kuh	v	fau	ä	äh
c	tseh	h	hah	m	emm	r	err	w	weh	ö	öh
d	deh	i	ih	n	enn	s	ess	x	iks	ü	üh
e	eh	j	jot	o	oh	t	teh	y	üpsilon	ß	ess-tsett

In speech, capital letters are indicated by using the word **groß: großes B, großes W.** Lower-case letters are referred to as **klein: kleines b, kleines w.**

C. Wie sagt man das? Pronounce the following abbreviations.   **Spelling**

VW (Volkswagen)
BMW (Bayerische Motorenwerke)
DDR (Deutsche Demokratische Republik)
USA (U.S.A.)
ADAC (Allgemeiner Deutscher Automobilclub)

D. Wie schreibt man das? Spell the following words.

Physik
preiswert
billig
Farbe
Hose
häßlich
Klassenzimmer
Bleistift

Int. Zelt-Musik-Festivale.V.

Aussprache

long vowel [o]   so, wohnen, Hose, Boot
short vowel [ɔ]   kommen, Socke

A.   Practice vertically in columns and horizontally in pairs.

[o]	[ɔ]
bog	Bock
Schote	Schotte
Moos	Most
Tone	Tonne
Ofen	offen
Sohne	Sonne

B.   Practice the following words horizontally in pairs.

[o]	[ø]	[ɔ]	[œ]
große	Größe	Kopfe	Köpfe
Hofe	Höfe	konnte	könnte
stoße	Stöße	Stocke	Stöcke
Gote	Goethe	Hocker	Höcker
Ofen	Öfen	Topfe	Töpfe

Doof bleibt doof, da helfen keine Pillen!

C. Practice the sounds [o] and [ɔ]. Read the sentences aloud.

1. Kommt Otto am Sonntag oder am Montag?
2. Lotte und Monika hören gern Rockmusik.
3. Hoffentlich kostet die Hose nicht zu viel.

Übungen

1. Telling time

Es ist zwei.
Es ist zwei Uhr.

Es ist eins.
Es ist ein Uhr.

A. Wann kommst du? Various friends want to know when you're coming to visit on Saturday. Inform them that you'll come an hour later than they expected.

▶ Kommst du um vier?   *Nein, um fünf.*

1. Kommst du um drei?
2. Kommst du um sechs?
3. Kommst du um eins?

4. Kommst du um elf?
5. Kommst du um neun?

Es ist Viertel° nach zwei.

Es ist Viertel vor° drei.

Um elf haben sie Musik.

B. Um Viertel nach . . . Tell Axel that you have classes a quarter hour later than he thinks.

▶ Hast du um drei Bio?   *Nein, um Viertel nach drei.*

1. Hast du um acht Deutsch?
2. Hast du um neun Mathe?
3. Hast du um elf Geschichte?

4. Hast du um eins Englisch?
5. Hast du um zehn Chemie?

C. Um Viertel vor . . . Inform Inge that you have classes a quarter hour earlier than she thinks.

▶ Hast du um acht Musik?   *Nein, um Viertel vor acht.*

1. Hast du um zehn Kunst?
2. Hast du um zwölf Sport?
3. Hast du um neun Latein?

4. Hast du um eins Erdkunde?
5. Hast du um elf Physik?

Es ist zehn vor fünf.
Es ist zehn Minuten vor fünf.

Es ist zehn nach sechs.
Es ist zehn Minuten nach sechs.

Wieviel Uhr ist es jetzt in New York? — Weltzeituhr in Berlin (Ost)

D. Wieviel Uhr ist es? Tell your friends that it's five minutes later than they thought.

▶ Ist es Viertel nach acht?   *Nein, es ist schon zwanzig nach acht.*

1. Ist es fünf nach elf?
2. Ist es sieben Uhr?
3. Ist es zehn nach sechs?
4. Ist es fünf vor neun?

5. Ist es zwanzig vor eins?
6. Ist es Viertel vor zwölf?
7. Ist es zehn vor acht?

Es ist halb drei.
Es ist zwei Uhr dreißig.

E. Wann gehst du nach Hause? Tell your friends that you're going home a half hour later than they thought.

▶ Gehst du um vier nach Hause?   *Nein, um halb fünf.*

1. Gehst du um elf nach Hause?
2. Gehst du um sieben nach Hause?
3. Gehst du um eins nach Hause?
4. Gehst du um neun nach Hause?
5. Gehst du um sechs nach Hause?
6. Gehst du um drei nach Hause?

Du hast das Wort

Wann? You need to find a time for a meeting. Find out when your classmates have various classes.

Discussing schedules

Hast du um acht [Bio]?
Wann hast du [Chemie]?
Du hast um halb zehn [Englisch], nicht?
Um wieviel Uhr hast du [Mathe]?

2. Direct object

Hast du **einen Bruder?**	Do you have *a brother?*
Kaufst du **die Hose?**	Are you buying *the pants?*

The direct object is the noun or pronoun that receives or is in some way affected by the action of the verb. The direct object answers the question *whom* (for example, **Bruder**) or *what* (for example, **Hose**).

3. Accusative case of **der, das, die**

NOMINATIVE	ACCUSATIVE
Der Mantel ist preiswert.	Meinst du **den** Mantel da?
Das Hemd ist toll.	Meinst du **das** Hemd da?
Die Hose ist klasse.	Meinst du **die** Hose da?
Die Schuhe sind spottbillig.	Meinst du **die** Schuhe da?

The direct object of a verb is in the accusative case. **Der** is the only definite article that has a different form before nouns in the accusative case: **der** > **den.**

F. Subjekt und Objekt. Indicate the subject and the direct object in the following sentences.

(subject)   *(direct object)*

▶ *Inge* findet *den Pullover* hübsch.

1. Ralph meint Evas Lehrer.
2. Meine Mutter findet Fußball langweilig.
3. Ich trage gern Jeans.
4. Die Schüler machen jetzt Hausaufgaben.
5. Karls Mutter findet Rockmusik nicht schlecht.
6. Wie findest du Tommy? Langweilig?
7. Wer findet Mathe doof?

G. Sehr hübsch! Say you find each article of clothing attractive.

▶ der Pulli   *Ich finde den Pulli hübsch.*

1. die Krawatte
2. der Gürtel
3. das Kleid
4. der Rock
5. der Mantel
6. die Bluse

H. Welche Sachen? Ute reacts favorably to a number of items in a clothing store. Ask her to specify which ones she means.

▶ Der Anzug ist preiswert.   *Meinst du den Anzug da?*

1. Der Gürtel ist klasse.
2. Die Bluse ist toll.
3. Der Rock ist spottbillig.
4. Das Hemd ist schön.
5. Der Mantel ist modisch.
6. Das Kleid ist hübsch.

4. Accusative case of **ein** and **kein**

NOMINATIVE	ACCUSATIVE
Da ist **ein** Bleistift. Da ist **kein** Bleistift.	Hast du **einen** Bleistift? Hast du **keinen** Bleistift?
Da ist **ein** Buch. Da ist **kein** Buch.	Hast du **ein** Buch? Hast du **kein** Buch?
Da ist **eine** Mappe. Da ist **keine** Mappe.	Hast du **eine** Mappe? Hast du **keine** Mappe?
Da sind Bleistifte. Da sind **keine** Bleistifte.	Hast du Bleistifte? Hast du **keine** Bleistifte?

The indefinite article **ein** and its negative form **kein** become **einen** and **keinen** before **der**-nouns in the accusative singular. **Ein** has no plural forms.

I. Schulsachen. You've misplaced several of your school supplies. Try to borrow the following articles from various friends.

▶ ein Bleistift   *Hast du einen Bleistift?*

1. ein Kuli
2. ein Radiergummi
3. ein Heft
4. eine Mappe
5. ein Buch
6. ein Bleistift

J. Was trägst du? Christa asks what you and your friends are wearing to the party. Tell her you all don't plan to wear what she expects.

▶ Trägst du heute abend eine Jacke?   *Nein, ich trage keine Jacke.*

1. Trägst du heute abend einen Pulli?
2. Trägt Erik einen Anzug?
3. Trägt Gisela ein Kleid?
4. Trägt sie einen Rock?
5. Trägt Günter Jeans?
6. Trägt er Schuhe?
7. Trägt er Socken?

Einmal im Monat geht die Klasse schwimmen.

5. Accusative case of possessive adjectives

Ich habe **einen** Bleistift.	Ich habe **meinen** Bleistift.
Ich habe **ein** Heft.	Ich habe **mein** Heft.
Ich habe **eine** Mappe.	Ich habe **meine** Mappe.
Ich habe Bücher.	Ich habe **meine** Bücher.

K. Im Klassenzimmer. You're always picking up after absent-minded Erik. When he asks where his school supplies are, say that you have them.

▶ Wo ist mein Kuli?   *Ich habe deinen Kuli.*

1. Wo ist mein Radiergummi?   4. Wo ist mein Bleistift?
2. Wo ist mein Heft?   5. Wo sind meine Bücher?
3. Wo ist meine Mappe?   6. Wo ist mein Papier?

L. Wo sind unsere Sachen? After an afternoon of swimming, everyone's clothes have become mixed up. Answer that you and Ulf have them.

▶ Wer hat unsere Socken?   *Wir haben eure Socken.*

1. Wer hat unsere Schuhe?   3. Wer hat unsere Jacken?
2. Wer hat unsere Hemden?   4. Wer hat unsere Gürtel?

M. Neue Sachen. Ilse points out that some of her friends are wearing new clothes. Ask what she thinks of them.

▶ Astrids Kleid ist neu.　*Wirklich? Wie findest du ihr Kleid?*

▶ Marks Jacke ist neu.　*Wirklich? Wie findest du seine Jacke?*

1. Christas Bluse ist neu.
2. Kirstins Rock ist neu.
3. Jochens Krawatte ist neu.
4. Kurts Pulli ist neu.

5. Thomas' Hemd ist neu.
6. Gerdas Mantel ist neu.
7. Herberts Schuhe sind neu.

Du hast das Wort

Wer ist es? Play a guessing game with your classmates. Think of a student in your class and name two or three articles of clothing that she/he is wearing. Your classmates will try to guess whom you have in mind.

Ich trage Hose und Hemd und einen Pulli.
Meine Hose ist braun.
Mein Pulli ist rot.
Wer bin ich?

6. Using **der, das, die** as pronouns

NOMINATIVE

Ist **der Gürtel** billig?
Nein, **der** ist teuer.

Is *that belt* inexpensive?
No, *it* is expensive.

ACCUSATIVE

Wie findest du **den Mantel** da?
Den finde ich schön.

How do you like *that* coat?
I think *that one* is nice.

Der, das, die are often used as pronouns to replace nouns. The forms of these pronouns are the same as the forms of the definite articles.

N. Wie sind die Sachen? Tell Stefan that each item is the opposite of what he thinks.

▶ Ist der Anzug billig?　*Nein, der ist teuer.*

1. Ist das Kleid schick?
2. Ist der Gürtel neu?
3. Ist die Jacke schön?
4. Ist der Mantel preiswert?

5. Ist das Hemd gut?
6. Sind die Schuhe modisch?
7. Sind die Handschuhe teuer?

O. Meine Meinung. You and Gabi are shopping. For some reason you don't seem to agree with any of her opinions.

▶ Ich finde den Pulli schön. Du auch?   *Nein, den finde ich nicht schön.*

1. Ich finde das Kleid hübsch. Du auch?
2. Ich finde die Bluse schick. Du auch?
3. Ich finde das Hemd teuer. Du auch?
4. Ich finde den Rock billig. Du auch?
5. Ich finde die Jacke hübsch. Du auch?

Grammatische Übersicht

Telling time (A–E)

	METHOD 1	METHOD 2
1.00 Uhr	Es ist eins. Es ist ein Uhr.	Es ist ein Uhr.
1.05 Uhr	Es ist fünf (Minuten) nach eins.	Es ist ein Uhr fünf.
1.15 Uhr	Es ist Viertel nach eins.	Es ist ein Uhr fünfzehn.
1.25 Uhr	Es ist fünf (Minuten) vor halb zwei.	Es ist ein Uhr fünfundzwanzig.
1.30 Uhr	Es ist halb zwei.	Es ist ein Uhr dreißig.
1.35 Uhr	Es ist fünf nach halb zwei.	Es ist ein Uhr fünfunddreißig.
1.45 Uhr	Es ist Viertel vor zwei.	Es ist ein Uhr fünfundvierzig.
1.55 Uhr	Es ist fünf (Minuten) vor zwei.	Es ist ein Uhr fünfundfünfzig.
2.00 Uhr	Es ist zwei (Uhr).	Es ist zwei Uhr.

German has two ways to indicate clock time. In conversational German, method one is used.

1. on the hour: 1.00   Es ist eins.
                              Es ist ein Uhr.

Notice that the **-s** of **eins** is dropped before the noun **Uhr.** Notice also that in written German a period is used after the numeral indicating the hour.

2. past the hour: 1.10   Es ist zehn (Minuten) nach eins.
                                1.15   Es ist Viertel nach eins.
                                1.30   Es ist halb zwei.

Notice that the expression with **halb** names the hour to come, not the preceding hour: **1.30 = halb zwei.**

Abfahrt – Departure

DB

Zeit Time	Zug Train Nr.	Richtung Destination	Gleis Track Nr.
7.00			
✕ **7.09** außer ⑥	4727 2. Kl 🧳	(In Kaufbeuren Anschluß nach Augsburg an 9.01)	
7.25	E 3774	Kempten-Ost 7.29–Dietmannsried 7.36– Grönenbach 7.43–Memmingen 7.53– **Ulm 8.41** (In Ulm Anschluß ◆ nach Stuttgart an 9.57–Frankfurt an 12.17– Hannover an 15.43–Hamburg-Altona an 17.24)	**1**
7.26 ⑥ und ⑦ sowie täglich vom 20. XII. bis 27. XII., und 3. bis 6. I., auch 1. und 4. IV., 12., 23. V.	E 2419 E 3771	Immenstadt 7.41–Sonthofen 7.58– **Oberstdorf 8.20** (In Immenstadt ✕ Anschluß nach Lindau an 8.56)	**2**
8.00			
† **8.30**	6782 2. Kl 🧳	**Isny 9.39**	**S 1**

Zeit Time	Zug Train Nr.	Richtung Destination	Gleis Track Nr.
12.00			
12.04	D 712 🍴 🧳	*Allgäu-Expreß* Memmingen 12.26–Ulm 13.05– Stuttgart 14.20–Mainz 16.53–Köln 19.12– Düsseldorf 19.49–**Dortmund 20.51**	**4**
12.26	D 269 ✕	*Bavaria* Buchloe 13.06–**München 13.46** (In Buchloe Anschluß nach Augsburg an 13.39)	**4**
19.00			
19.13	D 366 🍷 🧳	Immenstadt 19.29–Oberstaufen 19.45– Röthenbach 19.58–Lindau 20.28– Bregenz 20.46–St. Margrethen 21.03– Zürich-Flugh. 22.38–**Zürich HB 22.50**	**3**
22.00			
22.22 18. bis 24. XII., 26. XII., 1. bis 5. I., an ⑥ ab 8. I., auch 4. IV., nicht 2. IV	E 2418	Memmingen 22.45–**Ulm 23.24** 🛏 🚂 🛌 Stuttgart 0.59–Köln 6.15– Dortmund 7.56	**4**

3. before the hour: 1.40 Es ist zwanzig (Minuten) vor zwei.
1.45 Es ist Viertel vor zwei.

In official time, used for concerts, train and plane schedules, and schools, method two is used.

Ingrid hat **um 13 Uhr 30** Bio.   Ingrid has biology at 1:30 P.M.

Official time is indicated on a twenty-four hour basis:

  8.30 Uhr = 8:30 A.M.
20.30 Uhr = 8:30 P.M.

Direct object

Kaufst du **den Anzug** da?   Are you buying *the suit* there?
Nein, **den** kaufe ich nicht.   No, I'm not buying it *(that one)*.

A direct object receives or is in some way affected by the action of the verb. The direct object is a noun (like **Anzug**) or pronoun (like **den**) that answers the question *what* or *whom*.

Accusative case

Hast du **einen Bruder?**	Do you have *a brother?*
Ich kaufe **eine Jacke.**	I'm buying *a jacket.*
Petra trägt heute **keinen Pulli.**	Petra is wearing *no sweater* today.

A German noun has different cases, depending on how it is used in a sentence. When a noun is used as the direct object of a verb, it is in the *accusative case.*

Accusative case of **der, das, die** (F–H)

NOMINATIVE	ACCUSATIVE
Der Anzug ist billig.	Meinst du **den** Anzug da?
Das Kleid ist schick.	Meinst du **das** Kleid da?
Die Jacke ist klasse.	Meinst du **die** Jacke da?
Die Schuhe sind teuer.	Meinst du **die** Schuhe da?

Den is used instead of **der** in the accusative case. The other articles, **das** and **die,** have identical nominative and accusative forms.

Accusative case of **ein** and **kein** (I–J)

NOMINATIVE	ACCUSATIVE
Da ist **ein** Bleistift.	Sie hat **einen** Bleistift.
Da ist **kein** Bleistift.	Er hat **keinen** Bleistift.
Da ist **ein** Heft.	Sie hat **ein** Heft.
Da ist **kein** Heft.	Er hat **kein** Heft.
Da ist **eine** Mappe.	Sie hat **eine** Mappe.
Da ist **keine** Mappe.	Er hat **keine** Mappe.
Da sind Bleistifte.	Sie hat Bleistifte.
Da sind **keine** Bleistifte.	Er hat **keine** Bleistifte.

Ein changes to **einen** before a **der**-noun in the accusative singular. **Ein** has no plural forms.
Kein follows the pattern of **ein,** except that **kein** has plural forms. In the plural, the nominative and accusative forms are identical. They are both **keine.**

Accusative case of possessive adjectives (K–M)

NOMINATIVE		
Wo ist	ein mein	Kuli?
Wo ist	ein mein	Heft?
Wo ist	eine meine	Mappe?
Wo sind	meine	Bücher?

ACCUSATIVE		
Wer hat	einen meinen	Kuli?
Wer hat	ein mein	Heft?
Wer hat	eine meine	Mappe?
Wer hat	meine	Bücher?

The possessive adjectives — **mein, dein, sein, ihr** (her), **unser, euer, ihr** (their), **Ihr** (your, formal) — have the same endings as the indefinite article **ein**.

Using **der, das, die** as pronouns (N–O)

Kaufst du **den Mantel** da?
Nein, **der** ist zu teuer.

Are you going to buy *that jacket?*
No, *it* is too expensive.

Der, das, die are often used as pronouns to replace nouns. They are then called demonstrative pronouns. Demonstrative pronouns usually occur at or near the beginning of a sentence. The English equivalent is usually a personal pronoun.

	SINGULAR			PLURAL
Nominative	der	das	die	die
Accusative	den	das	die	die

The forms of the demonstrative pronouns are the same as the forms of the definite articles.

A. Ich trage . . . Take the role of the person in each picture. Tell what you are wearing.

▶ *Ich trage keine Jacke; ich trage einen Pullover.*

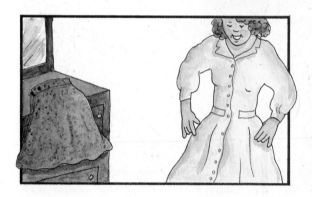
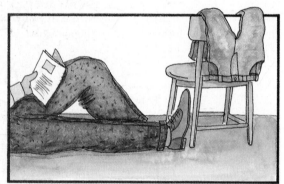

B. Nein, das nicht! Say everything is the opposite of what Gabi says.

▶ Ist dein Buch interessant? *Nein, es ist nicht interessant; es ist langweilig.*

1. Sind deine Matheaufgaben leicht?
2. Ist dein Kuli billig?
3. Ist deine Mappe neu?

4. Sind deine Englischaufgaben lang?
5. Ist dein Klassenzimmer groß?

Sie arbeiten gern am Computer.

C. Was sagen die Schüler? A German student is visiting your school. You overhear various snatches of conversation during lunch. Tell your German friend what people are saying.

1. Ingrid: I have math this afternoon.
   Math is my favorite subject.
2. Mark: I'm going to do my chemistry homework this afternoon.
   I think chemistry is interesting.
3. Erik: It's already a quarter after twelve.
   I'm going to be late again.
4. Christl: Gerd likes Petra.
   Sabine: Yes, but Petra doesn't like Gerd.
5. Robert: Does your pen pal live in Kiel?
   Tanja: No. He lives in Stuttgart now.

D. Was machst du? Find out from a classmate what she/he does after school on certain days.

▶ Was machst du am [Montag]? *Ich [spiele Fußball].*

E. Kurzes Gespräch.
Choose the phrase that best completes each statement, based on the dialogue.

PAUL   Hallo, Ursel! Wie geht's?
URSEL   Es geht. Ich habe heute nachmittag viel Hausaufgaben.
PAUL   Das ist ja doof. Ich spiele jetzt Tennis.
URSEL   Du, Paul . . . Wie spät ist es denn?
PAUL   Erst eins.
URSEL   Na gut. Ich spiele bis zwei.
PAUL   Das ist ja prima.

1. Es geht Ursel . . .
   a. gut.
   b. prima.
   c. nicht so gut.
2. Paul . . .
   a. geht jetzt nach Hause.
   b. macht Hausaufgaben.
   c. treibt heute nachmittag Sport.
3. Paul und Ursel . . .
   a. haben jetzt Schule.
   b. gehen jetzt nach Hause.
   c. spielen jetzt Tennis.

F. Mein Brieffreund.
Supply additional information to each of the following sentences by beginning with one of the words or expressions below.

abends   heute nachmittag   hoffentlich
jetzt   natürlich   morgens um halb neun

▶   Mein Brieffreund wohnt in   *Jetzt wohnt mein Brieffreund*
    Bergdorf.   *in Bergdorf.*

1. Er geht da in die Schule.   4. Er macht seine Hausaufgaben.
2. Er hat Chemie.   5. Er schreibt bald.
3. Er spielt Fußball.

G. Sag mir . . .
Interview a classmate about school. You may want to ask some of the following questions. Summarize your findings.

Was ist dein Lieblingsfach?
Wann hast du [Deutsch]?
Wie findest du [Erdkunde]? Ist es leicht? schwer?
Hast du viel Hausaufgaben?
Machst du gern [Chemie]aufgaben? Wann machst du sie?
Welches Fach hast du nicht gern?

You may wish to begin: *Gerdas Lieblingsfach ist Bio. Sie . . .*

H.   Das bin ich. You have changed schools and want to get to know your new classmates. Where are you from; what do you do in school; what kind of clothes do you wear? Once you have thought about who you are, prepare to talk about yourself to others.

I.   Land und Leute.

1. How does your school day differ from that of most German students?
2. Compare the emphasis on extra-curricular activities in your school and in German schools.

Kulturlesestück

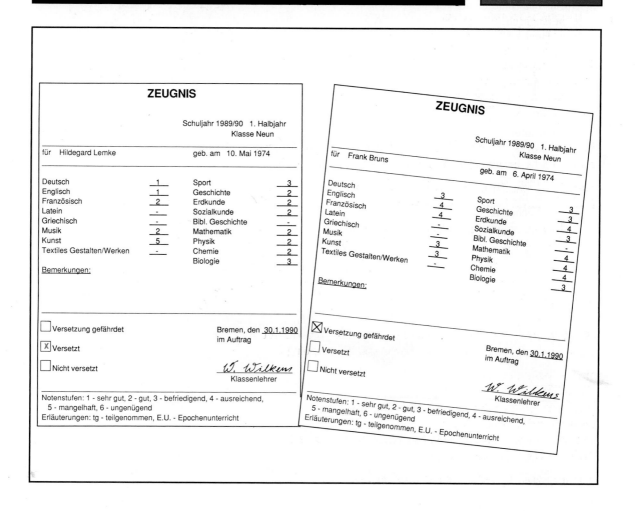

Zeugnis

Hilde geht in Bremen zur Schule. Sie ist in Klasse Neun. Links° ist ihr Zeugnis. In Deutsch und Englisch hat sie eine Eins. Das sind ihre Lieblingsfächer. Da ist sie sehr gut. In Mathe und Physik ist sie gut. Sie hat in beiden° eine Zwei. Nur in Kunst ist sie wirklich schlecht. Da hat sie eine Fünf. Sie findet Kunst langweilig.

5   Hildes Freund Frank ist nicht so gut. Er hat viele Dreien und Vieren. Er arbeitet nicht gern. Hoffentlich bekommt° er nächstes Mal° nicht nur Vieren und Fünfen. Mit° drei Fünfen zum Beispiel oder mit zwei Fünfen und ohne° Dreien bleibt er sitzen°. Dann° geht Hilde in Klasse Zehn, und er macht die ganze Klasse Neun noch einmal°.

Die Schüler Hilde und Frank. Answer the following questions, based on the reading.

1. Worin° hat Hilde eine zwei?
   a. in Englisch
   b. in Deutsch
   c. in Mathe
   d. in Kunst
2. Wie findet Hilde Kunst?
   a. interessant
   b. leicht
   c. nicht interessant
   d. schwer
3. Warum ist Franks Zeugnis nicht gut?
   a. Er findet alle Fächer langweilig.
   b. Er ist faul.
   c. Die Fächer sind zu schwer.
   d. Er spielt zuviel Fußball.

Margin notes:

on the left

in beiden: in both

gets / **nächstes Mal:** next time
with / without
bleibt . . . sitzen: he repeats
  a year / then
noch einmal: again

in what

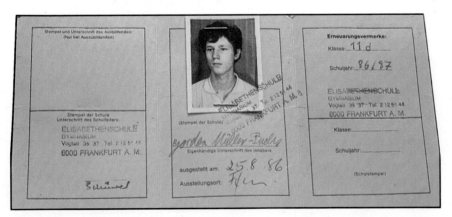

Schülerausweis (ID) *von Gordon Müller-Fuchs*

Vokabeln

Substantive

der **Bleistift**, —e pencil
der **Dienstag** Tuesday
der **Kugelschreiber**, — (der **Kuli**, —s) ballpoint pen
der **Mittwoch** Wednesday
der **Nachmittag**, —e afternoon; **am ~** in the afternoon
der **Plan**, ⁼e plan; schedule
der **Radiergummi**, —s eraser
der **Sport** sport
der **Stundenplan**, ⁼e class schedule

das **Buch**, ⁼er book
das **Englisch** English
das **Fach**, ⁼er (school) subject
das **Heft**, —e notebook
das **Klassenzimmer**, — classroom
das **Lieblingsfach**, ⁼er favorite subject
das **Papier** paper
das **Viertel**, — quarter

die **Aufgabe** lesson; **die Aufgaben** *(pl.)* homework; **die Chemieaufgaben** chemistry homework
die **Biologie** (*colloquial:* **die Bio**) biology
die **Chemie** chemistry
die **Erdkunde** geography
die **Geschichte** history; story
die **Klasse**, —n grade, class
die **Mappe**, —n briefcase, book bag
die **Mathematik** mathematics; **die Mathe** math
die **Pause**, —n break, intermission; recess
die **Physik** physics
die **Sache**, —n thing
die **Schule**, —n school
die **Stunde**, —n hour; class; lesson; **die Klavierstunde** piano lesson
die **Uhr**, —en clock, watch; **acht Uhr** eight o'clock

Andere Wörter

dick fat, thick
dies(er, es, e) this
fertig ready; finished
halb half
interessant interesting
ja *flavoring word (see p. 119)*
kurz short
lang long
langweilig boring
leicht easy; light
morgen tomorrow
nach after
schlimm bad
schwer difficult; heavy
später later
um at; around
vor before

Besondere Ausdrücke

Mensch! wow! brother! oh, boy!
klar! sure! of course!
du bist gut in Chemie you're good at chemistry
wie spät ist es? what time is it?
wieviel Uhr ist es? what time is it?
es ist zehn Uhr it's ten o'clock
um wieviel Uhr? at what time?
um ein Uhr at one o'clock
Viertel nach zwei quarter past two
Viertel vor zwei quarter till two
halb zwei one-thirty

Kapitel 7

Willst du ins Konzert?

Jazzfestival in Montreux, Schweiz

FRANKFURTER HOT DOGS IM JUGENDZENTRUM

7.-9. Januar   20.00^h

**Karten bei Buchhandlung Baumann
oder an der Kasse: geöffnet
täglich von 13^h bis 20^h**

Eintritt: DM 15, — 25, —

Fragen

1. Wo gibt° es ein Konzert°?
2. Wie heißt die Rockband°?
3. Wieviel Tage spielen die *Frankfurter Hot Dogs?*
4. Wann beginnt° die Vorstellung°?
5. Wieviel kosten die Karten?

Du hast das Wort

1. **Deine Lieblingsgruppe.** Ask a classmate to name the rock group she/he likes best.

   Asking about personal interests

   DU

   Wie heißt deine Lieblingsgruppe°?

   GESPRÄCHSPARTNER/IN

   [Die *Hot Dogs*].

The **Litfaßsäule** (a thick column on which advertising posters are displayed) was introduced to Germany in 1854 by Ernst Litfaß, a printer from Berlin. Litfaß had seen similar columns in other countries and recognized their value in advertising. The Berlin police gave Litfaß a monopoly on the poster columns; they saw them as a way of controlling the location of posters put up throughout the city. The **Litfaßsäulen** soon spread through the rest of Germany and are still in use today.

Litfaßsäule in Dresden, DDR: Möchtest du ins Theater, in die Philharmonie oder zu einem Kammerabend?

2. **Möchtest du . . .**   Ask a friend whether she/he would like to hear a concert by a certain rock group.

DU

Möchtest° du [die *Hot Dogs*] hören?

GESPRÄCHSPARTNER/IN

Ja, [sie sind] toll.
Ja, gern!
Klar!
Ja, hast du Karten?
Vielleicht°.
Nein, ich habe keine Lust°.

3. **Welches Rockkonzert?**   You want to give your friend a pair of concert tickets for her/his birthday. Find out what kind of concerts you could go to together. Your partner is in a bad mood; try to come up with a pair of tickets she/he couldn't refuse.

Konzert im Jugendzentrum

Dieter and Ingrid are trying to find a time when they can both go to the Hot Dogs *concert.*

INGRID   Du, Dieter, die *Hot Dogs* spielen heute abend.
DIETER   Das ist ja dumm. Ich kann leider heute abend nicht.
INGRID   Und morgen abend?
DIETER   Morgen abend geht's. Meinst du, wir bekommen noch Karten?
INGRID   Wir können's ja mal versuchen.

Fragen

1. Wer spielt heute abend?
2. Wann kann Dieter ins Konzert gehen?
3. Können die beiden noch Karten bekommen?
4. Hören sie die *Hot Dogs* gern?

Du hast das Wort

Heute abend wollen wir ins . . .   Create a dialogue between you and a friend.   **Making plans**
Try to make plans to go to a movie, play, or concert.

DU		FREUNDE	
Was macht ihr	heute abend?	Wir wollen	ins Kino°.
	am Samstag?		ins Theater°.
			ins Konzert.
Wann?		Um [8] Uhr.	Kommst du auch?
Um wieviel Uhr?			Hast du Lust?
Nein, ich habe	keine Zeit°.	Schade.	
	kein Geld°.	Das tut mir leid.	
Nein, ich muß Hausaufgaben machen.			
Ich habe schon Lust, aber keine Zeit.			
Nein, ich darf° nicht.			
Ja, gern. Gibt es noch Karten?		Ich glaube° ja.	
		Vielleicht, vielleicht auch nicht.	
		Wir können ja mal fragen°.	

Land und Leute

Rock music is very popular with teenagers in the German-speaking countries. Like Americans, they listen to hard rock, reggae, new wave, rockabilly, and rap, and spend much of their pocket money on records (**Schallplatten**) and cassettes (**Kassetten**).

The trends in rock music have shifted several times. For a long period rock music had to be American, British, or at least sung in English to be successful in the German-speaking countries. However, beginning in the 1970s, the number of rock musicians singing in German grew steadily and reached its peak in the early 1980s with the **Neue deutsche Welle** (New German Wave). Many songs were written in German, sometimes even in dialects. A trend back to English began in the mid-80s.

Berlin has become the focal point for German rock music. The city even appointed a **Rockbeauftragter** (a representative for rock music). Her/his task is to support unknown but talented musicians, helping them get started in the highly competitive music industry.

PRETTY BABY

Du bist so schön.
ich muß dich seh'n,
Heute noch seh'n,
Oh, pretty baby!

Du hast mein Herz.
Das ist kein Scherz.
Oh, welcher Schmerz
Ohne dich, baby!

Glücklich zu sein,
Mit dir allein,
Immer zu zwei'n,
Oh, pretty baby!

Es kann nicht sein.
Ich bin allein,
Immer allein
Ohne dich, baby.

An der Kasse

The Hot Dogs *are a popular group. Ingrid and Dieter have a hard time getting tickets.*

INGRID Haben Sie noch Karten für morgen abend?

HERR Es tut mir leid. Für morgen abend haben wir keine Karten mehr. Ich habe noch ein paar Karten für übermorgen.

INGRID *(zu Dieter)* Was meinst du?

DIETER Ich habe Zeit. Aber mußt du dann nicht arbeiten?

INGRID Das schon. Aber ich bekomme sicher frei. Ich muß die *Hot Dogs* einfach hören.

DIETER Also gut.

Fragen

1. Gibt es noch Karten für morgen abend?
2. Für wann gibt es noch Karten?
3. Warum will Ingrid übermorgen nicht arbeiten?

Du hast das Wort

Gibt es noch Karten? With a partner, make up a short dialogue about buying **Buying tickets** tickets to a performance. Use some of the questions and responses below.

DU

Haben Sie noch Karten für | heute abend?
morgen?
übermorgen?

Was kosten die Karten?

Ich nehme° [2] Karten zu [8] Mark.

Danke.

Oh, noch eine Frage°. Wann beginnt die Vorstellung?

FRAU/HERR

Es tut mir leid.
Es ist alles ausverkauft°.
Für [heute abend] haben wir nichts° mehr.
Für [heute abend] ist noch alles° da.
Für [übermorgen] haben wir noch Karten.

Wir haben Karten zu [5, 8, 12 und 16] Mark.
Wir haben noch ein paar Karten zu [8] Mark.

Bitte. Das macht° [16] Mark.

Um [20] Uhr.

Noun compounds

German has many noun compounds. Their meaning can often be guessed from their component parts.

der Abend + die Vorstellung = die Abendvorstellung
das Theater + die Karten = die Theaterkarten

A noun compound takes the definite article of the last noun in the compound.

A. Was ist das? What do the italicized words mean?

1. Die *Abendvorstellung* beginnt um acht Uhr.
2. Gibt es für heute noch *Theaterkarten*?
3. Welche *Schuhgröße* hast du?
4. Hast du morgen *Klavierstunde*?
5. Wann machst du deine *Hausaufgaben*?
6. Am *Wochenende* mache ich meine *Matheaufgaben*.
7. Wie heißt dein *Deutschlehrer*?
8. Wo ist das *Deutschbuch*?
9. Was sind deine *Lieblingsfächer*?

Flavoring word **mal**

Wir können's ja **mal** versuchen.

Let's *at least* give it a try.
 (We can try it *sometime*.)

Du kannst ja **mal** ins Kino gehen.

You can go to the movies *for a change*.

Bernd will **mal** in Hamburg arbeiten.

Bernd wants to work in Hamburg *someday*.

The flavoring word **mal** is often used in commands, suggestions, or in statements of intent. The time for carrying out the intended action is not stated precisely. To express the same idea in English one often uses *sometime* or *someday*.

Ruf doch mal an!

Die Telefon-Information für Österreich-Reisende

So einfach ist es, zu Hause anzurufen:
Von allen öffentlichen Telefonen. Ausgenommen sind Ortsmünztelefone.

Die Post findet es gut, wenn man mal einen Brief schreibt.

B. Kurze Dialoge. Choose the appropriate German response to complete each conversational exchange, based on the English guidelines.

a. Was können wir mal machen?
b. Möchtest du die *Hot Dogs* mal hören?
c. Das möchte ich auch mal machen.
d. Das muß ich auch mal lernen.
e. Ich muß bald mal neue Schuhe kaufen.
f. Ich muß Gerda auch mal schreiben.

1. *Jens says he also has to learn English someday.*
   Torsten: Dieses Jahr lerne ich Englisch.
   Jens: . . .
2. *Gerda would like to play more tennis, too.*
   Erika: Im Sommer spiele ich viel Tennis.
   Gerda: . . .
3. *Mark casually remarks that he needs new shoes soon.*
   Frank: Deine Schuhe sind kaputt.
   Mark: Ja. . . .
4. *Ursel asks what she and Barbara can do to relieve their boredom.*
   Barbara: Es ist heute so langweilig.
   Ursel: . . .
5. *Gerd asks whether Uwe wants to play a different record for a change.*
   Uwe: Du, diese Gruppe ist furchtbar langweilig.
   Gerd: . . .
6. *Barbara has been corresponding regularly with Gerda. Renate remembers that she owes Gerda a letter, too.*
   Barbara: Morgen muß ich wieder an Gerda schreiben.
   Renate: . . .

Aussprache

long vowel [a]   Vater, Staat, Frage
short vowel [A]   Kasse, alles, Mann

A. Practice vertically in columns and horizontally in pairs.

[a]	[A]
Bahn	Bann
kam	Kamm
Staat	Stadt
Schlaf	schlaff
lahm	Lamm

B. Practice the following words horizontally in pairs.

[a]	[ɔ]	[A]	[ɔ]
Bahn	Bonn	Bann	Bonn
kam	komm	Kamm	komm
stahlen	Stollen	Matte	Motte
Spaten	spotten	knalle	Knolle
fahl	voll	falle	volle

Ein Spatz in der Hand ist besser als eine Taube auf dem Dach.

C. Practice the sounds [a] and [A]. Read the sentences aloud.

1. Hast du Astrids Mappe?
2. Ich habe noch eine Karte zu acht Mark.
3. Kannst du heute abend tanzen gehen?

Übungen

1. Verbs with stem-vowel change **e** > **i**

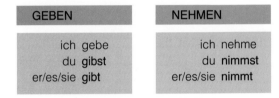

GEBEN	NEHMEN
ich gebe	ich nehme
du gibst	du nimmst
er/es/sie gibt	er/es/sie nimmt

Geben and **nehmen** have a stem-vowel change **e** > **i** in the **du-** and **er/es/sie-**forms of the present tense.

A. Wer braucht Karten? You are taking orders for tickets to a school dance. Ask whether the following people need tickets and how many tickets they want.

▶ Frau Lange   *Braucht Frau Lange Karten? Wieviel nimmt sie?*

1. Inge
2. du
3. Herr und Frau Wagner
4. ihr
5. Sie
6. wir

B. Wer gibt Christa Karten? Marita wonders how Christa can afford to go to so many concerts. Tell her that various people give her tickets.

▶ Erik   *Erik gibt Christa oft Karten.*

1. Inge
2. mein Bruder
3. ihre Schwester
4. wir
5. du
6. ihre Freunde
7. ihr
8. ich

2. Modal auxiliaries

können   can, to be able to

ich **kann**		wir **können**
du **kannst**	Sie **können**	ihr **könnt**
er/es/sie **kann**		sie **können**

Ich **kann** es ja mal **versuchen.**   I *can try* it.

Modal auxiliaries (for example, **können**) are irregular in the present-tense singular. They are usually used with dependent infinitives (for example, **versuchen**). The infinitive is in last position.

C.   Zu laut! (Too loud!)   The library seems very noisy today. Say that the following people can't work.

▶   Ich arbeite nicht.   *Ich kann nicht arbeiten.*

1. Bernd arbeitet nicht.
2. Ingrid arbeitet nicht.
3. Wir arbeiten nicht.
4. Du arbeitest nicht.
5. Frau Lange arbeitet nicht.
6. Ihr arbeitet nicht.

D.   Wer kann es machen?   Say who can (or can't) do the following things.

▶   Wir können es machen.   (Susanne)   *Susanne kann es machen.*

1. Die Jungen können es machen.   (du)
2. Du kannst das Buch nehmen.   (ihr)
3. Ihr könnt gut singen.   (ich)
4. Ich kann die Vokabeln nicht lernen.   (Erika)
5. Inge kann die Musik nicht hören.   (wir)
6. Wir können heute nicht arbeiten.   (Gisela)
7. Ich kann heute nicht ins Kino gehen.   (Ute und Jens)

sollen   to be supposed to

ich **soll**		wir **sollen**
du **sollst**	Sie **sollen**	ihr **sollt**
er/es/sie **soll**		sie **sollen**

Du **sollst** jetzt **beginnen.**   You're *supposed to begin* now.

E. Wer soll Musik machen? Decide which parts the members of your band should take.

▶ Wer soll Klarinette spielen?   *Ja, Jürgen soll Klarinette*
   Jürgen?   *spielen.*

1. Wer soll Gitarre spielen? Ich?
2. Wer soll Schlagzeug spielen? Jutta und Rainer?
3. Wer soll Klavier spielen? Kirstin?
4. Wer soll singen? Ich?
5. Wer soll Geige spielen? Stefan und Ute?

Reiner kann ausgezeichnet Schlagzeug spielen.

Du hast das Wort

Kannst du . . . sollst du? Say whether you can or should do the following things.

Kannst du	Gitarre	spielen?
	Klavier
	Flöte
	Geige
	Klarinette

Kannst du gut	schwimmen?
	laufen
	Fußball spielen
	Ski laufen°
	Volleyball spielen

Sollst du heute	kochen?
	Musik machen
	Theaterkarten kaufen
	zu Hause arbeiten

Sollst du heute abend	Mathe	lernen?
	Deutsch
	Physik
	Chemie
	Bio

müssen must, to have to

ich **muß**		wir müssen
du **mußt**	Sie müssen	ihr müßt
er/es/sie **muß**		sie müssen

Sie **muß** es bald **tun.**   She *has to do* it soon.

F. Sie müssen gehen. It's late. Say that the following people have to leave now.

▶ Gabi   *Gabi muß jetzt gehen.*

1. Hans-Jürgen
2. du
3. wir
4. ich
5. ihr
6. Stefan und Barbara

G. Viel Arbeit. Report to the class all the things you must do in the next few days.

▶ viel arbeiten   *Ich muß viel arbeiten.*

1. Mathe und Englisch machen
2. Vokabeln lernen
3. Briefe schreiben
4. Schuhe kaufen
5. morgen kochen
6. Karten kaufen

dürfen   may, to be permitted to

ich **darf**		Sie **dürfen**	wir **dürfen**
du **darfst**			ihr **dürft**
er/es/sie **darf**			sie **dürfen**

Wir **dürfen** jetzt **gehen.**   We're *allowed to go* now.

H. Darfst du denn? (Are you allowed to?)   Ask whether your friends really have permission to do what they plan.

▶ Ich gehe heute ins Kino.   *Darfst du denn heute ins Kino gehen?*

1. Ich gehe morgen ins Konzert.
2. Ich gehe übermorgen ins Theater.
3. Inge spielt heute Volleyball.
4. Bruno spielt heute Fußball.
5. Stefan und Bettina gehen morgen abend tanzen.
6. Wir gehen morgen schwimmen.

I. Verboten! (Forbidden!)   It's against the rules!
Respond to the following questions by saying the actions are not permitted.

▶ Warum spielst du nicht?   *Ich darf nicht spielen.*

1. Warum beginnst du nicht?
2. Warum schwimmst du nicht?
3. Warum kommt Ute nicht?
4. Warum bleibt Jens nicht?
5. Warum geht ihr nicht?
6. Warum kommen Inge und Jan nicht?

Windsurfer auf dem
Silsersee im Engadin,
Schweiz

Du hast das Wort

Wer muß . . . wer darf ? Form groups of five. Decide what certain people have
to do today and are allowed to do today.

Wer muß heute | Hausaufgaben machen?
Briefe schreiben
zu Hause helfen
zu Hause bleiben
einen Brief an [Tante° Emma] schreiben

Wer darf heute abend | ins Kino gehen?
ins Theater gehen
Musik hören
Sport treiben
ins Rockkonzert gehen

Wer darf nicht | Fußball spielen?
ins Kino gehen
Schlagzeug spielen
tanzen gehen
spät nach Hause kommen

Du darfst

Erfolgsrezepte
für die
schlanke Linie

wollen   to want, wish; to intend to

ich **will**		wir wollen
du **willst**	Sie wollen	ihr wollt
er/es/sie **will**		sie wollen

Ihr **wollt** hoffentlich **arbeiten.**   You *want to work,* I hope.

J. Pläne.   Say who is planning to do the following things.

▶   Will Erik Musik hören?   (du)   *Willst du Musik hören?*

1. Greta will heute nicht arbeiten.   (wir)
2. Wir wollen Tennis spielen.   (ich)
3. Ich will morgen schwimmen gehen.   (Monika)
4. Will Ute Englisch lernen?   (ihr)
5. Wollt ihr das Buch kaufen?   (Hans-Jürgen)
6. Willst du die *Hot Dogs* hören?   (Lore und Kai)

mögen   to like

ich **mag**		wir mögen
du **magst**	Sie mögen	ihr mögt
er/es/sie **mag**		sie mögen

Magst du meine neue Jacke?   *Do you like* my new jacket?
Ich **mag** Dieter **nicht.**   I *don't like* Dieter.

Mögen usually expresses a fondness or dislike for someone or something. With this meaning it usually does not have a dependent infinitive.

K.   Wer mag die Mitschüler?   You are planning a party with friends and want to be sure the guests are compatible. Discuss who likes whom.

▶   Ich / Andrea   *Ich mag Andrea.*

1. Du / Alex
2. Alex / Andrea
3. Wir / Petra
4. Alex und Andrea / Petra
5. Ihr / Julia
6. Ich / Julia
7. Du / Peter

Du hast das Wort

Was magst du? What do you like?

Welche Musik	magst du?
Welche Schulfächer	
Welche Farben	
Welches Musikinstrument	

möchte would like to

ich **möchte**		wir möchten
du **möchtest**	Sie möchten	ihr möchtet
er/es/sie **möchte**		sie möchten

Sie **möchten** es **kaufen.**   They would *like* to *buy* it.

Ich möchte, du möchtest, etc., are special forms of the verb **mögen** *(to like)* and are equivalent to *I would like, you would like,* etc.

L.   Ich möchte . . .   Tell your teacher that you would like to do the following things.

▶   jetzt Karten spielen   *Ich möchte jetzt Karten spielen.*

1. heute nachmittag Mathe machen
2. heute abend ins Kino gehen
3. morgen schwimmen gehen
4. am Wochenende wandern
5. die *Hot Dogs* hören

Du hast das Wort

Willst du . . . möchtest du . . . ?   Say whether you would like to do the following things.

Willst du	heute arbeiten?
	Schlagzeug spielen
	heute fleißig sein
	heute tanzen gehen

Möchtest du morgen	schwimmen gehen?
	Fußball spielen
	viel arbeiten
	zu Hause bleiben

M. Die Party. Your class is preparing a party. Discuss the party using the cued modals.

▶ Wann kommst du? (können) *Wann kannst du kommen?*

1. Erika spielt Klarinette. (sollen)
2. Kurt und Sibylle spielen Gitarre. (wollen)
3. Bernd singt sehr gut. (können)
4. Wann gehst du? (möchte)
5. Ich bleibe bis um 10 Uhr. (dürfen)
6. Aber erst mache ich meine Hausaufgaben. (müssen)

N. Schlechte Noten. (Bad grades.) Complete the dialogue using the German equivalents of the English cues.

1. „Wir _____ heute nachmittag Fußball spielen." *(want)*
2. „_____ du auch kommen?" *(want)*
3. „Hm. Ich _____ schon gern Fußball spielen. *(would like)*
4. Aber ich glaube, ich _____ jetzt nicht viel spielen." *(can)*
5. „Warum?" — „Ich _____ arbeiten." — „Was ist denn los?" *(have to)*
6. „Ich habe schlechte Noten." — „Ah, da _____ du jetzt erst mal lernen." *(have to)*
7. „Ja, ich _____ nicht ins Kino gehen und — " *(am not allowed to)*
8. „ — und du _____ nicht Fußball spielen." *(are not allowed to)*
9. „Ja, ich _____ erst eine Drei in Mathe schreiben. *(am supposed to)*
10. Dann _____ wir wieder spielen." *(can/may)*

Du hast das Wort

Haben Sie ein Hobby? Ask your teacher questions about leisure activities.

Können Sie [Klavier] spielen?
Möchten Sie am Wochenende [wandern]?
Wollen Sie heute abend [ins Kino] gehen?
Können Sie gut [schwimmen]?

3. Omission of the dependent infinitive with modals

Ich kann es nicht.	=	Ich kann es nicht tun.
Ich muß nach Hause.	=	Ich muß nach Hause gehen.
Du darfst nicht.	=	Du darfst es nicht tun.

In sentences with a modal, the dependent infinitive is often omitted when its meaning is clear.

O. Was bedeutet das? Give the English equivalents of the following conversational exchanges.

1. Es ist schon spät.
   Mußt du wirklich nach Hause?
2. Wir wollen ins Kino. Hast du Zeit?
   Nein, heute kann ich nicht. Ich muß arbeiten.
3. Ich kann die Aufgabe nicht machen. Ich habe keinen Bleistift.
   Möchtest du meinen Kuli?
4. Ist das nicht Christl Wagner da?
   Ja, was will sie denn hier?

Grammatische Übersicht

Verbs with stem-vowel change e > i (A–B)

GEBEN		
ich gebe		wir geben
du **gibst**	Sie geben	ihr gebt
er/es/sie **gibt**		sie geben

NEHMEN		
ich nehme		wir nehmen
du **nimmst**	Sie nehmen	ihr nehmt
er/es/sie **nimmt**		sie nehmen

Geben and **nehmen** have a stem-vowel change **e > i** in the **du-** and **er/es/sie-** forms. Note that an additional spelling change occurs in **nehmen: er/es/sie nimmt, du nimmst.**

Modal auxiliaries (C–O)

Er **muß** jetzt arbeiten.
Sie **kann** es tun.

He *must* work now.
She *can* do it.

English has modal auxiliary verbs such as *must* and *can* that indicate an attitude about an action, rather than expressing the action itself.

German also uses modal auxiliary verbs. German modals are irregular in the present-tense singular. They lack endings in the **ich-** and **er/es/sie-**forms, and most modals show stem-vowel change.

	DÜRFEN	KÖNNEN	MÜSSEN	SOLLEN	WOLLEN	MÖGEN	(MÖCHTE-forms)
ich	darf	kann	muß	soll	will	mag	(möchte)
du	darfst	kannst	mußt	sollst	willst	magst	(möchtest)
er/es/sie	darf	kann	muß	soll	will	mag	(möchte)
wir	dürfen	können	müssen	sollen	wollen	mögen	(möchten)
ihr	dürft	könnt	müßt	sollt	wollt	mögt	(möchtet)
sie	dürfen	können	müssen	sollen	wollen	mögen	(möchten)
Sie	dürfen	können	müssen	sollen	wollen	mögen	(möchten)

Soll ich die Karten **kaufen?**
Frank **will** nicht **arbeiten.**

Modal auxiliaries in German are usually used with dependent infinitives. The infinitive is in last position.

Ich **muß** nach Hause.   =   Ich **muß** nach Hause gehen.
Ich **will** mein Geld.   =   Ich **will** mein Geld haben.

The dependent infinitive may be omitted when the meaning of the sentence is clear from the context.

Meanings of modals

INFINITIVE/MEANING		EXAMPLES	ENGLISH EQUIVALENTS
dürfen	permission	Ich **darf** arbeiten.	I'm *allowed to* work.
können	ability	Ich **kann** arbeiten.	I *can* work.
mögen	liking	Ich **mag** es nicht.	I don't *like* it.
müssen	compulsion	Ich **muß** arbeiten.	I *must (have to)* work.
sollen	obligation	Ich **soll** arbeiten.	I'm *supposed to* work.
wollen	wishing, wanting, intention	Ich **will** arbeiten.	I *want (intend) to* work.

Welche Musik mögt ihr?

The modal **mögen** and the **möchte**-forms

Mögen Sie Frau Lenz?	*Do you like* Mrs. Lenz?
Ich **mag** Rockmusik **nicht.**	I *don't like* rock music.

Mögen is used to express a fondness or dislike for someone or something. With this meaning it usually does not have a dependent infinitive.

Ich **möchte** es versuchen.	I *would like to* try.

The **möchte**-forms are special forms of the modal **mögen.** They are used frequently and are equivalent to the English *would like.* The **möchte**-forms are often used with an infinitive.

The German film industry was extremely significant during the era of silent films and early "talkies" (1919–1932). Directors such as **Fritz Lang, F. W. Murnau,** and **G. W. Pabst** were considered among the finest in the world, and the German use of the "moving camera" was very influential.

During the Nazi era (1933–1945), many great German filmmakers emigrated to other countries — mainly the United States. Some of them never returned, and this loss of talent led to a period of mediocrity in German cinema, which lasted into the mid-sixties. At that point a generation of young filmmakers began to introduce the **Neuer deutscher Film** (New German Cinema). Many of those directors are now well known, including the late **Rainer Werner Fassbinder, Werner Herzog, Wim Wenders,** and **Wolfgang Petersen.** Since then other directors — **Margarethe von Trotta** and **Volker Schlöndorff,** among others — have gained international reputations. Their films explore profound issues relating to art, politics, and human nature.

above: Margarethe von Trotta, *below:* Rainer Werner Fassbinder

Wiederholung

A. Karten fürs Konzert. Christl and Peter are discussing the *Hot Dogs* concert. Answer the questions, based on the following dialogue.

CHRISTL   Die *Hot Dogs* geben morgen abend ein Konzert hier!
PETER   Das ist ja prima, aber ich kann sie nicht hören.
CHRISTL   Warum denn nicht? Mußt du arbeiten?
PETER   Nein. Ich habe kein Geld, und die Karten sind sehr teuer.
CHRISTL   Kein Problem! Mein Bruder arbeitet an der Kasse. Ich habe zwei Karten für das Konzert. Ich bekomme eine, und du bekommst eine.
PETER   Das ist ja klasse. Vielen Dank!

1. Wann geben die *Hot Dogs* ein Konzert?
2. Warum kann Peter nicht ins Konzert?
3. Wer arbeitet an der Kasse?
4. Wer gibt Peter eine Karte für das Konzert?

B. Ich auch. Inform Ingrid that you're going to do the same things she is doing, and use the cued modals.

▶   Ich mache heute abend   *Ich soll heute abend auch*
      Hausaufgaben. (sollen)   *Hausaufgaben machen.*

1. Ich spiele heute nachmittag Tennis. (können)
2. Ich gehe am Samstag ins Kino. (dürfen)
3. Ich kaufe morgen einen Pulli. (wollen)
4. Ich treibe am Sonntag Sport. (möchten)
5. Ich mache am Montag Chemie. (müssen)
6. Ich kaufe am Mittwoch Theaterkarten. (sollen)

Rockkonzert in Berlin (West)

C. Welches Wort? For each set of words below, pick out the three words that fit best into one category.

▶ Mark, tragen, kosten, wieviel   *Mark, kosten, wieviel*

1. Jugendzentrum, Konzert, Band, Lieblingsfach
2. wohnen, Karte, Kasse, ausverkauft
3. Stunde, Theater, Zeit, Uhr
4. Lust, Aufgabe, Geschichte, Englisch
5. Bleistift, Kuli, Geld, Radiergummi
6. Anzug, Schlagzeug, Größe, Farbe
7. Freund, Bruder, Schwester, Vater
8. Gitarre, Flöte, Geige, Fußball
9. Wochenende, Nachmittag, Café, Abend

D. Geburtstagsgeschenke. (Birthday presents.) It's Inge's birthday. Tell what she is getting from her family and friends.

▶ Erna / Bluse   *Erna gibt Inge eine Bluse.*

1. Carola / Kleid
2. Hans-Dieter / Pulli
3. ihr Vater / Schulmappe
4. ihre Mutter / Gitarre
5. Thomas / Kuli
6. Rüdiger / Buch

E. Wie bitte? Udo isn't speaking loudly enough. Ask about the part of the sentence you didn't hear.

▶ Ich gehe *heute abend* ins Konzert.   *Wann gehst du ins Konzert?*

1. *Meine Freundin Ute* kommt auch.
2. *Die Hot Dogs* spielen.
3. Sie spielen *im Jugendzentrum*.
4. Die Vorstellung beginnt *um halb acht.*
5. Die Karten kosten *fünfzehn Mark.*

F. Dein Kalender. Fill out your calendar for the week, indicating when you are going out, when you are doing your homework, etc. Your partner wants to invite you out. Try to find a mutually agreeable time.

Arranging free-time activities

WOCHE

Montag	Freitag
Dienstag	Samstag
Mittwoch	Sonntag
Donnerstag	

G. Schreib es auf! (Write it down!) Your teacher will have you draw the name of a classmate. Write an invitation to that person. Give her/him the invitation. Then answer the invitation you receive.

H. Du bist Kartenverkäufer/in. Take the role of the ticket seller in the illustration and answer the customers' questions.

1. Wer gibt das Rockkonzert am Samstag abend?
2. Wieviel kosten die Karten?
3. Haben Sie noch Karten zu fünfzehn Mark?
4. Wann beginnt die Vorstellung?
5. Wer spielt Donnerstag abend hier?
6. Kann ich noch Karten für Donnerstag abend bekommen?

I. Ein kurzes Gespräch. Write and practice a short dialogue using the German you have learned in Chapters 5–7. Use at least two of these sentences.

1. Gehst du ins Konzert?
2. Du kannst mein Buch nehmen.
3. Nein, ich habe keine Zeit.
4. Ich finde [Chemie] einfach.
5. Den finde ich schön.
6. Das Hemd ist schick, nicht?
7. Klasse!
8. Nein, ich muß Hausaufgaben machen.
9. Wir können ja mal fragen.
10. Gibt es noch Karten?

1. What role has English played in German rock music?
2. What are the highlights in the German film industry?
3. How are concerts and other cultural events advertised in the Bundesrepublik?

Kulturlesestück

Wer geht ins Kino?

Deutsche Teenager gehen gern ins Kino. Einige° deutsche Filme sind sehr gut und laufen° zum Beispiel° auch in Amerika. Aber die Deutschen sehen° auch amerikanische Filme gern. Amerikanische Stars sprechen° in deutschen Kinos Deutsch. Die Deutschen mögen Untertitel° nicht.

5   Die Karten für gute Plätze° sind teuer — sie können zehn Mark oder mehr kosten. Natürlich kann man auch billige Karten bekommen. Die guten Plätze sind hinten°, die billigen Plätze vorne°.

   Meistens° gibt es eine Vorstellung am Nachmittag und zwei Vorstellungen am Abend, zum Beispiel um 19 und um 21 Uhr. Und man muß dann auch um 7 oder 10 um 9 Uhr kommen.

some / run
for example / see, watch
speak
subtitles
seats

in the back / in the front
usually

Im Zoo Palast in Berlin (West) laufen oft amerikanische Filme.

A. Richtig oder falsch? Decide whether each statement is true (**richtig**) or false (**falsch**) based on the reading.

1. Deutsche Teenager dürfen nicht ins Kino gehen.
2. Deutsche sehen amerikanische Filme gern.
3. In deutschen Kinos haben amerikanische Filme Untertitel.
4. In deutschen Kinos kosten alle Karten zehn Mark.
5. Die Plätze vorne kosten mehr als° die Plätze hinten.   **mehr als** more than
6. Die Filme in deutschen Kinos laufen meistens nicht den ganzen Tag.

B. Deutsch und amerikanisch. Separate the following statements into two categories — those most typical of German movies and those most typical of American movies. If the statement is generally true of both German and American movies, put it in both categories: **deutsch und amerikanisch.**

1. Teenager gehen gern ins Kino.
2. Amerikanische Filme sind populär.
3. Die amerikanischen Stars sprechen Deutsch.
4. Die Stars sprechen Deutsch, aber der Film hat Untertitel.
5. Karten sind teuer.
6. Die Plätze vorne sind billig, denn° sie sind nicht so gut.   because
7. Die Vorstellung beginnt um sieben, aber man kann auch oft um acht hineingehen°.   go in
8. Es gibt eine Nachmittagsvorstellung.

Vokabeln

Substantive

das Geld money
das Jugendzentrum youth center, club
das Kino, —s movie theater; **ins Kino** to the movies
das Konzert, —e concert; **ins Konzert** to the concert
das Theater, — theater; **ins Theater** to the theater

die Band, —s band
die Frage, —n question
die Gruppe, —n group; **die Lieblingsgruppe** favorite group
die Karte, —n ticket
die Kasse, —n box office
die Lust pleasure, enjoyment

Substantive (cont.)

die Tante, —n aunt
die Vorstellung, —en performance
die Zeit, —en time

Verben

beginnen to start, to begin
bekommen to get, to receive
dürfen (darf) may, to be permitted to
fragen to ask
geben (i) to give; **es gibt** (+ *acc.*) there is, there are
glauben to believe; **ich glaube ja** I think so
können (kann) can, to be able to
möchte would like to
mögen (mag) to like

Verben (cont.)

müssen (muß) must, to have to
nehmen (nimmt) to take
Ski laufen to ski
sollen (soll) should, to be supposed to
versuchen to try
wollen (will) to want, to intend, to wish to

Andere Wörter

alles all, everything
an at
ausverkauft sold out
bei at (place of business); **bei Buchhandlung
  Baumann** at Baumann's Bookstore
bitte please; you're welcome
bitte schön please; you're very welcome
dann then
dumm dumb, stupid
ein paar a few, some
einfach simple, simply
frei free, not busy
ins to the; **ins Kino** to the movies

Andere Wörter (cont.)

mal *flavoring word (see p. 148)*
mehr more
morgen abend tomorrow evening
nichts nothing
sicher sure, certain(ly)
übermorgen the day after tomorrow
vielleicht maybe

Besondere Ausdrücke

hast du Lust? do you feel like . . . ?
ich habe keine Lust I don't feel like it; **ich
  habe schon Lust** I do feel like it
es geht it's possible
ich bekomme frei I'll get (the day) off
das schon that's true
Karten zu drei Mark tickets for three marks
das macht sechzehn Mark that's sixteen marks
nichts mehr nothing left
du darfst nicht you can't (may not) do that
an der Kasse at the box office

Kapitel 8

Was hast du vor?

Ein schönes Hobby — Schach (chess) *im Park*

Ansichtskarten sind interessant

Thomas is curious about Petra's choice of a hobby. He thinks old postcards are dull.

PETRA   Das ist ein Bild von Dresden.
THOMAS   Interessant. Sag mal, warum sammelst du gerade Ansichtskarten?
PETRA   Ich weiß nicht. Es macht Spaß.
THOMAS   Wirklich? Das verstehe ich nicht.
PETRA   Sehr einfach. Alte Ansichtskarten sind interessant und auch wertvoll.

Fragen

1. Was ist Petras Hobby?
2. Wie findet Thomas Petras Hobby?
3. Warum sammelt Petra alte Ansichtskarten?

Du hast das Wort

Sammelst du etwas?   Find someone else in the class who collects the same things you collect.

Asking about personal interests

DU

Sammelst du etwas?

GESPRÄCHSPARTNER/IN

Nein, ich sammle nichts.
Ja. Ich sammle | Briefmarken°.
                 Schallplatten°.
                 Poster.
                 Ansichtskarten°.
                 Bierdeckel°.

*Keramik ist ein Hobby
und auch ein
interessanter Beruf.*

Thomas braucht ein Hobby

Petra and Gerd think maybe Thomas needs a hobby, too.

GERD   Der Thomas ist wirklich eine lahme Ente.
PETRA   Ja, er ist immer müde. Und er findet immer alles langweilig.
GERD   Er hat aber auch zu nichts Lust.
PETRA   Was er braucht, ist ein Hobby.
GERD   Radioamateur vielleicht.
PETRA   Oder Keramik.

Richtig oder falsch?

1. Thomas ist immer müde.
2. Er findet alles interessant.
3. Er hat zu nichts Lust.
4. Er hat ein Hobby.
5. Er ist Radioamateur.

Du hast das Wort

1. **Hast du ein Hobby?** A classmate asks you whether you have a hobby. How would you respond?

Discussing hobbies

GESPRÄCHSPARTNER/IN

Hast du ein Hobby?

DU

Ja, ich spiele [Tennis].
Ja, ich fotografiere° sehr gern.
Ja, ich sammle Briefmarken.
Ja, ich lese° viel.
Ja, ich gehe gern spazieren.
Ja, ich repariere° alte Autos°.
Nein, ich habe kein Hobby.

2. **Du brauchst ein Hobby.** A friend suggests that you need a hobby. What are your excuses for not choosing the hobby she/he suggests?

Making excuses

GESPRÄCHSPARTNER/IN

Du brauchst ein Hobby.

DU

Ja, ich habe oft nichts zu tun°.
Ja, ich habe oft Langeweile°.
Meinst du?

Keramik	ist	vielleicht
Radioamateur		interessant.
Ansichtskarten	sind	
Briefmarken		

Ach, [Keramik] ist zu schwer.
Ach, [Radios°] sind zu kompliziert°.

Ach, [Ansichtskarten] sind so langweilig.
Ach, [Briefmarken] sind zu teuer.

3. **Welches Hobby?** Write down the names of five classmates. In a sentence write down a hobby you think would suit them and give a reason.

Asking about hobbies

Mark soll Tennis spielen.
Sonia soll fotografieren.

Er hat Sport gern.
Es macht Spaß.

Was habt ihr heute vor?

Astrid would like to know what Klaus and his friends have planned for the afternoon.

ASTRID Du, Klaus, was habt ihr heute nachmittag vor?
KLAUS Wir fahren nach Hamburg.
ASTRID Kauft ihr ein?
KLAUS Ja, wir kaufen Gerds Geburtstagsgeschenk.
ASTRID Wo?
KLAUS Ich weiß noch nicht. Bei Karstadt vielleicht.

Fragen

1. Wohin° fahren Klaus und seine Freunde?
2. Was wollen sie machen?
3. Wo kaufen sie ein?

Land und Leute

In the Federal Republic store hours are regulated to prevent competitors from taking advantage of each other and to maintain reasonable working hours. Monday through Friday stores are permitted to be open only between 7:00 A.M. and 6:30 P.M. With the exception of **langer Samstag** (the first Saturday of the month) and the four Saturdays before Christmas, when they remain open until 6:00 P.M., stores close between noon and 2 P.M. on Saturdays and are closed all day Sunday.

Stores in small towns and some city neighborhoods generally close for two hours during lunchtime on weekdays.

Dieses Geschäft macht auch am langen Samstag um eins zu.

Du hast das Wort

Was hast du vor?   Write down a plan of your activities for the week. A class-mate inquires about your plans. How would you respond?

GESPRÄCHSPARTNER/IN

Was hast du | heute
heute nachmittag
heute abend
am Wochenende | vor?

DU

Ich muß [arbeiten].
Ich muß [Deutsch] machen.
Ich gehe [ins Kino].
Ich spiele [Tennis].
Ich weiß noch nicht.
Nichts.
Ich habe zu nichts Lust.

Komm doch mit!

Astrid tries to persuade Erik to go shopping with her.

ASTRID   Kommst du heute nachmittag mit?
ERIK   Wohin?
ASTRID   In die Stadt. Zum Musikhaus Schumann.
ERIK   Heute, am Samstag?
ASTRID   Ja, heute ist doch langer Samstag.
ERIK   Ach ja, stimmt. Da machen die Geschäfte erst um sechs zu. Was willst du denn bei Schumann?
ASTRID   Die neue Platte von Katja Peters kaufen. Also, willst du nun mitkommen oder nicht?
ERIK   Ich habe eigentlich keine Zeit.
ASTRID   Ach, komm doch mit!
ERIK   Na gut.

Du hast das Wort

1. **Komm doch mit!**   You have plans for this evening. Invite a friend to come along, and inform her/him where you are going. Use the above dialogue as a model for your conversation, adapting it where necessary.

DU

Kommst du heute abend mit?

In die Disco°.
In die Stadt.
Ins Café°.
Ins Jugendzentrum.
Ins Theater.

GESPRÄCHSPARTNER/IN

Wohin?

Ja, gern.
Wann gehen wir?
Danke, ich kann nicht.

IMBISS   MetaCafé
1 Minute vom Adenauer Platz
Vegetarischer Imbiss + Stehcafé
Kurfürstendamm – Ecke Waitzstr. 15
1000 Berlin 12 · Telefon 324 80 08
Montag bis Freitag 9 bis 19 Uhr

2. **Viele Fragen.** You like to do different things with different friends. Ask a different classmate each set of questions.

    a. Wie findest du alte Ansichtskarten?
       Was sammelst du?
    b. Was machst du heute nachmittag?
       Was willst du bei [Schumann] kaufen?
    c. Wann gehst du ins Kino?
       Wieviel kosten die Kinokarten?

Land und Leute

In recent years the downtown areas of many cities in German-speaking countries have been converted to traffic-free pedestrian zones (**Fußgängerzonen**). In addition to attractive shops and boutiques, the **Fußgängerzone** has many restaurants and outdoor cafés. The streets are frequently lined with flowers or trees, and they often lead into small squares with fountains or sculpture. Throughout the **Fußgängerzone** there are benches where people can rest their tired feet or simply sit and watch people go by.

Fußgängerzone im Zentrum von München mit Rathaus *(town hall)* und Frauenkirche

Musikhaus Schumann

1. der Kassettenrecorder
2. das Radio
3. die Kassette
4. der Fernseher
5. die Schallplatte
   (die Platte)
6. die Stereoanlage
7. der Plattenspieler
8. der CD-Spieler

A. Siehst° du es? Answer the following questions based on the illustration.

1. Wie teuer ist die Stereoanlage?
2. Was kostet mehr — das Radio oder der Kassettenrecorder?
3. Ist der Fernseher preiswert?
4. Ist eine Schallplatte billig oder teuer?
5. Was kostet der CD-Spieler?

Sind Radios und Stereo-anlagen hier preiswert?

Du hast das Wort

Viel Musik.   Answer the questions for yourself, and then ask a classmate the same questions. Do you have similar interests?

Discussing personal preferences

Möchtest du einen Kassettenrecorder kaufen oder hast du schon einen?
Kaufst du viele Platten? Kassetten? Compact Discs?
Hörst du gern Radio?
Siehst du oft fern°?

Some useful commands

Mach die Tür bitte zu°!	Please close the door.
Mach das Fenster bitte auf°!	Please open the window.
Mach das Licht bitte an°!	Please turn on the light.
Mach das Licht bitte aus°!	Please turn out the light.
Steh bitte auf°!	Please stand up.

B.   Mach es!   Carry out the commands as your teacher gives them.

C.   Dein/e Freund/in soll es machen.   Tell a friend to carry out some of the commands above.

Flavoring word **mal** in commands

Sag **mal,** warum sammelst
  du gerade Ansichtskarten?
Schreib doch **mal!**

Say (Tell me), why do you collect
  postcards?
Why don't you write (sometime)?

Mal is frequently used to soften commands. The speaker leaves the time for carrying out the command vague and up to the receiver of the command.

Flavoring word **doch**

Komm **doch** mit!
Ja, heute ist **doch** langer Samstag.

Why don't you come along?
Today's the first Saturday of the
  month (remember?).

As a flavoring word **doch** has several meanings. In the first example the speaker uses **doch** to persuade the listener to do something. In the second example the speaker uses **doch** to imply that what is said is obvious and reminds the listener of something they both know.

D. Was bedeutet das? Give the English equivalents.

1. Sag mal! Gehen wir heute einkaufen oder nicht?
2. Hör mal! Das tut man doch nicht.
3. Wir gehen abends oft schwimmen. Komm doch mal mit!
4. Was machst du heute abend?
  Das weißt du doch.
5. Möchtest du mal die *Hot Dogs* hören?
6. Wir können es ja mal versuchen.
7. Schreib doch mal an Barbara!

Mein»Ruf-doch-mal-an-Geschenk«

Damit wir öfter
miteinander
sprechen...

Aussprache

[ai]   mein, Maier
[ɔi]   heute, Häuser
[ao] braun

A. Practice the following words horizontally in pairs.

[ai]	[ɔi]
leite	Leute
heiser	Häuser
Seile	Säule
Beile	Beule
Hai	Heu

[ao]	[ɔi]
Laute	Leute
blaue	Bläue
saure	Säure
Baume	Bäume
Haufen	häufen

[i]	[ai]
Liebe	Leibe
Wiese	Weise
siede	Seide
Biel	Beil
Wien	Wein

Aus den Augen, aus dem Sinn.

B. Practice the sounds [ai], [ɔi], and [ao]. Read the sentences aloud.

1. Meine Brüder spielen beide viel Fußball.
2. Das kleine Kind lernt fleißig Deutsch.
3. Warum gibt es so viele graue Häuser hier?

Übungen

1. The interrogatives **wo** and **wohin**

Wo ist Martina?	*Where* is Martina?
Wohin geht sie?	*Where* is she going (*to*)?

Wo is used to ask about location. **Wohin** is used to ask about direction.

A. Wo? Wohin? You didn't hear the last part of the conversation. Ask to have the last part of the conversation repeated, using **wo** and **wohin**.

▶ Utes Eltern wohnen in Mainz.   *Wo wohnen Utes Eltern?*

▶ Sie fahren am Wochenende   *Wohin fahren sie am*
nach Bremen.   *Wochenende?*

1. Utes Freund wohnt in Frankfurt.
2. Er fährt in die Stadt.
3. Er geht oft am Samstag ins Jugendzentrum.
4. Er arbeitet zu Hause.
5. Ute wohnt in Mainz.
6. Ute geht gern in die Schule.
7. Ihre Schule ist in Mainz.
8. Ute fährt am Wochenende nach Frankfurt.

2. Verbs with stem-vowel change **e** > **ie**

LESEN
ich lese
du **liest**
er/es/sie **liest**

SEHEN
ich sehe
du **siehst**
er/es/sie **sieht**

Lesen and **sehen** have a stem-vowel change **e** > **ie** in the **du-** and **er/es/sie-** forms of the present tense.

B. Was machen sie? Say that the following people read a lot.

▶ Dieter   *Dieter liest viel.*

1. Frau Weiß
2. ich
3. Monika
4. du
5. wir
6. ihr

C. Sie sehen oft fern. Say that the following people often watch television.

▶ Marita   *Marita sieht oft fern.*

1. Herr Hübner
2. ich
3. Torsten
4. du
5. wir
6. ihr

D. Hausaufgaben. Several people missed class and need help with homework. Fill in the appropriate form of the cued verb.

1. _____ du Sonja deine Mathe-Hausaufgabe? (geben)
2. Ja, ich _____ Sonja meine Mathe-Hausaufgabe. (geben)
3. _____ du heute abend Geschichte? (lesen)
4. Nein, ich _____. (fernsehen)
5. _____ du Erik später? (sehen)
6. Welche Hausaufgabe _____ du von Erik? (nehmen)
7. Ich _____ gar keine! (nehmen)

3. Present tense of **wissen**

ich **weiß**		wir wissen
du **weißt**	Sie wissen	ihr wißt
er/es/sie **weiß**		sie wissen

Wissen is irregular in the singular forms of the present tense.

E. Alle wissen es. You and your friends are going to a disco. Confirm that everyone knows when you're going.

▶ Jutta weiß, wann wir in die Disco gehen.   *Er weiß das auch.*
    Und Jürgen?

1. Und Benno?
2. Und Christl?
3. Und du?
4. Und Ulf und Jochen?
5. Und ihr?

Du hast das Wort

1. **Weißt du es?** Answer according to your personal knowledge or experience. Use **Ja, das weiß ich** or **Nein, das weiß ich nicht.**

Sharing personal knowledge

> Weißt du, wie alt deine Mutter ist?
> Weißt du, wann dein Vater Geburtstag hat?
> Weißt du, wann deine Freunde Geburtstag haben?
> Weißt du, wieviel Jeans kosten?
> Weißt du, wieviel eine Mappe kostet?
> Weißt du, wieviel Kinokarten kosten?

2. **Wissen Sie es?** Ask your teacher some of the questions in Exercise 1.

4. The imperative forms: du, ihr, Sie

Imperative forms are used to express commands. In both German and English, the verb is in first position. In written German an exclamation point is generally used after a command. A period may be used if the imperative sentence is said without emphasis.

du-imperative

Inge! **Frag(e)** bitte Frau Held!	Inge, *ask* Mrs. Held, please.
Dirk! **Arbeite** bitte jetzt!	Dirk, *work* now, please.

The **du**-imperative consists of the stem of a verb plus **-e.** The **-e** is often dropped in informal usage: **frage!** > **frag!** The **-e** may not be omitted if the stem ends in **-d** or **-t: arbeite!**

F.   Mach es heute! Frank is trying to put off repairing your car until tomorrow. Try to convince him to do it today.

▶ Ich repariere es morgen.   *Ach, repariere es doch heute!*

1. Ich versuche es morgen.
2. Ich mache es morgen.
3. Ich beginne morgen.
4. Ich komme morgen.

Petra! **Nimm** bitte das Buch da!	Petra, please *take* that book.
Lies es heute abend!	*Read* it this evening.

If the stem vowel of a verb changes from **e** to **i** or **ie,** the imperative has the same vowel change and has no final **-e: nehmen** > **nimm!**

G. Ja, sicher! Monika is working with you in the library. Tell her to do the things she asks about.

▶ Soll ich das Buch da nehmen?   *Ja, nimm das Buch da!*

1. Soll ich das Buch lesen?
2. Soll ich das Heft nehmen?

3. Soll ich Ute das Buch geben?
4. Soll ich Jan das Heft geben?

ihr-imperative

Günter! Peter! **Fragt** bitte
  Frau Held!
Arbeitet bitte jetzt!

Günter and Peter, please *ask* Mrs.
  Held.
Please *work* now.

The **ihr**-imperative is identical with the **ihr**-form of the present tense, except that the pronoun **ihr** is omitted.

H. Ja, sicher! You and your friends are in a record store. Advise them to do the things they ask about.

▶ Sollen wir die Platte hier kaufen?   *Ja, kauft die Platte!*

1. Sollen wir auch die Kassette nehmen?
2. Sollen wir die Platte spielen?
3. Sollen wir jetzt beginnen?
4. Sollen wir es versuchen?

Sie-imperative

Herr Schmidt! **Fragen Sie** Frau
  Held!
Arbeiten Sie bitte jetzt!

Mr. Schmidt, *ask* Mrs. Held.

Please *work* now.

The **Sie**-imperative is identical with the **Sie**-form of the present tense. The pronoun **Sie** is always stated and follows the verb directly.

I. Ja, machen Sie das. Frau Wagner is to pick up some theater tickets for you. Give her precise instructions on what to do.

▶ Soll ich die Karten heute kaufen?   *Ja, kaufen Sie bitte die Karten heute.*

1. Soll ich drei Karten kaufen?
2. Soll ich die Karten zu 30 Mark nehmen?
3. Soll ich heute abend ins Theater gehen?
4. Soll ich um sieben kommen?
5. Soll ich mit Frau Lange fahren?

Du hast das Wort

Sag, sie sollen das machen! Lead your class in a team game. Give various orders to individual members of each team. If they obey you, their teams gain a point. You may wish to use some of the commands from page 178.

Mach das Licht aus!
Mach das Fenster auf!
Mach die Tür zu!

Steh auf!
Nimm [Utes] Buch!
Gib [Erik] das Buch!

Giving commands

5. Imperative forms of the verb **sein**

Inge! | **Sei** um sieben da!
Günter! Peter! | **Seid** um sieben da! | *Be* here at seven.
Frau Lange! | **Seien Sie** um sieben da!

J. Sei/Seid/Seien Sie nicht so! Urge people to change their attitudes.

▶ Andrea, du bist aber faul.   *Sei nicht so faul!*

1. Astrid, du bist aber sauer.
2. Anton, du bist aber doof.
3. Bernd, du bist aber wirklich langweilig.

▶ Claudia! Gerd! Ihr seid ja so sauer.   *Seid nicht so sauer!*

4. Regina! Hugo! Ihr seid aber sehr faul.
5. Elke! Paul! Ihr seid so doof.
6. Inge! Franz! Ihr seid wirklich langweilig.

▶ Herr Kurz! Sind Sie sicher?   *Seien Sie nicht so sicher!*

7. Frau Lutz! Sie sind ja so fleißig.
8. Fräulein Weiß! Sie sind ja so sauer.
9. Herr Lehner! Warum sind Sie so langweilig?

6. Separable-prefix verbs

The separable prefix

mitkommen	Ingrid **kommt** heute **mit**.	Ingrid *is coming along* today.
zumachen	Wann **macht** das Geschäft **zu**?	When *does* the store *close*?

Many German verbs begin with prefixes such as **mit** and **zu**. Some prefixes are separable: in the present tense, they are separated from the base form of the verb and are in last position.

| Möchtest du heute **mitkommen?** | Would you like to *come along* today? |
| Kannst du die Tür **zumachen?** | Can you *shut* the door? |

In the infinitive form, the prefix is attached to the base form of the verb.

K. Was hast du vor? Ingrid asks what you and your friends have planned today. Verify her guesses.

▶ Kommst du heute nachmittag mit? *Ja, ich komme heute nachmittag mit.*

1. Kommt Axel auch mit?
2. Hat Helga etwas vor?

3. Kaufst du bei Karstadt ein?
4. Macht Karstadt um fünf zu?

L. Einkaufen für den Geburtstag. Ingrid and her sisters are discussing birthday shopping for their mother. Answer the questions using the cues given.

▶ Wann willst du morgen aufstehen? Spät? *Ja, ich stehe morgen spät auf.*

1. Wann willst du einkaufen? Heute nachmittag?
2. Wo willst du einkaufen? Bei Karstadt?
3. Wann soll Karstadt aufmachen? Um neun?
4. Was willst du einkaufen? Geburtstagsgeschenke für deine Mutter?
5. Wer will mitkommen? Ingrid?

Nicht with separable-prefix verbs

| mitkommen | Ingrid kommt heute **nicht** mit. |
| aufmachen | Warum machst du das Fenster **nicht** auf? |

In a negative sentence, the adverb **nicht** usually comes directly before the separable prefix.

M. Was habt ihr vor? Werner wants to know what plans you and Trudi have. Keep him guessing by answering his questions in the negative.

▶ Kommt ihr heute nachmittag mit? *Nein, wir kommen nicht mit.*

1. Kauft ihr heute nachmittag ein?
2. Kommt ihr heute abend mit?
3. Seht ihr heute abend fern?
4. Habt ihr vor, ins Kino zu gehen?

Imperative forms of separable-prefix verbs

Gerd! **Mach** die Tür bitte **zu!**
Peter! Claudia! **Kommt** jetzt **mit!**
Frau Stein! **Machen Sie** bitte das Fenster **auf!**

In an imperative sentence, the separable prefix is in last position.

N. Party im Jugendzentrum. You're getting the room ready for a party at the youth center. Tell each of your assistants what to do.

▶ Türen aufmachen   *Mach bitte die Türen auf!*

1. Fenster aufmachen
2. Licht anmachen
3. bei Karstadt einkaufen
4. Fenster wieder zumachen
5. Türen wieder zumachen
6. Licht ausmachen

O. Mach das! Tell the following people to do things.

▶ Inge — das Licht ausmachen   *Inge, mach bitte das Licht aus!*

1. Doris — die Tür zumachen
2. Werner — das Fenster aufmachen
3. Frau Schneider — mitkommen
4. Max — das Licht anmachen
5. Gerd und Astrid — bei Hertie einkaufen
6. Herr Klein — das Fenster wieder zumachen

Grammatische Übersicht

Interrogatives **wo** and **wohin** (A)

Wo ist Ingrid?   *Where* is Ingrid?
Wohin geht Dieter?   *Where* is Dieter going?

English uses the single word *where* for the two meanings *in what place* and *to what place*. German always distinguishes between these two meanings. **Wo** is used for *in what place* and **wohin** is used for *to what place*.

Verbs with stem-vowel change e > ie (B–D)

LESEN			
ich lese	Sie lesen	wir lesen	
du **liest**		ihr lest	
er/es/sie **liest**		sie lesen	

SEHEN			
ich sehe	Sie sehen	wir sehen	
du **siehst**		ihr seht	
er/es/sie **sieht**		sie sehen	

Lesen and **sehen** have a stem-vowel change **e > ie** in the **du-** and **er/es/sie-** forms of the present tense. Note that because the stem of **lesen** ends in a sibilant, the **-st** ending of the **du-**form contracts to **-t: du liest.**

Present tense of **wissen** (E)

ich **weiß**	Sie wissen	wir wissen	
du **weißt**		ihr wißt	
er/es/sie **weiß**		sie wissen	

Wissen is irregular in the singular forms of the present tense.

The imperative forms: **du, ihr, Sie** (F–I)

Ernst!	**Schreib** bald!	
Peter! Inge!	**Schreibt** bald!	*Write* soon.
Herr Schmidt!	**Schreiben Sie** bald!	

The imperative forms are used to express commands. As in English, the verb is in first position.

du-imperative

INFINITIVE	IMPERATIVE	PRESENT
beginnen	**Beginn(e)** jetzt!	Beginnst du jetzt?
arbeiten	**Arbeite** jetzt!	Arbeitest du jetzt?
nehmen	**Nimm** das Papier!	Nimmst du das Papier?

Diese Züricherin liest gern draußen.

The **du**-imperative consists of the stem of a verb plus **-e,** but the **-e** is often dropped in informal usage. If the stem of the verb ends in **-d** or **-t,** the **-e** may not be omitted in written German: **arbeite!**

If the stem vowel of a verb changes from **e** to **i** or **ie,** the **du**-imperative has the same vowel change and has no final **-e.** The pronoun **du** is not used in the imperative.

ihr-imperative

INFINITIVE	IMPERATIVE	PRESENT
beginnen	**Beginnt** jetzt!	Beginnt ihr jetzt?
nehmen	**Nehmt** das Papier!	Nehmt ihr das Papier?

The **ihr**-imperative is identical with the **ihr**-form of the present tense, except that the pronoun **ihr** is not used in the imperative.

Sie-imperative

INFINITIVE	IMPERATIVE	PRESENT
beginnen	**Beginnen Sie** jetzt! ↘	Beginnen Sie jetzt? ↗
nehmen	**Nehmen Sie** das Papier! ↘	Nehmen Sie das Papier? ↗

The **Sie**-imperative is identical with the **Sie**-form of the present tense. The pronoun **Sie** is always stated and follows the verb immediately.

In speech, one differentiates a command from a question by intonation. The voice falls at the end of a command and rises at the end of a general question.

Imperative forms of the verb **sein** (J)

Inge!	**Sei** um sieben Uhr da!	
Petra! Uwe!	**Seid** um sieben Uhr da!	*Be* here at seven o'clock.
Herr Braun!	**Seien Sie** um sieben Uhr da!	

Note that the **Sie**-imperative of **sein** is different from the **Sie**-form of the present tense.

Separable-prefix verbs (K–O)

to get up	I *get up* early.
to call up	Did you *call* your friend *up?*
to write down	Let me *write down* your address.

English has many two-word verbs, such as *to get up, to call up,* and *to write down.* These two-word verbs consist of a verb and a particle such as *up* or *down.* The participle is sometimes separated from the verb in sentences.

aufstehen	Warum **stehst** du nicht **auf?**
mitkommen	Erik **kommt** heute **mit.**
zumachen	**Mach** die Tür **zu!**

German has a large number of *separable-prefix verbs* that function like certain English two-word verbs. Examples are **aufstehen, mitkommen, zumachen.** In present-tense statements and questions and in imperative forms, the separable prefix (**auf, mit, zu,** and so on) is separated from the verb and is in last position.

Ute kann nicht **mitkommen.**

In the infinitive form, the prefix is attached to the base form of the verb.

Inge kommt heute **nicht** mit.

The adverb **nicht** usually comes directly before a separable prefix.

Frank möchte **mit′kommen.**
Petra kommt nicht **mit′.**

In spoken German, the stress falls on the prefix of separable-prefix verbs. In the vocabularies of this text, separable-prefix verbs are indicated by a raised dot between the prefix and the verb: **auf·stehen, ein·kaufen, mit·kommen, fern·sehen, vor·haben, zu·machen.**

Infinitives ending in **-eln**

SAMMELN		
ich **sammle**		wir sammeln
du sammelst	Sie sammeln	ihr sammelt
er/es/sie sammelt		sie sammeln

When the infinitive of a verb ends in **-eln,** the stem loses the **-e** in the **ich**-form.

Wiederholung

A. Eine lahme Ente. Erik is having a hard time getting Jürgen to do anything. Answer the questions based on the following dialogue.

ERIK Wir gehen heute abend zu Inge. Kommst du auch?
JÜRGEN Ach nein. Bei Inge ist es immer so langweilig. Da dürfen wir nicht richtig Musik machen.
ERIK Willst du vielleicht ins Kino?
JÜRGEN Ach nein. Filme finde ich doof.
ERIK Was möchtest du denn?
JÜRGEN Ich weiß es nicht. Ich habe zu nichts Lust.
ERIK Du bist aber eine lahme Ente!

1. Wohin möchte Erik heute abend?
2. Warum geht Jürgen nicht mit?
3. Will er ins Kino? Warum (nicht)?
4. Was will er denn?
5. Warum ist Jürgen eine lahme Ente?

B. Kurze Dialoge. Make up two-line dialogues by choosing a line from column A and an appropriate response from column B.

A	B
[Keramik] ist interessant.	Ich kann's ja mal versuchen.
Du brauchst ein Hobby.	Toll!
Ich sammle [alte Autos].	Meinst du?
Möchtest du [fotografieren] lernen?	Ich weiß es nicht.
Benno ist Radioamateur, nicht?	Vielleicht. Ich bin nicht sicher.
[Wanderst] du gern?	Nein, eigentlich nicht.
	Das kann sein.
	Ist das nicht furchtbar teuer?
	Nein, das ist zu langweilig.

C. Welches Wort? Complete the second line of each two-line exchange by choosing an appropriate flavoring word. Give an English equivalent of each exchange.

1. Ich wohne nicht in der Gartenstraße.
   Wo wohnst du _____? (denn, doch)
2. Fährst du nach Bergdorf?
   Ja, komm _____ mit! (denn, doch)
3. Der Anzug da kostet nur 100 Mark.
   Das ist _____ billig. (mal, ja)
4. Petra sammelt alte Ansichtskarten.
   Das ist _____ interessant! (ja, denn)
5. Ist das Buch interessant?
   Ja. Lies es doch _____! (mal, ja)
6. Der Rock hier ist zu klein.
   Welche Größe trägst du _____? (mal, denn)

D. Was bedeutet das? The following sentences contain some unfamiliar words that are either cognates or compounds of familiar words. Give the meaning of each italicized word.

1. Hast du die *Kinokarten* gekauft?
2. Weißt du, wann die *Abendvorstellung* beginnt?
3. Karl spielt gern Fußball, Basketball und Hockey. Er ist wirklich ein *Sportfreund.*
4. Eishockey spielen wir im *Wintersportzentrum.*
5. Volker braucht ein deutsch-englisches *Wörterbuch.*
6. Zum Geburtstag bekommt ein Baby viele *Spielsachen.*

E. Wir haben viel vor. You and Jürgen have plans for tomorrow. Form sentences using the cues provided.

1. Jürgen / müssen / aufstehen / morgen / um sechs
2. er / wollen / fahren / nach Hamburg
3. ihr / dürfen / mitkommen / auch /?
4. wir / können / einkaufen / da
5. Jürgen / möchten / kaufen / bei Schumann / eine Platte
6. die Platten / sollen / sein / da / sehr billig
7. du / wollen / kaufen / auch / eine Platte /?

F. Alles fertig? Thomas is in charge of a surprise party at his house this evening. Change the phrases in italics to the plural and restate his remarks.

1. Wer hat *das Geschenk?*
2. Hat Peter *den Bierdeckel?*
3. Ich brauche nun *die Schallplatte.*
4. Wer hat *die Kassette?*
5. Mach bitte *die Tür* auf!
6. Gib mir bitte *das Poster* da!
7. Hört ihr nicht *das Auto?*
8. Jetzt könnt ihr *die Tür* wieder zumachen.

G. Was sagst du?   Answer the following questions. Then ask your teacher the same questions.

1. Hast du ein Hobby?
2. Sammelst du etwas?
3. Liest du gern?
4. Welches Buch liest du jetzt?
5. Gehst du gern spazieren?
6. Treibst du gern Sport?
7. Fotografierst du gern?

H. Schulfächer und Hobbys.   Your friend Mark wants to become a banker **(Bankangestellte/r),** Sue wants to become an engineer **(Ingenieur/in),** Sally an architect **(Architekt/in),** and George a photographer **(Fotograf/in).** You're not surprised. What subjects do each of them like in school? What kinds of hobbies do they have?

▶ *Sue hat Mathematik und Physik gern. Sie repariert gern alte Radios.*

I. Land und Leute.

1. Describe how shopping in the U.S. might be different from shopping in Germany. Is there a pedestrian zone in your town?
2. Describe a pedestrian zone in a German-speaking country. Are you familiar with a pedestrian zone in the U.S.? Describe it.

Im Museum — Viele Leute finden Maschinen interessant.

194

Berlin (West) —
Museum for Transportation and Technology

Sammelfreuden°

Freude: joy, pleasure

Viele Menschen° sammeln etwas: Briefmarken, Bierdeckel, Bücher, Ansichtskarten, Schallplatten, Poster. Auch als° Gemeinschaft° sammeln die Menschen: Museen° findet man° in vielen Städten.

people
as / society
museums / one

    Viele Deutsche gehen am Sonntag ins Museum, denn dann kostet es nichts. Sie
5 sehen da Sammlungen° von Autos und Maschinen, von Bildern und Postern, von Briefmarken, Büchern, Keramik und Möbeln°. Es gibt auch besondere Museen, zum Beispiel das Gutenberg-Museum in Mainz, das Grimm-Museum in Kassel, ein Ledermuseum° in Offenbach, ein Uhrenmuseum in Furtwangen, ein Fahrradmuseum° in Neckarsulm und sogar ein Brotmuseum° in Ulm.

collections
furniture

leather museum
bicycle museum /
    bread museum

A. Welches Wort? Choose the phrase that best completes each statement, based on the reading.

1. Die Menschen sammeln als Gemeinschaft in . . .
    a. Möbeln   c. Bildern
    b. Geschäften   d. Museen
2. Man findet Museen in vielen . . .
    a. Städten
    b. Kassen   c. Sammlungen
                       d. Theatern

3. Am Sonntag sind viele Menschen im Museum, denn . . .
   a. die Karten sind am Sonntag sehr billig
   b. sie brauchen keine Karten zu kaufen
   c. am Samstag müssen sie arbeiten
   d. die Museen machen nur am Sonntag auf

B. Welches Wort paßt nicht? Below are lists of items, grouped so that two of them have something in common and might therefore be found in the same museum. Indicate which item does not belong in each group.

1. Briefmarken, Ansichtskarten, Autos
2. Möbel, Plattenspieler, Radios
3. Bilder, Brot, Poster
4. Autos, Schlagzeuge, Fahrräder
5. Kleider, Anzüge, Bierdeckel
6. Uhren, Geigen, Gitarren

Kunstmuseum in Wien

Land und Leute

Germans love to go to the museum. Each year some 35 million people visit the Federal Republic's two thousand museums. In addition to seeing fine art, people like to learn about other aspects of their history. Many towns, cities, and regions have a **Heimatmuseum,** which introduces visitors to their local culture and history. Also very popular are museums devoted to special collections such as hats, typewriters, salt, tobacco, bread, ivory, stoves, or shoes.

The **Gutenberg-Museum** in Mainz, for example, shows the evolution of book printing. The **Grimm Museum** in Kassel is devoted to the Grimm brothers, who became famous for their collection of fairy tales and for the first written German grammar rules.

Vokabeln

Substantive

der Bierdeckel, – coaster (*used under a glass or mug*)
der CD-Spieler, – compact disc player
der Fernseher, – television set
der Kassettenrecorder, – cassette recorder
der Plattenspieler, – record player, turntable
der Radioamateur, –e "ham" radio operator

das Auto, –s car
das Café, –s café
das Fenster, – window
das Geschäft, –e store
das Geschenk, –e present; **das Geburtstagsgeschenk** birthday present
das Licht, –er light
das (also **der) Poster, –** poster
das Radio, –s radio

die Ansichtskarte, –n picture postcard
die Briefmarke, –n postage stamp
die Compact Disc, –s compact disc
die Disco, –s dance club, discothéque
die Kassette, –n cassette
die Keramik ceramics, pottery
die Langeweile boredom
die Platte, –n record
die Schallplatte, –n record
die Stadt, ̈e city
die Stereoanlage, –n stereo system
die Tür, –en door

Verben

an·machen to switch on (*the light*)
auf·machen to open
auf·stehen to get up, to stand up
aus·machen to turn off (*the light*)
ein·kaufen to shop; **einkaufen gehen** to go shopping
fahren (ä) to drive; to go (by vehicle)
fern·sehen (ie) to watch TV

Verben (cont.)

fotografieren to photograph
lesen (ie) to read
mit·kommen to come along
reparieren to repair
sagen to say, to tell
sammeln to gather, to collect; **ich sammle** I collect
sehen (ie) to see, to watch, to look
tun to do
verstehen to understand
vor·haben to plan
wissen (weiß) to know
zu·machen to shut

Andere Wörter

doch *flavoring word (see p. 179)*
eigentlich really, actually
etwas something
gerade exactly, precisely; just
immer always
kompliziert complicated
na well
nach to (with cities and countries); **nach Hamburg** to Hamburg
noch nicht not yet
nun now
wertvoll valuable
wohin where (to)
zum to the; **zum Musikhaus** to the music store

Besondere Ausdrücke

eine lahme Ente a dull, boring person
er hat zu nichts Lust he doesn't feel like doing anything
ich habe Langeweile I am bored
das stimmt that's right
na gut well, o.k.
sag mal tell me

Kapitel 9

Ich habe zu Hause geholfen

Er muß zu Hause helfen.

Ich habe mein Zimmer aufgeräumt

Karin and Norbert found different ways to occupy their time over the weekend.

NORBERT	Was hast du am Wochenende gemacht?
KARIN	Ich habe geschlafen.
NORBERT	Mensch! Das ist doch nicht dein Ernst!
KARIN	Doch! Ehrenwort! Am Sonntag habe ich dann ein Flugzeugmodell gebastelt. Und was hast du gemacht?
NORBERT	Ich habe gearbeitet — wie immer.
KARIN	Was heißt das — du hast gearbeitet?
NORBERT	Ich muß zu Hause helfen. Ich habe mein Zimmer aufgeräumt und das Auto gewaschen.
KARIN	Das nennst du arbeiten?
NORBERT	Also, es ist wenigstens mehr als schlafen.

Fragen

1. Was hat Karin am Wochenende gemacht?
2. Was hat sie gebastelt?
3. Wer hat gearbeitet?
4. Welches Zimmer hat Norbert aufgeräumt?
5. Was hat Norbert sonst noch gemacht?

Du hast das Wort

1. **Was hast du gestern gemacht?** Find out what five of your classmates have done recently.

   Asking about recent activities

DU			GESPRÄCHSPARTNER/IN	
Was hast du	am Wochenende gestern°	gemacht?	Ich habe	Hausaufgaben gemacht. [Tennis] gespielt. viel gearbeitet. [mein Zimmer] aufgeräumt. das Auto gewaschen. viel geschlafen.

Which classmates have done the same activities? Your teacher will ask you to summarize what you have found out from your classmates.

[Andrea] hat [Hausaufgaben gemacht].

2. **Wirklich?** In groups of three, say how long you did certain things. Each person will increase the amount of the same claim until a fourth person expresses doubt or surprise.

Disputing claims

PERSON #1/#2/#3:

Ich habe gestern acht/zwölf/zwanzig
   Stunden geschlafen.
Ich habe am Wochenende _____/_____/_____
   Platten gekauft.
Ich habe am Wochenende _____/_____/_____
   Bücher gelesen.
Ich habe gestern _____/_____/_____
   Stunden gearbeitet.

PERSON #4:

Wirklich?

Mensch! Das ist doch nicht
   dein Ernst.
Das ist schwer zu glauben.
Du hast doch nicht _____
   Bücher gelesen.

Volksbuchhandel

WIR
LADEN
SIE EIN

Ich habe eine Torte gebacken

Paul feels he spent a constructive weekend, but Sabine seems to disagree.

SABINE   Was hast du am Wochenende gemacht?
PAUL   Ich habe für meine Mutter eine Torte gebacken. Sie hat meine Großeltern zum Kaffee eingeladen.
SABINE   Sehr interessant!
PAUL   Sei nicht so sarkastisch! Du hast doch gefragt.
SABINE   Hat die Torte wenigstens geschmeckt?
PAUL   Ich weiß nicht. Ich habe Gerda abgeholt, und wir haben einen Spaziergang gemacht. Wir haben dann bei Gerdas Eltern Kaffee getrunken.

Fragen

1. Was hat Paul gebacken?
2. Warum hat er die Torte gebacken?
3. Hat die Torte geschmeckt?
4. Was haben Gerda und Paul gemacht?
5. Wo haben sie Kaffee getrunken?

Du hast das Wort

Am Wochenende habe ich . . . Tell your neighbor everything you did over the weekend. When you're finished, listen to your neighbor.

Reporting on recent activities

Am Freitag abend habe ich [eine Geschichte gelesen].
Am Samstag . . .

Arbeitsplan fürs Wochenende

Herr und Frau Gerdes haben vier Kinder. Alle müssen zu Hause helfen. Jedes Wochenende macht Frau Gerdes einen Arbeitsplan. Hier ist der Plan für letztes Wochenende.

	Freitag	Samstag	Sonntag
Gudrun Werner	Badezimmer putzen	Geschirr spülen / Garage aufräumen	Tisch decken
	Tisch decken / Mülleimer raustragen	abtrocknen / Staub saugen	Geschirr spülen
Hilde	abtrocknen	Auto waschen / Tisch decken	Frühstück machen
Erik	Geschirr spülen	einkaufen	abtrocknen

Fragen

1. Wer hat am Freitag Geschirr gespült?
2. Wer hat abgetrocknet?
3. Wer hat den Mülleimer rausgetragen?
4. Wann hat Werner das Badezimmer geputzt?
5. Wer hat fürs Wochenende eingekauft?
6. Wann hat Hilde den Tisch gedeckt?
7. Wann hat Gudrun abgetrocknet?
8. Wer hat am Sonntag Frühstück gemacht? den Tisch gedeckt?

Du hast das Wort

Ein neuer Arbeitsplan. Make an **Arbeitsplan** with the name of your family members and the days of the week. Your partner will fill it in by asking who must do various chores next weekend and when.

Discussing future plans

Wer muß fürs Wochenende einkaufen?
Wer muß spülen?
Wer muß . . .

Look over the plan your partner has filled out. Make sure it is correct.

Wortschatzerweiterung

Doch as positive response

NORBERT	Das ist doch nicht dein Ernst!	You're not serious, are you?
KARIN	**Doch!**	*Of course I am!*
CAROLA	Gehst du denn nicht ins Kino?	Aren't you going to the movies?
OTTO	**Doch.**	*Why, sure I am.*

In Chapter 8 you learned that **doch** can function as a flavoring word. **Doch** may also be used as a one-word positive response to a negative statement or question. With **doch,** the speaker contradicts an assumption contained in a previous statement or question.

A. Doch. Helga is making a number of wrong suppositions. Correct her, using **doch.**

▶ Gehst du nicht einkaufen?   *Doch. Ich gehe einkaufen.*

1. Gehst du nicht in die Stadt?
2. Kaufst du keine Platten?
3. Arbeitest du heute nicht?
4. Du gehst also heute nicht spazieren.
5. Du meinst das nicht.

B. Ich habe das gemacht. Say you've done everything you were told to do.

▶ Hast du das Badezimmer geputzt?   *Ja, das habe ich geputzt.*

▶ Hast du den Tisch nicht gedeckt?   *Doch, den habe ich gedeckt.*

1. Hast du die Garage nicht aufgeräumt?
2. Hast du das Auto gewaschen?
3. Hast du die Torte gebacken?
4. Hast du deine Hausaufgaben nicht gemacht?

Was hast du zu Hause gemacht?

Ich habe die Möbel abgestaubt.

Ich habe den Tisch abgeräumt.

Ich habe Wäsche gewaschen.

Ich habe den Hund und die Katze gefüttert.

Ich habe Gartenarbeit gemacht.

Ich habe Kaffee gekocht.

C. Ich habe das gemacht. Confirm the fact that you've already done your chores for the day. Use **doch** or **ja** in your answer as appropriate.

► Hast du schon die Möbel abgestaubt?   *Ja, die habe ich schon abgestaubt.*

1. Hast du schon die Torte gebacken?
2. Hast du schon den Müll rausgetragen?
3. Hast du schon den Hund gefüttert?
4. Hast du schon die Gartenarbeit gemacht?

Du hast das Wort

Wer hat die Arbeit gemacht? Ein Rollenspiel. Each person in your family has designated chores. Ask them whether the work has been done. One overly zealous member constantly interrupts to say she/he has done everything! Work out the scene with your partners.

Land und Leute

A German **Torte** has several layers, often with a cream filling. Another favorite pastry in German-speaking countries is the **Kuchen,** which consists of a single layer and some-times has a fruit topping. The recipe below is for an **Apfelkuchen.**

Kleiner Apfel- und großer Zwetschgenkuchen

Zutaten	Ingredients
150 Gramm Butter	1⅓ sticks butter
125 Gramm Zucker	½ cup sugar
1 Ei	1 egg
Eine abgeriebene Zitronenschale	grated peel of 1 lemon
150 Gramm Mehl	¾ cup flour
1 Teelöffel Backpulver	1 teaspoon baking powder
2–3 große Äpfel, geschält und in Streifen geschnitten	2–3 large apples, peeled and sliced in thin wedges

Butter und Zucker schaumig rühren, dann das Ei und die Zitronenschale dazu rühren. Mehl und Backpulver langsam hinzufügen. Eine Form mit Butter einfetten und mit Mehl bestreuen, dann den Teig in die Form füllen. (Wenn nötig, die Hände mit Mehl bestreuen, damit der Teig nicht an den Händen kleben bleibt.) Die Apfelstreifen vorsichtig in den Teig stecken und etwas Zitronensaft darüber träufeln. Backzeit: Ungefähr 45 Minuten bei mittlerer Hitze (bis der Teig schön hellbraun ist).

Combine butter and sugar and beat until creamy, then stir in egg and grated lemon peel. Sift together flour and baking powder and add gradually to mixture. Grease and flour a spring-form pan and press dough into the pan. (Add flour as necessary to keep dough from sticking to hands.) Arrange apple slices in concentric circles on the crust and sprinkle with a few drops of lemon juice. Bake at 350°F for about 45 minutes or until crust is golden brown.

Aussprache

[ts]	ganz, Platz, geht's, zehn, zu
[z]	sein, sehr, Bluse, gesund
[s]	es, essen, weiß

The letter **z** is pronounced [ts]. Before a vowel the letter **s** represents the sound [z]. In most other positions **s** represents the sound [s]. The letters **ss** and **ß** are both pronounced [s].

A. Practice the sound [ts] in final position and initial position.

Tanz, schwarz, Schweiz   zehn, Zimmer, zu

B. Practice the following words horizontally.

[z]	[s]	[ts]
reisen	reißen	reizen
Kurse	Kurs	kurz
heiser	heißer	Heizer
Felsen	Fels	Filz

Wenn die Katze aus dem Haus ist,
tanzen die Mäuse.

C. Practice the sounds [ts], [z], and [s]. Read the sentences aloud.

1. Sie kommen um zwölf in die Klasse.
2. Gisela kauft eine Bluse und eine Hose.
3. Franz und Inge gehen zweimal die Woche tanzen.

Übungen

Conversational past with auxiliary **haben**

German has several past tenses. One of them is the *conversational past,* which is
commonly used in conversation to refer to past actions or states.

ich **habe** es **gehört**		wir **haben** es **gehört**	
du **hast** es **gehört**	Sie **haben** es **gehört**	ihr **habt** es **gehört**	
er/es/sie **hat** es **gehört**		sie **haben** es **gehört**	

The conversational past is made up of an auxiliary verb and a past participle. Most
verbs use **haben** as the auxiliary. The participle is in last position.

A. Hast du es schon gehört? Konrad is eager to pass on a bit of gossip. Explain to him that you and the other people have already heard it.

▶ Und du?   *Ich habe es schon gehört.*

1. Und Frau Weiß?
2. Und Herr Lange?
3. Und Jens und Inge?
4. Und Erika?
5. Und dein Bruder?
6. Und unsere Freunde?
7. Und ihr?
8. Und du?

Past participles of weak verbs

INFINITIVE	PAST PARTICIPLE	CONVERSATIONAL PAST
machen arbeiten	ge + mach + t ge + arbeit + et	Ingrid **hat** ihre Aufgaben nicht **gemacht**. Sie **hat** schwer **gearbeitet**.

German verbs may be classified as weak or strong according to the way in which they form their past tenses.

The past participle of a weak verb is formed by adding **-t** to the unchanged stem. The **-t** expands to **-et** in verbs ending in **-d** or **-t** (for example, **arbeiten**). In the past participle, most weak verbs also have the prefix **ge-**.

B. Was habt ihr gestern gemacht? Ilse asks whether you did certain things yesterday. Tell her you did.

▶ Habt ihr gestern Musik gehört?   *Ja, wir haben Musik gehört.*

1. Habt ihr Platten gespielt?
2. Habt ihr auch getanzt?
3. Habt ihr Vokabeln gelernt?
4. Habt ihr gearbeitet?
5. Habt ihr Geschirr gespült?
6. Habt ihr Staub gesaugt?

C. Schon gemacht! You've been very industrious. Say you've already done your chores.

▶ Machst du jetzt die Gartenarbeit?   *Nein, die Gartenarbeit habe ich schon gemacht.*

1. Putzt du jetzt das Badezimmer?
2. Spülst du jetzt Geschirr?
3. Deckst du jetzt den Tisch?
4. Machst du jetzt Frühstück?
5. Fütterst du jetzt den Hund?

D. Wie gestern. The following people are as busy today as they were yesterday. Tell what they did.

▶ Ich putze Fenster.   *Ich habe gestern Fenster geputzt.*

1. Ich spüle Geschirr.
2. Frank bastelt Flugzeugmodelle.
3. Thomas kocht Kaffee.
4. Ingrid und Sabine machen Mathe.
5. Gisela und Jan lernen Vokabeln.
6. Du arbeitest wirklich viel.
7. Du spielst Tennis.
8. Erik saugt Staub.

Past participles of strong verbs

INFINITIVE	PAST PARTICIPLE	CONVERSATIONAL PAST
schreiben	ge + schrieb + en	Ich habe den Brief geschrieben.
nehmen	ge + nomm + en	Hast du mein Heft **genommen**?

A strong verb is a verb that changes its stem vowel (and occasionally consonants) in at least one of the past tenses. The past participle of a strong verb is formed by adding **-en** to the stem. The past participles of most strong verbs have the prefix **ge-**.

INFINITIVE	PAST PARTICIPLE	CONVERSATIONAL PAST
geben	ge + geb + en	Ich **habe** Erika ein Radio **gegeben**.
lesen	ge + les + en	Ich **habe** gestern ein Buch **gelesen**.
sehen	ge + seh + en	Ich **habe** Ilse nicht **gesehen**.

Many verbs with stem vowel **e** in the infinitive have **e** in the past participle.

E. Wir haben Freunde besucht. Hans-Dieter asks about your visit with some old friends. Satisfy his curiosity.

▶ Was habt ihr Gisela gegeben?   *Ja, wir haben Gisela das*
  Das Poster?   *Poster gegeben.*

1. Was habt ihr Frank gegeben? Eine Platte?
2. Was habt ihr gelesen? Thomas' Buch?
3. Wann habt ihr sein Buch gelesen? Letzte Woche?
4. Wo habt ihr Erik gesehen? Im Jugendzentrum?
5. Wo habt ihr die *Hot Dogs* gesehen? In München?

INFINITIVE	PAST PARTICIPLE	CONVERSATIONAL PAST
backen	ge + back + en	Ich **habe** eine Torte **gebacken**.
schlafen	ge + schlaf + en	Ich **habe** gut **geschlafen**.
tragen	ge + trag + en	Ich **habe** eine Jacke **getragen**.
waschen	ge + wasch + en	Ich **habe** mein Auto **gewaschen**.

Many verbs with stem vowel **a** in the infinitive also have **a** in the past participle.

F. Haben sie . . . ? Restate in the conversational past.

▶ Wäscht Frank das Auto? *Hat Frank das Auto gewaschen?*

▶ Nein, Martina wäscht es. *Nein, Martina hat es gewaschen.*

1. Bäckt Ingrid die Torte?
   Nein, Thomas bäckt sie.
2. Schläfst du gut?
   Ja, ich schlafe gut.
3. Trägst du Jeans ins Konzert?
   Ja, und Udo trägt auch Jeans.
4. Wann wäschst du die Wäsche?
   Ich wasche sie am Samstag.

Innsbruck: man hat Wäsche gewaschen und am Balkon aufgehängt.

INFINITIVE	PAST PARTICIPLE	CONVERSATIONAL PAST
helfen	ge + holf + en	Ich **habe** zu Hause **geholfen**.
nehmen	ge + nomm + en	Ich **habe** das Heft **genommen**.
schreiben	ge + schrieb + en	Ich **habe** Erika **geschrieben**.
trinken	ge + **trunk** + en	Ich **habe** Kaffee **getrunken**.

Many strong verbs change their stem vowel (and occasionally consonants) in the formation of the past participle.

G. Wer hat . . . ? Sabine wants to know who did the following things. Confirm her guesses.

▶ Wer hat Rudi geschrieben? Eva? *Ja, Eva hat Rudi geschrieben.*

1. Wer hat Heike geschrieben? Udo?
2. Wer hat zu Hause geholfen? Stefan?
3. Wer hat Dieter geholfen? Ingrid?
4. Wer hat den Pulli genommen? Gerda?
5. Wer hat die Mappe genommen? Ulf?
6. Wer hat schon Kaffee getrunken? Mutter?
7. Wer hat noch nichts getrunken? Vater?

H. Bitte sag es. You still haven't received answers to your questions. Ask them again in the present tense.

▶ Warum hast du Beate die *Warum gibst du Beate die*
  Briefmarken gegeben? *Briefmarken?*

1. Warum hat Jan Gisela seinen Kassettenrecorder gegeben?
2. Was habt ihr in Englisch gelesen?
3. Wo hast du Tanja gesehen?
4. Warum hat Stefan soviel geschlafen?
5. Wer hat die Wäsche gewaschen?
6. Warum hast du keine Torte gebacken?
7. Warum hast du meinen Bleistift genommen?
8. Wer hat Heike geholfen?
9. Welche Jacke hast du getragen?

I. Sie haben das am Wochenende gemacht. Restate in the conversational past.

▶ Wir sehen unsere Großeltern *Wir haben unsere Großeltern*
  am Samstag. *am Samstag gesehen.*

▶ Wir trinken um vier Kaffee. *Wir haben um vier Kaffee*
  getrunken.

Am Wochenende wäscht dieser junge Berliner das Familienauto.

1. Hilft Gerd zu Hause?
   Ja, er wäscht die Wäsche.
2. Bäckt Frank die Torte?
   Nein, er schläft am Samstag bis elf.
3. Gibst du Gerda das Buch?
   Ja, sie liest es am Wochenende.

J. Das habe ich gemacht. Tell all the things you did yesterday.

▶ zu Hause helfen   *Ich habe gestern zu Hause geholfen.*

1. Geschirr spülen
2. den Tisch decken
3. einen Kuchen backen
4. Staub saugen
5. unser Auto waschen
6. einen Brief schreiben
7. eine deutsche Geschichte lesen
8. viel arbeiten
9. nicht schlafen

Past participles of separable-prefix verbs

INFINITIVE	PAST PARTICIPLE	CONVERSATIONAL PAST
abstauben	ab + **ge** + staubt	Kirstin **hat** die Möbel **abgestaubt**.
einladen	ein + **ge** + laden	Ihre Mutter **hat** Schmidts **eingeladen**.
fernsehen	fern + **ge** + sehen	Abends **haben** sie **ferngesehen**.

The prefix **ge-** of the past participle comes between the separable prefix and the stem of the participle.

K. Ute hat alles gemacht. Ute is a hard worker. Identify her as the one who did all the chores.

▶ Wer hat das Zimmer aufgeräumt?   *Ute hat das Zimmer aufgeräumt.*

1. Wer hat abgetrocknet?
2. Wer hat die Fenster aufgemacht?
3. Wer hat die Möbel abgestaubt?
4. Wer hat den Tisch abgeräumt?
5. Wer hat eingekauft?
6. Wer hat den Mülleimer rausgetragen?

L. Später. Your mother is checking whether you've done your chores yet. Inform her that you'll do them later.

▶ Hast du das Zimmer aufgeräumt?   *Nein, das räume ich später auf.*

1. Hast du die Garage aufgeräumt?
2. Hast du die Möbel abgestaubt?
3. Hast du die Fenster aufgemacht?
4. Hast du den Tisch abgeräumt?
5. Hast du das Geschirr abgetrocknet?
6. Hast du den Mülleimer rausgetragen?

M. Sag mal . . . Restate the following exchanges in the conversational past.

▶ Kaufst du heute ein?   *Hast du heute eingekauft?*

▶ Ja, ich kaufe bei Karstadt ein.   *Ja, ich habe bei Karstadt eingekauft.*

1. Kaufst du nur bei Karstadt ein?
   Nein, ich kaufe auch bei Hertie ein.
2. Wann macht Karstadt auf?
   Heute machen sie schon um neun auf.
3. Macht Karstadt um fünf zu?
   Nein, sie machen erst um halb sieben zu.

4. Siehst du Samstag nachmittag fern?
   Ja, und ich sehe auch am Abend fern.
5. Wann räumst du die Garage auf?
   Ich räume sie gar nicht auf.

Du hast das Wort

Was hast du am Wochenende gemacht? Ask various classmates what they did over the weekend.

Was hast du am Wochenende gemacht?
Hast du dein Zimmer aufgeräumt?
Hast du viel geschlafen?
Hast du etwas gebastelt?
Hast du gearbeitet? Wo?

Grammatische Übersicht

Conversational past (A–M)

Hast du schon Mathe **gemacht?**   *Have you done* your math?
Nein, **ich habe** Tennis **gespielt.**   No, *I played* tennis.

There are several past tenses in German. The conversational past, as the name implies, is common in conversation. It is used in many situations that require the simple past tense in English.

Auxiliary **haben**

ich **habe** Detlev **gefragt**		wir **haben** Stefan **gefragt**
du **hast** Petra **gefragt**	Sie **haben** Ingrid **gefragt**	ihr **habt** Silke **gefragt**
er **hat** Marta **gefragt**		sie **haben** Benno **gefragt**

The conversational past is made up of an auxiliary verb and a past participle. **Haben** is used as the auxiliary of most verbs. The past participle is always in last position.

Ich habe gestern **nicht** gearbeitet.

Nicht often comes directly before the past participle.

Past participles of weak verbs

INFINITIVE	PAST PARTICIPLE	CONVERSATIONAL PAST
kaufen	ge + kauf + t	Erik **hat** eine Platte **gekauft**.
kosten	ge + kost + et	Wieviel **hat** sie **gekostet**?

German verbs may be classified as weak or strong according to the way they form their past tenses. A weak verb is a verb with a stem that remains unchanged in the past-tense forms. The past participle of a weak verb is formed by adding the ending **-t** to the infinitive stem. The **-t** expands to **-et** in verbs with stems ending in **-d** or **-t** (for example, **kosten**). Most past participles have the prefix **ge-**.

Past participles of strong verbs

INFINITIVE	PAST PARTICIPLE	CONVERSATIONAL PAST
schreiben	ge + schrieb + en	Ich **habe** eine Karte **geschrieben**.
nehmen	ge + nomm + en	**Hast** du die Karte **genommen**?
sehen	ge + seh + en	Nein, ich **habe** sie nicht **gesehen**.

A strong verb is a verb that changes its stem vowel (and occasionally consonants) in at least one of the past tenses. The past participle of a strong verb is formed by adding **-en** to the stem. Most strong verbs also add the prefix **ge-** in the past participle. Since there is no way to guess how or even if the stem vowel changes from infinitive to past participle, you should memorize the past participles of strong verbs.

For a list of the strong verbs used in this book, with their past participles, see the Appendix. Past participles of strong verbs are noted in the vocabularies as follows: **schreiben (geschrieben).**

Past participles of separable-prefix verbs

INFINITIVE	PAST PARTICIPLE	CONVERSATIONAL PAST
aufräumen	auf + ge + räumt	**Hast** du das Zimmer **aufgeräumt**?
einladen	ein + ge + laden	Wir **haben** Schmidts **eingeladen**.

The prefix **ge-** of the past participle comes between the separable prefix and the stem of the participle.

A. Hausarbeit. Create captions that describe the activity in each picture.

B. Wie finden sie es? The following people recently went shopping. Say what they think of their purchases. Use a possessive adjective in each sentence.

▶ Peter / Pulli / schick   *Peter findet seinen Pulli schick.*

1. Frank / Mantel / klasse
2. Hannelore / Kleid / hübsch
3. wir / Jeans / prima
4. du / Gürtel / preiswert
5. ihr / Jacken / toll
6. ich / Hemd / schick

C. Was haben sie gemacht? Restate the following exchanges in the conversational past.

1. Hilft Bruno zu Hause?
   Ja. Er räumt die Garage auf.
2. Wann holt ihr Schmidts ab?
   Um vier. Wir trinken um halb fünf Kaffee.
3. Was machst du Samstag nachmittag?
   Ich spiele Tennis.
4. Petra bäckt eine Torte.
   Hoffentlich schmeckt sie.
5. Dieter räumt hoffentlich sein Zimmer auf.
   Leider nein. Er liest ein Buch.

D. Wo? Wohin? The following statements are all answers to questions beginning with **Wo?** or **Wohin?** Ask the questions.

1. Karsten wohnt in Hamburg.
2. Er fährt am Samstag in die Stadt.
3. Bei Karstadt kauft er einen Anzug.
4. Dann fährt er wieder nach Hause.
5. Er möchte heute abend ins Theater.

Die St. Michaelis Kirche ("Michel"), das Wahrzeichen (symbol) *Hamburgs*

Land und Leute

Unlike their counterparts in the United States, teenagers in the Federal Republic hardly ever work in part-time jobs. Child-labor laws prohibit girls and boys under the age of fourteen from working, and some restrictions last up to the age of eighteen (for example, they may not work weekends and holidays). Apprentices (**Auszubildende,** or **Azubis**) earn some money as they learn their trade, while students in a **Gymnasium** usually depend on their parents for pocket money (**Taschengeld**). As long as they are still in school, young people are expected to devote their time to homework. In those areas of the German-speaking countries where tourism is a major industry, more teenagers hold part-time and summer jobs, even though the summer vacation is only about six weeks long.

Im Sommer können Teenager im Einkaufszentrum *(shopping mall)* Hanse-Viertel in Hamburg arbeiten.

E. Mach das! Give orders to the people indicated.

▶ Peter: das Badezimmer putzen   *Putz bitte das Badezimmer!*

1. Karin: das Geschirr spülen
2. Norbert: abtrocknen
3. Werner und Dietmar: die Garage aufräumen
4. Herr Schwarz: die Wäsche waschen
5. Herr und Frau Weiß: das Auto waschen
6. Sabine: den Kaffee kochen
7. Inge: die Katze füttern

F. Welches Wort? You have learned several kinds of words that are in last position in a German sentence. Complete each of the following sentences with an appropriate word.

ab   auf   fahren   gefragt   gefüttert
gekauft   mit   spülen

1. Hat Gabi schon den Hund _____?
2. Muß sie noch das Geschirr _____?
3. Möchte sie morgen nach Frankfurt _____?
4. Ja. Sie steht früh _____.
5. Kommt ihr Freund Peter _____?
6. Hat er ein Auto _____?
7. Wann holt er Gabi _____?
8. Ich habe sie nicht _____.

G. Welches Wort? Complete the response for each conversational exchange with **Ja, Nein,** or **Doch,** as appropriate.

1. Hast du ein Hobby?
   _____, ich sammle Bierdeckel.
2. Kauft ihr heute ein?
   _____, wir bleiben zu Hause.
3. Fährt Detlev heute nicht mit?
   _____, er kommt mit.
4. Können Sie mein Auto reparieren?
   _____, ich habe leider keine Zeit.
5. Herr Siemens wohnt nicht in der Gartenstraße.
   _____, er wohnt da.
6. Spielst du oft Fußball?
   _____, es macht viel Spaß!

Sie wollen mit dem Auto von Würzburg nach Frankfurt fahren.

218

H. Wie sagt man das? Your German guest wants to know what your American friends are saying. Translate the following conversational exchanges for your guest.

1. What did you do yesterday?
   Gerda and I went for a walk.
2. Didn't you work?
   Not much. I washed our car.
3. When did you pick up Gerda?
   I picked Gerda up at four.
4. Why didn't you watch TV yesterday?
   I didn't have time.

I. Eine Geburtstagsparty. Your partner had a birthday party yesterday for someone (friend, mother, brother). Develop a conversation about the party.

J. Land und Leute.

1. What are some ways young people in the United States earn pocket money? If you were a young German, what would the possibilities be?
2. What is the difference between apple pie and **Apfelkuchen?** What kinds of cakes do you like? Would they classify as **Torte** or **Kuchen?** Why?

Kulturlesestück

Taschengeld und Jobs

Taschengeld° ist oft ein Problem für deutsche Schüler. Viele bekommen Taschengeld von den Eltern. Und in vielen Familien bekommen sie auch Geld für gute Zeugnisse°. Und zum Geburtstag und zu Weihnachten°. Aber das ist natürlich oft nicht genug° für Kino und Konzerte, für Kassetten und Schallplatten, für
5 Klassenfahrten° und Sport.
   Viele Schüler wollen also etwas Geld verdienen°. In Deutschland ist das aber nicht so leicht. Es gibt nur wenige Jobs als Babysitter. Ein paar Schüler können Nachhilfestunden° geben. In den Supermärkten° gibt es auch Jobs, aber sie sind nicht leicht zu bekommen. Jobs bei Zeitungen° gibt es auch, aber nicht für Schüler.
10 In Deutschland kommen die Zeitungen am Morgen. Am Morgen haben die Schüler natürlich keine Zeit. So bleibt für sie die Reklame°: Sie können Reklame austragen°.

pocket money

grades / Christmas
enough
class trips
earn

tutoring sessions / supermarkets / newspapers

advertisements
distribute

Ein Azubi bei der Arbeit

Deutsch oder amerikanisch? Below is a list of statements about teenagers, jobs, and spending money. Indicate which statements seem more characteristic of German-speaking countries, which of the United States, which of both.

1. Taschengeld ist oft ein Problem für Teenager.
2. Barbara hat jede Woche einen Babysitterjob.
3. Viele Schüler arbeiten in den Supermärkten.
4. Paula kann keinen Babysitterjob finden. Ihre Freundinnen auch nicht.
5. Thomas arbeitet abends und am Wochenende im Supermarkt.
6. Paul macht jede Woche Gartenarbeit. So bekommt er Geld von seinen Eltern. Wenn er extra Geld braucht, räumt er die Garage auf, oder er putzt die Fenster.
7. Claudia kauft zwei neue Schallplatten. Sie bekommt das Geld von ihren Eltern, denn sie hat ein sehr gutes Zeugnis.
8. Jens kann keine Zeitungen austragen. Er muß am Morgen in die Schule.
9. Zum Geburtstag hat Inge Geld bekommen. Jetzt kann sie das kaufen, was sie haben will.
10. Erik trägt am Dienstag und am Freitag Reklame aus.

Vokabeln

Substantive

der Arbeitsplan, ∸ work schedule
der Eimer, − pail
der Hund, −e dog
der Kaffee coffee
der Müll garbage; der Mülleimer, − garbage pail
der Spaziergang, ∸e walk, stroll; einen machen to go for a walk
der Staub dust
der Tisch, −e table

das Badezimmer, − bathroom
das Flugzeugmodell, −e model airplane
das Frühstück breakfast
das Geschirr dishes
das Haus, ∸er house
das Zimmer, − room

die Arbeit, −en work; die Arbeit machen to do the work
die Garage, −n garage
die Gartenarbeit gardening, yard work
die Geschichte, −n story; history
die Katze, −n cat
die Torte, −n (fancy layer) cake
die Wäsche laundry

die Eltern (pl.) parents
die Großeltern (pl.) grandparents
die Möbel (pl.) furniture

Verben

ab·holen to call for, to pick up
ab·räumen to clear, to remove
ab·stauben to dust
ab·trocknen to dry up, to wipe dry
auf·räumen to put in order
backen (ä; gebacken) to bake
basteln to tinker (with), to work at a hobby
decken to set (the table)
ein·laden (ä; eingeladen) to invite
füttern to feed
helfen (i; geholfen) to help
nennen (genannt) to name, to call

Verben (cont.)

putzen to clean
raus·tragen (ä; rausgetragen) to carry out
schlafen (ä; geschlafen) to sleep
schmecken to taste (good)
spülen to rinse; Geschirr spülen to wash dishes
Staub saugen to vacuum
trinken (getrunken) to drink
waschen (ä; gewaschen) to wash

Andere Wörter

alle all, everyone
als than
bei with; at (home of); bei Gerdas Eltern with Gerda's parents (at their home)
fürs = für das for the
gestern yesterday
jed(-er, -es, -e) each, everyone
letzt last
sarkastisch sarcastic
wenigstens at least
wie (immer) as (always)

Besondere Ausdrücke

was heißt das? what do you mean? what does that mean?
das ist doch nicht dein Ernst! you can't be serious!
doch! yes (in answer to a question containing a negative word)
Ehrenwort! honest! on my honor!
Kaffee trinken to drink coffee (with breakfast or with afternoon pastries)
zum Kaffee einladen to invite for coffee and cake
fürs Wochenende for the weekend
das ist schwer zu glauben that's hard to believe

Kapitel 10   **Sport und Freizeit**

Segelboote auf dem Thuner See, Schweiz

Wer hat gewonnen?

Jan is on the Bergdorf soccer team. He tells Gisela the outcome of yesterday's game against Oberndorf.

GISELA   Was hast du gestern gemacht?
JAN   Wir haben Fußball gespielt.
GISELA   Gegen wen?
JAN   Gegen Oberndorf.
GISELA   Habt ihr gewonnen?
JAN   Nein, wir haben zwei zu drei verloren.
GISELA   Ach, Mensch. Das tut mir leid. Aber zwei zu drei gegen Oberndorf ist ja nicht so schlecht.
JAN   Das stimmt. Oberndorf ist gut.
GISELA   Na, vielleicht spielt ihr nächstes Mal wenigstens unentschieden.

Fragen

1. Gegen wen hat Bergdorf gespielt?
2. Wer hat gewonnen? Wie hoch° haben sie gewonnen?
3. Wie spielt Bergdorf vielleicht nächstes Mal?

Du hast das Wort

Wer hat gewonnen? Ask your partner which team won a particular game, and ask about the score.

Discussing sports

Wer hat das [Fußball]spiel gewonnen?
Wie hoch haben sie/wir gewonnen?
Wie hoch haben sie/wir verloren?

Ich lade dich ein

Ingrid is reluctant to go to a party to which she wasn't invited.

INGRID   Was hast du heute abend vor?
DIETER   Ich gehe auf eine Fete. Was machst du denn?
INGRID   Eigentlich nichts.
DIETER   Nichts? Das ist ja prima. Dann komm doch mit!
INGRID   Wohin? Auf die Party?
DIETER   Natürlich.
INGRID   Du gibst doch nicht die Party!
DIETER   Nein. Gerd. Aber ich kann dich einladen.
INGRID   Ach Quatsch! Das geht doch nicht.
DIETER   Doch. Natürlich geht das. Du kennst ihn doch gut, nicht?
INGRID   Ja . . . Also schön. Wann geht's denn los?
DIETER   Ich glaube, um acht. Ich rufe dich noch an.
INGRID   O.K. Tschüß. Bis später.

Fragen

1. Was hat Dieter heute abend vor?
2. Was hat Ingrid vor?
3. Wer gibt die Fete? Dieter?
4. Warum darf Ingrid mitkommen?
5. Wann geht die Fete eigentlich los?
6. Wen ruft Dieter an? Wann?

Du hast das Wort

1. **Was hast du vor?** A friend asks what you have planned for this evening. How would you respond?

Discussing free-time activities

Was hast du heute abend vor?	Ich gehe	auf eine Party.
		ins Kino.
		ins Jugendzentrum.
		tanzen.

Ich sehe fern.
Ich höre Musik.
Ich will [Briefe schreiben].
Ich trainiere°.
Ich muß Hausaufgaben machen.
Ich muß Wäsche waschen.

2. **Du gibst eine Fete?**   React to a classmate's announcement that she/he is giving a party.

Ich gebe am [Samstag abend] eine Fete.

Echt?
Super!
Prima!
Schön!
Toll!
Wann geht's los?
Wirklich?
Schade, ich habe schon Pläne für [Samstag].

3. **Wirklich?**   Suppose you find out that a friend of yours hasn't been invited to a party. How would you react?

Jan gibt eine Fete. Er hat aber [Dieter] nicht eingeladen.

Mensch! Das geht doch nicht.
Was!? Warum denn nicht?
Was ist denn los?
Wirklich?
Na und°?
Natürlich nicht.
Das ist ja prima.

Freizeit

Im Winter gehen Ute und Bernd Ski laufen.

Bernd kann auch gut Schlittschuh laufen.

Im Frühling zelten Paul und Norbert oft. Camping macht Spaß.

Gisela und Jan machen gern Picknicks. Dann gibt's viel zu essen.

Im Sommer gehen Gisela und Jan windsurfen. Jan fällt oft ins Wasser.

Ralf und seine Freunde gehen oft segeln. Ilse segelt nicht gern.

Im Herbst gehen Karin und Uwe oft bergsteigen.

Ilse reitet gern, Ralf aber nicht.

A. Freizeit. Answer the following questions based on the illustrations.

1. Was machen Karin und Uwe oft im Herbst?
2. Was macht Ute im Winter?
3. Wer kann gut Schlittschuh laufen?
4. Wer zeltet gern?
5. Warum machen Gisela und Jan gern Picknicks?
6. Wer geht oft windsurfen?
7. Wer kann nicht gut windsurfen?
8. Wer geht mit Ralf segeln?
9. Wer geht nicht mit Ralf segeln?
10. Was macht Ilse gern, Ralf aber nicht?

Frühlingszauber

Du hast das Wort

1. **Was machst du gern?** What do you like to do in different seasons? Ask the student next to you, and fill out your grid with her/his answers. Try to find activities in common.

	FRÜHLING	SOMMER	HERBST	WINTER
1. Ich	reiten			.
2. Barbara	reiten	schwimmen		
3. _____				

Your teacher will ask you to summarize your findings.

Im Frühling reiten Barbara und ich gern.
Im Sommer schwimmt Barbara gern.

2. **Was machen Sie gern?** Ask your teacher five questions about what she/he likes to do in various seasons. For example:

Was machen Sie gern im Winter? Treiben Sie gern Sport?

B. Aktive Leute. Your teacher will ask you to repeat a bit of information to another classmate. Note that in requests of this kind, the verb comes at the end of the sentence.

▶ Sag [Kai], daß du oft reitest.   *Ich reite oft.*

1. Sag [Ute], daß Gerd oft segeln geht.
2. Sag [Kai], daß du morgen zelten gehst.
3. Sag [Ute], daß sie mitkommen kann!
4. Sag [Kai], daß ihr oft Picknicks macht.

Suffixes -er and -er + -in

| fahren | to drive | fahr + er | = | der Fahrer | driver (*m.*) |
| | | fahr + er + in | = | die Fahrerin | driver (*f.*) |

The suffix **-er** is often added to a verb stem to form a noun that indicates the male doer of an activity. The additional suffix **-in** indicates the female doer of an activity.

| segeln | | segl + er | = | der Segler |
| | | segl + er + in | = | die Seglerin |

To form a noun from a verb ending in **-eln,** the **-e** before the **-l** is dropped.

| Skilaufen | | der Skiläufer |
| | | die Skiläuferin |

Some nouns formed from verbs have an umlaut.

Land und Leute

Most young people in German-speaking countries are interested in a sport of some kind. Physical education is required in all schools, but compared to the United States sports play a smaller role in school life.

Those wishing to play competitively can join a sports club **(Sportverein)**. The Federal Republic has 60,000 such clubs, to which a quarter of the population belongs. Most clubs offer memberships students can afford. Soccer is a national obsession, and traditionally Saturday afternoon is spent playing or watching a soccer game. Recently women's soccer teams have become more common. Other popular sports include gymnastics **(Turnen)**, tennis, track-and-field **(Leichtathletik)**, swimming, table tennis, skiing, wind-surfing, and **Handball. Handball** resembles soccer, but the ball is thrown instead of kicked.

Boris Becker, deutscher Tennissuperstar

Skiläufer/innen in den Schweizer Alpen bei St. Moritz

C. Er und sie. Name the male and female doers of the activities related to the following verbs and verb phrases.

▶ Tennis spielen   *der Tennisspieler, die Tennisspielerin*

1. schwimmen
2. arbeiten
3. Briefmarken sammeln
4. basteln
5. bergsteigen
6. reiten
7. backen (ä)
8. tanzen (ä)
9. verkaufen (ä)

Rainer ist Verkäufer.	Rainer is *a* salesman.
Sabine ist Verkäuferin.	Sabine is *a* saleswoman.

German does not use **ein** or **eine** with a noun used to identify a member of a profession or someone temporarily engaged in an activity.

D. Was sind sie? Complete each sentence with a noun derived from the verb.

1. Lutz und Anja arbeiten bei VW.
   Er ist _____. Sie ist _____.
2. Frau Krupp und Herr Anders backen viel.
   Sie ist _____, und er ist _____.
3. Herr und Frau Braun sammeln Briefmarken.
   Er ist schon vier Jahre Briefmarken_____; sie ist erst zwei Jahre Briefmarken_____.
4. Volker und Katrin tanzen sehr gut.
   Er ist Ballett_____; sie ist _____ in Musicals.

Aussprache

[R]   **R**ock, P**r**eis, wa**r**um

The German **r** can be pronounced in two different ways. Some German speakers use a tongue-trilled [r] in which the tip of the tongue vibrates against the gum ridge behind the upper front teeth, like the **rrr** that small children often make in imitation of a car or truck starting up. Most German speakers, however, use a uvular [R] in which the back of the tongue is raised toward the uvula (the little flap of skin hanging down in the back of the mouth). It may help you to pronounce the uvular [R] if you make a gargling sound before the sound [a]: **ra.** Keep the tip of your tongue down and out of the way. It plays no role in the pronunciation of the uvular German [R].

Wer anderen eine Grube gräbt, fällt selbst hinein.

A. Practice vertically in columns and then horizontally.

[R]	[R]	[R]
fragt	warum	ragt
Krokodil	barock	Rock
trugen	führen	rufen
Preis	Nieren	Reis
bring	darin	Ring
grünen	schüren	rühmen

B. Practice the sound [R]. Read the sentences aloud.

1. Frau Braun trägt heute einen neuen Rock.
2. Können Sie mein Radio reparieren, Herr Grün?
3. Frag mal Rita, warum sie nicht schreibt!
4. Wer hat Frau Krüger das gefragt?

Übungen

1. The verbs **kennen** and **wissen**

Ich **kenne** Frau Hofer.   Ich **weiß,** wer Frau Hofer ist.
Ich **kenne** Rainers Haus.   Ich **weiß,** wo Rainer wohnt.

Kennen means to know (to be acquainted with) a person, place, or thing. **Wissen** means to know something as a fact.

A. Wer ist Jörg Schneider?   Answer Torsten's questions in the negative.

▶ Weißt du, wo Jörg Schneider wohnt?   *Nein, das weiß ich nicht.*

▶ Kennst du seine Schwester?   *Nein, seine Schwester kenne ich nicht.*

1. Weißt du, wie alt Jörg ist?
2. Weißt du, wie Jörgs Schwester heißt?
3. Kennst du Jörgs Eltern?
4. Weißt du, wo Jörgs Schule ist?
5. Kennst du Jörgs Deutschlehrer?
6. Weißt du, wo Jörgs Freundin wohnt?
7. Kennst du Jörgs Freundin?
8. Kennst du denn Jörg Schneider?

Du hast das Wort

Asking what someone knows

Was weißt du? Ask a classmate whether she/he is acquainted with certain people, places, or things or knows certain facts. When you have finished with these questions, you and your classmate will prepare five more questions of your own. Share them with your teacher.

Kennst du [Ingrid/Thomas]?
Weißt du, wo [sie/er] wohnt?
Weißt du, wie alt [sie/er] ist?
Kennst du [meine Schwester/meinen Bruder]?
Kennst du [meine Freundin Erika/meinen Freund Thomas]?
Kennst du [Berlin]?
Kennst du die Musik von [Beethoven]?

2. Verbs with stem-vowel change au > äu

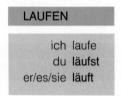

LAUFEN

ich laufe
du läufst
er/es/sie läuft

Laufen has a stem-vowel change **au > äu** in the **du-** and **er/es/sie**-forms of the present tense.

B. Sie sind gute Skiläufer. Margit is trying to recruit members for a ski club. Tell her that the following people ski well.

▶ Peter   *Peter läuft gut Ski.*

1. Uschi
2. Gerd und Paul
3. du

4. deine Freunde
5. Silke
6. ihr

C. Joschi lädt ein. Joschi is inviting friends for the weekend. Complete the sentences using the cued verbs.

1. Joschi Pfeifer _____ seine Freunde aus° München und Salzburg _____. °from
   (einladen)
2. Sie _____ am Samstag nach Garmisch. (fahren)
3. Herr Pfeifer _____ die Wäsche und _____ eine Torte für die Freunde.
   (waschen / backen)
4. Joschi _____ die Musikinstrumente in sein Zimmer, und sie spielen viel
   Musik. (tragen)

5. Sie _____ alle in Joschis Zimmer, nur Herr Pfeifer _____ nicht da. (schlafen / schlafen)
6. Am Sonntag _____ Peter wieder nach München, und Erik _____ nach Salzburg.   (fahren / fahren)

3. Accusative case of **wer**

NOMINATIVE	ACCUSATIVE
Wer kommt heute abend?	**Wen** laden wir ein?

The accusative of **wer** is **wen.**

D.   Wie bitte?   Helga is chatting about various people, but you don't hear her clearly. Ask who she is referring to.

▶   Ich habe Erik im Jugendzentrum gesehen.   *Wen hast du gesehen?*

1. Ich habe Christl im Kino gesehen.
2. Ich habe Dieter für heute abend eingeladen.
3. Ich habe Ingrid angerufen.
4. Ich habe die *Hot Dogs* gehört.

E.   Wer oder wen?   Complete the questions with the appropriate interrogative. Use **wer** or **wen.**

1. _____ hat angerufen?
2. _____ hast du im Kino gesehen?
3. _____ geht heute abend mit?
4. _____ kommt am Samstag?
5. _____ sollen wir einladen?
6. _____ willst du anrufen?

Wen hat Peter zum Rodeln (sledding) *eingeladen?*

4. Accusative case of personal pronouns

mich/dich

NOMINATIVE	ACCUSATIVE
Ich verstehe Christl. Du verstehst Christl.	Christl versteht **mich.** (Christl understands *me.*) Christl versteht **dich.** (Christl understands *you.*)

F. Wirklich? Express surprise at your classmate's statements.

▶ Ich kenne dich gut. *Wirklich? Du kennst mich gut?*

1. Ich verstehe dich.
2. Ich meine dich.
3. Ich höre dich.
4. Ich frage dich.

G. Doch! Karl is feeling rejected today. Reassure him that what he says isn't true.

▶ Du lädst mich nicht ein. *Doch, ich lade dich ein.*

1. Du rufst mich nicht an.
2. Du hast mich nicht gern.
3. Du kennst mich nicht gut.
4. Du fährst mich nicht nach Hause.

uns/euch

NOMINATIVE	ACCUSATIVE
Wir verstehen Frank. Ihr versteht Frank.	Frank versteht **uns.** (Frank understands *us.*) Frank versteht **euch.** (Frank understands *you.*)

H. Ja, natürlich! Answer the following questions in the affirmative.

▶ Kennt ihr uns? *Ja, natürlich kennen wir euch.*

1. Hört ihr uns?
2. Meint ihr uns?
3. Fragt ihr uns?
4. Versteht ihr uns?
5. Braucht ihr uns?

I. Doch! Petra and Erik are feeling gloomy today. Try to cheer them up.

▶ Ihr nehmt uns nicht mit   *Doch, wir nehmen euch mit.*
ins Konzert.

1. Ihr ladet uns nicht ein.   3. Ihr ruft uns nicht an.
2. Ihr habt uns nicht gern.   4. Ihr braucht uns nicht.

ihn/es/sie

NOUN	PRONOUN
Kennst du **meinen Bruder**?	Ja, ich kenne **ihn**. (Yes, I know *him*.)
Kaufst du **den Fernseher**?	Ja, ich kaufe **ihn**. (Yes, I'm buying *it*.)
Kennst du **das Kind**?	Ja, ich kenne **es**. (Yes, I know *her/him*.)
Kaufst du **das Radio**?	Ja, ich kaufe **es**. (Yes, I'm buying *it*.)
Kennst du **meine Schwester**?	Ja, ich kenne **sie**. (Yes, I know *her*.)
Kaufst du **die Uhr**?	Ja, ich kaufe **sie**. (Yes, I'm buying *it*.)
Kennst du **meine Freunde**?	Ja, ich kenne **sie**. (Yes, I know *them*.)
Kaufst du **die Platten**?	Ja, ich kaufe **sie**. (Yes, I'm buying *them*.)

J. Gisela ruft an. Gisela is in charge of invitations to Gerd's party. Say that she intends to call the following guests later.

▶ Wann ruft Gisela meinen   *Später. Sie ruft ihn später an.*
Bruder an?

1. Wann ruft sie Erik an?
2. Wann ruft sie meine Schwester an?
3. Wann ruft sie ihren Freund Peter an?
4. Wann ruft sie meine Freunde an?
5. Wann ruft sie Petra und Jens an?

K. Willst du es oder nicht? After an hour in the music store, Jan impatiently urges you to make up your mind. Decide that you don't want the things after all.

▶ Willst du nun den Kassetten-   *Nein, ich will ihn nicht.*
recorder oder nicht?

1. Willst du nun den Plattenspieler oder nicht?
2. Willst du die Stereoanlage oder nicht?
3. Willst du den CD-Spieler oder nicht?
4. Willst du das Radio oder nicht?
5. Willst du die Platte oder nicht?
6. Willst du die Kassetten oder nicht?

Public telephones in the Federal Republic are usually installed in bright yellow booths. A flashing number indicates how much money to

insert, and the caller is warned when time and money are running out. The telephone system is run by the **Deutsche Bundespost** (German Federal Postal System). Every post office maintains public telephones, which are either coin-operated or billed through a clerk.

The standard way to answer the phone is by identifying oneself at once. The caller then gives her/his name before asking for the person she/he is trying to reach. In recent years there has been a trend toward answering the phone with **Ja, bitte** or **Hallo,** and then waiting for the caller to identify her/himself. Whereas people ending a telephone conversation formally say **Auf Wiederhören** (literally: until we hear each other again), friends would use an informal **Tschüß** or **Bis dann** to say good-by. For example:

— Ja, bitte?
— Kann ich bitte mit Thomas sprechen? Hier ist Gerda.
— Hallo, Gerda. Ich bin's (*it's me*), Ingrid. Thomas ist nicht zu Hause. Er spielt heute Fußball.
— Ach ja, richtig. Ich rufe später wieder an. Bis dann, Ingrid.
— Tschüß.

Sie

NOMINATIVE	ACCUSATIVE
Verstehen Sie **mich?**	Ja, ich verstehe **Sie.** (Yes, I understand *you*.)

L. Ja, ich habe . . . Answer your teacher's questions in the affirmative.

▶ Hast du mich gehört? *Ja, ich habe Sie gehört.*

1. Hast du mich gemeint?
2. Hast du mich gefragt?

3. Hast du mich angerufen?
4. Hast du mich zum Kaffee eingeladen?

M. Wer weiß es? Angela is having difficulty with a math problem. Suggest that she ask various friends and classmates for the answer.

▶ Frank weiß es.   *Warum fragt sie ihn denn nicht?*

1. Wir wissen es.
2. Ingrid weiß es.
3. Du weißt es.
4. Heike weiß es.
5. Ihr wißt es.
6. Mein Bruder weiß es.
7. Meine Freunde wissen es.

N. Wen lädst du ein? Who is going to be at Lisa's tonight? Complete the sentences with the correct personal pronoun. Use the cues.

▶ Hast du *ihn* gefragt?   (*him*)

1. Der Günther ist doof, ich lade _____ nicht ein.   (*him*)
2. Aber seine Schwester ist sehr nett. Ich will _____ einladen.   (*her*)
3. Lädst du _____ auch ein?   (*us*)
4. Klar, ich lade _____ ein.   (*you, pl.*)
5. Kannst du _____ bitte anrufen?   (*me*)
6. Ja, wann soll ich _____ anrufen?   (*you, sg.*)
7. Was ist mit Gabi und Fred? — Ach, ich kann _____ ja mal anrufen.   (*them*)

5. Conversational past of inseparable-prefix verbs

INFINITIVE	PAST PARTICIPLE	CONVERSATIONAL PAST
beginnen	begonnen	Wann **hat** das Spiel **begonnen?**
bekommen	bekommen	**Hast** du noch Karten **bekommen?**
gewinnen	gewonnen	Oberndorf **hat** das Spiel **gewonnen.**
verlieren	verloren	Wir **haben** das Spiel **verloren.**
verstehen	verstanden	**Habt** ihr das **verstanden?**
versuchen	versucht	Wir **haben** alles **versucht.**

Some prefixes (including **be-, ge-, ver-**) are never separated from the verb stem.

Inseparable-prefix verbs do not add **ge-** in the past participle. Both weak and strong verbs may have inseparable prefixes.

O. Das Fußballspiel. Werner has a few questions about yesterday's soccer game. Answer in the affirmative.

▶ Hast du wirklich eine Karte bekommen?

    Ja, ich habe wirklich eine Karte bekommen.

1. Hat Marta auch eine Karte bekommen?
2. Hat das Spiel erst um vier begonnen?
3. Hat München wirklich gewonnen?
4. Und Hamburg hat verloren?
5. Hast du das Spiel verstanden?

luck

P. Kein Glück°. Astrid and Klaus had some problems getting to the soccer game on time yesterday. Tell what happened by restating in the conversational past.

▶ Astrid bekommt kein Geld von zu Hause.

    Astrid hat kein Geld von zu Hause bekommen.

1. Astrid versucht alles.
2. Klaus bekommt Geld von zu Hause.
3. Aber sie bekommen keine guten Karten.
4. Sie versuchen alles.
5. Das Spiel beginnt schon um sieben.

Land und Leute

German soccer cheers:

Zicke-Zacke, Zicke-Zacke
Hoi, Hoi, Hoi!

Tempo, Tempo, Tempo!

Ha, Ho, He
Hertha BSC! (BSC: Berliner Sport-Club)

Die Nationalmann-schaft der Bundes-republik im Welt-meisterschaftsspiel gegen Argentinien 1986

Du hast das Wort

Wie war das Spiel? Discuss a recent school game with your classmates.

Discussing a sports event

Hast du Karten bekommen?
Wann hat das Spiel begonnen?
Wer hat gewonnen? Wer hat verloren?
Wie hoch haben sie gewonnen/verloren?

Grammatische Übersicht

The verbs **kennen** and **wissen** (A)

Ich **kenne** Frau Braun gut.   I *know* Mrs. Braun well.
Ich **weiß,** wer Herr Braun ist. I *know* who Mr. Braun is.

The English equivalent of both **kennen** and **wissen** is *to know.* **Kennen** means to be acquainted with a person, place, or thing. **Wissen** means to know something as a fact.

Verbs with stem-vowel change **au > äu** (B–C)

LAUFEN		
ich laufe		wir laufen
du **läufst**	Sie laufen	ihr lauft
er/es/sie **läuft**		sie laufen

Laufen has a stem-vowel change **au > äu** in the **du-** and **er/es/sie-**forms of the present tense.

Accusative case of **wer** (D–E)

Nominative	**Wer** hat Detlev gefragt?	*Who* asked Detlev?
Accusative	**Wen** hat Detlev gefragt?	*Whom* did Detlev ask?

The accusative of **wer** is **wen.**

Accusative case of personal pronouns (F–N)

Ralf kennt **mich** gut.	Ralf knows *me* well.
Er kennt **dich** auch, nicht?	He also knows *you,* doesn't he?

Pronouns used as direct objects are in the accusative case. Nominative and accusative forms of personal pronouns correspond as follows:

Nominative	ich	du	er	es	sie	wir	ihr	sie	Sie
Accusative	mich	dich	ihn	es	sie	uns	euch	sie	Sie

Note that **es, sie,** and **Sie** are the same in the nominative and accusative.

ACCUSATIVE NOUN	ACCUSATIVE PRONOUN
Kennst du **den Mann?**	Ja, ich kenne **ihn.**
Kaufst du **den Plattenspieler?**	Ja, ich kaufe **ihn.**
Kennst du **das Kind?**	Ja, ich kenne **es.**
Kaufst du **das Radio?**	Ja, ich kaufe **es.**
Kennst du **die Frau?**	Ja, ich kenne **sie.**
Kaufst du **die Platte?**	Ja, ich kaufe **sie.**
Kennst du **die Kinder?**	Ja, ich kenne **sie.**
Kaufst du **die Platten?**	Ja, ich kaufe **sie.**

The accusative pronouns **ihn, es,** and **sie** can refer to either persons or things.

Conversational past of inseparable-prefix verbs (O–P)

INFINITIVE	PRESENT TENSE	CONVERSATIONAL PAST
beginnen	Wann **beginnt** das Spiel?	Wann **hat** das Spiel **begonnen?**
verlieren	Wir **verlieren** oft.	Wir **haben** oft **verloren.**
versuchen	Ute **versucht** alles.	Ute **hat** alles **versucht.**

The prefixes **be-, emp-, ent-, er-, ge-, ver-,** and **zer-** are never separated from the verb stem. These inseparable prefixes may occur with both weak and strong verbs. Inseparable-prefix verbs do not add the prefix **ge-** in the past participle.

In spoken German, inseparable prefixes are unstressed: **begin'nen, versu'chen.**

A. Dieters Tagebuch. (Dieter's diary.) Read the excerpts from Dieter's diary and answer the questions that follow.

MONTAG

Ein prima Tag! In Englisch habe ich eine Zwei bekommen und in Deutsch eine Eins. In Mathe habe ich leider eine Vier. Aber Mathe ist schwer. Und für mich ist eine Vier eigentlich nicht schlecht.

DIENSTAG

Die *Hot Dogs* geben am Samstag abend ein Konzert. Ich habe aber keine Karten mehr bekommen. Ausverkauft! Ich bin wirklich sauer.

DONNERSTAG

Ich habe Jörg im Jugendzentrum gesehen. Er hat zwei Karten für die *Hot Dogs*. Erika kann nicht mitkommen, und er braucht jetzt nur noch eine Karte. Ich habe Erikas Karte gekauft. Ute gibt am Freitag eine Fete. Sie hat mich eingeladen.

SAMSTAG

Eine tolle Fete. Ich habe viel mit Ute getanzt. Sie tanzt wirklich gut. Und heute abend gehen wir ins Konzert. Ute hat auch eine Karte. Jörg und ich holen sie um sieben ab.

1. Was hat Dieter in Mathe bekommen?
2. Warum kann Dieter am Dienstag keine Karten bekommen?
3. Wen hat er im Jugendzentrum gesehen?
4. Warum braucht Jörg nur eine Karte?
5. Wer hat Dieter eingeladen?
6. Wer geht mit Dieter ins Konzert?
7. Wann holen Jörg und Dieter Ute ab?

B. Eine Party bei Jörg. You and Sabine are chatting about Jörg and his forthcoming party. Answer Sabine's questions in the affirmative.

▶ Kennst du Jörgs Freundin Uschi? *Natürlich kenne ich sie.*

1. Hast du Jörg gesehen?
2. Hat er dich eingeladen?
3. Darf meine Schwester auch mitkommen?
4. Kannst du uns abholen?
5. Rufst du mich am Nachmittag an?
6. Brauchst du meine Kassetten?

C. Wie sagt man das? Express the following conversational exchanges in German.

1. Christl bought a dress.
   What did it cost?
2. Last night Peter called Meike.
   What did she say?
3. You didn't see Erika this morning?
   No, I had no time.
4. Did you invite Jörg?
   Yes, but he can't come.
5. What did you do yesterday afternoon?
   We watched television.
6. We played against Oberndorf yesterday.
   Who won?

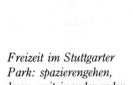

D. Was machst du gern? Prepare five or six sentences about activities you like to do. You may wish to include answers to the following questions.

Treibst du gern Sport? Hast du ein Hobby? Sammelst du etwas? Läufst du gern Ski? Liest du gern? Schläfst du viel?

*Freizeit im Stuttgarter
Park: spazierengehen,
lesen, miteinander reden*

E. Wie sollen wir es machen? You are thinking about having a party this weekend. Which night will it be? You can only invite half of your German class. Ask your neighbor about her/his party plans. She/he will then ask you about yours. Negotiate and develop *one* plan together.

F. Freizeit. Describe the activities in the illustration. What are the people doing? What time of year is it?

G. Telefongespräch. You are having a party and have to phone your friends. Arrange your chairs back to back and phone your friends! Remember your parents don't want you out every night! When you're finished, tell your teacher about your social schedule.

Phoning your friends

H. Land und Leute.

1. What sports are popular in the German-speaking countries? Which sports are popular in the United States and in Germany? Which are not?
2. Where do you and your friends go to relax and have fun? Where do German teenagers go?
3. What are some differences between the telephone system in the Federal Republic and the U.S.? Compare the manner of answering the telephone in the two countries.

König Fußball

Im deutschen Sport ist der Fußball König°. Man° kann sagen, daß Fußball *der* Nationalsport ist. Und das ist er nicht nur in Deutschland. Man kann sicher sagen, daß Fußball der beliebteste° Sport der Welt° ist.

     Überall° in Deutschland kann man sehen, daß Fußball sehr beliebt ist. Was
5 spielen die Kinder auf der Straße? Fußball. Was spielen sie im Park? Fußball. Wohin gehen viele Männer, Frauen und Kinder am Samstag- oder Sonntagnachmittag? Zum Fußballplatz° oder ins Fußballstadion°. Oder sie sehen Fußball im Fernsehen. Auch kleine Dörfer° haben einen Fußballplatz, und die großen Städte haben große Stadien°.
10   In den Schulen und Universitäten gibt es auch Fußballmannschaften°, aber da spielen sie fast keine Rolle°. Die großen Fußballmannschaften und Fußballspieler kommen aus den Sportvereinen°. Und jedes Kind kennt die Namen der großen Fußballspieler. Die besten° Spieler spielen in der Nationalmannschaft. Weltmeisterschaften° gibt es alle° vier Jahre.

king / one

favorite / **der Welt:** in the world

everywhere

soccer field / soccer stadium

villages

stadiums

soccer teams

spielen . . . Rolle: are not important

sports clubs

best

world championships / every

Welches Wort? Choose the word or phrase that best completes each statement, based on the reading.

1. Der beliebteste Sport der Welt ist . . .
     a. Basketball   b. Fußball   c. Segeln   d. Ski laufen
2. Im Park spielen deutsche Kinder . . .
     a. Golf   b. Baseball   c. Basketball   d. Fußball

Der Ball rollt, das Spiel hat begonnen — Argentinien : Bundesrepublik

3. Viele Deutsche sehen am . . . ein Fußballspiel.
   a. Sonntagnachmittag   b. Sonntagabend   c. Samstagmorgen
   d. Samstagabend
4. Auch kleine Dörfer haben . . .
   a. große Stadien   b. eine Universitätsfußballmannschaft
   c. einen Fußballplatz   d. viele Sportvereine
5. Die großen Fußballmannschaften kommen aus den . . .
   a. Schulen   b. Sportvereinen   c. Universitäten   d. Dörfern
6. Die besten Spieler können alle . . . Jahre in den Weltmeisterschaften spielen.
   a. zwei   b. drei   c. vier   d. fünf

Vokabeln

Substantive

der Frühling spring
der Herbst autumn, fall
der Schlittschuh, —e ice skate
der Ski, —er (*also* **Schi**) ski
der Sommer summer
der Winter winter

das Camping camping
das Fußballspiel, —e soccer game
das Mal time, occasion; **nächstes Mal** next time
das Picknick, —s picnic
das Spiel, —e game
das Wasser water

die Fete, —n party
die Freizeit leisure time
die Party, —s party

Verben

an·rufen (angerufen) to call, to telephone
bergsteigen gehen to go mountain-climbing
essen (i; gegessen) to eat
fallen (ä) to fall
gewinnen (gewonnen) to win
kennen (gekannt) to know, to be acquainted with
laufen (äu) to run, to walk
los·gehen to go, to take off

Verben (cont.)

reiten to ride (horseback)
Schlittschuh laufen (äu) to ice-skate
segeln to sail
Ski laufen (äu) to ski
trainieren to practice a sport, to train
verlieren (verloren) to lose
windsurfen to go wind-surfing
zelten to camp

Andere Wörter

gegen (*+acc.*) against
hoch high
nächst next
ok okay
unentschieden undetermined; tied (*in scoring*)
wen (*acc. of* **wer**) whom

Besondere Ausdrücke

wir haben zwei zu drei verloren we lost 2–3
wie hoch hat Oberndorf gewonnen? by how much did Oberndorf win?
auf eine Fete/Party gehen to go to a party
wann geht's los? when does it start?
das geht nicht that doesn't work; that won't do
Quatsch! nonsense! rubbish!
super! great!
na und? so what?

NOCH EINMAL

A

Eine deutsche Zeitung. Publish a newspaper (**die Zeitung**) in German with features, interviews, and ads. The following list may give you some ideas on what kinds of articles to include:

- Calendar of school events for a month
- Interview of student or teacher about a hobby

- Interview of a foreign student, giving her/his impressions of American schools
- Sports report
- Poll of students listing chores they do at home, favorite school subjects, favorite music or band
- Ad from bookstore for books and school supplies, listing prices in **Mark, Schilling,** or **Franken**

B

Junge Deutsche. The class is divided into several groups. Using pictures from German magazines, each group prepares a display. Topics can be clothing, sports, entertainment, and teenagers at parties, school, or home. Each group may include illustrations on all of these subjects, or single topics can be assigned: one group takes clothing, another sports, and so on.

C

Ein/e Brieffreund/in. At the end of Stage 1, one of the suggested activities was to write a short autobiography to be submitted to a panel. Use some of that information — age, appearance, family — to begin a letter to a German-speaking friend. Continue to tell about your school subjects, hobbies, interests, and activities. Describe a typical school day; tell what you and your friends like to do after school or on weekends.

If you would like to have a real German pen pal, ask your teacher for the names of some organizations that can arrange such contacts. It might be possible for your class as a whole to correspond with an English class in a school in Austria, Germany, or Switzerland.

Hier und dort. Look at the pictures in this Stage and select the features in them that seem to you more characteristic of German-speaking countries than of life in America. Discuss the differences.

Tagebuch. In German, keep a diary (**das Tagebuch**) — one which you can read aloud or discuss in class, if requested. Include topics such as (1) school — classes you most enjoyed or disliked, amount of homework, any tests or special programs; (2) home — chores, family activities; (3) free time — shopping trips, hobbies you worked on or records you enjoyed listening to, friends you saw, and movies, concerts, or sports events you attended.

Für Schnorchler

Für Kunstfans

Für Strandläufer

Schicke Sachen. With several classmates, prepare a skit in which you go shopping for clothes. You will need a salesperson, and you may want to have a friend accompany you. Dialogues may include a discussion of sizes, colors, prices, and style; possible settings may concern a somewhat pushy salesperson, an indecisive customer, or an urgent phone call home to request additional spending money.

Stufe 3

Zum Städtele hinaus

Kapitel 11 — Bäcker, Metzger, Supermarkt

Samstags kauft man auf dem Mainzer Markt ein.

Einkaufen in Deutschland

Barbara Braun besucht ihren Brieffreund in Nürnberg. Sie schreibt einen Brief an ihre Deutschklasse.

Nürnberg, den 3. März

Liebe Klasse!

Ich habe hier schon viel gesehen und gelernt. Meine Gastfamilie°, Herr und Frau Kraft, Ingrid und Michael, ist sehr nett. Letzte Woche bin ich dreimal° mit Frau Kraft einkaufen gegangen. Die Supermärkte sind hier fast so wie zu Hause. Nur darf man das Obst und Gemüse hier nicht anfassen°. Das habe ich natürlich falsch gemacht. Ich habe die Tomaten angefaßt. Da hat die Verkäuferin gesagt: „Einen Moment, bitte! *Ich* gebe Ihnen° die Tomaten. Die Tomaten kann doch schließlich° nicht jeder anfassen." — „Entschuldigung! Das habe ich nicht gewußt."

Wir haben alle Sachen in einen Einkaufswagen° gepackt und bezahlt, wie in Amerika. Aber dann hat Frau Kraft alle Lebensmittel selbst eingepackt. Fast alle Kunden haben nämlich große Einkaufstaschen. Große Papiertüten gibt es nicht. Und für Plastiktüten° muß man bezahlen.

Das Fleisch, das Brot und den Kuchen fürs Wochenende hat Frau Kraft aber nicht im Supermarkt gekauft. Fleisch, Wurst und Schinken haben wir beim Metzger gekauft und den Kuchen und das Brot beim Bäcker. Frau Kraft hat da „ihren" Metzger und „ihren" Bäcker. Beim Bäcker und beim Metzger sagen alle Kunden immer schön „Grüß Gott" und „Auf Wiederschauen". Und die Verkäufer antworten jedes Mal. Wie oft sagen sie wohl jeden Tag „Auf Wiederschauen"?

Am Samstag sind wir dann noch zum Markt gegangen und haben dort eingekauft. Wir waren schon früh dort, denn dann ist noch alles frisch. Und es ist noch viel da. Aber auch hier darf man Obst und Gemüse nicht anfassen.

Das ist alles für heute. Bald mehr!

Herzliche Grüße

Barbara

host family
three times
handle, touch
to you
after all
shopping cart
plastic bags

Fragen

1. Wie oft ist Barbara letzte Woche einkaufen gegangen?
2. Ist sie allein° gegangen?
3. Was hat Barbara falsch gemacht?
4. Wer hat die Lebensmittel eingepackt?
5. Warum hat Frau Kraft keine Plastiktüte genommen?
6. Was hat Frau Kraft beim Metzger gekauft? Und beim Bäcker?
7. Was sagen die Verkäufer jeden Tag sehr oft?
8. Warum ist Frau Kraft am Samstag schon früh zum Markt gegangen?

Du hast das Wort

1. **Entschuldigung.** With a partner prepare a mini-skit in which you say or do something for which you must excuse yourself.

Excusing oneself

GESPRÄCHSPARTNER/IN	DU
Du hast [meine Platte] kaputtgemacht.	Entschuldigung.
	Habe ich das gemacht? Ach, Entschuldigung.
Du, das ist [mein Buch].	Entschuldigung. Das habe ich nicht gewußt.
	Das tut mir leid.

2. **Ein Brief nach Amerika.** Summarize the letter from Barbara. Use the questions above as guidelines.

Summarizing

3. **Einkaufen.** In German, list four differences in shopping at a small German store and shopping in a supermarket in the United States or Canada. Share them with the rest of the class.

Discussing cultural differences

Land und Leute

In the German-speaking countries much of the food shopping is done in supermarkets. These tend to be smaller than supermarkets in the United States, but most are within walking distance of home. Although they are self-service stores, fresh foods (cheese, sausage, bread, and vegetables) are sold by clerks at separate counters.

The convenience of supermarkets is causing the number of small neighborhood stores to decrease. However, small specialty stores **(Fachgeschäfte)** such as bakeries and butcher shops are still very popular, for their merchandise is always fresh and is sometimes prepared according to special recipes. Some customers also prefer the more personal atmosphere there.

Viele Leute kaufen Brot bei „ihrem" Bäcker.

Sag!

1. Sag [Kai], daß du einkaufen gehst!
2. Sag [Ute], daß du Tomaten brauchst!
3. Sag [Kai], daß du Wurst beim Metzger kaufst!
4. Sag [Ute], daß du Kuchen beim Bäcker kaufst!
5. Sag [Kai], daß du alles in die Einkaufstasche packst!
6. Sag [Ute], daß du keine Plastiktüte kaufen willst!

Beim Metzger

Frau Kraft kauft bei ihrem Metzger ein.

HERR LANGE	Grüß Gott, Frau Kraft! Was darf es sein?
FRAU KRAFT	Wieviel kosten die Schweinskoteletts?
HERR LANGE	7 Mark 50 das Pfund.
FRAU KRAFT	Ich brauche fünf Stück.
HERR LANGE	Gern. Sonst noch was?
FRAU KRAFT	Ich hätte gern zehn Wiener Würstchen.
HERR LANGE	So. Haben Sie noch einen Wunsch?
FRAU KRAFT	Nein. Das ist alles für heute.
HERR LANGE	Danke . . . So, bitte schön. Das macht zusammen 24 Mark 50 . . . So, Sie bekommen 50 Pfennig zurück.
FRAU KRAFT	Danke schön.
HERR LANGE	Bitte. Auf Wiedersehen, Frau Kraft.
FRAU KRAFT	Auf Wiedersehen, Herr Lange.

Fragen

1. Wieviel kosten die Schweinskoteletts?
2. Wieviel Koteletts braucht Frau Kraft?
3. Was kauft Frau Kraft noch?
4. Wieviel kostet alles zusammen?
5. Wieviel bekommt Frau Kraft zurück?

Wurst and **Würstchen** are very popular in German-speaking countries. Almost every town, and certainly every region, has one or more sausage specialties of its own. **Würstchen** are among the foods most commonly sold at snackbars, where they are served on an unbuttered roll or with a piece of bread, often with a dab of mustard **(Senf).**

The snackbars are called by many different names, such as **Imbißstube, Kaltes Buffet,** and **Bier Würstl,** and they can be found almost everywhere — in the marketplace, in a railroad station, or in a shopping area. Besides many varieties of **Würstchen,** popular snacks include ham, cheese, or fish sandwiches, French fries, hamburgers, and pizza.

Schnellimbiß bei Neuschwanstein: Würstchen, usw.

Was gibt's heute auf dem Markt?

1. der Apfel, ¨
2. die Banane, –n
3. die Orange, –n
4. die Erdbeere, –n

5. die Kartoffel, –n
6. der Spinat
7. die Erbse, –n
8. die Karotte, –n

9. der Saft, ¨e
10. die Milch
11. das Ei, –er
12. die Butter
13. der Käse

A. Wie findest du das? You are with your friend at an open-air market. The vendor doesn't have his prices out yet. Ask how much something is and then ask your friend for her/his opinion of the price.

Asking for and receiving opinions

DU

Was kosten die Kartoffeln?

VERKÄUFER/IN

Drei Mark und neun Pfennig das Kilo.

DU

Wie findest du das — teuer oder billig?

DEIN/E FREUND/IN

Das ist teuer.

B. Ich gehe in den Supermarkt und kaufe . . . How good is your memory? Start with a simple statement about food and pass it on. Your neighbor repeats it and adds one more item. The next person repeats the entire statement and adds another item.

Schüler 1: Ich gehe in den Supermarkt und kaufe Brot.
Schüler 2: Ich gehe in den Supermarkt und kaufe Brot und Kaffee.
Schüler 3: Ich gehe in den Supermarkt und kaufe Brot, Kaffee und . . .

Units of measurement and quantity

Ich möchte vier **Kilo** Kartoffeln.
I'd like four *kilos* of potatoes.

Ich nehme fünf **Pfund** Orangen.
I'll take five *pounds* of oranges.

Er kauft zwei **Liter** Milch.
He's buying two *liters* of milk.

Sie trinkt jeden Tag vier **Glas** Wasser.
She drinks four *glasses* of water every day.

Er kauft zwei **Flaschen** Saft.
He's buying two *bottles* of juice.

In German, **der**-nouns and **das**-nouns expressing measure, weight, or number are in the singular. **Die**-nouns, for example **Flasche,** are in the plural.

Land und Leute

In German-speaking countries, the metric system is used to measure volume and weight. The basic measure of volume is the **Liter (l)**, and the basic measures of weight are the **Gramm (g)** and the **Kilogramm (kg).** German speakers also use the older term **Pfund (Pfd.)** for half a **Kilogramm,** or 500 **Gramm.** A **Pfund** is equivalent to 1.1 American pounds. One **Liter** equals 1.056 U.S. quarts.

Ein Liter Milch und zweihundert Gramm Käse

In diesem Lebensmittelgeschäft ist alles frisch.

C. Wieviel möchtest du? Have a classmate take the part of a clerk. Tell her/him how much you want to buy.

▶ Wieviel Kilo Orangen   *Ja, ich nehme drei Kilo*
   möchten Sie? Drei?   *Orangen.*

1. Wieviel Gramm Butter möchten Sie? Hundert?
2. Wieviel Pfund Äpfel möchten Sie? Fünf?
3. Wieviel Kilo Kartoffeln möchten Sie? Zehn?
4. Wieviel Stück Kuchen möchten Sie? Zwei?
5. Wieviel Stück Torte möchten Sie? Vier?
6. Wieviel Flaschen Saft möchten Sie? Drei?
7. Wieviel Gramm Käse möchten Sie? Fünfhundert?

Du hast das Wort

Wieviel? Think about the quantities of different kinds of foods you consume. Using the following questions ask your classmate her/his eating and drinking habits.

Discussing eating habits

DU

Wieviel Glas Milch trinkst du
  jeden Tag?
Wieviel Liter Milch kauft deine
  Familie jede Woche? Wieviel
  Liter Saft?
Wieviel Stück Brot ißt du jede Woche?
Wieviel Eier ißt du jede Woche?
Wieviel Gramm Käse ißt deine Familie
  jede Woche?
Wieviel Obst ißt du jede Woche?

GESPRÄCHSPARTNER/IN

Zwei. Wieviel Glas Milch trinkst du?

Aussprache

[ʌ]   Uhr, Klavier, fährt

When the German **r** is not followed by a vowel, it tends to be pronounced like the final sound in British English *here (hee-uh), there (thay-uh)*. The symbol [ʌ] represents this **uh**-sound. In German, the sound [ʌ] occurs in the unstressed final position.

A. Practice the following words horizontally in pairs.

[R]	[ʌ]
Tiere	Tier
Paare	Paar
Uhren	Uhr
Türen	Tür
fahren	fährt
fahre	fahr
Klaviere	Klavier
schwere	schwer

Glücklich ist, wer vergißt,
was nicht mehr zu ändern ist.

B. Practice the sounds [ʌ] and [R]. Read the sentences aloud.

1. Warum brauchen wir soviel Papier?
2. Birgit sammelt gern Bierdeckel.
3. Jörg, darf ich die Tür hier aufmachen?
4. Hannelore spielt wirklich gut Klavier.

Übungen

1. Conversational past with auxiliary **sein**

Erika **ist** spät nach Hause **gekommen.**	Erika *came* home late.
Sie **ist** erst um acht **aufgestanden.**	She *didn't get up* until eight.
Ich **bin** gestern in die Stadt **gefahren.**	I *went* into town yesterday.

Some verbs require **sein** as an auxiliary in the conversational past. These verbs have no direct object and denote a change in location (for example, **kommen**) or a change in condition (for example, **aufstehen**).

ich **bin** gefahren		wir **sind** gefahren
du **bist** gefahren	Sie **sind** gefahren	ihr **seid** gefahren
er/es/sie **ist** gefahren		sie **sind** gefahren

A. Wer und wohin? Deine Freunde fahren am Samstag in die Stadt. 1) Bitte sag, wer allein in die Stadt gefahren ist! 2) Frag, wohin deine Freunde gefahren sind!

▶ Jürgen und Paul   *Jürgen und Paul sind allein gefahren.*

1. ich
2. die Jungen
3. Erika
4. wir

▶ Udo   *Wohin ist Udo gefahren?*

5. du
6. ihr
7. deine Freundin Inge
8. Richard

INFINITIVE	PAST PARTICIPLE	CONVERSATIONAL PAST
aufstehen	(ist) aufgestanden	Sie **sind** spät **aufgestanden.**
fahren	(ist) gefahren	Sie **sind** in die Stadt **gefahren.**
gehen	(ist) gegangen	Sie **sind** ins Kino **gegangen.**
kommen	(ist) gekommen	Sie **sind** um acht **gekommen.**
laufen	(ist) gelaufen	Sie **sind** nach Hause **gelaufen.**
wandern	(ist) gewandert	Sie **sind** durch die Stadt **gewandert.**

B. Freizeit. Deine Freunde machen immer viel in der Freizeit. Frag, was sie gemacht haben!

▶ Wandert ihr im Sommer viel?   *Seid ihr im Sommer viel gewandert?*

Ja, wir wandern ziemlich viel.   *Ja, wir sind ziemlich viel gewandert.*

1. Wohin fährst du?
   Ich fahre in die Stadt.
2. Wir gehen ins Kino.
   Gehen eure Freunde mit?
3. Lauft ihr jeden Tag?
   Nein, wir laufen nur am Samstag.
4. Wann kommst du nach Hause?
   Ich komme erst um acht.
5. Gehst du im Winter Ski laufen?
   Ja, ich gehe ziemlich oft Ski laufen.
6. Stehst du spät auf?
   Nein, ich stehe um sieben auf.

Du hast das Wort

Wann hast du das gemacht? You and a classmate are discussing some of the things you did this week. Ask the following questions. She/he will respond and then ask you the same questions.

Discussing daily routines

DU

Wann bist du heute morgen
   aufgestanden?

Wann bist du in die Schule gegangen?
Bist du gefahren oder gelaufen?
Wann bist du in die Stadt gefahren?
Wo bist du einkaufen gegangen?
Wann bist du nach Hause gekommen?
Wohin bist du am Wochenende gegangen?

GESPRÄCHSPARTNER/IN

Um [sieben]. Und wann bist du
   aufgestanden?

2. Narrative past of sein

ich	war müde
du	warst müde
er/es/sie	war müde
wir	waren müde
ihr	wart müde
sie	waren müde
Sie	waren müde

I	was tired
you	were tired
he/she	was tired
we	were tired
you	were tired
they	were tired
you	were tired

Although **sein** does have a conversational past, the most commonly used past-tense forms are **war, warst,** and so on. These forms are called the *narrative past.*

C. Letztes Wochenende. Gerd möchte wissen, was seine Freunde am Wochenende gemacht haben. Sag, wie es war! Folge dem Mustersatz°!

model sentence

▶   Wie ist das Fußballspiel?   *Wie war das Fußballspiel?*
    Es ist langweilig.   *Es war langweilig.*

1. Wo bist du Samstag abend?
   Ich bin im Jugendzentrum, wie immer.
2. Wo seid ihr am Sonntag?
   Wir sind zu Hause.
3. Wie ist das Konzert?
   Es ist klasse.
4. Warum sind die Jungen am Wochenende zu Hause?
   Sie sind doch nicht zu Hause.

3. Special **der**-nouns in the accusative singular

NOMINATIVE	ACCUSATIVE
Wie heißt **der Junge** da? Wie heißt **der Herr** da?	Kennst du **den Jungen**? Kennst du **den Herrn**?

A few **der**-nouns add **-n** in the accusative singular.

D. Viele Leute. Jörg erzählt° von einigen° Leuten°. Frag ihn nach° anderen Leuten!

tells about / several / people / about

▶ Ich habe Frau Braun einge-   *Hast du auch Herrn Braun*
    laden. (Herr Braun)   *eingeladen?*

1. Ich habe Frau Wagner angerufen.   (Herr Wagner)
2. Ich habe Frau Lenz gesehen.   (Herr Lenz)
3. Ich kenne das Mädchen dort.   (der Junge)
4. Ich finde das Mädchen doof.   (der Junge)
5. Ich kenne die Kundin dort.   (der Kunde)
6. Ich finde Frau Klein nett.   (Herr Klein)

Frisches Obst im Supermarkt in Karlsruhe: „Nicht anfassen!"

E. Mehr Leute. Jörg erzählt von noch mehr Leuten. Sag etwas über° andere   about
Leute!

▶ Ich finde Frau Schuster nett. (Herr Schuster)   *Ich finde Herrn*
                                                  Schuster nett.

1. Ich habe meine Freundin eingeladen. (mein Freund)
2. Ich finde das Mädchen nett. (der Junge)
3. Ich habe meine Mutter angerufen. (mein Vater)
4. Ich kenne die Frau da nicht. (der Herr)
5. Ich finde die Verkäuferin doof. (der Kunde)
6. Ich kenne die Ärztin nicht. (der Arzt)
7. Ich habe Frau Grün gern. (Herr Grün)

Alles für den schönen Garten

4. Prepositions with the accusative case

durch	through	Gabi geht **durch das** Geschäft.
für	for	Gabi kauft ein Buch **für ihren** Vater.
gegen	against	Sie hat nichts **gegen ihren** Freund.
ohne	without	Frank macht die Hausaufgaben **ohne mich.**
um	around	Er geht **um das** Haus.

The prepositions **durch, für, gegen, ohne,** and **um** are always followed by the
accusative case.

F. Man kann doch nicht . . . ! Gerd möchte durch die Gebäude° gehen, weil   buildings
er wenig Zeit hat. Sag Gerd, es geht nicht!

▶ Versuchen wir mal das Café!   *Man kann doch nicht durch das*
                                       Café gehen.

1. Versuchen wir mal den Supermarkt!
2. Versuchen wir mal das Lebensmittelgeschäft!
3. Versuchen wir mal das Musikgeschäft!
4. Versuchen wir mal das Jugendzentrum!
5. Versuchen wir mal das Sportgeschäft!

G. Für wen ist das? Du hast Geschenke gekauft. Sag Sabine,
für wen sie sind!

▶ Ist die Bluse für deine Mutter   *Für [meine Mutter].*
   oder deine Schwester?

1. Ist der Pulli für deinen Vater oder deinen Bruder?
2. Ist das Buch für Herrn Lenz oder Frau Lenz?
3. Ist die Platte für deine Freundin oder deinen Freund?
4. Ist der Kuli für deinen Bruder oder deine Schwester?

H. Was hat sie gegen diese Leute? Frau Lerner mag viele Leute nicht. Frag bitte, was Frau Lerner gegen alle hat!

▶ Frau Lerner mag ihren   *Was hat sie denn gegen*
  Apotheker nicht.   *ihren Apotheker?*

1. Sie mag auch ihren Bäcker nicht.
2. Auch ihren Metzger mag sie nicht.
3. Ihren Elektriker findet sie schlecht.
4. Sie findet auch ihren Friseur schlecht.
5. Sie mag ihren Arzt nicht.

I. Dann gehen wir ohne sie. Ihr macht ein Picknick, aber viele Freunde arbeiten. Sag, ihr geht ohne sie!

▶ Jürgen muß arbeiten.   *Dann gehen wir ohne ihn.*

1. Bruno muß arbeiten.   4. Lore und Jutta müssen arbeiten.
2. Heidi muß arbeiten.   5. Frank und Udo müssen arbeiten.
3. Ich muß arbeiten.

J. Hast du etwas gegen sie? Viele Leute kommen auf Juttas Party. Sag, du hast nichts gegen die Leute!

▶ Hast du etwas gegen Franz?   *Nein, ich habe nichts gegen ihn.*

1. Hast du etwas gegen Marianne?
2. Hast du etwas gegen Herrn Lenz?
3. Hast du etwas gegen mich?
4. Hast du etwas gegen uns?
5. Hast du etwas gegen Stefan und Thomas?

K. Sag das! Christa sagt etwas. Du sagst auch etwas, aber mit dem anderen Wort!

▶ Ursel geht durch *das Geschäft.*   *Ursel geht durch den Supermarkt.*
  (der Supermarkt)

1. Walter geht durch *das Haus.*   (die Stadt)
2. Warum läuft Toni um *das Haus?*   (der Markt)
3. Volker will nichts gegen *seine Freundin* sagen.   (sein Freund)
4. Ingrid hat etwas gegen *ihren Bruder.*   (ihre Schwester)
5. Trudi kauft den Pulli für *ihre Mutter.*   (ihr Vater)
6. Sie kauft die Platte für *ihre Freundin.*   (ihr Freund)
7. Christl kommt ohne *ihre Schwester.*   (ihr Bruder)
8. Warum läuft der Hund um *den Tisch?*   (der Stuhl)
9. Ich möchte einmal ohne *meinen Bruder* zelten gehen.   (meine Eltern)
10. Arbeitest du für *deine Mutter?*   (dein Vater)

Viele Leute kaufen Fleisch bei „ihrem" Fleischer.

Du hast das Wort

Geburtstagsgeschenke. Tell your classmates what you would like to buy as a birthday present for some of your friends and relatives.

▶ dein Vater   *Für meinen Vater möchte ich [ein Buch] kaufen.*

deine Mutter   dein Freund [Ralf]
dein Bruder [Volker]   deine Freundin [Ilse]
deine Schwester [Margit]

5. Accusative prepositional contractions

Frank geht **durchs** Geschäft.	durch das > **durchs**
Ute kauft etwas **fürs** Haus.	für das > **fürs**
Ingrid geht **ums** Haus.	um das > **ums**

The prepositions **durch, für,** and **um** often contract with the definite article **das** to form **durchs, fürs,** and **ums.**

L. Mach es kurz! Ingrid sagt, was ihre Freunde gemacht haben. Sag es noch einmal, aber kürzer°!

shorter

▶ Eva ist durch das Haus gegangen.   *Eva ist durchs Haus gegangen.*

1. Hugo ist durch das Geschäft gegangen.
2. Petra hat das Geld für das Radio bekommen.
3. Hast du die Karten für das Konzert gekauft?
4. Hast du schon den Arbeitsplan für das Wochenende gemacht?
5. Michael hat einen Spaziergang um das Haus gemacht.

Du hast das Wort

Was hast du vor? Prepare eight questions about a classmate's plans for the weekend, modelled on the questions below. Then ask a classmate the questions.

Asking about planned activities

Was hast du fürs Wochenende vor?
Gehst du ins Kino?
Hast du Geld fürs Kino?

Grammatische Übersicht

Conversational past with auxiliary **sein** (A–B)

ich **bin gekommen**		wir **sind gekommen**
du **bist gekommen**	Sie **sind gekommen**	ihr **seid gekommen**
er/es/sie **ist gekommen**		sie **sind gekommen**

Wir **sind** zu spät **gekommen.**	We *came* late.
Gabi **ist** spät **aufgestanden.**	Gabi *got up* late.

Some verbs require **sein** instead of **haben** as an auxiliary in the conversational past. Verbs that require **sein** must meet two conditions:

1. They must be intransitive verbs (verbs without a direct object).
2. They must indicate a change of location (as in **kommen**) or a change of condition (as in **aufstehen**).

In the vocabularies of this book, verbs that require **sein** are indicated as follows: **kommen (ist gekommen).**

The following verbs require **sein** as an auxiliary in the conversational past.

INFINITIVE	PAST PARTICIPLE
aufstehen	(ist) aufgestanden
fahren	(ist) gefahren
fallen	(ist) gefallen
gehen	(ist) gegangen
kommen	(ist) gekommen

INFINITIVE	PAST PARTICIPLE
laufen	(ist) gelaufen
reiten	(ist) geritten
schwimmen	(ist) geschwommen
segeln	(ist) gesegelt
wandern	(ist) gewandert

Narrative past of **sein** (C)

ich **war**		wir **waren**
du **warst**	Sie **waren**	ihr **wart**
er/es/sie **war**		sie **waren**

Wo **warst** du gestern?   Where *were* you yesterday?

The most commonly used past-tense forms of **sein** are **war, warst,** and so on. These forms are called *narrative past.* **Sein** also has a conversational past, which you will learn in *German Today, Two.*

Special **der**-nouns in the accusative singular (D–E)

Wie heißt **der Junge?**   Meinst du **den Jungen** da?
Wie heißt **der Kunde?**   Meinst du **den Kunden** da?
Herr Altmann ist unser Metzger.   Ich kenne **Herrn Altmann** nicht.

Most nouns have the same form in the nominative and the accusative. A few **der**-nouns, including **Junge, Kunde,** and **Herr,** add **-n** in the accusative singular. Note that the **-n** must be added even when **Herr** is used as a title.

In the vocabularies of this book, special **der**-nouns will be followed by two endings: **der Herr, -n, -en.** The first ending is the accusative singular; the second ending is the nominative plural.

KALBSKÄSE u.
GELBWURST
je 100 gr. **0.79**
FLEISCHSALAT u.
WURSTSALAT
je 100 gr. **0.69**
BAVARIA BLU
100 gr. **1.98**

Metzgerei Altmann
Gundelindenstraße 3
Mü. 40, Tel. 36 99 02
SCHWEINEKOTELETT
100 gr. **0.79**
PUTENSCHNITZEL
100 gr. **1.69**

Prepositions with the accusative case (F–K)

durch	Tanja geht **durch** die Stadt.	Tanja is going *through* the city.
für	**Für** wen kauft sie die Platte?	*For* whom is she buying the record?
gegen	Sie hat nichts **gegen** den Jungen.	She has nothing *against* the boy.
ohne	Sie beginnt **ohne** Herrn Bauer.	She's beginning *without* Mr. Bauer.
um	Sie geht **um** das Haus.	She's going *around* the house.

Accusative prepositional contractions (L)

Erika geht **durchs** Zimmer.
Jörg kauft ein Geschenk **fürs** Kind.
Torsten geht **ums** Haus.

durch das > **durchs**
für das > **fürs**
um das > **ums**

The prepositions **durch, für,** and **um** may contract with the definite article **das.**

"**Himmel und Erde**" (Heaven and Earth), "**Butterblume**" (Buttercup), and "**Milchstraße**" (Milky Way) are among the colorful names for a special kind of store in the Federal Republic: the health food store, usually called **Naturkostladen** (natural food store)

Land und Leute

or **Bioladen** (organic food store). These stores sell food without preservatives and with only natural ingredients. Their fruit, vegetables, and grains are grown without insecticides and chemical fertilizers. They also sell natural cosmetic products: herbal hair-care products, make-up, body creams and oils, and many other items. Although the **Reformhäuser** have been selling natural products in Germany since the beginning of this century, the **Bioläden** have become more popular.

Natural healing methods have long been used in the German-speaking countries. People often seek relief from their illnesses at a **Kurort** (health spa) or **Heilbad** (healing bath). Depending on their location, the spas might feature mineral waters for drinking or bathing, mud baths, herbal medicines, and good clean air.

Wiederholung

A. Wer hat das gemacht? Your grandmother wants to know who's done various tasks. Confirm her guesses.

▶ Wer hat den Bäcker angerufen? Du? *Ja, ich habe ihn angerufen.*

1. Wer hat den Metzger angerufen? Du?
2. Wer hat das Haus aufgeräumt? Ihr?
3. Wer hat die Möbel abgestaubt? Karin?
4. Wer hat das Geschirr abgetrocknet? Karl und Erik?
5. Wer hat die Fenster aufgemacht? Du?
6. Wer hat die Wurst eingepackt? Deine Mutter?

B. Was ist logisch? Read the following statements about various foods and quantities of foods. Correct the statements that aren't logical.

▶ Ich möchte zwei Meter Bananen. *Ich möchte zwei Pfund Bananen.*

1. Ich möchte zwei Liter Würstchen bitte.
2. Sind die Tomaten frisch?
3. Fleisch und Schinken kaufe ich immer beim Bäcker.
4. Ich brauche auch fünf Stück Milch bitte.
5. Kartoffeln kosten eine Mark das Gramm.
6. Im Supermarkt darf man das Obst nicht anfassen.
7. Butter kostet 6 Mark 50 der Kilometer.
8. Ich trinke jeden Tag zwei Glas Milch.

C. Jeder muß helfen. Everyone has chores to do today. Form complete sentences in the present tense, using the cues provided.

1. Andrea / müssen / spülen / Geschirr
2. ich / sollen / decken / Tisch
3. Werner / aufräumen / Garage
4. du / füttern / Katze
5. wir / abstauben / Möbel
6. Werner / backen / Kuchen
7. ich / müssen / raustragen / Mülleimer

D. Was machst du? List at least five things you sometimes do after school or in the evening. You may wish to include some of the following activities.

Hausaufgaben machen **einkaufen gehen** **zu Hause helfen**
tanzen gehen **ins Konzert gehen** **fernsehen**

E. Was machen sie? What are the following people and animals doing? Write
a sentence related to each picture, using the preposition given.

▶ um   *Sie laufen um die Frau herum°.*   around

1. ohne

3. für

2. gegen

4. durch

F. Wer hat die Antwort°? You and each of your classmates should prepare two cards — one with a question and one with the answer to the question. Your teacher will shuffle and distribute the cards. The students with the questions must go around the room and ask them until they find the person who has an appropriate answer. When you have finished, look at the questions again. Are there other possible answers to them? As a class give some examples.

answer

G. Eine Einkaufsliste. Prepare a shopping list of food you will need to buy to survive for one week. Include the quantity and price of each item. You have only 40 DM to spend.

H. Hier kaufe ich ein. Draw a map showing the stores in your town, neighborhood or shopping center. Show the map to a friend and explain to her/him what you buy where, how much things cost, and what you think of quantity and/or price. For additional types of stores, see *Appendix.*

Da ist die Bäckerei. Das Brot ist gut. Ein Pfund kostet fünfundsiebzig Pfennig.

I. Land und Leute.

1. What kinds of snacks do Germans like to eat? Where would they buy them? Are any of these snacks also popular in America? What snack popular in the United States was originally a German food?
2. Review all the cultural notes in the chapter. List the major similarities and differences between **einkaufen** in Germany and shopping in the United States.
3. What can Germans do to stay healthy?

Sie hat im Supermarkt eingekauft.

Der Markt

Viele Deutsche gehen nicht nur einmal° in der Woche einkaufen. Sie gehen zweimal oder öfter°, denn sie wollen frisches Obst und Gemüse haben.

    Sie kaufen ihr Obst und Gemüse oft auf dem Markt. Hier kann man es direkt von den Bauern° kaufen. Der Markt ist meistens° im Zentrum einer° Stadt, auf
5 dem Marktplatz° vor dem Rathaus°. Die Verkäufer haben ihre Waren unter° großen Schirmen°. Diese Schirme haben viele Farben — rot, blau oder grün. So sieht der Markt schön bunt° aus.

    In großen Städten ist jeden Tag Markt, in kleinen Städten ein- oder zweimal in der Woche. Man findet da oft auch Brot, Käse und Eier, Fleisch und Wurst und
10 Fisch°. Und Blumen°. Viele Blumen. Einige° Städte haben sogar° einen besonderen° Blumenmarkt.

one time	
more often	
farmers / mostly / of a	
market place / town hall / under	
umbrellas	
colorful	
fish / flowers / some / even	
special	

A. Auf dem Markt. Choose the phrase that best completes each sentence, based on the reading.

1. Viele Deutsche gehen zweimal oder öfter in der Woche einkaufen, denn . . .
   a. sie wollen nicht soviel tragen.
   b. sie wollen immer alles frisch haben.
   c. sie haben kein Auto.
   d. man kann Gemüse nur von den Bauern kaufen.
2. Die Deutschen kaufen gern auf dem Markt, denn . . .
   a. im Supermarkt ist alles frisch.
   b. in kleinen Geschäften ist alles billig.
   c. die Bauern haben alles frisch.
   d. man muß nicht so weit gehen.
3. Auf dem Markt sieht man viele bunte . . .
   a. Bauern
   b. Verkäufer
   c. Rathäuser
   d. Schirme
4. In . . . ist jeden Tag Markt.
   a. großen Städten
   b. kleinen Städten
   c. allen Städten
   d. keiner Stadt

B. Was gibt es auf dem Markt? Which of the following would generally be available at an open-air market in a German-speaking country?

Möbel, Äpfel, Kartoffeln, Kassetten, Fernseher, Käse, Eier, Wurst, Briefmarken, Blumen, Flugzeugmodelle, Fisch, Gemüse, Brot.

Vokabeln

Substantive

If two other entries follow a noun, the first one indicates the accusative singular, the second, the plural. For example: **der Kunde, —n** *(acc.),* **—n** *(pl.)*

der Bäcker, —/die Bäckerin, —nen baker
der Kunde, —n, —n/die Kundin, —nen customer
der Metzger, —/die Metzgerin, —nen butcher

der Apfel, ⸚ apple
der Käse, — cheese
der Kuchen, — cake
der Liter, — liter
der Markt, ⸚e market
der Pfennig, —e *(abbr.* **Pf***)* German coin

Substantive (cont.)

der Saft, ⸚e juice
der Schinken, — ham
der Spinat spinach
der Supermarkt, ⸚e supermarket
der Wunsch, ⸚e wish, desire

das Brot, —e (loaf of) bread
das Ei, —er egg
das Fleisch meat
das Gemüse, — vegetable
das Glas, ⸚er glass
das Gramm gram
das Kilo(gramm) kilogram
das Obst fruit

Substantive (cont.)

das Pfund, −e (*abbr.* **Pfd.**) pound
das Schweinskotelett, −s pork chop
das Stück, −e piece
das Wiener Würstchen, − frankfurter

die Banane, −n banana
die Butter butter
die Einkaufstasche, −n shopping bag
die Erbse, −n pea
die Erdbeere, −n strawberry
die Flasche, −n bottle
die Karotte, −n carrot
die Kartoffel, −n potato
die Milch milk
die Orange, −n orange
die Tasche, −n bag; purse; pocket
die Tomate, −n tomato
die Tüte, −n bag
die Wurst, ̈e sausage, cold cuts

die Lebensmittel (*pl.*) food, groceries

Verben

besuchen to visit
bezahlen to pay
ein·packen to pack
packen to pack
war (*past tense of* **sein**) was

Andere Wörter

allein alone
denn (*conjunction*) for, because
dort there
durch (+ *acc.*) through
fast almost
frisch fresh
früh early
man (*indef. pronoun*) one, you, they, people
nämlich namely, you know
nett nice
ohne (+ *acc.*) without
selbst oneself, myself, etc.
so . . . wie as . . . as
wohl indeed, probably
zurück back
zusammen together

Besondere Ausdrücke

einen Moment just a moment
Entschuldigung excuse me, sorry
Grüß Gott hello
auf Wiederschauen good-by
was darf es sein? what would you like?
ich hätte gern . . . I would like . . .
sonst noch was? anything else?
das macht zusammen 10 Mark that comes to
   10 Marks
auf dem Markt at the open-air market

Kapitel 12

Guten Appetit!

Das Mittagessen ist warm.

Essen bei Familie Wolf

Was gibt's zum Frühstück?

Familie Wolf frühstückt um sieben. Zum Frühstück gibt es Brot und Brötchen mit Butter und Marmelade, manchmal auch ein Ei, Käse oder Wurst. Der Vater und die Mutter trinken Kaffee, und Gabi trinkt Schokolade oder Milch.

Fragen

1. Wann frühstücken Wolfs?
2. Was essen und trinken Wolfs zum Frühstück?
3. Was ißt und trinkst du zum Frühstück? Eier? Corn-flakes? Brot? Toast? mit Butter und Marmelade? Saft? Milch? Kaffee?

Was gibt's zum Mittagessen?

Um ein Uhr ißt Familie Wolf zu Mittag. Zum Mittagessen gibt es Suppe, dann Fisch oder Fleisch mit Kartoffeln und Gemüse und manchmal auch Salat. Zum Essen trinken sie gewöhnlich nichts. Als Nachtisch gibt es vielleicht Orangen oder Bananen oder einen Pudding.

Fragen

1. Wann essen Wolfs zu Mittag?
2. Was essen Wolfs zu Mittag?
3. Was ißt du mittags°? Thunfisch°? Schinkenbrote°? Wurst? Würstchen?
   Salat? Suppe? Pommes frites°? Kartoffelchips°? Pizza?
4. Was trinkst du zum Mittagessen?

Was gibt's zum Abendessen?

Um sieben ißt die Familie zu Abend. Zum Abendessen gibt es Brot mit Wurst und
Käse. Der Vater und die Mutter trinken eine Tasse Tee. Gabi trinkt ein Glas
Limonade oder Cola. Wasser mögen sie nicht, denn es schmeckt nicht so gut wie
Cola oder Tee.

Fragen

1. Wann essen Wolfs zu Abend?
2. Was essen Wolfs zu Abend?
3. Was ißt du abends? Steak? Rindsbraten? Schweinskoteletts? Huhn? Fisch?
   Würstchen? Kartoffeln? Gemüse? Nachtisch?
4. Was trinkst du zum Abendessen?

Land und Leute

One of Gabi Wolf's chores is to set the table
before each meal: fork **(die Gabel)** on the left
of the plate, knife **(das Messer)** on the right,
and spoon **(der Löffel)** above the plate. When
people in German-speaking countries eat, they
keep the fork in the left hand and the knife in
the right, using both utensils at once. Germans
keep their left hand on the table instead of in
their lap, as people in the United States do.

Before beginning to eat, one of the parents
may say **Guten Appetit** or **Mahlzeit,** short
for **Gesegnete Mahlzeit** ("wishing everyone
a good meal"). The rest of the family often re-
sponds with **Danke, gleichfalls** (same to
you).

Im Restaurant

OBER	Guten Tag! Möchten Sie etwas trinken?
FRAU WOLF	Ach ja. Ich habe so einen Durst. Ein Mineralwasser bitte.
HERR WOLF	Ich trinke auch ein Mineralwasser.
OBER	Zwei Mineralwasser.
GABI	Ich möchte eine Cola bitte.
OBER	Danke.
HERR WOLF	Und die Speisekarte bitte.

Der Ober bringt die Getränke.

OBER	Möchten Sie jetzt bestellen?
FRAU WOLF	Ja bitte. Ist der Rindsbraten zart?
OBER	Oh ja. Den kann ich empfehlen.
FRAU WOLF	Also, dreimal Rindsbraten mit Kartoffelpüree und Salat.
GABI	Ich möchte kein Kartoffelpüree.
FRAU WOLF	Hast du denn keinen Hunger?
GABI	Doch. Aber ich esse lieber Pommes frites.

* * *

OBER	So, hat's geschmeckt?
FRAU WOLF	Ja. Der Braten war ausgezeichnet.
HERR WOLF	Ich möchte gern zahlen.
OBER	Bitte sehr. Das macht zusammen 43 Mark und 50 Pfennig.
HERR WOLF	Machen Sie es 45.
OBER	Vielen Dank.

Land und Leute

Most restaurants in German-speaking countries post the menu outside so that customers may decide whether they wish — or can afford — to eat there. The price includes a value-added tax **(Mehrwertsteuer)** and a service charge **(Bedienung)** of 15 percent. To ask for the bill one can say **Die Rechnung, bitte!**, **Zahlen bitte!**, or **Ich möchte gern zahlen.** The waiter or waitress will total the bill and usually make change right at the table. Although no extra tip is normally left, the customer often rounds up the bill to the next appropriate figure.

Fragen

1. Ißt Familie Wolf immer zu Hause? Wo essen sie auch gern?
2. Warum bestellt Frau Wolf ein Mineralwasser?
3. Was trinkt Gabi?
4. Wer bringt die Speisekarte?
5. Was empfiehlt der Ober?
6. Was bestellt Frau Wolf?
7. Warum will Gabi kein Kartoffelpüree?
8. Wie hat der Braten geschmeckt?
9. Wer bezahlt?

Du hast das Wort

1. **Was ißt du gern?** Ask a classmate whether she/he likes to eat certain foods.

Asking about personal preferences

DU		GESPRÄCHSPARTNER/IN
Ißt du gern	Kartoffelpüree?	Ja, sehr gern.
	Fisch?	Ja, [Kartoffelpüree] schmeckt gut.
	Gemüse?	Ich esse es, aber nicht gern.
		Nein, [Kartoffelpüree] esse ich nicht gern.
		Nein, [Kartoffelpüree] mag ich nicht.

2. **Was ißt du lieber?** You are doing a poll of your classmates on their preferences for foods and beverages. With a partner prepare your survey following the examples given below. When you are ready, go and ask your classmates!

Expressing preferences

Was ißt du lieber:

    Kartoffelpüree oder Pommes frites?

    Eier oder Corn-flakes?

Sie/er ißt lieber:

_____

_____

Was trinkst du lieber:

    Cola oder Kaffee?

    Saft oder Milch?

    Tee oder Wasser?

Sie/er trinkt lieber:

_____

_____

_____

TEEKANNE AUS DEM HAUSE TEEKANNE FÜR TEEKENNER

3. **Frühstück — Mittagessen — Abendessen.** Ask two classmates what they like and don't like for three daily meals. Was ißt du gern zum Frühstück? Was ißt du nicht gern? After you have filled out a chart like the one below, report your findings to two other classmates.

Asking about personal preferences

NAME _____	ißt gern	ißt nicht gern
Zum Frühstück	_____	_____
Zum Mittagessen	_____	_____
Zum Abendessen	_____	_____

► Zum Frühstück ißt Tanja gern Corn-flakes.

INTERHOTEL „ASTORIA" LEIPZIG

Wertbon - Frühstück
10,00 M
Frühstückszeit 6.00 bis 10.00 Uhr
Datum

Wortschatzerweiterung

Speisekarte

Suppen

Hühnersuppe	DM 3,20
Gemüsesuppe	DM 3,50
Tagessuppe	DM 2,80

Fleisch und Fisch

Filetsteak	DM 18,–
Rindsbraten	DM 16,50
Schweinskotelett	DM 14,–
Wiener Schnitzel	DM 16,20
Schinkenbrot	DM 8,50
Würstchen	DM 6,–
Fischfilet	DM 13,50
Wurstsalat	DM 5,–

Gemüse und Salate

Erbsen	DM 3,50
Karotten	DM 3,50
Spinat	DM 3,50
Pommes frites	DM 2,50
Kartoffelpüree	DM 2,50
Salat	DM 5,–
Tomatensalat	DM 5,–

Getränke

1 Tasse Kaffee	DM 2,50
1 Glas Tee	DM 2,50
1 Tasse Schokolade	DM 2,80
0,20 l Apfelsaft	DM 2,30
0,20 l Cola	DM 2,30
0,20 l Limonade	DM 2,30
0,20 l Milch	DM 1,50
0,25 l Mineralwasser	DM 2,30
0,50 l Bier	DM 3,50

zum Nachtisch

Eis	DM 3,50
Pudding	DM 2,50
Apfelkuchen	DM 3,–
Erdbeertorte	DM 3,–
Käseplatte	DM 6,50

A. Was möchtest du? You have been given twenty-five German marks (DM 25,00) to spend on a restaurant meal. The restaurant you have chosen offers the items shown on the menu above. What will you eat? Begin with *Ich möchte* . . . and list the items you wish to order.

Ordering in a restaurant

A **Frühstück** ordered in a restaurant or hotel usually consists of a hot beverage, an assortment of rolls and breads, butter, and jam or jelly. This is what is referred to in the United States as a "continental breakfast." Many breakfasts include an egg and/or cold cuts. When people in German-speaking countries have eggs for breakfast, they generally have soft-boiled eggs **(weichgekochte Eier)**. Scrambled eggs **(Rühreier)** and fried eggs **(Spiegeleier)** are eaten mostly at supper.

Pancakes are generally not a breakfast food in German-speaking countries. German **Pfannkuchen** are thinner and lighter than American pancakes, more like French **crêpes.** They are often filled with apple pieces or jam and then rolled up and dusted with sugar.

In vielen kleinen Hotels gibt es Frühstückszimmer.

B. Im Restaurant. Using the cues below, create a skit with a partner. One of you takes the role of a waiter or waitress. The other orders dinner or a snack from the menu.

FRÄULEIN°/OBER	GAST°/GÄSTE
Guten Tag! Möchten Sie etwas trinken?	Ja, eine Cola.
Möchten Sie jetzt bestellen?	Ja, bitte. Ich möchte (ein) Eis. Ist [die Tagessuppe] gut? Was können Sie empfehlen?
Hat's geschmeckt?	Ja, sehr. Es war ausgezeichnet. Ich möchte gern zahlen. Zahlen bitte. Die Rechnung° bitte.
Das macht zusammen [19] Mark.	Machen Sie es [20].

Kleine Kochschule

der Löffel	spoon	**bedecken**	to cover
der Teelöffel	teaspoon	**bestreichen**	to spread
der Eßlöffel	tablespoon	**bestreuen**	to sprinkle
die Prise	pinch	**erhitzen**	to heat
die Pfanne	pan	**gießen**	to pour
der Topf	pot	**schneiden**	to cut
die Schüssel	bowl	**verrühren**	to stir, to beat
die Zutaten	ingredients		
der Teig	dough		

The list above includes some of the more common German terms used in cooking. It should help you to understand the following recipe for **Pfannkuchen.**

Zutaten

375 Gramm Mehl°   flour
3 Eier
1 Prise Salz°   salt
¾ Liter Milch
Butter oder Margarine
150 Gramm Marmelade
Puderzucker° zum Bestreuen   confectioner's sugar

Mehl, Eier, Milch und Salz zu einem dünnen, glatten° Teig verrühren. In einer   smooth
Pfanne etwas° Butter oder Margarine erhitzen, den Boden° dünn mit Teig be-   some/bottom
decken und die Pfannkuchen auf beiden Seiten° goldgelb backen.   sides

    Dies so lange wiederholen°, bis der Teig aufgebraucht° ist. Jeden Pfannkuchen   repeat/used up
mit Marmelade bestreichen, einrollen° und mit Zucker bestreuen.   roll up

[ə]	bitt**e**, bestimmt
[ən]	spiel**en**, geh**en**
[ər]	Spiel**er**, bitt**er**, Verkäuf**er**

The [ə] sound occurs in unstressed **-en** and **-e** endings and is similar to English *e* in *boxes, pocket.*

The [ər] sound occurs when the sequence **er** stands at the end of a word, before a consonant, or in an unstressed prefix. The **-r** is not pronounced as an [R], but sounds much like the final *-a* in English *sofa.*

A. Practice the following words horizontally.

[ən]	[ə]	[ər]
bitten	bitte	bitter
denken	denke	Denker
fahren	fahre	Fahrer
fehlen	fehle	Fehler
leiden	leide	leider
nennen	nenne	Nenner

B. Practice the sounds [ə], [ən], and [ər]. Read the sentences aloud.

1. Wo haben Sie diese Platten gekauft, Frau Leber?
2. Unser Kassettenrecorder ist wieder kaputt.
3. Die Hose ist nicht teuer, aber ich kann sie nicht kaufen.

Morgen, morgen, nur nicht heute,
sagen alle faulen Leute.

1. Dieser-words in the nominative and accusative

dieser

NOMINATIVE		ACCUSATIVE		
Der Dieser	Fernseher ist preiswert.	Kaufst du	den diesen	Fernseher?
Das Dieses	Radio ist preiswert.	Kaufst du	das dieses	Radio?
Die Diese	Stereoanlage ist preiswert.	Kaufst du	die diese	Stereoanlage?
Die Diese	Kassetten sind preiswert.	Kaufst du	die diese	Kassetten?

Dieser follows the same pattern of endings in the nominative and accusative as the definite article.

A. Billige Sachen. Du gehst mit Marina einkaufen. Sie sieht viele schöne Sachen und fragt, ob die teuer sind. Sag ja, und sag, daß° andere Sachen nicht so   that teuer sind!

▶ Ist die Jacke da teuer?   *Ja, aber diese Jacke hier ist nicht teuer.*

1. Ist die Hose da teuer?
2. Ist der Gürtel da teuer?
3. Ist der Pulli da teuer?
4. Ist das Hemd da teuer?

5. Ist das Kleid da teuer?
6. Sind die Schuhe da teuer?
7. Sind die Jeans da teuer?

B. Ich kann es empfehlen. Du arbeitest im Supermarkt. Alles ist sehr gut, und du kannst alles empfehlen. Bitte sag das!

▶ Ist dieser Salat frisch?   *Ja, ich kann diesen Salat empfehlen.*

1. Ist diese Wurst gut?
2. Ist dieser Käse gut?
3. Ist dieser Schinken frisch?
4. Ist dieses Brot frisch?
5. Sind diese Brötchen frisch?
6. Sind diese Tomaten gut?

Hier ist jedes Kleidungsstück 50% billiger.

welcher/jeder

Welcher Fernseher **Welches** Radio **Welche** Stereoanlage	ist teuer?

Jeder Fernseher **Jedes** Radio **Jede** Stereoanlage	ist teuer.

Welcher and **jeder** have the same endings as **dieser. Jeder** is used in the singular only.

C. Was meint Matthias? Matthias macht oft nicht alles sehr klar. Frag Matthias, was er meint!

▶ Ich habe das Buch zweimal gelesen.   *Welches Buch?*

1. Ich habe das Poster nicht gekauft.
2. Ich habe den Kugelschreiber leider verloren.
3. Ich habe den Pulli gestern getragen.
4. Ich habe die Platte schon gehört.
5. Ich habe das Spiel natürlich gewonnen.
6. Ich habe die Schuhe nicht gekauft.
7. Ich habe die Uhr selbst bezahlt.

D. Dein Hobby. Sammeln ist dein Hobby. Du findest viele Sachen schön oder interessant. Bitte sag das!

▶ Findest du diese Uhr schön? *Ja, für mich ist jede Uhr schön.*

1. Findest du diese Ansichtskarte interessant?
2. Findest du diesen Bierdeckel interessant?
3. Findest du diese Briefmarke schön?
4. Findest du dieses Poster schön?
5. Findest du diese Platte gut?

mancher/solcher

Manche Bücher sind zu teuer.	*Some* books are too expensive.
Solche Bücher kaufe ich nicht.	I wouldn't buy *such* books.

Solcher and **mancher** have the same endings as **dieser,** but they are used almost exclusively in the plural.

E. Auf dem Markt. Auf dem Markt sind Obst und Gemüse heute nicht sehr gut. Sag, du kaufst solche Sachen nicht!

▶ Möchten Sie diese Kartoffeln? *Nein, solche Kartoffeln kaufe ich nicht.*

1. Möchten Sie diese Erdbeeren?
2. Möchten Sie diese Orangen?
3. Möchten Sie diese Äpfel?
4. Möchten Sie diese Tomaten?
5. Möchten Sie diese Erbsen?

F. Das ist oft so. Sag es noch einmal, im Plural!

▶ Das Mädchen trägt Jeans. *Manche Mädchen tragen Jeans.*

1. Die Frau kauft im Supermarkt ein.
2. Der Junge kocht gern.
3. Das Geschäft ist teuer.
4. Das Haus ist klein.
5. Die Platte ist schlecht.
6. Die Party ist langweilig.

2. Time expressions in the accusative case

Wann kommt Karl-Heinz?	**Diesen** Sommer.
Wie oft spielt er Tennis?	**Jeden** Samstag.
Wie lange arbeitet er im Geschäft?	**Einen** Monat.

Time expressions that answer the questions **wann?, wie oft?,** and **wie lange?** are in the accusative case. Such expressions indicate a definite time or period of time.

G. Ja, das stimmt! Deine Freundin fragt viel, und sie antwortet° oft selbst. Ihre Antwort° stimmt immer. Sag das!

answers
answer

▶ Wie oft kommt Michael?   *Ja, er kommt jeden Abend.*
  Jeden Abend?

1. Wie oft schreibt Frau Weiß? Jede Woche?
2. Wie oft geht Herr Neumeier einkaufen? Jeden Tag?
3. Wie lange arbeitet Erika schon? Einen Monat?
4. Wann gehen wir spazieren? Diesen Samstag?
5. Wie oft kommen Ingrids Freunde? Jedes Jahr?
6. Wann gehst du tanzen? Jedes Wochenende?

Du hast das Wort

1. **Was machst du immer?** Ask your classmates the following questions about their routine activities.

Asking personal questions

▶ Arbeitest du jeden Abend?   *Ja, jeden Abend. / Nein, nicht jeden Abend. Ich arbeite [nur am Montagabend].*

Frühstückst du jeden Morgen?
Gehst du jeden Tag tanzen?
Trägst du jeden Tag Jeans?
Gehst du jede Woche einkaufen?
Siehst du jeden Abend fern?
Treibst du jeden Nachmittag Sport?

2. **Was machen Sie immer?** Ask your teacher the following questions.

▶ Frag, ob sie/er jeden   *Treiben Sie jeden*
  Samstag Sport treibt!   *Samstag Sport?*

Frag, ob sie/er jeden Abend arbeitet!
Frag, ob sie/er jeden Morgen frühstückt!
Frag, ob sie/er jede Woche einkaufen geht!
Frag, ob sie/er jeden Abend fernsieht!

Intercity. Jede Stunde. Jede Klasse.

Deutsche Bundesbahn

3. Present tense to express duration of time

Wie lange **lernst** du **schon** Deutsch?	How long *have* you *been studying* German?
Erik **arbeitet schon** zwei Monate im Supermarkt.	Erik *has been working* for two months in the supermarket.

To express action that started in the past and extends into the present, German uses the present tense plus a time indication, usually accompanied by **schon**.

H. Wie lange schon? Gerd fragt, wie lange sie das schon machen. Was er glaubt, stimmt. Sag das!

▶ Wie lange arbeitest du schon im Supermarkt? Zwei Wochen?   *Ja, ich arbeite schon zwei Wochen im Supermarkt.*

1. Wie lange lernst du schon Deutsch? Sechs Monate?
2. Wie lange wohnt Beate schon in München? Zwei Jahre?
3. Wie lange sammelt Dirk schon Bierdeckel? Ein Jahr?
4. Wie lange sammelt Heike schon Briefmarken? Drei Jahre?
5. Wie lange arbeitet Rudi schon im Musikgeschäft? Einen Monat?

Du hast das Wort

Wie lange schon? An exchange student wants to know more about you, and asks how long you have been doing the following. Tell her or him.

▶ Wie lange lernst du schon Deutsch?   *Ich lerne schon sieben Monate Deutsch.*

Wie lange kannst du schon Ski laufen?
Wie lange spielst du schon ein Musikinstrument?
Wie lange gehst du schon in diese Schule?
Wie lange wohnst du schon hier?
Wie lange kennst du schon [deine Freundin]?
Wie lange spielst du schon [Fußball]?

4. Coordinating conjunctions: **aber, denn, oder, sondern, und**

Uwe trinkt Kaffee, **aber** ich trinke lieber Milch.
Ich trinke morgens Milch, **denn** ich mag keinen Kaffee.

Coordinating conjunctions are used to connect two independent clauses. They do not affect word order of subject and verb.

*Sie sind schon zwei Jahre
zusammen im Orchester.*

I. Warum haben sie die Aufgaben nicht gemacht? Der Lehrer will wissen, warum die Schüler die Hausaufgaben nicht gemacht haben. Sag es!

▶ Ingrid hat Tennis gespielt. *Ingrid hat die Aufgaben nicht gemacht,
denn sie hat Tennis gespielt.*

1. Jan hat keine Zeit gehabt.
2. Dieter ist ins Kino gegangen.
3. Gisela hat Musik gehört.
4. Erik hat Platten gespielt.
5. Astrid hat gearbeitet.
6. Gabi ist tanzen gegangen.
7. Ich war auf einer Party.

J. Nächste Woche. Die Klasse will wissen, was du nächste Woche machst.
Sag es für jeden Tag!

▶ Samstag gehen wir einkaufen. *Samstag gehen wir einkaufen,*
Dann gehen wir ins Kino. *und dann gehen wir ins Kino.*

1. Sonntag wandern wir. Dann trinken wir Kaffee.
2. Montag abend mache ich Mathe. Dann sehe ich fern.
3. Mittwoch arbeite ich im Supermarkt. Dann gehe ich tanzen.
4. Donnerstag spielen wir Tennis. Dann machen wir Hausaufgaben.
5. Freitag gehe ich einkaufen. Dann mache ich Abendessen.

Zum Mittagessen gibt es Fleisch und Gemüse.

K. Was machst du jetzt? Sabine hat gesagt, was sie jetzt machen will. Du weißt aber nicht mehr, was es ist. Also frag Sabine!

▶ Arbeitest du? Gehst du   *Arbeitest du, oder gehst du*
   jetzt schwimmen?   *jetzt schwimmen?*

1. Kommst du mit? Hast du keine Zeit?
2. Möchtest du jetzt essen? Hast du keinen Hunger?
3. Trinkst du jetzt eine Cola? Hast du keinen Durst?
4. Gehst du auf den Markt? Kaufst du im Supermarkt ein?
5. Spielst du jetzt Volleyball? Machst du Hausaufgaben?
6. Rufst du Volker an? Besuchst du ihn?

aber and sondern

Wir möchten heute abend fernsehen,   We'd like to watch TV this evening,
   aber unser Fernseher ist kaputt.   *but* our TV set is broken.
Wir sehen heute abend nicht fern,   We aren't going to watch TV this
   sondern gehen ins Kino.   evening; *instead* we're going to
                                           the movies.

Aber as a coordinating conjunction is equivalent to *but, nevertheless.* It may be used after either a positive or a negative clause. **Sondern** is a coordinating conjunction that is equivalent to *but, instead, on the contrary.* It is used after a negative clause only, and then only if the second clause contradicts the first clause. Otherwise **aber** is used.

L. Aber . . . Gabi sagt etwas in zwei Sätzen. Sag es in einem Satz. Benutze° *aber!*   use

▶ Frau Meier geht jeden Tag   *Frau Meier geht jeden Tag*
   einkaufen. Sie kauft   *einkaufen, aber sie kauft*
   nicht viel.   *nicht viel.*

1. Ich möchte einkaufen gehen. Die Geschäfte sind zu°.   closed
2. Ich möchte ins Kino gehen. Ich habe kein Geld.
3. Die *Hot Dogs* spielen diesen Samstag. Ich möchte sie nicht hören.

M. Welches Wort? Mach einen logischen° Satz! Benutze° *sondern* oder *aber!*   logical / use

1. Erikas Zimmer ist nicht groß, _____ sehr klein.
2. Ihr Zimmer ist klein, _____ schön.
3. Erika arbeitet heute abend nicht, _____ geht ins Konzert.
4. Sie hat viele Hausaufgaben, _____ sie macht sie nicht.
5. Die Schuhe sind nicht teuer, _____ sehr billig.
6. Die Schuhe sind nicht teuer, _____ ich kaufe sie nicht.

Land und Leute

When Germans eat dessert with the main meal at noon, it is often pudding or fruit rather than baked goods. Cakes and pastries are eaten during the **Kaffeestunde** later in the afternoon. Sunday afternoon in particular is the time to have a **Kaffeestunde** with friends or relatives, whether at home or in a café.

Zum Kaffee gibt es eine gute Orangentorte. Auf dem Tisch stehen Blumen *(flowers)* und schönes Geschirr.

Dieser-words in the nominative and accusative

(A–F)

	NOMINATIVE	ACCUSATIVE
der Pulli	Dieser Pulli ist toll.	Inge kauft **diesen** Pulli.
das Hemd	Dieses Hemd ist toll.	Erik kauft **dieses** Hemd.
die Jacke	Diese Jacke ist toll.	Jan kauft **diese** Jacke.
die Schuhe	Diese Schuhe sind toll.	Anna kauft **diese** Schuhe.

Dieser, jeder, welcher, solcher, and **mancher** (called **dieser**-words) follow the same pattern of endings in the nominative and accusative as the definite articles **der, das,** and **die.** Meanings of **dieser**-words are as follows:

dieser	this; these (*pl.*)	**solcher**	such (mainly *pl.*)
jeder	each, every (*sg.* only)	**welcher**	which?
mancher	many a, several (mainly *pl.*)		

Time expressions in the accusative case (G)

Wann kommt Katrin wieder?
Wie oft spielt Jan Tennis?
Wie lange bleibt Beate?

Sie kommt **dieses Jahr** wieder.
Er spielt **jeden Tag** Tennis.
Sie kann nur **einen Tag** bleiben.

Time expressions that indicate a definite time (answering the questions **wann?, wie oft?**) or a period of time (answering the question **wie lange?**) are in the accusative case.

Present tense to express duration of time (H–I)

Nun **sind** wir **schon drei Wochen** in Deutschland.

Now *we've been* in Germany *for three weeks.*

Ingrid **arbeitet schon ein Jahr** im Supermarkt.

Ingrid *has been working* in the supermarket *for a year.*

To express action that started in the past and extends into the present, German uses the present tense plus a time indication, usually accompanied by **schon.** To express the same concept, English uses such forms as *have been, has been . . . -ing.*

Independent clauses

INDEPENDENT CLAUSE	COORDINATING CONJUNCTION	INDEPENDENT CLAUSE
Wir möchten einkaufen gehen,	aber	wir haben kein Geld.
Ich kaufe die Jacke nicht,	denn	sie ist zu teuer.

An independent clause can make sense standing alone. When used as parts of sentences, two independent clauses may be connected with each other by coordinating conjunctions.

Coordinating conjunctions (J–M)

Ich habe Hunger, **aber** das Essen ist noch nicht fertig.
Wir können im Restaurant essen, **denn** ich habe heute Geld.
Nimmst du den Fisch, **oder** magst du keinen Fisch?
Er geht nicht ins Restaurant, **sondern** ins Café.
Du nimmst ein Eis, **und** ich bestelle den Pudding.

Five common coordinating conjunctions are **aber, denn, oder, sondern,** and **und.** Coordinating conjunctions do not affect the word order of subject and verb. The conjunctions are generally preceded by a comma.

Ich schreibe Ute einen Brief **oder besuche** sie nächste Woche.

I'll write Ute a letter *or visit* her next week.

Sie arbeiten bis sieben **und gehen** dann ins Kino.

They'll work until seven *and* then *go* to the movies.

Oder and **und** are not preceded by a comma when the subject in both independent clauses is the same. The subject usually is not repeated in the second clause.

aber and sondern

Ich möchte im Restaurant essen,
  aber ich habe kein Geld.
Wir gehen heute nicht ins
  Restaurant, **sondern** essen
  zu Hause.

I'd like to eat in a restaurant,
  but I don't have any money.
We're not going to a restaurant
  today; *instead* we'll eat at home.

Aber as a coordinating conjunction is equivalent to *but, however, nevertheless.* It may be used after either a positive or a negative clause. **Sondern** is a coordinating conjunction that expresses a contrast or contradiction. It is equivalent to *but, instead, on the contrary.* **Sondern** is used after a negative clause only. When the subject is the same in both clauses, it is not repeated.

Wir gehen nicht ins Restaurant, sondern **essen** zu Hause.

Wiederholung

A. Dein Lieblingsrestaurant. Answer the following questions, based on your own experience or preferences. Then ask your teacher the same questions.

1. Ißt du lieber zu Hause oder im Restaurant?
2. Wie heißt dein Lieblingsrestaurant?
3. Ist es da teuer oder billig?
4. Wie oft ißt du dort?
5. Was bestellst du gewöhnlich?
6. Welchen Nachtisch ißt du gern?

B. Wie sagt man das? Ilse is talking to her friends about a dinner she had last night at a restaurant. Express their conversational exchanges in German.

1. Did you eat in a restaurant yesterday?
   Yes. Sabine and Ralf also went along.
2. Why didn't you invite me?
   We called you up. You weren't home.
3. Did you order the roast beef?
   Yes. The waiter recommended it.
4. Did it taste good?
   Yes. It was very tender.
5. What did Ralf eat?
   He had the ham.
6. How much did you pay?
   Nothing. We didn't have any money.
7. And why did you come home so late?
   We washed the dishes.

C. Welches Wort? Ask the questions that the following sentences answer.
Use the following interrogatives:

Wann? Wen? Wer? Was? Wie? Wo? Wohin?
Wie oft? Wie lange?

1. Detlev sammelt *alte Ansichtskarten*.
2. Benno findet Ansichtskarten *langweilig*.
3. Kurt segelt *jeden Samstag*.
4. Martina geht oft *ins Jugendzentrum*.
5. Ute arbeitet schon *ein Jahr* im Supermarkt.
6. Gerd kauft seine Briefmarken *in Hamburg*.
7. *Petra* hat kein Hobby.
8. Lothar ruft *seine Freunde* oft an.
9. Frank sieht *abends* fern.

D. Was macht Peter? Begin each sentence with the word or phrase in italics,
and make the necessary changes in word order.

1. Peter spielt *jeden Tag* Tennis.
2. Er sieht *abends* fern.
3. Er hat *gestern* Gartenarbeit gemacht.
4. Seine Schwester Petra hat *heute morgen* das Auto gewaschen.
5. Sie fahren *am Wochenende* nach Bremen.
6. Sie kommen *Sonntag abend* wieder nach Hause.

E. Welches Wort? Replace each word in italics with the appropriate antonym.

einfach frisch hübsch kaputt
langweilig leicht verloren

1. Unser Fernseher ist wieder *repariert*.
2. Wir haben das Fußballspiel *gewonnen*.
3. Dieses Hobby ist wirklich *interessant*.
4. Unsere Matheaufgabe ist heute *kompliziert*, nicht?
5. Chemie finde ich aber *schwer*.
6. Ist das Brot da *alt*?
7. Die Bluse da ist wirklich *häßlich*, nicht?

FISCHERS FRITZ
FISCHT FRISCHE FISCHE.

ALNO® *...die Welt der Küche.*

F. Wie sagt man das? Change one German word to another by changing a single letter. Use the English cues as guidelines.

▶ we > how   *wir > wie*

1. then > because
2. beautiful > already
3. then > thin
4. of course > you *(acc.)*
5. now > only

6. four > much
7. go > against
8. still > after
9. butter > mother
10. can > know

G. Die Fete. In six to eight sentences describe a party you gave recently. You may wish to include answers to the following questions.

Wieviel Personen hast du eingeladen?
Wann hat die Fete begonnen?
Was habt ihr alles gemacht?
Habt ihr getanzt? Musik gehört?
Was habt ihr gegessen und getrunken? Wie war die Fete?

H. Eine Party für die Klasse. In groups of three, plan a party for the class. Consider the following arrangements.

Wer gibt die Party?
Wieviel Gäste wollt ihr einladen?
Was wollt ihr machen? Tanzen?
Wer bringt die Musik?
Was wollt ihr essen? Trinken?
Wer bringt was?

Present your ideas to the class. Whichever group comes up with the best ideas gets to send out invitations!

I. Lebensmittel. With a partner, group as many foods as you can into categories of your own choosing. When you have your list ready, read it to other teams. They have to guess what your category is. You may want to categorize according to food groups, color, spelling considerations, things that can be eaten for certain meals, and so on.

J. Land und Leute.

1. What is usually offered for breakfast in a German-speaking country? Does it differ from what you would normally eat?
2. Assume you are going to the German-speaking countries. Compared to the U.S., what differences will you experience in table manners and while dining at a restaurant?
3. In the cultural notes there are four items that you would eat at a different time of day or for a different meal if you were in a German-speaking country. What are they?

Kaffeestunde

Kaffeestunde mit
Freundinnen

Am Sonntag trinken viele Deutsche nachmittags Kaffee. Sie trinken aber natürlich nicht nur Kaffee, sondern sie essen auch Kuchen. Manche Familien trinken fast jeden Nachmittag Kaffee, nicht nur am Sonntag.

Es ist besonders° schön, nachmittags in ein Café oder in eine Konditorei° zu
5 gehen. Da gibt es viele Torten und Kuchen. Alles schmeckt ausgezeichnet, besonders mit Sahne°.

Oft kommen Freunde zum Kaffee zusammen. Frau Weiß lädt Familie Kuhn ein: „Können Sie am Sonntag zu uns zum Kaffee kommen? Sagen wir° um halb fünf?"

Pünktlich° um halb fünf stehen° Herr und Frau Kuhn vor der Tür. Herr Kuhn
10 hat Blumen° in der Hand. Er gibt sie Frau Weiß. Der Kaffeetisch sieht° sehr schön aus: Auf dem Tisch ist eine schöne weiße Tischdecke°; Tassen und Teller° sind aus Porzellan°; die Blumen sind frisch; und natürlich gibt es viel Kuchen und Sahne. Ein schöner Nachmittag.

especially / shop serving
   pastries and coffee

whipped cream

let's say

punctually / stand

flowers / **sieht . . . aus:**
   looks

tablecloth / plates /
   china

A. Choose the word or phrase that best completes each statement, based on the reading.

1. . . . jeden Tag Kaffee.
   a. Kein Deutscher trinkt
   b. Viele Deutsche trinken
   c. Alle Deutschen trinken
   d. Alte Deutsche trinken

2. Wenn man „zum Kaffee" kommt, bekommt man . . .
   a. nur Kaffee.
   b. ein warmes Essen.
   c. Kaffee und Kuchen.
   d. nur Kuchen.

3. „Kaffee" trinkt man . . .
   a. morgens.
   b. abends.
   c. zu Mittag.
   d. nachmittags.

4. . . . gibt es nachmittags viele Torten und Kuchen.
   a. Auf dem Markt
   b. In einem Geschäft
   c. In einem Supermarkt
   d. In einer Konditorei

5. Wenn man zum Kaffee eingeladen ist, bringt man oft . . .
   a. Blumen.
   b. Tassen und Teller.
   c. Bücher.
   d. einen Kuchen.

6. Ein Stück Torte schmeckt besonders gut mit . . .
   a. Butter.
   b. Sahne.
   c. Porzellan.
   d. Tischdecken.

B. Which of the following things would you expect to find when invited **zum Kaffee?**

Torte, eine weiße Tischdecke, Wurst, Tomaten, Teller aus Porzellan, Pudding, frische Blumen, Tee, Speisekarte, Salat, Sahne, Kaffee.

Vokabeln

Substantive

der **Durst** thirst
der **Fisch, —e** fish
der **Gast, ⁻e** guest
der **Hunger** hunger
der **Kartoffelchip, —s** potato chip
der **Mittag** noon
der **Nachtisch** dessert
der **Ober, —** waiter; **Herr Ober!** Waiter!
der **Pudding** pudding
der **Rindsbraten, —** roast beef, pot roast
der **Salat, —e** (head of) lettuce; salad
der **Tee** tea
der **Thunfisch, —e** tuna

das **Abendessen** supper
das **Brot, —e** sandwich; das **[Schinken]brot** [ham] sandwich
das **Brötchen, —** hard roll
das **Eis** ice cream; ice
das **Essen** meal
das **Fräulein** (term of address for a waitress)
das **Getränk, —e** beverage
das **Huhn, ⁻er** chicken
das **Kartoffelpüree** mashed potatoes
das **Mineralwasser** mineral water
das **Mittagessen** lunch
das **Restaurant, —s** restaurant

die **Cola** (*also* das **Cola**) cola drink
die **Limo(nade)** soft drink
die **Marmelade** jam
die **Rechnung, —en** check (bill)
die **Schokolade, —n** chocolate, hot chocolate; bar of chocolate
die **Speisekarte, —n** menu
die **Suppe, —n** soup
die **Tasse, —n** cup

die **Pommes frites** *(pl.)* French fries

Verben

bestellen to order
bringen (gebracht) to bring
empfehlen (ie; empfohlen) to recommend
frühstücken to have breakfast
zahlen to pay; **zahlen, bitte!** the check please!

Andere Wörter

als as
ausgezeichnet excellent
gewöhnlich usually
manch(-er, -es, -e) *(sg.)* many a; **manche** *(pl.)* some, several
manchmal sometimes
mittags at noon, at lunch time
nachmittags in the afternoon
nicht nur . . . sondern auch not only . . . but also
solch(-er, -es, -e) *(sg.)* such a; **solche** *(pl.)* such
sondern but (on the contrary)
zart tender, delicate

Besondere Ausdrücke

Durst haben to be thirsty
Hunger haben to be hungry
guten Appetit! enjoy your meal
ich esse lieber . . . I prefer to eat . . .
zum Frühstück for breakfast
zum Mittagessen for lunch
zum Abendessen for supper
zu Abend essen to have supper
zu Mittag essen to have lunch
bitte sehr certainly
vielen Dank! thank you very much
wie lange? how long?

Kapitel 13

Über das Wetter kann man immer sprechen

Gewitter (storm) *überm Genfer See bei Montreux*

Ein Quiz

Was weißt du über das Wetter in Deutschland?

Weißt du,

wo es im Sommer wärmer ist — in Ohio oder in Deutschland?
was wärmer ist — 60 Grad Fahrenheit oder 20 Grad Celsius?
wo es im Winter kälter ist — in Pittsburgh oder in Bonn?
welche Stadt nördlicher liegt — New York oder München?
welche Stadt südlicher liegt — Chicago oder Frankfurt?
wo es im Winter mehr schneit — in Minnesota oder in Norddeutschland?
wo es öfter regnet — in den Smoky Mountains oder im Schwarzwald°? Black Forest

How did you do? Answers are printed on page 304.

In Deutschland ist das Wetter anders

Jim aus° St. Louis besucht seinen Freund Klaus in Kassel. Klaus findet es heiß — from
Jim findet es warm.

Es ist Juli. In Kassel ist das Wetter gut. Die Sonne scheint. Jim ist gerade erst drei
Tage in Kassel, da° sagt Klaus: „Heute ist es wirklich heiß, furchtbar heiß." Jim at that time
aber denkt: Heiß? Hier? Jetzt? Nein! Schön warm.

 In Deutschland ist das Wetter anders, denn Deutschland liegt weiter nördlich
als Amerika. Bonn, die Hauptstadt der° Bundesrepublik Deutschland, liegt circa° of the / approximately
1300 Kilometer weiter nördlich als Washington, die amerikanische Hauptstadt.
Auch beeinflußt° der Atlantische Ozean das Klima°. So ist das Wetter oft kühl im influences / climate
Sommer und nicht so kalt im Winter. Der Wind kommt gewöhnlich von Westen
und bringt vom Atlantischen Ozean Regen mit. Es regnet also viel; und Jim lernt,
daß man einen Regenschirm mitnimmt, wenn man spazierengeht.

Fragen

1. Liegt St. Louis oder Kassel weiter nördlich?
2. Wie heißt die Hauptstadt der Bundesrepublik?
3. Wie heißt die Hauptstadt der USA?
4. Wie ist das Wetter oft im Sommer in Deutschland?
5. Was kommt von Westen?
6. Was bringt der Wind mit?
7. Was nimmt Jim mit, wenn er spazierengeht?

Wie ist das Wetter?

Im Frühling

STEFAN	Was meinst du? Regnet es morgen wieder?
KARIN	Wahrscheinlich.
STEFAN	Das ist wirklich dumm!
KARIN	Warum?
STEFAN	Mein Regenschirm ist kaputt.

Im Sommer

DIETER	Heute ist es schön, nicht?
INGRID	Ja, endlich ist es mal warm.
DIETER	Hoffentlich wird es nicht zu heiß.
INGRID	Lieber zu heiß als zu kalt.

Im Herbst

FRAU KRAFT	Schönes Wetter, nicht?
HERR WOLF	Ja, ich habe diese Jahreszeit besonders gern. Es ist so schön° kühl.
FRAU KRAFT	Das ist gutes Wanderwetter.
HERR WOLF	Zu dumm, daß wir arbeiten müssen.

Im Winter

RALF	Der Wind ist aber ganz schön° kalt heute morgen.
ILSE	Ja, es hat letzte Nacht gefroren.
RALF	Heute nachmittag soll es schneien.
ILSE	Das ist ja prima. Dann können wir rodeln gehen.

Fragen

1. Warum ist Stefan unglücklich?
2. Hat Ingrid es lieber warm oder kalt?
3. Warum findet Herr Wolf den Herbst schön?
4. Was macht Ilse gern im Winter?

Wannsee, Berlin (West): Möchtest du bei diesen Temperaturen schwimmen?

Du hast das Wort

1. **Das Wetter.** Ask two classmates their preferences concerning the weather. Make notes so you can compare the results.

   Discussing preferences

   Hast du es lieber kalt oder warm?
   Hast du den Winter oder den Sommer lieber? Den Frühling oder den Herbst?
   Magst du Regen? Schnee°?
   Welchen Sport treibst du im Frühling? Im Herbst?
   Welchen Sport treibst du im Winter? Im Sommer?

2. **Wie ist das Wetter?** Half the class (Group A) gets cards with comments on the weather. The other half (Group B) gets cards with responses that express agreement or disagreement. Students in Group A make comments to students in Group B, who may respond with one of the sentences on the cards or make up their own.

   Agreeing or disagreeing

GROUP A (COMMENTS)	GROUP B (RESPONSES)
Morgen soll es wieder regnen.	Das stimmt.
Heute ist es schön.	Das finde ich auch.
Es hat letzte Nacht gefroren.	Du hast recht°.
Heute soll es schneien.	Das glaube ich nicht.
Jetzt regnet es schon eine Woche.	Das kann nicht stimmen.
Morgen soll es wieder heiß werden.	Du spinnst°.
Schönes Wetter heute, nicht?	Meinst du?
	Glaubst du?

Das Thermometer

37°C = 98.6°F

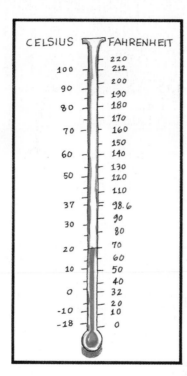

100°C = 212°F

–18°C = 0°F

0°C = 32°F

In German-speaking countries the Celsius thermometer is used. To find out the temperature, a German asks: **Wieviel Grad haben wir heute?** The answer may be **Es sind [15] Grad** or **Heute haben wir [15] Grad.**

A. Wieviel Grad? What's the temperature in degrees Celsius? *Wieviel Grad Celsius sind . . .*

1. 12°F
2. 98.6°F
3. 68°F
4. 32°F
5. 212°F
6. 80°F

Answers to the weather-quiz:
1. Ohio   2. 20 Grad Celsius   3. Pittsburgh   4. München
5. Chicago   6. Minnesota   7. Schwarzwald

Das Wetter und ein Wetterbericht

Es schneit.
Die Straßen sind glatt.

Es regnet.
Die Straßen sind naß.

Es ist windig.
Es ist kalt.

Es ist bewölkt.
Es ist kühl.

Die Sonne scheint.
Es ist warm.

Es ist heiß.
Es ist trocken.

B. Wie ist das Wetter? You're looking at pictures of friends. Judging from their clothing or activities tell what the weather was probably like.

Reporting on the weather

▶ Katrin läuft Ski.   *Es war kalt. Es hat geschneit.*

1. Ralf geht schwimmen.
2. Cornelia trägt einen Pullover.
3. Veronika trägt einen Regenmantel.
4. Axel will nicht aus dem Haus gehen.
5. Sandra versucht, braun zu werden.
6. Doris und Ulf spielen Tennis.
7. Rudi trägt eine leichte Jacke.
8. Renate und Jens rodeln.
9. Matthias trägt eine Badehose°.

C. Meine Stadt: das Wetter. Christa, a Swiss exchange student, is going to spend a year at your school. Tell her what the weather is like during the following months.

▶ August   *Im August ist es sehr heiß und trocken.*

1. Oktober   3. Dezember   5. März   7. Juli
2. November   4. Februar   6. Mai

D. Tag für Tag. Jim made a report of the weather in Kassel in early March for his class at home. Using his report as a model, keep your own daily record of the weather for a week, recording the temperature in degrees Celsius.

Montag	Es hat den ganzen Tag geregnet. Es war kalt; nur 6 Grad.
Dienstag	Bewölkt und kühl. Es waren 8 Grad.
Mittwoch	Die Sonne hat endlich geschienen. Es war fast warm — 12 Grad.
Donnerstag	Es war wieder kühl und windig. Es waren 10 Grad. Furchtbares Wetter.
Freitag	Es war sehr kalt. Es hat wieder geregnet. Temperatur: 7 Grad.
Samstag	Am Morgen war es noch kühl. Aber am Nachmittag hat die Sonne geschienen. Es waren 13 Grad. Abends ist es wieder kühl geworden.
Sonntag	Es war sehr schön — die Sonne war fast heiß. Es waren 18 Grad.

Im Frühling und im Herbst ist es oft sehr windig.

Aussprache

[χ] ach, noch, Buch, auch

The sound [χ] is made in the back of the mouth, where the sound [k] is pronounced. It is produced by forcing air through a narrow opening between the back of the tongue and the back of the roof of the mouth. To produce the sound [χ], keep the tongue below the lower front teeth and, without moving the tongue or lips, make a gentle gargling noise. Do not substitute the [k] sound for the [χ] sound.

A. Practice the following words horizontally in pairs.

[k]	[χ]	[k]	[χ]
nackt	Nacht	locken	lochen
back!	Bach	Pocken	pochen
lacken	lachen	buk	Buch
Dock	doch	Hauke	hauche

The sound [χ] is represented by the letters **-ch** and occurs after the vowels **a, o, u,** and **au.**

B. Practice the following words.

ach, machen, nach
noch, **d**och, kochen

Buch, **K**uchen, versuchen
auch, brauchen, tauchen

Wer zuletzt lacht, lacht am besten.

C. Practice the sound [χ]. Read the sentences aloud.

1. Frau Meier bäckt jede Woche einen Kuchen.
2. Was machen wir noch?
3. Heute nachmittag besuchen wir Herrn Luckenbach.

Übungen

1. Comparison of adjectives and adverbs

Comparison of equality

Bernd ist **so alt wie** Jens.	Bernd is *as old as* Jens.
Er arbeitet aber nicht **so viel wie** Jens.	He doesn't work *as much as* Jens, however.

The German construction **so . . . wie** is equivalent to the English construction *as . . . as.*

A. Gut in Sport. Inge sagt, ihre Freunde sind gut in Sport. Sag, du bist nicht so gut wie sie!

▶ Ulrike spielt gut Tennis.   *Ich spiele nicht so gut wie sie.*

1. Dieter schwimmt gut.
2. Anja spielt oft Volleyball.
3. Kerstin reitet schön.
4. Benno geht oft bergsteigen.
5. Jörg segelt viel.
6. Inge spielt viel Hockey.
7. Klaus läuft gut.

Comparison of inequality

Base form	klein	Ute ist klein.	Ute is *small.*
Comparative	kleiner	Ute ist **kleiner als** Petra.	Ute is *smaller than* Petra.

The comparative of an adjective or adverb is formed by adding **-er** to the base form. The word **als** is equivalent to *than.*

B. Wie sind die Sachen? Du gehst mit Gerda einkaufen. Du findest viele Sachen anders als sie. Sag das bitte!

▶ Der Pulli da ist schön.   *Ja, aber der Pulli hier ist noch schöner.*

1. Die Bluse da ist schön.
2. Das Hemd da ist dünn.
3. Der Gürtel da ist toll.
4. Der Mantel da ist leicht.
5. Die Krawatte da ist furchtbar.
6. Die Jacke da ist billig.
7. Die Schuhe da sind schwer.
8. Die Socken da sind billig.

Base form	groß	Petra ist groß.	Petra is *tall.*
Comparative	größer	Petra ist größer als Ute.	Petra is *taller than* Ute.

Many one-syllable adjectives and adverbs add an umlaut in the comparative:
älter/jünger; kürzer/länger; wärmer/kälter; größer; dümmer.

C. Das stimmt nicht! Michael weiß nicht alles. Sag, alles ist anders als er meint!

▶ Ulf ist älter als Katja, nicht?   *Unsinn, er ist jünger.*

1. Aber Katja ist jünger als Susanne, nicht?
2. Katja ist kleiner als Susanne, nicht?
3. Aber Katja ist kleiner als Ulf, nicht?
4. Es ist heute wärmer als gestern, nicht?
5. Aber gestern war es kälter als am Samstag, nicht?
6. Dieses Jahr ist es wärmer als letztes Jahr, nicht?

Base form	gern	gut	viel	hoch
Comparative	lieber	besser	mehr	höher

A few adjectives and adverbs are irregular in the formation of their comparatives.

D. Du weißt mehr. Du sprichst mit Klaus über eure Freunde. Gib Klaus mehr Information!

▶ Liese spielt gern Basketball. — Und Tennis?   *Sie spielt lieber Tennis.*

1. Ernst spielt gern Klavier. — Und Gitarre?
2. Jens reitet gut. — Und Erik?
3. Eva tanzt gut. — Und Cornelia?
4. Ingrid singt hoch. — Und Heike?
5. Dietmar arbeitet viel. — Und sein Bruder?
6. Karin liest viel. — Und ihre Schwester?

Du hast das Wort

1. **Was machst du gern?** Complete the following sentences according to what you like to play, do, listen to, and so on.

Expressing preferences

Ich spiele gern _____.   Ich höre gern _____.
          _____.   _____.
Ich gehe gern ins _____.   Ich mache gern _____.
          _____.   _____.
Ich trinke gern _____.   Ich esse gern _____.
          _____.   _____.

When you are finished, show your list to a partner. She/he will ask you which of the two you prefer doing.

Was spielst du lieber — Tennis oder Basketball?

2. **Was machst du besser?** List five things you can do better than someone else.

Ich kann besser singen als mein Vater.

3. **Was machst du nicht so gut?** List five things you can't do as well as someone else.

Ich kann nicht so gut Tennis spielen wie Peter.

2. The verb **werden**

Present tense of **werden**

ich werde		wir werden
du **wirst**	Sie werden	ihr werdet
er/es/sie **wird**		sie werden

The verb **werden** is irregular in the **du-** and **er/es/sie**-forms of the present tense.

E. Sie werden müde. Ihr treibt viel Sport auf dem Picknick. Alle werden müde. Sag es bitte!

▶ Erik   *Erik wird müde.*

1. Petra
2. ich
3. Christl
4. du

5. wir
6. ihr
7. Hans und Karin

Wenn es mal spät wird ...

... mit unseren BVG-Nachtbussen kommen Sie immer gut nach Hause.

Conversational past of **werden**

Ich **bin** müde **geworden.**	I've become tired.
Herr Lenz **ist** alt **geworden.**	Mr. Lenz has grown old.

Because the verb **werden** expresses a change of condition, it requires **sein** as an auxiliary in the conversational past.

F. Sie sind anders geworden. Karin spricht von Freunden. Sie sind nicht wie sie waren. Sag, sie sind wirklich anders geworden!

▶ Herr Fischer ist aber alt, nicht?   *Ja, er ist wirklich alt geworden.*

1. Dieter ist aber groß, nicht?
2. Herr Schmidt ist aber dick, nicht?
3. Frau Meier ist furchtbar dünn, nicht?
4. Peter ist sehr faul, nicht?
5. Ingrid ist schön schlank, nicht?

Du hast das Wort

Wie alt wirst du? Ask five classmates two questions about their age. Keep track of the answers.

Asking for personal information

DU	GESPRÄCHSPARTNER/IN
Wann hast du Geburtstag?	Im [August].
Wie alt wirst du?	Ich werde [16].
Wann wirst du 20?	[19__].

3. Indirect statements

Direct statement	Petra sagt: „Jan spielt morgen Tennis."
Indirect statement	Petra sagt, **daß** Jan morgen Tennis spielt.

An indirect statement is a dependent clause. A dependent clause is introduced by a subordinating conjunction, for example **daß.** In a dependent clause, the verb is in final position.

G. Was sagt und macht Jens? Sag, was Jens meint und was er macht!

▶ Der Pulli ist häßlich.   *Jens sagt, daß der Pulli häßlich ist.*

1. Er kauft ihn nicht.
2. Er findet die Jacke aber schön.

3. Sie kostet zuviel.
4. Sie ist zu teuer.
5. Er kauft sie auch nicht.

| Direct statement | Petra sagt: „Jan ruft uns später an." |
| Indirect statement | Petra sagt, **daß** Jan uns später **anruft**. |

In a dependent clause, the separable prefix is attached to the base form of the verb, which is in final position.

H. Was sagen Ingrid und Gisela? Sag Carola, was Ingrid und Gisela gesagt haben!

▶ Stehen Ingrid und Gisela   *Sie sagen, daß sie immer*
      immer früh auf?   *früh aufstehen.*

1. Kommen sie heute mit?   3. Kaufen sie morgen ein?
2. Rufen sie uns später noch an?   4. Haben sie Samstag etwas vor?

| Direct statement | Petra sagt: „Jan muß jetzt gehen." |
| Indirect statement | Petra sagt, **daß** Jan jetzt **gehen muß**. |

In a dependent clause, the modal auxiliary follows the infinitive and is in final position.

I. Was macht Marianne heute? Jens fragt, was Marianne heute machen will. Du glaubst, es stimmt, was er sagt. Sag das!

▶ Will sie arbeiten?   *Ja, ich glaube, daß sie arbeiten will.*

1. Muß sie zu Hause helfen?
2. Soll sie das Essen kochen?
3. Will sie dann fernsehen?
4. Muß sie noch Mathe machen?
5. Kann sie um zehn Uhr anrufen?

| Direct statement | Petra sagt: „Jan hat Mathe gemacht." |
| Indirect statement | Petra sagt, **daß** Jan Mathe **gemacht hat**. |

In a dependent clause in the conversational past, the auxiliary verb **haben** or **sein** follows the past participle and is in final position.

J. Frank war fleißig. Deine Eltern möchten wissen, wer soviel zu Hause gearbeitet hat. Frank sagt, daß er alles gemacht hat. Sag das!

▶ Wer hat die Garage *Frank sagt, daß er die*
  aufgeräumt? *Garage aufgeräumt hat.*

1. Wer hat die Fenster geputzt?
2. Wer hat Staub gesaugt?
3. Wer hat die Wäsche gewaschen?
4. Wer hat die Torte gebacken?

4. Indirect questions

Specific questions

Direct question	**Wer ist** das Mädchen?
Indirect question	Paul möchte wissen, **wer** das Mädchen **ist.**

An indirect question is a dependent clause; therefore, the verb is in final position. In indirect *specific* questions (that is, questions introduced by an interrogative like **wer**), the interrogative functions as a subordinating conjunction.

K. Günter gibt eine Party. Günter hat bald Geburtstag, und er gibt eine Party. Du willst viele Sachen wissen. Frag deine Klassenfreunde!

▶ Wo ist die Party? *Weißt du, wo die Party ist?*

1. Wen hat Günter eingeladen?
2. Was machen wir?
3. Was gibt es zu essen?
4. Wer soll den Kuchen backen?
5. Was soll ich mitbringen?
6. Wie alt wird Günter?

General questions

Direct question	**Kommt** Inge zur Party?
Indirect question	Günter möchte wissen, **ob** Inge zur Party **kommt.**

In indirect *general* questions (that is, questions that can be answered by **ja** or **nein**), the indirect-question clause is introduced by **ob** *(whether, if).*

Weißt du, ob diese junge Berlinerin ins Kino gehen möchte?

L. Ich weiß es nicht. Heute ist Montag. Was haben Petra und Rainer am Wochenende gemacht? Sag, du weißt nicht, was sie gemacht haben!

▶ Hat Rainer gearbeitet?   *Ich weiß nicht, ob er gearbeitet hat.*

1. Hat Petra zu Hause geholfen?
2. Sind sie schwimmen gegangen?
3. Sind Dieter und Inge mitgefahren?
4. Haben sie einen Spaziergang gemacht?
5. Sind sie zusammen ins Kino gegangen?

Grammatische Übersicht

Comparison of adjectives and adverbs (A–D)

Regular forms

| Base form | leicht | easy | schön | beautiful |
| Comparative | leichter | easier | schöner | more beautiful |

German forms the comparative of adjectives and adverbs by adding the suffix **-er** to the base form. Note that English can form the comparative either by adding *-er* to the base form or by using the modifier *more*.

Forms with umlaut

Base form	alt	groß	jung
Comparative	älter	größer	jünger

Many one-syllable adjectives and adverbs add an umlaut in the comparative: **älter, dümmer, größer, jünger, kälter, kürzer, länger, wärmer.** From now on, adjectives and adverbs of this type will be listed in the vocabularies of this book as follows: **kalt (ä).**

Irregular forms

Base form	gern	gut	hoch	viel
Comparative	lieber	besser	höher	mehr

A few adjectives and adverbs are irregular in the comparative form.

so . . . wie

Bernd spielt nicht **so gut wie** Jens.

Bernd doesn't play *as well as* Jens.

The construction **so . . . wie** with the base form of the adjective or adverb is used to make comparisons of equality. It is equivalent to English *as . . . as.*

Comparative with als

Jens ist **größer als** Erik.
Petra tanzt **besser als** Gretl.

Jens is *taller than* Erik.
Petra dances *better than* Gretl.

The comparative form of the adjective or adverb with **als** is used to make comparisons of inequality. **Als** is equivalent to English *than.*

Ständig gut sortiertes Neuwagenlager.

Kommen Sie zur unverbindlichen Probefahrt.

Autohaus [OPEL] [GM] **Breisgau**

Mit uns fahren Sie besser.

Autohaus Breisgau · Prinz zu Fürstenberg KG a. A.
Zähringer Str. 40 · 7800 Freiburg · Tel 0761/50511

The verb **werden** (E–F)

Present tense

ich werde	Sie werden	wir werden
du **wirst**		ihr werdet
er/es/sie **wird**		sie werden

Werden is irregular in the **du-** and **er/es/sie**-forms of the present tense.

Ich **werde** müde.	I *am getting* tired.
Der Mann **wird** alt.	The man *is growing* old.
Wie alt **wirst** du?	How old *are* you *going to be?*
Was möchtest du **werden?**	What would you like *to be?*

English uses a number of different verbs to express the many ideas of **werden.**

Conversational past

Frank **ist** krank **geworden.**   Frank *became* ill.

Because the verb **werden** expresses a change of condition, it requires **sein** as an auxiliary in the conversational past.

Word order in dependent clauses (G–L)

INDEPENDENT CLAUSE	SUBORDINATING CONJUNCTION	DEPENDENT CLAUSE
Ute sagt,	daß	sie morgen Tennis spielt.
Sie möchte wissen,	ob	du auch spielen willst.

A dependent clause cannot stand alone as a complete sentence. It is introduced by a subordinating conjunction, such as **daß** or **ob.** The conjunction is always preceded by a comma.

Verb in final position

1. In a dependent clause, the verb is in final position:

   Ingrid sagt, daß sie in die Stadt **fährt.**

2. A separable prefix is attached to the base form of the verb, which is in final position:

   Sie sagt, daß Astrid **mitfährt.**

3. A modal auxiliary follows the infinitive and is in final position:

   Sie sagt, daß sie in die Stadt **fahren müssen.**

4. In the conversational past, the auxiliary verb **haben** or **sein** follows the past participle and is in final position:

   Sie sagt, daß sie gestern nicht **gefahren sind.**

Indirect statements

Direct statement	Ingrid sagt: „Jan macht jetzt Mathe."
Indirect statement	Ingrid sagt, **daß** Jan jetzt Mathe **macht.**

Indirect statements are introduced by the subordinating conjunction **daß** *(that).*

Indirect specific questions

Direct question	**Wann** macht Jens Mathe?
Indirect question	Ich möchte wissen, **wann** Jens Mathe **macht.**

Indirect specific questions are introduced by the same interrogatives that are used to introduce direct specific questions.

Indirect general questions

Direct question	**Macht** Ingrid jetzt Mathe?
Indirect question	Ich weiß nicht, **ob** Ingrid jetzt Mathe **macht.**

Indirect general questions are introduced by the subordinating conjunction **ob** *(whether, if).*

Wenn ich weiß

Zu 3 Stimmen

Franz Lachner (1803–1890)

Wenn ich weiß, was du weißt, und du weißt, was
ich weiß, dann weiß ich, was du weißt, und du weißt, was
ich weiß. Dann weiß ich, was du weißt, dann weiß ich, was
du weißt, und du weißt, und du weißt, was ich weiß,
wenn ich weiß, was du weißt, und du weißt, was ich weiß,
dann weiß ich, was du weißt, und du weißt, was ich weiß.

Wiederholung

A. Drei Sätze. Make three sets of comparisons for each pair of sentences.

▶ Ich bin 1,40 m groß. Mein
   Bruder ist 1,30.

        Ich bin größer als mein Bruder.
        Mein Bruder ist kleiner als ich.
        Mein Bruder ist nicht so groß wie ich.

1. Ich bin sechzehn Jahre alt.
   Meine Schwester ist erst dreizehn.
2. Dieser Bleistift ist 17 cm lang.
   Dieser Kugelschreiber ist nur 13 cm lang.
3. Im August haben wir oft 30 Grad.
   Im Januar haben wir oft 0 Grad.
4. Gisela läuft einen Kilometer in drei Minuten.
   Jan läuft einen Kilometer in vier Minuten.

B. Eine fleißige Familie. Form sentences in the present tense, using the cues provided.

1. Trudi / helfen / viel / zu Hause
2. sie / raustragen / der Mülleimer
3. am Wochenende / sie / waschen / das Auto
4. sie / müssen / auch / machen / Gartenarbeit
5. sie / werden / einfach / nicht / müde
6. sie / tragen / gern / alte Jeans
7. ihr Vater / lesen / abends / gern
8. ihr Bruder / fernsehen / lieber

C. Letztes Wochenende. Jörg and Sabine are discussing a typical weekend. Restate their conversation in the conversational past.

1. Stehst du früh auf?
   Nein, ich schlafe bis neun.
2. Fährst du in die Stadt?
   Nein. Birgit und ich gehen windsurfen.
3. Macht das Spaß?
   Ja. Aber ich falle zu oft ins Wasser.
4. Wann kommt ihr nach Hause?
   Um fünf. Wir essen um sechs zu Abend.
5. Seht ihr fern?
   Nein. Wir gehen ins Kino.

D. Welches Wort? Complete each sentence with one of the following prepositions.

durch   für   gegen   ohne   um

1. Gerd geht _____ den Supermarkt.
2. Er kommt oft _____ seine Familie.
3. _____ seinen Bruder Otto kauft er ein Stück Apfelkuchen.
4. Er kauft nichts _____ Trudi.
5. Hat er etwas _____ seine Schwester?
6. _____ drei Uhr kommt er wieder nach Hause.

E. Heute abend. Choose the appropriate conjunction to connect each pair of sentences.

▶ Willst du heute abend fernsehen?   *Willst du heute abend fernsehen,*
   (oder, aber)   *oder willst du lieber ins Kino?*
   Willst du lieber ins Kino?

1. Ich kann ins Kino.   (oder, denn)
   Ich habe meine Hausaufgaben schon gemacht.
2. Meine Hausaufgaben sind nicht fertig.   (sondern, aber)
   Ich kann sie später machen.

3. Ich lade Paula ein. (und, sondern)
   Du kannst Heidi einladen.
4. Ich möchte nicht Heidi einladen. (aber, sondern)
   Ich möchte Ute einladen.
5. Ruf sie jetzt an! (denn, oder)
   Es wird zu spät.

F. Was bedeutet das? Give the individual words that make up the compounds, and supply the definite article for each noun. Then give the English equivalents of the compounds.

▶ die Wintersonne   *der Winter, die Sonne (winter sun)*

1. der Sonnenschirm   3. die Windjacke   5. der Schneemann
2. der Wetterbericht   4. der Stadtplan   6. der Regenmantel

*Ein Wintertag in
Rothenburg ob der
Tauber (Bayern)*

G. Wie sagt man das? Express the following conversation in German.

DIETER	Hi, Gisela. How are you?
GISELA	Hi, Dieter. Fine, thanks.
DIETER	Do you have anything planned for today?
GISELA	This morning I have to wash our car and clean out the garage. But this afternoon I'm free.
DIETER	Would you like to go swimming?
GISELA	Glad to. It's hot.
DIETER	I'll pick you up at two-thirty.
GISELA	Great. See you later.

H. Was machst du, wenn . . . ? You are in charge of planning a week with your friends, either in the winter or in the summer. Ask five classmates what they like to do during certain weather conditions. Try to come up with a few activities you could share.

1. Was machst du gern, wenn es sehr heiß ist?
2. Was machst du, wenn die Sonne scheint und es nicht zu heiß ist?
3. Was machst du, wenn es regnet?
4. Was machst du, wenn es sehr kalt ist?

Regenmäntel und Regenschirme–Regentag am Kölner Dom

Geographie

An der Nordseeküste–Wasser und flaches Land

Deutschland liegt im Zentrum Europas und hat neun Nachbarländer°: im Norden Dänemark; im Westen die Niederlande, Belgien, Luxemburg und Frankreich; im Süden die Schweiz und Österreich; und im Osten die Tschechoslowakei und Polen. Man spricht nicht nur in Deutschland Deutsch, sondern auch in Österreich und in einem Teil° der° Schweiz. Seit° 1949 gibt es zwei deutsche Staaten — im Osten die Deutsche Demokratische Republik (DDR) und im Westen die Bundesrepublik Deutschland.

    In Deutschland ist das Land im Norden flach°. In der Mitte gibt es die Mittelgebirge°. Im Süden liegen die Alpen, ein Hochgebirge°. Die großen Flüsse° — der Rhein, die Weser, die Elbe und die Oder — fließen° von Süden nach Norden in die Nordsee und in die Ostsee. Nur die Donau fließt von Westen nach Osten.

Margin glosses:
neighboring countries

part / of the / since

flat
low mountains / high mountains / rivers
flow

In den bayerischen Alpen–hohe Berge und enge Täler (narrow valleys)

Im Norden sind die großen Hafenstädte°: Bremen an der Weser, Hamburg an der Elbe und Rostock an der Ostsee. In der Mitte gibt es im Westen viel Kohle°. Daher° ist an der Ruhr das deutsche Schwerindustriezentrum°. Nur ein kleiner Teil von Deutschland liegt in den Alpen. Aber Österreich und die Schweiz sind vor allem° Alpenländer. Hier findet man daher die international bekannten° Wintersportzentren wie Zermatt und St. Moritz, oder Innsbruck und Kitzbühel.

port cities
coal
therefore / center of mining and iron and steel industry
above all / famous

Richtig oder falsch?

1. In Deutschland liegen die Berge im Norden.
2. Das Land im Süden ist flach.
3. Die Weser und die Elbe sind Flüsse.
4. Die Donau und die Oder fließen von Westen nach Osten.
5. Der Rhein fließt von Süden nach Norden.
6. Hamburg ist eine Hafenstadt.
7. Die Ruhr ist ein Alpenland.
8. Die deutsche Schwerindustrie liegt im Hochgebirge.
9. Kitzbühel liegt in den Alpen.

Substantive

der Atlantische Ozean Atlantic Ocean
der Bericht, —e report
der Grad degree
der Norden north
der Osten east
der Regen rain
der Regenschirm, —e umbrella
der Schnee snow
der Süden south
der Westen west
der Wetterbericht, —e weather report
der Wind wind

das Thermometer, — thermometer
das Wetter weather

die Badehose, —n bathing trunks
die Hauptstadt, ⸚e capital city
die Jahreszeit, —en season, time of the year
die Sonne, —n sun
die Temperatur, —en temperature

Verben

denken (gedacht) to think
frieren (gefroren) to freeze, to be very cold
liegen (gelegen) to lie; to be (situated)
mit·bringen (mitgebracht) to bring along
mit·nehmen (i; mitgenommen) to take along
regnen to rain
rodeln (ist gerodelt) to toboggan
scheinen (geschienen) to shine
schneien to snow
sprechen (i; gesprochen) to speak
werden (wird; ist geworden) to become

Andere Wörter

amerikanisch American
anders different
besonders particularly, especially
bewölkt cloudy, overcast
daß *(conj.)* that
endlich finally
glatt slippery
heiß hot
kalt (ä) cold
kühl cool
naß wet
nördlich northern, north of
ob *(conj.)* whether, if
südlich southern, south of
trocken dry
über about; above; over
wahrscheinlich probably
weiter further
wenn *(conjunction)* if; when
windig windy

Besondere Ausdrücke

du hast recht you're right
du spinnst you're crazy
ganz schön kalt quite cold
lieber haben to like better, to prefer
noch [schöner] even more [beautiful]
schön kühl nice and cool

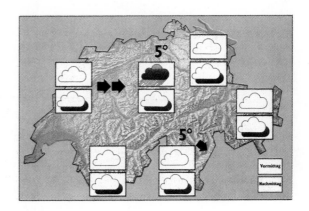

Kapitel 14

Christa macht den Führerschein

Sie ist über 18 und kann ihren Führerschein machen.

Aus Briefen an Jochen

Christa wird bald achtzehn und darf dann den Führerschein machen. Sie schreibt oft an ihren Freund Jochen und erzählt von ihren Fortschritten°. progress

Mittwoch, den 16.° Januar **sechzehnten:** sixteenth

. . . Du weißt, ich werde am Samstag 18. Dann kann ich endlich meinen Führerschein machen. Heute haben meine Eltern mich gefragt, was ich zum Geburtstag haben möchte. Vielleicht bezahlen sie ja das Geld oder wenigstens etwas Geld für die Fahrschule. . . .

Samstag, den 19. Januar

. . . Ich bin sehr glücklich. Ich habe von meinen Eltern das Geld für die Fahrschule bekommen. Vielleicht kann ich nächste Woche den Sehtest° machen eye test
und mit dem Erste-Hilfe-Kurs° beginnen. . . . first aid course

Dienstag, den 5. Februar

. . . Mit dem Erste-Hilfe-Kurs bin ich fertig. Mit dem Sehtest auch. Ich bin zur Fahrschule gegangen. Am Montag beginnt der theoretische° Unterricht; meine theoretical
erste Fahrstunde ist am Dienstag. . . .

Montag, den 18. Februar

. . . Der theoretische Unterricht ist furchtbar langweilig. Niemand macht ihn gern, aber er muß ja wohl sein. Die theoretische Prüfung soll sehr kompliziert sein. Hast Du auch gehört, daß 40%° durchfallen? . . . **Prozent:** percent

Freitag, den 7. März

. . . Der Fahrlehrer ist sehr nett. (Brauchst aber nicht eifersüchtig zu werden!) Es ist nur gut, daß er auch eine Bremse hat. Ich habe zu meinen Freunden schon gesagt, sie sollen abends zwischen 6 und 7 zu Hause bleiben. Da mache ich die Straßen unsicher . . .

Mittwoch, den 23. April

. . . Morgen ist die praktische Prüfung. Halt mir die Daumen, daß ich sie bestehe . . .

Donnerstag, den 24. April

. . . Heute habe ich die Fahrprüfung bestanden. Endlich! Die Prüfungsfahrt° ist road test
gut gegangen. Ich habe aber auch etwas Schwein gehabt. Nicht viele Autos auf den Straßen . . .

Dienstag, den 6. Mai

. . . Heute habe ich einen gebrauchten° VW gekauft. Was sagst Du nun? Jetzt kann ich endlich an den See fahren, wenn *ich* es will. Jetzt bin ich am Wochenende endlich unabhängig. . . .

used

Mittwoch, den 7. Mai

. . . große Diskussion mit meinen Eltern: Soll ich mit dem Auto zur Arbeit fahren? Es ist natürlich toll, mit dem Auto in die Stadt zu fahren. Aber Zug und Straßenbahn sind billiger. Je° weniger wir in der Woche fahren, desto° mehr können wir am Wochenende fahren. Ich fahre also jeden Tag mit dem Zug. Und dann mit der Straßenbahn. Leider! . . .

je (weniger) . . . desto (mehr) the (less) . . . the (more)

Richtig oder falsch?

1. In Deutschland macht man gewöhnlich erst mit achtzehn den Führerschein.
2. Christa möchte nichts zum Geburtstag.
3. Christa beginnt die Fahrschule mit dem praktischen Unterricht.
4. Christa kann gut sehen.
5. Der theoretische Unterricht ist interessant.
6. Die theoretische Prüfung soll nicht schwer sein.
7. Christa fällt in der theoretischen Prüfung durch.
8. Christa bleibt abends zwischen sechs und sieben zu Hause.
9. Christa hält die Bremse mit den Daumen.
10. Das Auto macht Christa am Wochenende unabhängiger.
11. Christa will nicht mit dem Auto zur Arbeit fahren.
12. Christa fährt mit dem Zug und mit der Straßenbahn, denn es ist billiger.

Du hast das Wort

1. **Machst du den Führerschein?** Ask a classmate about driver's education.

   Wieviel kostet die Fahrschule hier?
   Hast du Fahrunterricht gehabt?
   Hast du schon die Fahrprüfung gemacht? Hast du sie bestanden? Wieviel sind durchgefallen?
   Wieviel Bremsen hat dein Auto?

Talking about cars

2. **Was für ein Auto?**   Ask five classmates about their family cars. Make up a form to keep track of the answers.

Hast du oder hat deine Familie ein Auto?
Ist das Auto alt oder neu?
Welche Farbe hat dein Auto?
Was für ein Auto ist es? Ein amerikanisches? Ein japanisches? Ein deutsches? Ein französisches?

Land und Leute

Although some young people in the German-speaking countries have cars, most teenagers take public transportation, use mopeds or bicycles, or walk to school and work. The minimum age for a driver's license is eighteen (though exceptions are sometimes made for a sixteen-year-old who needs a car to make a living). Taking a course in a private driving school **(Fahrschule)** and passing a test are requirements for getting a license. In addition to taking driving lessons, the driving student **(Fahrschüler)** has to go to class one or two evenings a week and pass a written test. The final test is the **Fahrprüfung,** a thirty-minute driving test. The total cost of a license **(Führerschein)** is at least 1500 Marks, but once obtained it is valid for life.

Straßenbahnfahren ist oft einfacher und billiger als Autofahren. (Innsbruck, Österreich)

Dein Auto, dein Traumauto

Manche Teenager kaufen oder bekommen ein Auto, wenn sie den Führerschein machen. Wie ist es bei dir°? Hast du ein Auto? Oder hast du vielleicht nur ein Traumauto? Beschreibe° es!

bei dir: in your case

1. Was für ein Auto hast du? Was für ein Auto möchtest du haben?
2. Hast du das Auto gebraucht oder neu gekauft?
3. Ist das Auto groß oder klein?
4. Braucht das Auto viel Benzin? 7 Liter auf 100 Kilometer? 1 Gallone auf 20 Meilen°?

   eine Gallone auf 20 Meilen: 20 miles to the gallon

5. Läuft es gut?
6. Reparierst du gern alte Autos? Ist das dein Hobby?
7. Fährst du gern schnell oder lieber langsam?
8. Wie schnell fährst du auf der Landstraße°? Auf der Autobahn? In der Stadt? 90 Kilometer pro° Stunde? 55 Meilen pro Stunde?

   country road

   per

Land und Leute

The Federal Republic has an extensive highway system. Superhighways **(Autobahnen)** link major cities, and numerous other roads crisscross the country. With few exceptions, there is no speed limit **(Geschwindigkeitsbegrenzung)** on the **Autobahn,** and some people tend to drive at very high speeds when traffic and weather conditions permit.

The large number of vehicles in circulation (about one car for every two people) results in numerous traffic jams **(Staus),** especially on weekends and holidays. The traffic jams on the **Autobahn** are particularly bad at the beginning and end of school vacations, despite the fact that each German state has different vacation dates — an attempt to stagger arrivals and departures. School vacations begin as early as the middle of June and end as late as mid-September, depending on the state students live in.

Solche Staus gibt es auf der Autobahn oft.

Land und Leute

The letters before the dash on a German license plate tell you where the car is registered. A large city usually has one letter (**K** for **Köln**, **M** for **München**); three letters identify the smallest townships.

Dieses Auto kommt aus einer mittelgroßen Stadt. Landsberg am Lech ist in Bayern.

Du hast das Wort

Mein Traumauto. Think about your dream car. Your neighbor is going to try to guess what it is.

Describing your dream car

Ist dieses Auto alt oder neu?
Welche Farbe hat dein Auto?
Was für ein Auto ist es?
Läuft es gut?
Warum hast du dieses Auto gern?

Wie fährt man?

das Fahrrad (das Rad)

das Mofa

das Motorrad

der Zug

das Flugzeug

das Schiff

der Bus

die Straßenbahn

die U-Bahn

A. Wie oft fährst du? Find out from three classmates how often they use various means of transportation.

Discussing means of transportation

DU		GESPRÄCHSPARTNER/IN
Wie oft fährst du mit dem	Fahrrad?	oft
	Mofa?	nicht sehr oft
	Motorrad?	nie
	Bus?	
	Zug?	
	Schiff?	
Wie oft fährst du mit der	Straßenbahn?	
	U-Bahn?	

Wie oft fliegst du?

B. Wie fährst du? Ask a classmate the following questions.

1. Hast du ein Fahrrad? Ist es neu? Alt?
2. Fährst du gern mit dem Rad?
3. Möchtest du eine lange Radtour machen? Wohin?
4. Hast du letzten Sommer eine Radtour gemacht? Wohin?
5. Hast du ein Motorrad? Ein Mofa? Ist es neu? Alt?
6. Fährst du gern mit dem Motorrad? Mit dem Mofa?
7. Bastelst du gern am Fahrrad oder am Motorrad?
8. Hat deine Stadt eine Straßenbahn?

C. Wie fahren Sie? Ask your teacher some questions about transportation.

1. Wie fahren Sie zur Schule? Mit dem Bus? Mit dem Rad? Mit dem Auto?
2. Wie kann man von Österreich in die Schweiz kommen? Von Deutschland in die Schweiz?
3. Fliegen Sie gern? Wie oft sind Sie schon geflogen? Wohin?
4. Wie möchten Sie nach Europa fahren? Mit dem Schiff oder mit dem Flugzeug? Warum?

Kilometer und Meile

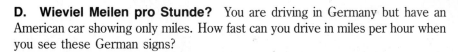

1 (ein) Kilometer = 0,62 Meilen
1 (eine) Meile = 1,6 Kilometer

D. Wieviel Meilen pro Stunde? You are driving in Germany but have an American car showing only miles. How fast can you drive in miles per hour when you see these German signs?

▶ 50 km   *31 Meilen pro Stunde*

1. 80 km   2. 100 km   3. 20 km   4. 120 km

[ç] Mil**ch**, schle**ch**t, Bü**ch**er

The sound [ç] is similar to that used by many Americans for the *h* in such words as *hue, huge, Hugh.* The sound [ç] is represented by the letters **-ch** when they occur after the vowel sounds written as **e, i, ie, ü, äu, eu,** and **ö,** and after consonants.

A. Practice the following words.

mi**ch**	re**ch**t	eu**ch**	man**ch**	Bü**ch**er
endli**ch**	mö**ch**te	Bräu**ch**e	dur**ch**	Tü**ch**er

B. Practice the following words horizontally in pairs, to contrast [ʃ] (as in **Fisch** and **waschen**) with [ç].

[ʃ]	[ç]	[ʃ]	[ç]
Kirsche	Kirche	Mensch	Mönch
fischte	Fichte	Büsche	Bücher
frisch	frech	misch	mich

C. Practice the following words horizontally in pairs.

[χ]	[ç]	[χ]	[ç]
doch	dich	Buch	Bücher
Dach	Dächer	Brauch	Bräuche
Tochter	Töchter	Loch	Löcher

Gleich und gleich gesellt sich gern.

D. Practice the sound [ç]. Read the sentences aloud.

1. Hoffentlich hast du nichts gegen Bücher!
2. Er spricht gut Deutsch.
3. Ich möchte ein Glas frische Milch, bitte.

Übungen

1. Dative case of definite articles and nouns

Singular

NOMINATIVE
Der Fernseher ist kaputt.
Das Radio spielt nicht.
Die Platte ist schlecht.

DATIVE
Was hast du mit **dem Fernseher** gemacht?
Was hast du mit **dem Radio** gemacht?
Was hast du mit **der Platte** gemacht?

The dative case is used with certain prepositions, one of which is **mit.** The definite article changes form in the dative case.

A.   So fahre ich nicht.   Jörg sagt, warum du nicht so fahren sollst. Sag, daß du gar nicht so fährst!

▶   Der Bus ist zu langsam.   *Ich fahre doch nicht mit dem Bus.*

1. Die Straßenbahn fährt nach zwölf nicht mehr.
2. Die U-Bahn fährt um diese Zeit nicht.
3. Das Auto läuft nicht.
4. Das Motorrad ist kaputt.
5. Und das Fahrrad ist leider auch kaputt.

Plural

NOMINATIVE
Die **Fernseher** sind kaputt.
Die **Radios** spielen nicht.
Die **Platten** sind schlecht.

DATIVE
Was hast du mit **den Fernsehern** gemacht?
Was hast du mit **den Radios** gemacht?
Was hast du mit **den Platten** gemacht?

The dative plural form of the definite article is **den.** In the dative plural, an **-n** is added to the plural form of the noun, unless the plural already ends in **-n** or in **-s.**

B. Was hast du mit der Sammlung gemacht? Christl hat viele Sachen gesammelt. Sie sammelt sie aber nicht mehr. Frag, was sie mit den Sachen gemacht hat!

▶ Ich sammle keine Briefmarken mehr.

Was hast du denn mit den Briefmarken gemacht?

1. Ich sammle keine Ansichtskarten mehr.
2. Ich sammle keine Poster mehr.
3. Ich sammle keine Bierdeckel mehr.
4. Ich sammle keine Schallplatten mehr.
5. Ich sammle keine Flugzeugmodelle mehr.

2. Dative case of **dieser**-words

Von **welchem** Fernseher sprichst du?	Von **diesem.**
Von **welchem** Radio sprichst du?	Von **diesem.**
Von **welcher** Stereoanlage sprichst du?	Von **dieser.**
Von **welchen** Platten sprichst du?	Von **diesen.**

Dieser-words (**dieser, jeder, solcher, mancher, welcher**) follow the same pattern of endings in the dative case as the definite articles. The dative case is used with the preposition **von.**

C. Auf einer Fete. Auf einer Fete fragt Ingrid, ob du etwas essen willst. Sag: „Ja, bitte", und nimm von allem ein Stück!

▶ Möchtest du etwas Käse?

Ja, bitte. Ich nehme ein Stück von diesem hier.

1. Möchtest du etwas Wurst?
2. Willst du etwas Brot?

3. Möchtest du etwas Kuchen?
4. Willst du etwas Torte?

D. Im Kleidungsgeschäft. Hans-Jürgen spricht von den Sachen im Geschäft. Du siehst sie aber nicht. Frag, von welchen Sachen er spricht!

▶ Dieser Anzug ist aber teuer.   *Von welchem Anzug sprichst du?*

1. Diese Jacke ist ja toll.
2. Dieser Pulli ist wirklich klasse.
3. Diese Schuhe sind aber billig.
4. Diese Krawatte ist aber häßlich.
5. Dieser Mantel ist zu dick.
6. Diese Handschuhe sind wirklich warm.

3. Dative case of indefinite articles and ein-words

Erika hat das von **einem** Mann im Geschäft gehört.
Dieter hat das von **einem** Mädchen im Café gehört.
Uwe hat das von **einer** Frau im Supermarkt gehört.

Gabi hat das von **ihren** Freunden gehört.

Indefinite articles and **ein**-words (**mein, dein, sein,** and so on) follow the same pattern of endings in the dative as **dieser**-words.

E. Der neue Film. Gisela will wissen, wie der neue Film im *Olympia* ist. Du weißt es nicht, und du hast auch noch niemand gefragt. Sag das!

▶ Was denkt dein Bruder?   *Mein Bruder? Mit meinem Bruder habe ich noch nicht gesprochen.*

1. Was denkt deine Schwester?
2. Was denkt dein Vater?
3. Was denkt deine Mutter?
4. Was denken deine Freunde?

F. Wirklich? Silke und Sabine haben von einigen° Leuten gehört, wie das   some
Wetter wird. Frag, ob sie das wirklich von *diesen* Leuten gehört haben!

▶ Unser Metzger hat es gesagt.   *Wirklich? Von eurem Metzger habt ihr es gehört?*

1. Unser Bäcker hat es auch gesagt.
2. Unser Elektriker hat es auch gesagt.
3. Und unsere Friseurin hat es gesagt.
4. Unser Lehrer hat es gesagt.
5. Und unsere Ärztin hat es gesagt.

Du hast das Wort

Ist das Unsinn? Make a series of statements to a classmate. Your classmate will tell you whether the statements make sense and correct them if they don't.

DU

Man schreibt mit einem Buch, nicht?

Man spült Geschirr mit Wasser, nicht?

GESPRÄCHSPARTNER/IN

Unsinn! Man schreibt mit einem Bleistift.

Ja, das stimmt.

Man fährt mit dem Rad von hier nach Österreich, nicht?
Man bäckt eine Torte mit Eiern, nicht?
Man spricht mit dem Deutschlehrer Deutsch, nicht?
Du fährst mit der Straßenbahn zur Schule, nicht?

4. Dative case of special **der**-nouns

Nominative	Wie heißt der Herr da?
Accusative	Kennst du **den Herrn** da?
Dative	Willst du mit **dem Herrn** arbeiten?

Special **der**-nouns that add an **-n** or **-en** in the accusative also add **-n** or **-en** in the dative singular. The special **der**-nouns you know are **Herr, Junge, Kunde.**

G. Mit wem? Gisela fragt, ob du dies oder das mit jemand° gemacht hast. Sag, du hast es mit jemand anders gemacht! °someone

▶ Hast du mit dem Mädchen da gearbeitet? (Junge)   *Nein, mit dem Jungen da.*

1. Bist du mit der Frau da gefahren? (Herr)
2. Hast du mit dem Verkäufer da gesprochen? (Kunde)
3. Hast du mit dem Jungen da Tennis gespielt? (Herr)
4. Hast du mit dem Mädchen da gegessen? (Junge)

H. Gabi hat mit vielen gesprochen. Gabi hat mit vielen Personen gesprochen. Sag das! Folge dem Mustersatz!

▶ die Frau da   *Gabi hat mit der Frau da gesprochen.*

1. der Herr da
2. der Junge da
3. der Friseur da
4. der Kunde da

5. die Männer da
6. die Verkäuferin da
7. die Frauen da
8. das Mädchen da

5. Dative case of wer

Nominative	**Wer** ist das?	*Who* is that?
Dative	Mit **wem** spricht Gabi?	With *whom* is Gabi speaking?

The dative form of the interrogative pronoun **wer** is **wem**.

I. Mit wem? Christl sagt, was ihre Freunde fürs Wochenende vorhaben. Du verstehst aber nicht, mit wem sie das vorhaben. Frag Christl! Folge dem Mustersatz.

▶ Erik geht mit seinem Bruder ins Kino.   *Mit wem geht er ins Kino?*

1. Andrea spielt mit ihrer Schwester Tennis.
2. Eva geht mit einer Freundin schwimmen.
3. Volker geht mit seiner Freundin einkaufen.
4. Dirk fährt mit seinen Freunden an den See.
5. Karin kommt mit Paul zur Fete.
6. Ingrid fährt mit Dieter in die Stadt.

J. Wer/wem/wen? Tina hat viele Fragen, aber sie sagt nicht den ganzen Satz. Sag den Satz! Benutze wer/wem/wen!

1. _____ kommt morgen?
2. _____ meinst du?
3. Mit _____ kommst du?
4. _____ rufst du an?
5. _____ wohnt hier?
6. Für _____ ist die Platte?
7. _____ ladet ihr ein?
8. Mit _____ gehst du ins Kino?
9. _____ ist doof?

Du hast das Wort

Mit wem? As a class make a list of fun activities on the board:

einkaufen gehen
ins Kino gehen
tanzen gehen
zum Basketballspiel gehen

Ask a classmate if she/he has done these things and with whom.

DU	GESPRÄCHSPARTNER/IN
Bist du letzte Woche einkaufen gegangen?	Ja, ich bin letzte Woche einkaufen gegangen.
Mit wem bist du einkaufen gegangen?	Mit meiner Freundin.

Dative case of articles and nouns (A–F)

	SINGULAR			PLURAL
Nominative	der	das	die	die
Accusative	den	das	die	die
Dative	**dem**	**dem**	**der**	**den**
	dies**em**	dies**em**	dies**er**	dies**en**
	ein**em**	ein**em**	ein**er**	—
	sein**em**	sein**em**	sein**er**	sein**en**

In addition to nominative and accusative, German has a third case called dative. It is used with certain prepositions, two of which are **mit** and **von**.

The definite article has three forms in the dative case: **dem, der,** and **den. Dieser**-words (**dieser, jeder, welcher, solcher, mancher),** the indefinite article, and **ein**-words (**kein, mein, dein, sein,** and so on) follow the same pattern of endings in the dative case as the definite article.

NOMINATIVE	DATIVE
Der Fernseher ist kaputt.	Was hast du mit **dem Fernseher** gemacht?
Das Radio spielt nicht.	Was hast du mit **dem Radio** gemacht?
Die Platte ist schlecht.	Was hast du mit **der Platte** gemacht?
Die Fernseher sind kaputt.	Was hast du mit **den Fernsehern** gemacht?
Die Radios spielen nicht.	Was hast du mit **den Radios** gemacht?
Die Platten sind schlecht.	Was hast du mit **den Platten** gemacht?

In the singular, the dative form of a noun is identical with the nominative and accusative forms.

In the plural, the dative form of a noun adds an **-n** unless the plural form of the noun already ends in **-n** or in **-s**.

Dative case of special **der**-nouns (G–H)

Nominative	der Herr	der Junge	der Kunde
Accusative	den Herr**n**	den Jung**en**	den Kund**en**
Dative	dem Herr**n**	dem Jung**en**	dem Kund**en**

Special **der**-nouns that add **-n** or **-en** in the accusative also add **-n** or **-en** in the dative singular.

Dative case of **wer** (I–J)

Nominative	**Wer** ist das?	*Who* is that?
Dative	Mit **wem** gehst du?	With *whom* are you going?

The dative form of the interrogative pronoun **wer** is **wem**.

Wiederholung

A. Wo ist dein Mofa? Lore was quite surprised when she saw Dieter yesterday. Read the following dialogue and then relay the content of the dialogue to a friend from Lore's point of view.

LORE	Mensch, Dieter, habe ich richtig gesehen?
DIETER	Wie soll ich das wissen? Was hast du denn gesehen?
LORE	Du bist ja mit dem Rad gefahren.
DIETER	Na und?
LORE	Tu nicht so! Du weißt schon, was ich meine. Wo ist denn dein Mofa?
DIETER	Kaputt.
LORE	Aha! Und jetzt bist du sauer.
DIETER	Ja, natürlich, und wie! Komm, ich fahr dich zu Großinger. Ich lade dich zu einer Cola ein.
LORE	Schön. Aber nicht mit dem Fahrrad. Ich nehme dich auf° meinem Mofa mit.

on

Keine Mofas

You may want to begin your narrative as follows:

▶ *Gestern habe ich Dieter gesehen. Er ist . . .*

B. Mit wem spricht er? Indicate with whom Mr. Wolf is speaking. Base your choice on the content of Mr. Wolf's statements.

**Ärztin   Bäcker   Elektriker   Fahrlehrer
Metzger   Verkäuferin**

▶ „Haben Sie noch Brot von gestern?"   *Er spricht mit dem Bäcker.*

1. „Das Licht im Badezimmer ist kaputt. Können Sie es heute noch reparieren?"
2. „Ich möchte ein Kleid in Blau für meine Frau. Ich glaube, sie trägt Größe 40."
3. „Das habe ich wieder falsch gemacht, nicht? Autofahren ist nicht leicht zu lernen."
4. „Ich bin den ganzen Tag müde und habe keinen Appetit."
5. „Ich hätte gern ein Pfund von dem Schinken da."

C. Im Kleidungsgeschäft. Form sentences about clothes shopping, using the cues provided.

1. ich / möchten / kaufen / jedes Hemd hier
2. warum / manche Kleider / sein / so teuer / ?
3. was / ich / sollen / machen / mit / dieser Mantel / ?
4. welcher / Rock / ich / sollen / nehmen / ?
5. du / können / bezahlen / dieser Anzug / ?
6. du / finden / solche / Schuhe / schön / ?

D. Wie sagt man das? Change each English word to its German equivalent by changing one or two letters.

▶ milk   *Milch*

1. word
2. friend
3. water
4. thick
5. for

6. long
7. green
8. new
9. half
10. was

E. Autofahren. Complete each of the following sentences with the appropriate form of the words in parentheses.

1. Christa und Jochen sind durch _____ gefahren.   (die Stadt)
2. Du hast doch hoffentlich _____ nicht wieder verloren!   (dein Führerschein)
3. Frank muß für _____ lernen.   (die Fahrprüfung)
4. Er ist durchgefallen, aber er hat nichts gegen _____.   (sein Fahrlehrer)
5. Mußt du für _____ viel lernen?   (dein Führerschein)
6. Petra kann nicht ohne _____ fahren, denn sie hat noch keinen Führerschein.   (ihr Fahrlehrer)

F. Welches Wort? Complete the following dialogue with the words below.

Karten   Kino   Lust   sicher   teuer   Vorstellung

FRANK   Hast du _____, heute abend ins Konzert zu gehen?
PAUL   Wann beginnt die _____?
FRANK   Ich bin nicht _____. Ich glaube, um halb acht.
PAUL   Was kosten die _____?
FRANK   25 Mark.
PAUL   Mensch, das ist viel zu _____. Ich gehe ins _____.

G. An der Bushaltestelle°. Join with three classmates to prepare a narrative   bus stop
based on the picture. One person will write down the story you agree on. You may
wish to include answers to some of these questions.

1. Wie ist das Wetter heute? Scheint die Sonne? Regnet es?
2. Welche Jahreszeit ist es?
3. Wieviel Personen sind hier?
4. Wer sind sie?
5. Was tragen sie? Warum?
6. Wohin wollen sie fahren?
7. Was haben sie vor? Gehen sie Ski laufen? Zelten sie? Besuchen sie
   Freunde?
8. Wie lange bleiben sie?
9. Wann kommen sie zurück?

1. Summarize the information about automobile travel in the German-speaking countries. What are some of the similarities and differences between automobile travel in these countries and the U.S.?
2. Many of the requirements for getting a driver's license in a German-speaking country are different from those of the U.S. Summarize the differences. Which features in each system do you like or dislike?

Kulturlesestück

Die Bahn

In den deutschsprachigen° Ländern gibt es viele Autos. Aber viele Leute° fahren auch noch mit der Bahn°. Die Züge sind modern, schnell und fast immer pünktlich°. Man kann alle Städte und fast alle Städtchen° mit dem Zug erreichen°. Und es gibt jeden Tag genug° Züge, so daß man nicht viele Stunden warten° muß.

5   Viele Leute fahren mit dem Zug zur Arbeit. Sie nehmen den Nahverkehrszug°. Zwischen den großen Städten gibt es die Intercity-Züge. Durch ganz Westeuropa fahren die TEE°- und die EuroCity-Züge. In diesen Zügen ist der Service besonders gut. Man kann gut essen, man kann telefonieren, man kann Briefe diktieren°. Natürlich sind diese Züge teuer. Billiger sind die D-Züge

10 (Schnellzüge)° für weitere Reisen° und die Eilzüge° für kürzere Reisen. Aber auch für diese Züge sind die Karten nicht gerade billig. Trotzdem° produziert die Bahn jedes Jahr ein Defizit. Der Staat° deckt° dieses Defizit und bezahlt jedes Jahr viele Millionen, denn alle Bahnen sind staatlich°.

German-speaking / people
railroad
punctual / small towns / reach
enough / wait
local train

TEE = Trans-Europ-Express

dictate
express trains / trips / semi-fast trains
nevertheless
state / covers
owned by the state

DB = Deutsche Bundesbahn — TransEuropExpress in Köln-Hauptbahnhof

Richtig oder falsch?

1. In den deutschsprachigen Ländern fahren viele Leute mit der Bahn, denn es gibt wenige Autos.
2. Die Züge sind fast immer pünktlich.
3. Mit dem Zug kann man alle Großstädte erreichen.
4. Leider muß man oft lange warten, denn es gibt nicht genug Züge.
5. Zur Arbeit nehmen alle Leute einen Intercity-Zug.
6. Von der Schweiz nach Dänemark kann man mit einem TEE-Zug fahren.
7. Für lange Reisen fährt man mit dem Eilzug.
8. Es ist nicht teuer, mit dem Zug zu fahren, denn der Staat bezahlt jedes Jahr Millionen.
9. Die Bahn verliert jedes Jahr viel Geld.
10. Alle Bahnen in den deutschsprachigen Ländern sind privat.

Land und Leute

On most trains in the German-speaking countries the cars **(Wagen)** consist of a long corridor **(Gang)** on one side, with doors leading into a series of compartments **(Abteile)**. Each compartment has luggage racks **(Gepäck- netze)** and seats for six passengers. Most trains have two classes; first class offers bet- ter service, has more comfortable seats, and is usually less crowded than second class. Modern **Intercity** trains are not divided into small compartments but have two seats on each side with a long aisle in the middle. Most long-distance trains have a dining car **(Speisewagen)**.

Vokabeln

Substantive

der Fahrlehrer, –/ die Fahrlehrerin,
  –nen driving instructor

der Bus, –se bus
der Fahrunterricht driving instruction
der Führerschein, –e driver's license; **den**
  Führerschein machen to get a driver's
  license
der Kurs, –e course
der See, –n lake
der Traum, ⁻e dream
der Unterricht lesson, instruction
der VW Volkswagen
der Zug, ⁻e train

das Benzin gasoline
das Fahrrad, ⁻er bicycle
das Flugzeug, –e airplane
das Mofa, –s moped, motorbike
das Motorrad, ⁻er motorcycle
das Rad, ⁻er bike (*short for* **das Fahrrad**);
  wheel
das Schiff, –e ship

die Autobahn, –en expressway, freeway
die Bremse, –n brake
die Diskussion, –en discussion, debate
die Fahrschule, –n driving school
die Fahrstunde, –n driving lesson
die Prüfung, –en exam, test
die Straßenbahn, –en streetcar
die Tour, –en tour, trip
die U-Bahn, –en subway

Verben

beschreiben (beschrieben) to describe
bestehen (bestanden): die Prüfung
  bestehen to pass a test
durch·fallen (ä; ist durchgefallen) to fail, to
  flunk; **in der Prüfung durchfallen** to fail the
  test
erzählen [von] to tell [about]
fliegen (ist geflogen) to fly
halten (hält; gehalten) hold

Andere Wörter

eifersüchtig jealous
langsam slowly
mir (*dative of* **ich**) me
mit (+ *dat.*) with; by (*of vehicles*); **mit dem**
  Auto by car
nie never
niemand no one
praktisch practical
pro per
schnell fast
unabhängig independent
unsicher dangerous; unsure, insecure
was für ein what kind of
zur to the; **zur Arbeit** to work
zwischen (+ *acc. or dat.*) between

Besondere Ausdrücke

halt mir die Daumen cross your fingers for me
  (*literally:* hold your thumbs for me)
Schwein haben (*colloq.*) to be lucky
7 Liter auf 100 Kilometer 100 kilometers to 7
  liters
an den See to the lake

Die neue Bahn

Fahr & Spar.
Die neuen
Preise der
neuen Bahn.

Deutsche
Bundesbahn

Kapitel 15

Ein Stadtbesuch

München: Marienplatz, Rathaus, Frauenkirche

Wohin gehen wir denn nun?

Kai, Lore und Dieter gehen in Frankfurt zur Schule. Fast jedes Jahr macht ihre Klasse eine Klassenfahrt. Dieses Jahr sind sie nach Bayern gefahren, nach München. Am Tag besuchen sie Museen und Kirchen; oder sie bummeln durch die Fußgängerzone, vom Rathaus zum Karlsplatz und zurück. Aber abends wollen sie keine Museen und Kirchen sehen; abends wollen sie tanzen gehen.

Jetzt stehen Kai und Lore vor ihrem Hotel.

KAI	Wollen wir hier noch lange stehen? Wohin gehen wir denn nun?
LORE	Dieter sagt, daß die Musik im *Western Club* ganz toll ist. Aber wo ist denn der *Western Club*?
KAI	Da kommt der Dieter. Frag ihn doch! Er weiß ja immer alles.
LORE	Dieter, sag mal, wo ist der *Western Club*?
DIETER	In Schwabing.
KAI	Mensch, das ist aber weit! Wie kommen wir denn nach Schwabing?
DIETER	Ihr könnt mit der U-Bahn fahren, mit der Drei oder der Sechs. Ihr könnt aber auch laufen.
KAI	Zu Fuß nach Schwabing?
DIETER	Ja, es ist nur eine halbe Stunde von hier.
LORE	Willst du nicht mitkommen?
DIETER	Ach nein.
LORE	Warum denn nicht?
DIETER	Weil ich zu müde bin.
KAI	Das kannst du doch sehen, Mensch. Er schläft ja schon fast.
LORE	Na gut, dann gehen wir also allein. Gute Nacht, Dieter, schlaf gut!

Fragen

1. Wo wohnen Kai und Lore?
2. Wie oft macht ihre Klasse eine Klassenfahrt?
3. Wo sind die Schüler dieses Jahr?
4. Was besuchen die Schüler? Wo bummeln sie?
5. Was machen sie am Abend?
6. Wo ist die Musik ganz toll?
7. Mit welcher U-Bahn können Lore und Kai fahren?
8. Warum geht Dieter nicht tanzen?

Du hast das Wort

1. **Wie bist du gekommen?** Find out how your classmates came to school today. Possible answers are provided.

Discussing transportation

DU

Wie bist du heute zur Schule gekommen?

GESPRÄCHSPARTNER/IN

Zu Fuß.
Mit dem [Rad/Bus/Auto].
Mit der [Straßenbahn/U-Bahn].
[Mein Vater] hat mich gefahren.

2. **Stadtplan: München.** You are going to visit a friend in Munich, and your friend has sent you a map so you can decide what you wish to see. Make a list of the following places by name.

Consulting a map

Museen   Theater   Märkte   Kirchen   Tore   (Was sonst?)

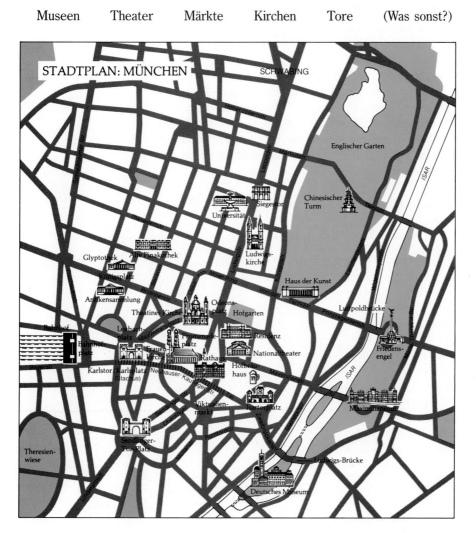

3. **Eine Stadtrundfahrt.** (A sightseeing trip.) Assume you have been in Munich for a month and your parents are going to be with you for a week. Make a program of what they should see and when.

Tag	Zeit	Was und wo
Montag	9–13 Uhr	Deutsches Museum
Dienstag . . .	————	————

Wie kommen wir zum Western Club?

Jetzt sind Kai und Lore in Schwabing, aber sie können den Western Club *nicht finden.*

KAI   Ich bin froh, daß wir mit der Bahn gefahren sind.

LORE   Ja, aber wo ist denn nun der *Western Club?*

KAI   Schau doch mal auf den Stadtplan!

LORE   Ich habe ihn nicht. Hast du ihn denn vergessen?

KAI   Ich glaube ja. Dann müssen wir wohl jemanden fragen. Entschuldigung! Können Sie uns sagen, wie wir zum *Western Club* kommen?

STUDENT   Ja, das kann ich. Ihr geht geradeaus bis zur Ampel. Bei der Ampel geht ihr rechts. Dann wieder geradeaus, bis ihr zu einem Platz mit einem Brunnen kommt. Da geht ihr links. Dann seht ihr schon das Schild mit dem großen Stiefel.

KAI   Vielen Dank!

STUDENT   Bitte schön. Oh, Moment mal. Da fällt mir gerade ein — der *Western Club* hat heute zu.

LORE   Nein, so ein Pech! Was machen wir denn nun?

STUDENT   Geht doch zu *Alfons.* Bei *Alfons* ist auch viel los. Das ist auch ein Studentenlokal.

Fragen

1. Wie sind Kai und Lore nach Schwabing gekommen?
2. Wer hat den Stadtplan?
3. Wen fragen sie, wo der *Western Club* ist?
4. Wie kommen sie zum Brunnen?
5. Was für ein Schild hat der *Western Club?*
6. Warum können Lore und Kai nicht in den *Western Club?*
7. Was für ein Lokal ist *Alfons?*
8. Warum geht man zu *Alfons?*

Munich **(München),** the capital of Bavaria **(Bayern),** has over a million inhabitants. It is regarded as one of the most attractive cities in the Federal Republic: it is close to the Alps, to Austria and Italy, to famous lakes such as the **Tegernsee, Chiemsee,** and **Starnberger See,** and to the romantic nineteenth-century castles of King Ludwig II **(König Ludwig II.).** The city itself has many beautiful churches and palaces, important museums, excellent theaters, and extensive parks:

The **Deutsches Museum,** devoted to science and technology, has many working models and demonstrations.

The **Alte Pinakothek** contains one of the most famous art collections in the world.

The **Frauenkirche,** with its twin onion domes, has long been a symbol of Munich.

The **Hofbräuhaus** is a popular tourist attraction, offering music, beer, sausages, and Bavarian atmosphere.

The **Englischer Garten** is one of Europe's largest city parks. Its lakes, streams, and wooded areas invite everybody to rest, sunbathe, or buy refreshments in one of the outdoor cafés.

Particularly interesting is **Schwabing,** a district of Munich that is often compared with the Latin Quarter in Paris. Its proximity to the university and the Academy of Fine Arts attracts many people with artistic and intellectual interests.

The streets come alive in the early afternoon, and during the **Kaffeestunde** the many sidewalk cafés are filled with people. Sidewalk artists attract onlookers, and young people peddle paintings, jewelry, and other handmade items.

By evening it is often hard to make one's way through the crowded streets as local inhabitants and tourists head for the more than three hundred restaurants or pubs. Like Lore and Kai, young people also come to Schwabing to hear jazz or rock or to dance in the clubs.

In Schwabing sitzt man bei schönem Wetter gern draußen.

Englischer Garten und Münchener Türme (towers)

Du hast das Wort

1. **Tourist in München.** Now that you know Munich you are able to help German visitors who ask for directions. Five students will take the role of tourists. Each will ask for directions from one place to another.

Asking for and giving directions

TOURIST/IN	DU
Entschuldigung, wie komme ich vom Bahnhof° [zum Karlsplatz]?	Gehen Sie immer geradeaus!
Entschuldigung, ich suche° [die Marienkirche].	Gehen Sie um die Ecke°!
	Gehen Sie die nächste Straße [rechts].
	Gehen Sie diese Straße entlang°, bis Sie zu [einer Kirche/einem Tor] kommen!
	An der Kreuzung° biegen° Sie [links] ab!

2. **Bei der Auskunft.°** You are at the information desk in a train station. Where do you want to go? When? When you and your partner have thought through the details, prepare your role-play and present it to another group.

information

Ich möchte morgen nach . . .

Frag, | wann du abfahren° kannst.
       | wann du ankommst°.
       | wie teuer die Fahrkarte° ist.

Bahnhof, Museen, Kirchen, Tore, Rathaus —auf dem Stadtplan findet man sie.

Was findet man in einer Stadt?

1. die Bank
2. die Kirche
3. das Museum
4. der Park

5. die Post
6. das Rathaus
7. die Schule
8. der Supermarkt

9. die Tankstelle
10. das Kaufhaus

A. Meine Stadt. You are expecting some exchange students from Austria. Give them some advance information about your town.

Make a list of the things to see.   Draw a route on the map.
Prepare a map.   Describe the tour.

Word families

die **Arbeit**	the work
arbeiten	to work
die **Arbeit**er/in	the worker

Like English, German has many words that belong to "families" that are derived from a common stem.

B. Was bedeutet das? Give the English equivalents of the following words.

1. die Klasse, die Klassenfahrt, der Klassenlehrer, die Klassenarbeit.
2. einkaufen, kaufen, der Käufer, die Verkäuferin, verkaufen, das Kaufhaus, der Einkäufer, der Kauf, der Verkauf.

Aussprache

[l]   alle, lese, viel, kühl
[ŋ]   Junge, Hunger, Sänger

To produce the German **l,** place the tip of the tongue against the upper gum ridge, as in English, but keep the tongue flat. A very tight smile helps. Many Americans use this *l*-sound in such words as *million, billion,* and *William.*

The combination **ng** is pronounced [ŋ], as in English *singer.* It does not contain the sound [g] as in English *finger.*

A. Practice the following words vertically in columns.

[l]		[ŋ]	
alle	lassen	Junge	Finger
Juli	lesen	Frühling	länger
weil	Lehrer	Vorstellung	Hunger
Film	Blume	klingeln	singen
toll	Flamme	Dinge	hängen

Aller guten Dinge sind drei.

B. Practice the sounds [l] and [ŋ]. Read the sentences aloud.

1. Im Frühling werden die Tage länger.
2. Der Junge kauft eine tolle Platte.
3. Du hast das Flugzeugmodell wohl selbst gebastelt.

Übungen

1. Prepositions with the dative case

The prepositions **aus, außer, bei, mit, nach, seit, von,** and **zu** are always used with the dative case.

mit with; by means of (transportation)

Ingrid fährt **mit** dem Zug.	Ingrid goes *by (means of)* train.
Sie fährt **mit** ihrer Schwester.	She goes *with* her sister.

A. Zum Olympiagelände°. Erik will zum Olympiagelände. Er ist nicht sicher, wie er fahren kann. Sag, welche Transportmittel° er benutzen kann!

Olympic village
means of transportation

▶ die Straßenbahn   *Natürlich kannst du mit der Straßenbahn fahren!*

1. der Bus
2. die U-Bahn
3. das Auto
4. das Rad

bei   at (place of business); with (at the home of)

Brigitte arbeitet **bei** einem Bäcker.   Brigitte works *at* a bakery.
Kurt wohnt **bei** seinen Großeltern.   Kurt lives *with* his grandparents.

B. Bei wem? Deine Freundin Gisela will wissen, was du vorhast. Sag Gisela, bei wem du dies und das machst!

▶ Ißt du bei deinen Großeltern   *Ja, bei meinen Großeltern.*
   zu Mittag?

1. Trinkst du bei deiner Schwester Kaffee?
2. Siehst du bei deinem Bruder fern?
3. Spielst du bei Rudi Karten?
4. Hörst du bei Monika Musik?

Du hast das Wort

1. **Bei wem?** Ask a classmate with whom she/he has done various things.

   DU   GESPRÄCHSPARTNER/IN

   Bei wem hast du | zu Abend gegessen?   Bei meinen Großeltern.
                          | Musik gehört?
                          | ferngesehen?
                          | Hausaufgaben gemacht?

2. **Willst du da arbeiten?** Ask classmates whether they would like to work in certain places and why: **„Möchtest du bei einem [Bäcker/Metzger/Elektriker] arbeiten? Warum (nicht)?"**

aus   out of, from (= is a native of)

Udo kommt **aus** dem Haus.   Udo comes *out of* the house.
Monika kommt **aus** Frankfurt.   Monika comes *from* Frankfurt.

C. Woher kommen sie? Sag, woher diese Leute gerade kommen.

▶ Paul und Dieter / Lokal   *Paul und Dieter kommen gerade*
aus dem Lokal.

1. Lore und Frank / Café
2. Paula und Regina / Kaufhaus
3. Gerd und Ilse / Restaurant
4. Grete und Liese / Bank
5. Ingrid und Jan / Post

Frische aus deutschen Landen

SPAR

D. Woher kommen sie? Erik möchte wissen, wer die Leute sind und woher
die Leute kommen. Du weißt es. Sag es!

▶ Maria / München   *Das ist Maria. Sie kommt aus München.*

1. Gerhard / Frankfurt
2. Anja / Hamburg
3. Günter / Wien
4. Rudi / Bern
5. Helga / Berlin

von from; of

Was hörst du **von** deiner Freundin Meike?	What do you hear *from* your friend Meike?
Viele **von** meinen Freunden gehen auf die Fete.	Many *of* my friends are going to the party.

An dieser Tankstelle
muß man selbst tanken.

E. Wirklich? Jan hat gehört, daß am Montag keine Schule ist. Er sagt, von
wem er das gehört hat. Frag ihn, ob er das wirklich von diesen Leuten gehört hat!

▶ Mein Bruder hat es gesagt.   *Hast du das wirklich von*
deinem Bruder gehört?

1. Meine Schwester hat es gesagt.
2. Mein Vater hat es gesagt.
3. Meine Lehrerin hat es gesagt.
4. Meine Großeltern haben es gesagt.

zu to (people and some places)

Ich fahre am Samstag **zu** einer Tankstelle.	I'm going *to* a service station Saturday.
Ich gehe heute abend **zu** meinem Freund Udo.	I'm going *to* my friend Udo's this evening.

F. Um wieviel Uhr? Du bist bei deiner Brieffreundin in Frankfurt. Ihr seid oft eingeladen. Frag, um wieviel Uhr ihr eingeladen seid!

▶ Mein Freund Jochen hat   *Um wieviel Uhr gehen wir*
    uns für Dienstag eingeladen.   *zu deinem Freund?*

1. Meine Freundin Christl hat uns für Donnerstag eingeladen.
2. Meine Großeltern haben uns für Samstag eingeladen.
3. Meine Schwester hat uns für Sonntag eingeladen.
4. Mein Bruder hat uns für Montag eingeladen.
5. Mein Lehrer hat uns für Mittwoch eingeladen.

nach   after; to (a city or country)

Wir fahren **nach** München.   We're driving *to* Munich.

The preposition **nach,** used with cities and countries, is equivalent to English *to (in the direction of).*

Nach dem Essen gehen wir ins Kino.   *After* dinner we'll go to the movies.

The preposition **nach** is also equivalent to English *after.*

G. Du willst viel sehen. Du willst immer viel Neues sehen. Sag, wohin du im Sommer fährst und was du besuchen willst!

▶ Möchtest du Deutschland sehen?   *Ja. Ich fahre im Sommer*
                                  nach Deutschland.

1. Besuchst du auch Bayern?
2. Dann besuchst du sicher auch München?
3. Du möchtest dann auch Österreich sehen, nicht?
4. Und Wien?
5. Und Salzburg?

H. Kommen sie dann zurück? Viele Leute fahren im Sommer weg°. Frag,   away
wann sie zurückkommen!

▶ Schmidts bleiben zwei   *Kommen sie dann nach*
    Monate in Berlin.   *zwei Monaten zurück?*

1. Schneiders bleiben einen Monat in Zürich.
2. Hofers bleiben zwei Wochen in Zermatt.
3. Langes bleiben zehn Tage in Salzburg.
4. Wagners bleiben eine Woche in Kiel.

Du hast das Wort

Was machst du? Think about what you do after school, after work, after lunch/dinner, and after you've finished your homework. Then try to find out what your classmates do at these times.

Was machst du nach der Schule? Ich spiele Tennis.
Was machst du nach dem Abendessen? Ich mache meine Hausaufgaben.

seit since (time), for (referring to time)

Christl ist **seit** einem Monat in München.
Christl has been in Munich *for* a month.
Tanja ist **seit** Montag in Hamburg.
Tanja has been in Hamburg *since* Monday.

To express an action or condition that started in the past but is still continuing in the present, German often uses the present tense and a time phrase with **seit**.

I. Wie lange schon? Lore will wissen, wie lange es schon so ist. Du weißt es. Sag, seit wann!

▶ Wie lange ist Gerd schon in Hamburg? Einen Monat?   *Ja, seit einem Monat.*

1. Wie lange ist Gabi schon in Österreich? Ein Jahr?
2. Wie lange ist Frank schon krank? Vier Wochen?
3. Wie lange hat er nichts gegessen? Drei Tage?
4. Wie lange ist dein Auto schon kaputt? Eine Woche?

außer besides, except

Was hast du **außer** dem Museum gesehen?
What did you see *besides* the museum?
Ich habe **außer** dem Museum nichts gesehen.
I saw nothing *except* the museum.

Städt. Galerie im Lenbachhaus
8 München 2, Luisenstraße 33
04973
Eintritt 1.50 DM
Auf Verlangen vorzeigen
ABRISS 04973

Das Hofbräuhaus in München ist weltbekannt.

J.   Was noch°?   Birgit und ihre Klasse haben in München viel gesehen. Frag   What else?
Birgit, was sie noch gesehen haben.

▶   Wir haben das Rathaus gesehen.   *Was habt ihr außer dem
                                          Rathaus gesehen?*

1. Wir haben das Hofbräuhaus gesehen.
2. Wir haben die Fußgängerzone gesehen.
3. Wir haben die Frauenkirche gesehen.
4. Wir haben die Isar gesehen.
5. Wir haben die Straßencafés gesehen.
6. Wir haben die Theater gesehen.

K.   Mein Freund Rainer.   David erzählt von seinem Freund Rainer. Er vergißt
manchmal ein paar Wörter. Sag die Sätze mit den Wörtern!

▶   Rainer kommt immer erst um   *Rainer kommt immer erst um
    eins ____. (from school)   eins aus der Schule.*

1. Er arbeitet ____ hier. (for 8 months)
2. Was hat er heute ____ gemacht? (besides homework)
3. Er hat heute nachmittag ____ Kaffee getrunken. (at his grandmother's)

4. Er geht _____ spazieren. *(after dinner)*
5. Heute abend geht er _____ ins Kino. *(with his sister)*
6. Hast du _____ sonst noch etwas gehört? *(from your friend Rainer)*
7. Ja, er fährt am Sonntag _____. *(to Berlin)*

L. Ein Geschenk für den Lehrer. Jan und Bernd wollen ein Geschenk für den Lehrer kaufen. Astrid erzählt, was sie machen. Aber sie vergißt oft, was sie sagen will. Sag die Sätze mit den richtigen Wörtern!

▶ Jan arbeitet für _____ _____. (sein Vater)   *Er arbeitet für seinen Vater.*

   Jan arbeitet mit _____ _____. (sein Vater)   *Er arbeitet mit seinem Vater.*

1. Oliver geht mit _____ _____ durch _____ _____. (sein Freund / die Stadt)
2. Sie suchen ein Geschenk für _____ _____. (ihr Lehrer)
3. Sie wollen es schon seit _____ _____ kaufen. (eine Woche)
4. Als sie gerade bei _____ _____ um _____ _____ gehen, sehen sie Gerhard. (die Post / die Ecke).
5. Er ist auch aus _____ _____. (ihre Klasse)
6. Gerhard sieht Oliver und Bernd und läuft zu _____ _____. (seine Freunde)
7. „Hallo! Gehst du mit?" Aber Gerhard kommt gerade von _____ _____ und muß schnell nach Hause gehen. (ein Fußballspiel)
8. Also gehen sie ohne _____ _____ weiter. (ihr Freund)

Land und Leute

Once or twice a year schools in the Federal Republic have **Wandertage.** On such occasions, a teacher might take her/his class on a hiking trip or visit a local place of interest — Roman ruins, an old castle, or a diamond manufacturer, for example.

Eighth-, tenth-, and twelfth-grade classes take a **Klassenfahrt** (a longer class trip) with their teacher. Depending on the season, they might go on a week-long skiing trip or visit a city to explore its museums and see the historical sites. Excursions outside the German-speaking countries allow students to practice the foreign language they are studying. These trips are part of the school program, and costs are kept down by subsidies from the town.

Die Porta Nigra, ein römisches Tor in Trier, ist eine besonders bekannte Ruine aus der Römerzeit.

2. Dative prepositional contractions

Unser Radio ist **beim** Elektriker. Ich komme gerade **vom** Elektriker. Gehst du jetzt **zum** Supermarkt? Ja, ich gehe auch **zur** Bank.	bei dem > **beim** von dem > **vom** zu dem > **zum** zu der > **zur**

The contractions **beim, vom, zum,** and **zur** are frequently used.

M. Da war ich schon. Dein Freund fragt, wohin du gehst. Er nennt viele Geschäfte. Sag, daß du schon da warst!

▶ Gehst du jetzt zum Bäcker?   *Nein, beim Bäcker war ich schon.*

1. Gehst du jetzt zum Metzger?
2. Gehst du jetzt zum Elektriker?
3. Gehst du jetzt zum Friseur?
4. Gehst du jetzt zum Arzt?

N. Entschuldigung . . . Du wohnst nicht in dieser Stadt, und du willst hier viel sehen. Du weißt aber nicht, wo alles ist. Frag, wie du gehen mußt!

▶ die Post   *Können Sie mir sagen, wie ich zur Post komme?*

1. die Bank
2. das Museum
3. das Rathaus
4. der Bahnhof
5. die Fußgängerzone
6. der *Western Club*
7. das Theater

O. Wie weit ist es? Du willst mit Petra in die Stadt gehen, aber du bist müde. Frag, wie weit alles ist!

▶ Ich muß zum Bäcker und zur Apotheke.   *Wie weit ist es vom Bäcker zur Apotheke?*

▶ Dann gehe ich zum Metzger.   *Wie weit ist es von der Apotheke zum Metzger?*

1. Ich muß zum Rathaus und zum Markt.
2. Dann gehe ich zum Kaufhaus.
3. Und dann gehe ich zum Elektriker.
4. Ich gehe dann zur Post.
5. Dann muß ich noch zur Bank.

Schönes zum Anfassen. WMf

Du hast das Wort

1. **Logische Sätze.** With three classmates make as many logical sentences as you can in five minutes.

▶ *Rita geht zum Bäcker. Sie braucht Brot.*

ich
du
Rita
ihr
Andrea und Günter

zum Bäcker
zum Bahnhof
zur Bank
zum Elektriker
zum Metzger
zur Post
zur Tankstelle
zum Supermarkt
in die Disco
ins Kleidungsgeschäft
ins Café
ins Kaufhaus
ins Kino
ins Museum
auf den Markt

tanzen gehen
Brot brauchen
nach Hamburg fahren
Bilder von Picasso sehen
Butter/billiger sein
mit Freunden sprechen
einen neuen Pulli kaufen
neue Gläser brauchen
einen guten Film sehen
eine Fete geben
Radio/kaputt sein
ein Picknick machen
Geld brauchen
Wurst/besser sein
Benzin brauchen
frisches Gemüse kaufen
Briefmarken kaufen
eine Cola trinken
Musik/toll sein

Am neuen Rathaus in München spielt das Glockenspiel jeden Tag um 11 Uhr.

2. **Wohin?** Form a group with three classmates. They will take turns telling you of a need or a problem. Tell them where they should go.

Helping with problems

GESPRÄCHSPARTNER/IN

Ich bin krank.
Ich möchte mit dem Zug fahren.
Ich möchte einen guten Film sehen.
Ich möchte alte Bilder sehen.
Ich brauche | Aspirin.
einen neuen Fernseher.
eine neue Hose.
frische Wurst.
Brot.
Briefmarken.
Milch.
Geld.
Benzin.
frisches Obst.

DU

Geh [zum Arzt!]

Prepositions with the dative case (A–L)

aus	Udo geht **aus** dem Haus. Andrea kommt **aus** Wien.	Udo goes *out of* the house. Andrea comes *from* Vienna.
außer	**Außer** meinem Freund war mein Bruder da. Ich esse alles gern **außer** Fisch.	*Besides* my friend, my brother was there. I like everything *except* fish.
bei	Sonja wohnt **bei** ihrer Tante. Sie kauft ihr Brot **beim** Bäcker.	Sonja lives *with* her aunt (at her house). She buys her bread *at* the bakery.
mit	Rita spricht **mit** dem Verkäufer. Udo fährt **mit** dem Bus.	Rita is speaking *with* the salesman. Udo is going *by* bus.
nach	Gabi fliegt **nach** Berlin. **Nach** dem Essen gehen wir schwimmen.	Gabi is flying *to* Berlin. *After* dinner we're going swimming.
seit	**Seit** dem Essen habe ich Durst. Schmidts wohnen **seit** einem Jahr in Berlin.	I've been thirsty *since* dinner. The Schmidts have been living in Berlin *for* a year.
von	Günter kommt gerade **von** der Party. Das Geschenk ist **von** seinen Eltern. Sprichst du **von** meinem Freund?	Günter is just coming *from* the party. The present is *from* his parents. Are you speaking *of* my friend?
zu	Petra geht **zu** ihrer Freundin. Sie hat sie **zu** einer Party eingeladen.	Petra is going *to* her friend's. She invited her *to* a party.

The prepositions **aus, außer, bei, mit, nach, seit, von,** and **zu** are always used with the dative case.

Bei/mit. One meaning of both **bei** and **mit** is *with*. However, they are not interchangeable. **Bei** means *at the home of.* **Mit** expresses the idea of doing something together.

Nach/zu. One meaning of both **nach** and **zu** is *to.* **Nach** is used with cities and countries. **Zu** is used to show movement toward people and many places.

Seit + present tense is used in German to express an action or condition that started in the past but is still continuing in the present. English uses the present perfect tense (e.g. has been living) with *since* or *for.*

Dative prepositional contractions (M–O)

Unser Fernseher ist **beim** Elektriker.
Ich komme gerade **vom** Elektriker.
Gehst du **zum** Supermarkt?
Ja, und dann gehe ich **zur** Post.

bei dem > **beim**
von dem > **vom**
zu dem > **zum**
zu der > **zur**

The contractions **beim, vom, zum,** and **zur** are frequently used.

Wiederholung

A. Welches Wort paßt? Choose the place in column B that is associated with each statement in column A. Supply the definite article for each noun in column B.

A	B
1. Ich brauche Geld.	a. Bahnhof
2. Ich habe Briefmarken gekauft.	b. Bank
3. Ich möchte einen neuen Mantel kaufen.	c. Café
4. Am Sonntag machen wir immer einen schönen Spaziergang.	d. Kino
	e. Park
5. Orangen sind heute besonders preiswert.	f. Post
6. Frank ist leider durchgefallen.	g. Schule
7. Die Vorstellung beginnt um sieben Uhr.	h. Supermarkt
8. Möchtest du eine Cola trinken?	i. Kaufhaus
9. Wir fahren mit dem Zug nach Salzburg.	

B. Ein Besuch in München. Complete each sentence with an appropriate dative preposition.

1. Am Montag bin ich _____ meinem Bruder gefahren. Er wohnt in München.
2. Ich habe _____ meinem Bruder und seiner Frau in Schwabing gewohnt. Sie wohnen _____ einem Jahr da.
3. Mein Bruder hat nicht immer in München gewohnt. Er kommt _____ Köln, wie ich.
4. Ich bin oft _____ meinem Bruder und seiner Frau im Englischen Garten spazierengegangen.
5. _____ seinem Haus bis zum Englischen Garten ist es nicht so weit.
6. In die Stadt sind wir dann _____ der U-Bahn gefahren.
7. Am Freitag muß ich _____ Köln zurück.
8. In den fünf Tagen habe ich sehr viel _____ München gesehen.

C. Kann das sein? Make sense out of the following sentences by replacing the italicized phrase with the phrase in parentheses. Make any other necessary changes.

1. Frau Wächter geht mit *ihrer Geige* einkaufen. (ihr Mann)
2. Sie bummelt durch *den Brunnen*. (die Fußgängerzone)
3. Frau Wächter arbeitet bei *der Ampel*. (die Post)
4. Frau Wächter schreibt ihre Briefe mit *einer Flöte*. (ein Kugelschreiber)
5. Sie kauft oft Geschenke für *ihren Metzger*. (ihre Familie)
6. Sie geht nicht ohne *ihren Fernseher* in die Stadt. (ihre Einkaufstasche)
7. Frau Wächter trinkt Cola aus *einer Socke*. (ein Glas)

D. Sag das! Compare the following items, using the adjective or adverb in parentheses.

1. Schallplatten sind _____ als Kassetten. (billig)
2. Dieses Radio ist nicht so _____ wie dieser Kassettenrecorder. (teuer)
3. Kostet der Kassettenrecorder so _____ wie der Plattenspieler? (viel)
4. Dieser Plattenspieler ist viel _____ als der Plattenspieler da. (gut)
5. Der Preis im Radiogeschäft ist viel _____ als der Preis im Kaufhaus. (hoch)
6. Ich spiele Platten _____ als Kassetten. (gern)

E. Was sagen Kai und Lore? Complete the second sentence in each pair by reporting what Kai and Lore said.

▶ Kai sagt: „Ich bin mit meiner Klasse nach München gefahren." *Kai sagt, daß er mit seiner Klasse nach München gefahren ist.*

1. Kai sagt: „Wir haben eine Klassenfahrt gemacht."
   Kai sagt, daß sie . . .
2. Lore fragt: „Habt ihr viele Museen und Kirchen besucht?"
   Lore fragt, ob sie . . .
3. Kai sagt: „Wir sind ins Deutsche Museum gegangen."
   Kai sagt, . . .
4. Lore fragt: „Seid ihr auch durch die Fußgängerzone gebummelt?"
   Lore fragt, . . .
5. Kai sagt: „Ich habe Platten und Poster gekauft."
   Kai sagt, . . .

F. Wie sagt man das? Express the following dialogue in German.

GISELA   Do you know where the *Western Club* is?
SABINE   Naturally. In Schwabing.
TORSTEN   Is that far from here?
SABINE   To Schwabing? No. You can go by subway.
GISELA   Can we go on foot?
SABINE   Sure. I'll come along.
TORSTEN   Ask Anke whether she wants to come along, too.
SABINE   All right. She likes to dance.

G. Postkarten aus München. Write two postcards from Kai and Lore telling about the highlights of their class trip to Munich. Have Kai write to his parents, while Lore writes to one of her friends. You may want to mention some of the following places and activities.

Schwabing
Museen
Fußgängerzone
mit der U-Bahn fahren
bummeln
tanzen

H. Land und Leute.

1. Your class is going on a **Klassenfahrt** to Munich. Make a list of what you will see.
2. Assume your school is in a small suburb outside of Munich. Where could you go on your **Klassenfahrt?** Depending on the season, what would you do there?

Wien

Touristen in Österreich wollen oft *eine* Stadt unbedingt° sehen: Wien, die Hauptstadt. Wien hat viele alte Kirchen wie zum Beispiel° den Stephansdom. Und es hat schöne Schlösser°. Schloß Schönbrunn ist die frühere° Sommerresidenz der Kaiser°. Mitten° in der Stadt steht die Hofburg, die frühere Winterresidenz
5 der Kaiser.

Wien hat berühmte° Cafés. Das Kaffeehaus *Zur blauen Flasche* soll das älteste° in der deutschsprachigen Welt° sein. Und Wien hat Theater und Museen. Das Kunsthistorische Museum gehört° zu den besten Museen in der Welt.

Wenn man an Wien denkt, denkt man vor allem° an Musik. Viele kennen die
10 Wiener Operetten und den „Walzerkönig"° Johann Strauß. Mozart und Beethoven haben lange in Wien gelebt°. Die Wiener Sängerknaben° geben Konzerte in Wien und in der ganzen Welt.

Touristen besuchen Wien gern. Aber auch für die Österreicher spielt Wien eine große Rolle°. Es liegt am Rand° von Österreich, ziemlich weit im Osten.
15 Trotzdem° ist es das politische und das kulturelle Zentrum von Österreich.

definitely
for example
palaces / former
der Kaiser: of the emperors / in the middle
famous / oldest
world
belongs
vor allem: above all
Waltz King
lived / Boys' Choir

spielt . . . Rolle: is important / edge
nevertheless

Match the items in column B with the information in column A.

A	B
1. eine schöne alte Kirche	a. Wien
2. der Walzerkönig	b. der Stephansdom
3. die Hauptstadt von Österreich	c. die Hofburg
4. dieses Schloß steht mitten in der Stadt	d. ein Wiener Kaffeehaus
5. viele Touristen besuchen es	e. Musik in Wien
6. Operetten	
7. liegt ziemlich weit im Osten	
8. die frühere Winterresidenz der Kaiser	
9. Mozart	
10. das politische und kulturelle Zentrum von Österreich	
11. Sängerknaben	
12. das älteste in der deutschsprachigen Welt	

Vokabeln

Substantive

der Student, —en, —en/die Studentin,
  —nen student (at a university)
der Tourist, —en, —en/die Touristin,
  —nen tourist

der Bahnhof, ⁻e train station
der Besuch, —e visit
der Brunnen, — fountain, well, spring
der Club, —s club
der Park, —s park
der Platz, ⁻e square
der Stadtplan, ⁻e city map
der Stiefel, — boot

(das) Bayern Bavaria
das Kaufhaus, ⁻er department store
das Lokal, —e place to eat, drink, dance;
  restaurant; **das Studentenlokal** pub
  frequented by students
das Museum, die Museen museum
das Rathaus, ⁻er town hall
das Schild, —er sign
das Schloß, ⁻sser castle, palace
das Tor, —e gate

die Ampel, —n traffic signal
die Bahn, —en train, railway; track
die Bank, —en bank
die Ecke, —n corner
die Fahrkarte, —n (train) ticket
die Fußgängerzone, —n pedestrian zone
die Kirche, —n church
die Klassenfahrt, —en class trip
die Kreuzung, —en intersection
die Post post office; mail
die Tankstelle, —n service station, gas station
die Universität, —en university

Verben

ab·biegen (ist abgebogen) to make a turn
ab·fahren (ä; ist abgefahren) to leave, to depart
an·kommen (ist angekommen) to arrive
bummeln (ist gebummelt) to go for a stroll, for
  a walk
schauen to look
stehen (gestanden) to stand
suchen to look for
vergessen (i; vergessen) to forget

Andere Wörter

aus (+ *dat.*) out of; from
außer (+ *dat.*) besides, except for
bis zu up to
entlang (+ *acc.*) along (entlang *follows the
  object:* die Straße entlang along the street)
froh glad, happy
jemand someone
links (to the) left
rechts (to the) right
seit (+ *dat.*) since, for
weil *(sub. conj.)* because
zu shut, closed; **die Tür ist zu** the door is
  closed

Besondere Ausdrücke

Moment mal just a moment
da fällt mir gerade ein it just occurs to me
es ist viel los there is a lot going on
so ein Pech what bad luck, how unfortunate
zu Fuß on foot
immer geradeaus straight ahead
die Straße entlang along (down) the street

NOCH EINMAL

Besuch. Your pen pal (from the end of Stage 2) has just written that she/he will soon have the opportunity to visit you and would like to know what to expect. Write a reply in which you explain what your friend may find different in your area. You may wish to compare some or all of the following: geography, landscape, weather, food, meals, transportation to school and into town, and town landmarks such as a market, pedestrian zone, town hall, museums.

Guten Appetit! As a class project, assemble a German meal. Plan a menu, with individual students or small groups volunteering to prepare the various foods. At the dinner, each student should receive a booklet in English and German containing the menu and the recipes for each dish. Be sure to set the table and to eat as a German family would.

As an extension of this activity, or as an alternative, your class may want to compile a cookbook of favorite German recipes. If there are German-speaking people in the community, members of the class could ask them for suggestions as to what to include.

Ein Spiel. The class is divided into two teams. Each team has fifteen minutes to compile a list of questions regarding information from Chapters 10–15. The questions may concern either the introductory reading material in each chapter, or the **Kulturlesestücke.** For example, a question from Chapter 14 might be, "Mit wieviel Jahren darf man in Deutschland Auto fahren?" Members of both teams take turns asking the questions of members of the opposing team. The team with the most correct answers wins.

Wo möchtest du sein? Look at the photographs in this Stage. In which place would you most like to be? Which person would you most like to meet? Would you choose a situation in which you feel at home and comfortable, or one which is new and different? In German, discuss your answers and the reasons for them. Then pretend that you are actually in one of the situations shown, and make up and enact a suitable dialogue. As necessary, select several classmates to work with you.

Im Verkehrsamt. Because you can speak German, you have been given a job in an information center (**das Verkehrsamt**) of the city of your choice (for example, Hamburg, Berlin, Salzburg, or Basel). Your task is to assist strangers in town. Learn about the sights in these cities. Several of your classmates will then play the role of tourists. When they ask which sights you recommend and how to get there, you give them the correct information. You may want to begin by asking how long they are staying and what their particular interests are — museums, theater, shopping, and so on.

Ein Geschenk. You've been spending the summer with a family in Switzerland. Now that you're about to leave, you want to get them a present to express your gratitude; but you're not sure what to buy. Choose a partner to take the role of a salesperson in a department store. Create a dialogue in which the salesperson tries to help you make a decision by asking questions about the family's tastes and interests. As the salesperson finds out more about the family, she/he can offer various suggestions. You may want to bring in props to help you perform the dialogue.

Ein Kreuzworträtsel. In small groups, prepare a crossword puzzle (**das Kreuzworträtsel**), using a single category of words: vocabulary relating to weather, transportation, buildings, food, shopping, and so on. When the puzzles are finished, each group exchanges its puzzle for that of another and tries to solve it.

H

Wer kann das sein? Find classmates who fit the following descriptions.

- ißt gern Spinat
- trinkt keine Cola
- trinkt jeden Tag einen Liter Milch
- frühstückt
- mag Regen
- mag den Winter lieber als den Sommer
- war schon einmal in Deutschland
- hat den Führerschein
- spielt Geige
- hat ein Mofa oder Motorrad
- ist schon einmal mit dem Zug gefahren
- ist dieses Jahr geflogen
- tanzt gern
- hat einen Freund oder eine Freundin in Österreich
- spült gern/oft Geschirr
- macht gern Gartenarbeit
- trägt Schuhe ohne Socken
- hat einen weißen Hund

POSTLEIT-ZAHLEN!

$1.50

REPUBLIK ÖSTERREICH

I

Eine deutsche Stadt. In groups of four to five, prepare poster displays of a city in a German-speaking country. Provide a map of the city; draw or cut out of magazines pictures of famous buildings, and label them. Select a speaker to present a brief report on the city, using the poster.

REFERENCE

Es war ein alter König
Heinrich Heine (1797–1856)

Es war[1] ein alter König,[2]
Sein Herz[3] war schwer, sein Haupt[4] war grau;
Der arme[5] alte König,
Er nahm[6] eine junge Frau.

Es war ein schöner Page,[7]
Blond[8] war sein Haupt, leicht[9] war sein Sinn;[10]
Er trug[11] die seidne[12] Schleppe[13]
Der jungen Königin.[14]

Kennst du das alte Liedchen?[15]
Es klingt[16] so süß,[17] es klingt so trüb;[18]
Sie mußten[19] beide sterben,[20]
Sie hatten sich viel zu lieb.[21]

1. **Es war:** there was 2. king 3. heart 4. head (of hair)
5. poor 6. took 7. page 8. blond 9. light, cheerful
10. disposition, temperament 11. carried 12. silken
13. train of a dress 14. queen 15. little song 16. sounds
17. sweet 18. dark, gloomy 19. had to 20. die 21. **Sie
. . . lieb:** they loved each other too much

Erinnerung[1]
Johann Wolfgang von Goethe (1749–1832)

Willst du immer weiter schweifen?[2]

Sieh, das Gute[3] liegt so nah.[4]

Lerne nur das Glück[5] ergreifen,[6]

Denn das Glück ist immer da.

1. reminder 2. wander, rove 3. the good 4. near
5. good fortune, happiness 6. seize

Septembermorgen
Eduard Mörike (1804–1875)

Im Nebel[1] ruhet noch die Welt,

Noch träumen Wald und Wiesen:[2]

Bald siehst du, wenn der Schleier[3] fällt,

Den blauen Himmel unverstellt,[4]

Herbstkräftig[5] die gedämpfte[6] Welt

In warmem Golde fließen.[7]

1. fog, mist 2. meadows 3. veil 4. unconcealed 5. full
of autumnal vigor 6. muted, quieted 7. to flow, be awash

Ein Jüngling[1] liebt ein Mädchen
Heinrich Heine

Ein Jüngling liebt ein Mädchen
Die hat einen andern erwählt;[2]
Der andre liebt eine andre,
Und hat sich mit dieser vermählt.[3]

Das Mädchen heiratet aus Ärger[4]
Den ersten besten Mann,[5]
Der ihr in den Weg gelaufen;[6]
Der Jüngling ist übel dran.[7]

Es ist eine alte Geschichte,
Doch bleibt sie immer neu;
Und wem sie just[8] passieret,[9]
Dem bricht das Herz[10] entzwei.[11]

1. young man 2. chose 3. married 4. **aus Ärger:** from
vexation 5. **den . . . Mann:** the first man 6. **der . . .
gelaufen:** who crossed her path 7. **ist . . . dran:** is in a
bad fix 8. by chance 9. happens to 10. heart
11. **bricht . . . entzwei:** breaks in two

Der Mond ist aufgegangen

1. moon 2. risen 3. little stars 4. sparkle, shine 5. heaven 6. bright(ly) 7. forest 8. is silent 9. meadows 10. rises 11. fog, mist 12. wondrously

Himmel und Erde müssen vergehen   (Kanon)

1. heaven 2. earth 3. pass away 4. musicians 5. last, continue

Ich bin ein Musikante[1]

Vorsänger: Ich bin ein Mu-si-kan-te und komm aus Schwa-ben-land.[2]
Alle: Wir sind die Mu-si-kan-ten und kom-men aus Schwa-ben-land.

Vorsänger: Ich kann auch spie-len,
Alle: wir kön-nen auch spie-len,

auf der Trom.-pe-te, auf der Trom-pe-te.

Vorsänger: Teng — teng-te-reng, teng-teng-te-reng, teng-teng-te-reng, teng — teng — te-reng!

Alle: Teng — teng-te-reng, teng-teng-te-reng, teng-teng-te-reng, teng — teng!

2. Auf meiner Geige,
vidi-gei-gei-gei.

3. Auf meiner Flöte,
didi-lid-lid-lid.

4. Auf der Klarinette,
didi-dum-dum-dum.

5. Auf meiner Trommel,
ti-rom-dom-dom.

6. Auf meiner Pauke,[3]
bum-bum-de-rum.

7. Auf dem Klaviere,
greif hier mal hin, greif da mal hin.[4]

1. musician 2. Swabia 3. drum 4. **greif . . . hin:** hit this key here, hit that key there

Heim, heim, heim

(Kanon)

① Heim, heim, heim, heim, heim, heim, heim woll'n wir gehen. ② Lied[1] ist aus[2], Spiel ist aus,

Tanz[3] ist aus, al-les ist aus! Heim, heim, heim, heim, heim, heim, heim woll'n wir gehen!

1. song 2. over 3. dance

Jugendsprache

ich bin total abgeschlafft I'm worn out

ein Schlaffi someone without much energy

Alte/Alter mother/father

anmachen: ich mache ihn an I'm trying to get to know him

mach mich nicht an! leave me alone!

das macht mich an that turns me on

Bock: ich hab' Bock auf Rock I like rock, I'm into rock

ich hab' null Bock auf Hausaufgaben I don't like homework

brettern: wir sind über die Autobahn gebrettert we drove fast down the highway

drauf sein: ich bin heute schlecht drauf I'm in a bad mood today

er ist ja heute irre drauf he's in a great mood today

echt very

echt gut! really good!

echt? really?

also echt (protest) aw, come on!

die Gurke slow motorcycle

heißer Ofen fast motorcycle

du tickst wohl nicht richtig! you must be out of your mind!

das ist ein/der Hammer that's unbelievable

die Karre, die Kiste automobile

die Kohle, Knete, Pinke, Schotter, Kies money

labern to talk nonsense

nerven: das nervt mich that gets on my nerves

das schafft mich that exhausts me

der schafft mich he drives me nuts

ich bin total geschafft I'm worn out

das ist echt ein Schlauch that's exhausting

schnallen: das hab' ich geschnallt I understood it

stark, spitze, super, irre, scharf, ausgeflippt great, really nice

mir stinkt's I've had enough, I'm tired of it

da blick' ich voll durch! I get it!

tote Hose: alles (ist) tote Hose nothing's going on

Trouble haben, bekommen, machen to have, get, make trouble

der Typ guy, man

ausflippen to lose it (one's nerve)

ich flip' gleich aus I'm losing it (my nerve)

German First Names

The following list includes some of the most popular German names. It is not a complete list of first names.

girls

Alexandra	Gabi	Michaela
Andrea	Gabriele	Monika
Anita	Gisela	Nadine
Anja	Gudrun	Nicole
Anke	Hannelore	Nina
Anna	Heidi	Petra
Anne	Heike	Regina
Antje	Ilse	Renate
Astrid	Inge	Rita
Barbara	Ingrid	Ruth
Beate	Irene	Sabine
Bettina	Iris	Sandra
Birgit	Isabelle	Sarah
Brigitte	Julia	Silke
Carola	Jutta	Sonja
Christa	Karin	Stephanie
Christina	Katharina	Sybille
Christine	Katja	Sylvia
Claudia	Katrin	Susanne
Cornelia	Kerstin	Suse
Dagmar	Margit	Tanja
Daniela	Margret	Ulla
Doris	Maria	Ulrike
Elisabeth	Marianne	Ute
Elke	Marion	Veronika
Ellen	Martina	Yvonne
Erika	Meike	
Eva	Melanie	

boys

Alex	Holger	Rainer
Alexander	Jan	Ralf
Andreas	Jens	Reinhard
Axel	Joachim	Richard
Benjamin	Jochen	Robert
Benno	Johannes	Rolf
Bernd	Jörg	Rudi
Burkhard	Jürgen	Sascha
Christian	Kai	Sebastian
Christoph	Karl	Stefan
Daniel	Karsten	Thilo
Detlev	Klaus	Thomas
Dieter	Kurt	Till
Dietmar	Lars	Tobias
Dirk	Lothar	Torsten
Erik	Lutz	Udo
Felix	Manfred	Ulf
Florian	Mark	Ulrich
Frank	Markus	Urs
Georg	Martin	Uwe
Gerd	Matthias	Volker
Gerhard	Michael	Werner
Günter	Niels	Wim
Hannes	Olaf	Wolfgang
Hans	Oliver	
Hartmut	Paul	
Heinz	Peter	
Helmut	Phillip	

Below you will find English equivalents of the dialogues in this book. Because the English dialogues are not literal translations they sometimes contain words that do not have exact equivalents in the German text. Don't let this bother you. Two languages often express the same idea in different ways.

chapter 1   Hi! How are you?

What's your name?

UTE BRAUN	What's your name?
UTE SCHMIDT	Ute.
UTE BRAUN	Amazing! My name is Ute, too.
UTE SCHMIDT	Really?

How are you?

INGRID	Hi, Gisela. How are you?
GISELA	Hello, Ingrid.
INGRID	Hi, Dieter. How are you?
DIETER	Bad.
INGRID	Well, what's the matter?
DIETER	I'm sick.
INGRID	I'm sorry.

Are you well again?

UTE	Hello, Mrs. Weiß. How are you?
MRS. WEISS	Hello, Ute. I'm OK again.
UTE	Are you well again?
MRS. WEISS	Yes, I'm only very tired.

chapter 2   How old are you?

Young or old?

HEIKE	How old is Michael?
DIRK	Sixteen.
HEIKE	And you?
DIRK	Sixteen too. We're both sixteen.
HEIKE	Are you both *really* sixteen?
DIRK	Yes. Why?
HEIKE	You're so young.
DIRK	Well, how old are *you*?
HEIKE	Already seventeen.
DIRK	That really is very old!

When is your birthday?

PETRA   My birthday's in March. Yours too, isn't that right?
DIRK   No.
PETRA   Well, when is your birthday?
DIRK   In April.
PETRA   Oh. Isn't Gerd's birthday in April, too?
DIRK   No, it's not until May.
PETRA   Oh yes, that's right.

chapter 3   This afternoon

Where do you live?

ERIK   Are you going home now?
SABINE   Yes.
ERIK   Where do you live?
SABINE   On Garden Street.
ERIK   Is that far from here?
SABINE   No, just ten minutes.

What are you going to do?

JAN   Are you staying home this afternoon?
GISELA   Yes.
JAN   What are you going to do?
GISELA   Homework. What else?

chapter 5   Do you need new clothes?

That's too expensive

ASTRID   How expensive is that dress over there?
GISELA   100 marks, and that's too expensive.
ASTRID   What do you mean by that?
GISELA   I think it's ugly.
ERIK   Those jeans are really terrific.
ASTRID   You think so? How much do they cost?
ERIK   60 marks.
ASTRID   60 marks! That's a bargain. Are you going to buy them?
ERIK   Yes.

What size do you wear?

ASTRID   Here's a coat in brown. Nice, isn't it?
ERIK   Yes, terrific. It's also nice and warm.
ASTRID   Does it fit?
ERIK   Unfortunately not. It's too big.
ASTRID   What size do you wear?

ERIK	Size 40.
ASTRID	Here's your size.
ERIK	But that's not a coat. That's a jacket.
ASTRID	Oh yes. Too bad.

chapter 6   The school day

In the classroom

GISELA	What do we have at nine? Chemistry?
DIETER	No, we don't have chemistry today. We have math.
GISELA	Oh, great!
DIETER	You think math is great?
GISELA	Yes, I think math is interesting. Math's my favorite subject.

During recess

KARIN	Have you finished your homework assignments yet?
NORBERT	Which one? The math assignment?
KARIN	No, the chemistry assignment.
NORBERT	That I'll do tonight. What are you doing this afternoon?
KARIN	I'm doing biology.
NORBERT	Oh, man! Do we have biology tomorrow, too?
KARIN	Of course.

What time is it?

DIETER	What time is it?
SABINE	It's five after ten.
DIETER	Oh no! I'm going to be late again!
SABINE	That's not so bad. You're good in chemistry after all.

chapter 7   Do you want to go to the concert?

Concert at the youth center

INGRID	Hey, Dieter, the *Hot Dogs* are playing tonight.
DIETER	Boy, that's dumb. I can't go tonight, unfortunately.
INGRID	And tomorrow night?
DIETER	Tomorrow night will be all right. Do you think we can still get tickets?
INGRID	Well, we can give it a try.

At the box office

INGRID	Do you still have tickets for tomorrow night?
MAN	I'm sorry. There are no tickets left for tomorrow night. I do have a couple of tickets for the day after tomorrow.
INGRID	*(To Dieter)* What do you think?

DIETER *I* can make it. But don't you have to work then?

INGRID Yes, I do. But I can certainly get time off. I just have to hear the *Hot Dogs*.

DIETER OK, that's settled.

chapter 8 What are your plans?

Picture postcards are interesting

PETRA That's a picture of Dresden.

THOMAS Interesting. Say, just why do you collect picture postcards?

PETRA I don't know. It's fun.

THOMAS Really? I don't understand that.

PETRA It's very simple. Old postcards are interesting and valuable as well.

Thomas needs a hobby

GERD That Thomas is really a bore.

PETRA Yes, he's always tired. And he always thinks everything is boring.

GERD He never feels like doing anything, either.

PETRA What he needs is a hobby.

GERD Maybe ham radio operator.

PETRA Or ceramics.

What are you planning to do today?

ASTRID Hey, Klaus, what are you going to do this afternoon?

KLAUS We're going to Hamburg.

ASTRID Are you going shopping?

KLAUS Yes, we're going to buy Gerd's birthday present.

ASTRID Where?

KLAUS I don't know yet. At Karstadt's maybe.

Why don't you come along?

ASTRID Are you coming along this afternoon?

ERIK Where to?

ASTRID Downtown. To *Musikhaus Schumann*.

ERIK Today, on Saturday?

ASTRID Yes, today is "long Saturday," you know.

ERIK Oh yes, that's right. The stores won't close until six. What do you want at Schumann's?

ASTRID To buy the new record by Katja Peters. All right, do you want to come along now or not?

ERIK I really don't have time.

ASTRID Oh, come on!

ERIK Well, OK.

I straightened up my room

NORBERT	What did you do over the weekend?
KARIN	I slept.
NORBERT	Oh, come on! You can't be serious!
KARIN	Yes. I am! Honest! Then on Sunday I built a model airplane. And what did you do?
NORBERT	I worked — as usual.
KARIN	What do you mean you worked?
NORBERT	I have to help at home. I straightened up my room and washed the car.
KARIN	You call that working?
NORBERT	Well, at least it's more than sleeping.

I baked a layer cake

SABINE	What did you do last weekend?
PAUL	I baked a cake for my mother. She invited my grandparents over for coffee and cake.
SABINE	How interesting!
PAUL	Don't be so sarcastic! You did ask, you know.
SABINE	Did the cake at least taste good?
PAUL	I don't know. I picked up Gerda and we took a walk. Then we had coffee and cake with Gerda's parents.

Who won?

GISELA	What did you do yesterday?
JAN	We played soccer.
GISELA	Against whom?
JAN	Oberndorf.
GISELA	Did you win?
JAN	No, we lost two to three.
GISELA	Oh man, I'm really sorry. But two to three against Oberndorf isn't really so bad.
JAN	That's true. Oberndorf is good.
GISELA	Well, maybe next time you can at least play a tie game.

I'm inviting you

INGRID	What do you have planned for tonight?
DIETER	I'm going to a party. What are you going to do?
INGRID	Nothing, actually.
DIETER	Nothing? That's great. Then you can come along.
INGRID	Where? To the party?
DIETER	Of course.

INGRID	But you're not giving the party.
DIETER	No, Gerd is. But I can invite you.
INGRID	Don't be silly. You can't do that.
DIETER	Sure I can. You know him pretty well, don't you?
INGRID	Yes . . . Well, all right. When does it start?
DIETER	At eight, I think. I'll call you.
INGRID	OK. So long. See you later.

chapter 11   Baker, butcher, supermarket

At the butcher shop

MR. LANGE	Hello, Mrs. Kraft. May I help you?
MRS. KRAFT	How much are the pork chops?
MR. LANGE	7 marks 50 a pound.
MRS. KRAFT	I'll need five chops.
MR. LANGE	Fine. Anything else?
MRS. KRAFT	I would like ten frankfurters.
MR. LANGE	There you are. Would you like something else?
MRS. KRAFT	No. That's all for today.
MR. LANGE	Thank you . . . So, here you are. That will be 24 marks 50 all together.
	***
	Here you go. You get 50 pfennigs back.
MRS. KRAFT	Thank you very much.
MR. LANGE	You're welcome. Good-by, Mrs. Kraft.
MRS. KRAFT	Good-by, Mr. Lange.

chapter 12   Enjoy your meal!

At the restaurant

WAITER	Good day, would you care for something to drink?
MRS. WOLF	Oh yes. I am so thirsty. One mineral water, please.
MR. WOLF	I'll have a mineral water too.
WAITER	Two mineral waters.
GABI	I'd like a cola, please.
WAITER	Thank you.
MR. WOLF	And the menu, please.
	The waiter brings the drinks.
WAITER	Would you like to order now?
MRS. WOLF	Yes, please. Is the roast beef tender?
WAITER	Oh yes. I can recommend it.
MRS. WOLF	Well then, three roast beef dinners with mashed potatoes and salad.
GABI	I don't want any mashed potatoes.
MRS. WOLF	Aren't you hungry?
GABI	Yes, I am, but I'd rather eat French fries.
	***
WAITER	Well now, did you enjoy your meal?

MRS. WOLF	Yes. The roast was excellent.
MR. WOLF	I'd like the check, please.
WAITER	Very well. All together it comes to 43 marks and 50 pfennigs.
MR. WOLF	Make it 45.
WAITER	Thank you very much.

chapter 13   You can always talk about the weather

How's the weather?

In the spring

STEFAN	What do you think? Is it going to rain tomorrow?
KARIN	Probably.
STEFAN	That is really dumb!
KARIN	Why?
STEFAN	My umbrella is broken.

In the summer

DIETER	Nice today, isn't it?
INGRID	Yes, it's finally getting warm.
DIETER	I hope it won't get too hot.
INGRID	I'd rather have it hot than cold.

In the fall

MRS. KRAFT	Beautiful weather, isn't it?
MR. WOLF	Yes, I really like this season. It's so nice and cool.
MRS. KRAFT	This is good hiking weather.
MR. WOLF	Too bad that we have to work.

In the winter

RALF	The wind is rather cold this morning.
ILSE	Yes, there was a frost last night.
RALF	This afternoon it's supposed to snow.
ILSE	That's great. Then we can go sledding.

chapter 15   A city visit

Where shall we go now?

KAI	Are we going to stand here forever? Where are we going to go now?
LORE	Dieter says that the music at the Western Club is terrific. But where in the world is the Western Club?
KAI	Here comes Dieter now. Why don't you ask him. He always knows everything.

LORE	Dieter, tell us, where is the Western Club?
DIETER	In Schwabing.
KAI	Boy, that's a long way from here. How are we going to get to Schwabing?
DIETER	You can go by subway — take the 3 or the 6. You can also walk.
KAI	To Schwabing on foot?
DIETER	Yes, it's only about a half an hour from here.
LORE	Don't you want to come along?
DIETER	No.
LORE	Why not?
DIETER	Because I'm too tired.
KAI	You can see that, man. He's almost asleep already.
LORE	Well OK, then we'll just go alone. Good night, Dieter. Sleep well (pleasant dreams).

How do we get to the Western Club?

KAI	I'm glad that we took the subway.
LORE	Yes, but now where is the Western Club?
KAI	Why don't you look at the map!
LORE	I haven't got it. Did you forget it?
KAI	I believe so. Then we'll just have to ask someone. Excuse me. Can you tell us how we can get to the Western Club?
STUDENT	Yes, I can. You go straight ahead to the traffic light. Turn right at the light. Then go straight ahead again until you come to a square with a fountain. There you turn left. Then you'll see the sign with the big boot.
KAI	Thanks a lot.
STUDENT	Don't mention it. Oh, wait a minute. It just occurred to me — the Western Club is closed today.
LORE	No, what rotten luck. What are we going to do now?
STUDENT	Why don't you go to Alfons. At Alfons there's always something going on. It's also a student hangout.

Pronouns

personal pronouns

	SINGULAR					PLURAL			FORMAL
Nominative	ich	du	er	es	sie	wir	ihr	sie	Sie
Accusative	mich	dich	ihn	es	sie	uns	euch	sie	Sie
Dative	mir	dir	ihm	ihm	ihr	uns	euch	ihnen	Ihnen

interrogative pronouns

Nominative	wer	was
Accusative	wen	was
Dative	wem	

demonstrative pronouns

	SINGULAR			PLURAL
Nominative	der	das	die	die
Accusative	den	das	die	die
Dative	dem	dem	der	denen

Words that introduce nouns

definite article

	SINGULAR			PLURAL
Nominative	der	das	die	die
Accusative	den	das	die	die
Dative	dem	dem	der	den

dieser-words

	SINGULAR			PLURAL
Nominative	dieser	dieses	diese	diese
Accusative	diesen	dieses	diese	diese
Dative	diesem	diesem	dieser	diesen

The **dieser**-words are: **dieser, jeder, mancher, solcher,** and **welcher.**

indefinite article and ein-words

	SINGULAR			PLURAL
Nominative	ein	ein	eine	keine
Accusative	einen	ein	eine	keine
Dative	einem	einem	einer	keinen

The **ein**-words are **kein** and the possessive adjectives:

mein	my	**unser**	our
dein	your (*fam.sg.*)	**euer**	your (*fam.pl.*)
sein	his, its	**ihr**	their
ihr	her, its	**Ihr**	your (*formal*)

Noun plurals

		SINGULAR	PLURAL
Pattern 1	no change in plural	das Mädchen	die Mädchen
	plural adds umlaut	der Bruder	die Brüder
Pattern 2	plural adds -e	der Freund	die Freunde
	plural adds -e and umlaut	der Rock	die Röcke
Pattern 3	plural adds -er	das Kind	die Kinder
	plural adds -er and umlaut	der Mann	die Männer
Pattern 4	plural adds -n	die Familie	die Familien
	plural adds -en	die Frau	die Frauen
	plural adds -nen	die Schülerin	die Schülerinnen
Pattern 5	plural adds -s	der Pulli	die Pullis

Special der-nouns

	SINGULAR	PLURAL
Nominative	der Herr	die Herren
Accusative	den Herrn	die Herren
Dative	dem Herrn	den Herren

The special **der**-nouns include **der Junge, der Kunde,** and **der Student.**

Comparison of irregular adjectives and adverbs

Base form	gern	gut	viel	hoch
Comparative	lieber	besser	mehr	höher

Prepositions

WITH ACCUSATIVE	CONTRACTIONS
durch	durch das > durchs
für	für das > fürs
gegen	um das > ums
ohne	
um	

WITH DATIVE	CONTRACTIONS
aus	bei dem > beim
außer	von dem > vom
bei	zu dem > zum
mit	zu der > zur
nach	
seit	
von	
zu	

Numbers

0 = null	11 = elf	22 = zweiundzwanzig	60 = sechzig
1 = eins	12 = zwölf	23 = dreiundzwanzig	70 = siebzig
2 = zwei	13 = dreizehn	24 = vierundzwanzig	80 = achtzig
3 = drei	14 = vierzehn	25 = fünfundzwanzig	90 = neunzig
4 = vier	15 = fünfzehn	26 = sechsundzwanzig	100 = hundert
5 = fünf	16 = sechzehn	27 = siebenundzwanzig	101 = hunderteins
6 = sechs	17 = siebzehn	28 = achtundzwanzig	102 = hundertzwei
7 = sieben	18 = achtzehn	29 = neunundzwanzig	121 = hunderteinundzwanzig
8 = acht	19 = neunzehn	30 = dreißig	500 = fünfhundert
9 = neun	20 = zwanzig	40 = vierzig	1.000 = tausend
10 = zehn	21 = einundzwanzig	50 = fünfzig	

Verbs

regular verbs

Infinitive	kommen	finden[1]	tanzen[2]
Present	ich komme	finde	tanze
	du kommst	findest	tanzt
	er/sie kommt	findet	tanzt
	wir kommen	finden	tanzen
	ihr kommt	findet	tanzt
	sie kommen	finden	tanzen
	Sie kommen	finden	tanzen
Imperatives	komm!	finde!	tanz!
	kommt!	findet!	tanzt!
	kommen Sie!	finden Sie!	tanzen Sie!
Conversational past	ich bin gekommen	habe gefunden	habe getanzt

1. A verb with stem ending in **-d** or **-t** has an **-e** before the **-st** and **-t** endings.
2. The **-st** of the **du**-form ending contracts to **-t** when the verb stem ends in a sibilant (**-s, -ss, -ß, -z,** or **-tz**). Thus, the **du-** and **er/sie**-forms are identical.

verbs with stem-vowel change

Infinitive	geben (e > i)	lesen (e > ie)	fahren (a > ä)
Present	ich gebe	lese	fahre
	du gibst	liest	fährst
	er/sie gibt	liest	fährt
	wir geben	lesen	fahren
	ihr gebt	lest	fahrt
	sie geben	lesen	fahren
	Sie geben	lesen	fahren
Imperatives	gib!	lies!	fahr!
	gebt!	lest!	fahrt!
	geben Sie!	lesen Sie!	fahren Sie!
Conversational past	ich habe gegeben	habe gelesen	bin gefahren

The following verbs used in this text have stem-vowel changes:

e > i: essen, geben, helfen, nehmen, sprechen, vergessen
e > ie: empfehlen, lesen, sehen
a > ä: backen, einladen, fahren, fallen, schlafen, tragen, waschen
au > äu: laufen

irregular verbs

Infinitive	sein	haben	werden	wissen
Present	ich bin	habe	werde	weiß
	du bist	hast	wirst	weißt
	er/sie ist	hat	wird	weiß
	wir sind	haben	werden	wissen
	ihr seid	habt	werdet	wißt
	sie sind	haben	werden	wissen
	Sie sind	haben	werden	wissen
Imperatives	sei!	habe!	werde!	
	seid!	habt!	werdet!	
	seien Sie!	haben Sie!	werden Sie!	
Conversational past	ich bin gewesen	habe gehabt	bin geworden	habe gewußt

present tense of modal auxiliaries

	dürfen	können	müssen	sollen	wollen	mögen	
ich	darf	kann	muß	soll	will	mag	möchte
du	darfst	kannst	mußt	sollst	willst	magst	möchtest
er/sie	darf	kann	muß	soll	will	mag	möchte
wir	dürfen	können	müssen	sollen	wollen	mögen	möchten
ihr	dürft	könnt	müßt	sollt	wollt	mögt	möchtet
sie	dürfen	können	müssen	sollen	wollen	mögen	möchten
Sie	dürfen	können	müssen	sollen	wollen	mögen	möchten

principal parts of irregular weak verbs

INFINITIVE	PAST PARTICIPLE	ENGLISH EQUIVALENT
bringen	gebracht	to bring
denken	gedacht	to think
kennen	gekannt	to know
nennen	genannt	to name
wissen	gewußt	to know

principal parts of strong verbs used in this text

Compound verbs (like **mitgehen**) are not included when the basic form of the verb (like **gehen**) is included, since the principal parts are the same. Stem-vowel changes in the present tense are indicated in parentheses after the infinitive. For additional meanings, see the German-English Vocabulary.

INFINITIVE	PAST PARTICIPLE	ENGLISH EQUIVALENT
ab·biegen	(ist) abgebogen	to turn
an·rufen	angerufen	to telephone
backen (ä)	gebacken	to bake
beginnen	begonnen	to begin
bekommen	bekommen	to get, to obtain
bestehen	bestanden	to pass (a test)
bleiben	(ist) geblieben	to stay
ein·laden (ä)	eingeladen	to invite
empfehlen (ie)	empfohlen	to recommend
essen (i)	gegessen	to eat
fahren (ä)	(ist) gefahren	to drive
fallen (ä)	(ist) gefallen	to fall
finden	gefunden	to find
fliegen	(ist) geflogen	to fly
frieren	gefroren	to freeze
geben (i)	gegeben	to give
gehen	(ist) gegangen	to go
gewinnen	gewonnen	to win
heißen	geheißen	to be called
helfen (i)	geholfen	to help
kommen	(ist) gekommen	to come
laufen (äu)	(ist) gelaufen	to run
lesen (ie)	gelesen	to read
liegen	gelegen	to lie
nehmen (nimmt)	genommen	to take
reiten	(ist) geritten	to ride (horseback)
scheinen	geschienen	to shine
schlafen (ä)	geschlafen	to sleep
schreiben	geschrieben	to write
schwimmen	(ist) geschwommen	to swim
sehen (ie)	gesehen	to see
sein	(ist) gewesen	to be
singen	gesungen	to sing
sprechen (i)	gesprochen	to speak
stehen	gestanden	to stand
tragen (ä)	getragen	to wear; to carry
trinken	getrunken	to drink
tun	getan	to do
vergessen (i)	vergessen	to forget
waschen (ä)	gewaschen	to wash
werden (wird)	(ist) geworden	to become

The following word lists will help you to increase the number of things you can say and write during your study of each chapter. Some of the words may be introduced as active vocabulary later than the chapters for which they are given here.

chapter 1

Adjectives for mood or personality

ausgezeichnet excellent
erstklassig first-rate
furchtbar horrible
klasse terrific
miserabel miserable
schrecklich dreadful
spitze tops, first-rate

Descriptive adjectives

clever clever
doof idiotic
dumm stupid
fies disgusting
klug smart
lahm tired
langsam slow
langweilig boring
launisch moody
nett nice
verrückt crazy

Farewells

auf Wiederhören! good-by *(on the telephone)*
bis bald! see you soon
bis dann! see you later
mach's gut! take it easy
tschau! so long

chapter 3

Musical instruments

das Akkordeon accordion
die Blockflöte recorder
das Cello cello
das Fagott bassoon
die Harfe harp
der Kontrabaß double bass
die Oboe oboe
die Orgel organ
das Saxophon saxophone
die Posaune (+blasen) trombone
die Trompete (+blasen) trumpet
die Tuba (+blasen) tuba
das Waldhorn (+blasen) French horn

Sports and games

Billard billiards
Dame checkers
Eishockey ice hockey
Federball badminton
Golf golf
Handball (Hallenhandball) handball
Hockey field hockey
Mühle Chinese checkers
Schach chess
Tischtennis ping pong (table tennis)
Wasserball water polo

chapter 4

Professions

ein Angestellter/eine Angestellte employee
der Arzthelfer/die Arzthelferin medical assistant
der Bankkaufmann/die Bankkauffrau banker
der Dolmetscher/die Dolmetscherin interpreter
der Fremdsprachenkorrespondent/die —— korrespondentin foreign language correspondent
der Industriekaufmann/die —— kauffrau business employee
der Informatiker/die Informatikerin computer engineer

der Ingenieur/die Ingenieurin engineer
der Krankenpfleger/die Krankenschwester
  nurse
der Mechaniker/die Mechanikerin mechanic
der Programmierer/die Programmiererin
  (computer) programmer
der Rechtsanwalt/die Rechtsanwältin lawyer
der Sekretär/die Sekretärin secretary
der Steward/die Stewardeß steward(ess)

Family members

die Tante aunt
der Onkel uncle
die Kusine cousin (f.)
der Cousin (der Vetter) cousin (m.)
die Oma grandma
der Opa grandpa
die Großmutter grandmother
der Großvater grandfather
der Neffe nephew
die Nichte niece
der Sohn son
die Stiefmutter stepmother
der Stiefvater stepfather
die Schwägerin sister-in-law
der Schwager brother-in-law
die Tochter daughter

Physical description of people

attraktiv attractive
blond blond
dick fat
brünett brunette
häßlich ugly
hübsch pretty
mager thin
normal normal
schwach weak
stark strong
süß sweet

chapter 5

Clothing for men and women

der Anorak jacket with hood
der Hut hat
die Kniestrümpfe (pl.) knee socks

die Latzhose overalls
die Lederjacke leather jacket
der Motorradanzug motorcycle outfit
die Mütze cap
der Parka parka
der Regenmantel raincoat
der Rollkragenpullover turtleneck
die Sandalen (pl.) sandals
der Schlafanzug pajamas
die Shorts shorts
der Stiefel boot
die Strickjacke cardigan
das T-Shirt t-shirt
der Trainingsanzug warm-up suit
der Turnschuh gym shoe, sneaker
die Unterwäsche underwear
die Weste vest
der Wintermantel winter coat

Clothing for women

das Abendkleid evening gown
der Badeanzug bathing suit
der Hosenanzug pants suit
der Hosenrock culottes
das Partykleid party dress
die Pumps (pl.) pumps, dress shoes
das Sonnentop halter top
das Kostüm suit
das Trägerkleid jumper

Clothing for men

die Badehose bathing trunks
der Blazer blazer
das Freizeithemd casual shirt
das Polohemd polo shirt
der Sakko sport coat
der Smoking dinner jacket

Colors

lila lilac
orange orange
purpurrot crimson
rosa pink
türkis turquoise
violett violet
hell(blau) light (blue)
dunkel(blau) dark (blue)

chapter 6

School subjects

Französisch French
Gemeinschaftskunde social studies
Geographie geography
Griechisch Greek
Informatik computer science
Italienisch Italian
Kunsterziehung art
Musik music
Religion(skunde) religion
Spanisch Spanish
Werken shop

Classroom objects

der Computer computer
die Diskette computer disk
die Federmappe pencil case
der Filzstift felt pen
das Klassenbuch record book
der Klassenschrank cupboard
das Klassenzimmer classroom
die Kreide chalk
der Kurs course
die Landkarte (Wandkarte) map
das Lineal ruler
der Notizblock note pad
der Overheadprojektor overhead projector
der Papierkorb wastebasket
das Ringbuch loose leaf binder
der Schwamm sponge
das Sprachlabor language lab
die Sprachkassette language tape
die (Wand)tafel chalkboard

Schoolrooms

die Aula auditorium
der Musiksaal music room
die Turnhalle gymnasium
der Werkraum shop
der Zeichensaal art room

Physical attributes of objects

aus Glas glass
aus Holz wooden

aus Metall metal
aus Papier paper
aus Stein stone
dunkel dark
hell light
farbig (bunt) colorful
glatt smooth
hart hard
massiv massive, solid
rauh rough
weich soft
biegsam pliable
bequem comfortable
gemütlich cozy

chapter 8

Stereo and audio-visual equipment

der Farbfernseher color television
der Kopfhörer headphone
der Lautsprecher loudspeaker
das Mikrophon microphone
der Schwarzweißfernseher black-and-white television
der Stereorecorder stereo recorder
das Tonband tape
das Tonbandgerät tape recorder (reel-to-reel)
der Tuner tuner
der Verstärker amplifier
die Videokassette video cassette
der Videorecorder video recorder
der Walkman walkman

Hobbies

angeln to fish
basteln to tinker with something, to work at a hobby
Blumen (z.B. Rosen, Dahlien, Lilien) flowers (e.g., roses, dahlias, lilies)
der Garten garden
malen to paint
Musik hören to listen to music
schreiben (Gedichte, Geschichten) to write (poems, stories)
zeichnen to draw

Collectibles

alte Bücher   old books
alte Flaschen   old bottles
alte Fotos   old photos
Antiquitäten   antiques
Autogramme   autographs
Comics   comic books
Glas   glass
Münzen   coins
Pflanzen (getrocknet)   plants (dried)
Puppen   dolls
Silber   silver
Streichholzschachteln   match covers
altes Zinn   old pewter

chapter 9

Chores

(die) Fenster putzen   to clean windows
(das) Mittagessen kochen   to cook dinner
(das) Abendessen vorbereiten/machen   to
  prepare supper
meinem Vater helfen   to help my father
meiner Mutter helfen   to help my mother
(die) Wäsche bügeln   to iron (clothes)
Wäsche/Kleider flicken   to mend clothes
das Haus/den Zaun/das Boot streichen   to paint
  the house/the fence/the boat
(den) Rasen mähen   to mow the lawn
(den) Rasen sprengen   to water the lawn
(die) Bäume beschneiden/pflanzen/fällen   to
  prune/to plant/to cut trees
die Blumen gießen   to water the flowers
die Hecke schneiden   to trim the hedge
(das) Unkraut jäten   to pull out weeds
(das) Holz sägen/spalten/hacken   to saw/to split/
  to chop wood
(den) Schnee fegen (kehren)/schippen   to sweep/
  to shovel snow
das Treppenhaus putzen   to clean the stairway (in
  an apartment building)

chapter 10

sports

angeln   to fish
Badminton spielen   to play badminton

das Boxen   boxing
das Drachenfliegen   hang gliding
das Fallschirmspringen   parachute jumping
fechten   to fence
das Gewichtheben   weightlifting
das Jagen   hunting
Kanu fahren   to canoe
das Kegeln   bowling
die Leichtathletik   track and field
das Minigolf   miniature golf
der Radsport   bicycling
das Ringen   wrestling
rudern   to row
das Schießen   shooting
das Segelfliegen   glider flying
der Selbstverteidigungssport   martial arts
Squash spielen   to play squash
das Tanzen   dancing
das Tauchen   diving
das Turnen   gymnastics
Volleyball spielen   to play volleyball
Wasserski fahren   to go waterskiing
das Yoga   yoga

chapter 11

Small specialty shops

die Apotheke   pharmacy
das Blumengeschäft   florist
die Chemische Reinigung   dry cleaner
die Drogerie   drugstore
das Eisenwarengeschäft   hardware store
das Elektrogeschäft   appliance store
das Feinkostgeschäft   delicatessen
das Fotogeschäft   camera store
das Handarbeitsgeschäft   needle-craft shop
der Juwelier   jeweler
der Klempner (Spengler)   plumber
die Konditorei   pastry shop
das Lederwarengeschäft   leather goods store
das Milchgeschäft   dairy store
der Optiker   optician
das Papiergeschäft   stationery
das Sportgeschäft (Sportausrüstungen)   sporting
  goods store (sporting goods)
der Zeitungskiosk   newsstand

chapter 12

Breakfast

die **Corn-flakes** cornflake cereal
das **weichgekochte Ei** soft-boiled egg
der **Haferbrei** oatmeal porridge
der **Honig** honey
der **Joghurt** yogurt
der **Käse** cheese
die **Margarine** margarine
das **Müsli** mixed-grain cereal
der **Orangensaft** orange juice
der **Tomatensaft** tomato juice
das **Graubrot** light rye bread
der **Pumpernickel** pumpernickel bread
das **Schwarzbrot** dark rye bread
der **Toast** toast
das **Vollkornbrot** coarse whole grain bread
das **Weißbrot** white bread
der **Aufschnitt** cold cuts

Noon meal

die **Erbsensuppe** pea soup
die **Fruchtsuppe (kalt)** fruit soup (cold)
die **Kartoffelsuppe** potato soup
der **Bratfisch** fried fish
das **Fischfilet** filet of fish
der **Kochfisch** boiled fish
der **Bohnensalat** bean salad
der **gemischte Salat** vegetable salad plate
der **grüne Salat** tossed (green) salad
die **Ente** duck
die **Gans** goose
das **Reh** venison
das **Gulasch** beef goulash
der **Hackbraten** chopped steak
die **Kasseler Rippchen** smoked pork chops
die **Roulade** beef rolls filled with bacon
die **Kohlroulade** cabbage roll
Königsberger Klopse meatballs
der **Sauerbraten** sauerbraten (marinated beef)
die **Schweinshaxe** pigs' knuckles
die **Klöße** *(pl.)*/**Knödel** *(pl.)* dumplings
die **Kartoffelknödel** *(pl.)* potato dumplings
der **Kartoffelpuffer** potato pancake
die **Leberknödel** *(pl.)* liver dumplings
die **Dampfnudeln** *(pl.)* steamed dumplings
die **Spätzle** *(pl.)* noodles

das **Sauerkraut** sauerkraut
der **Blumenkohl** cauliflower
die **Bohnen** *(pl.)* beans
die **Erbsen** *(pl.)* peas
der **Lauch** leek
die **Paprikaschote** green pepper
die **Pilze** *(pl.)* mushrooms
der **Rosenkohl** brussel sprouts
der **Rotkohl** red cabbage
der **Sellerie** celery
der **Spargel** asparagus
die **Tomate** tomato
die **Zucchini** zucchini
die **Zwiebel** onion

Evening meal

das **(Beefsteak) Tatar** spiced, raw ground beef
der **Speck** bacon
der **Quark** *(similar to)* cottage cheese
der **Schnittkäse** sliced cheese
der **Streichkäse** spreadable cheese
der **Senf** mustard
die **Bratwurst** frying sausage
die **Fleischwurst** *(similar to)* baloney
die **Knackwurst** knackwurst
die **Weißwurst** white veal sausage
die **Zunge** tongue
der **(Wurst)aufschnitt** cold cuts

Desserts

der **Fruchtsalat (der Obstsalat)** fruit salad
die **Melone** melon
die **Rote Grütze** red fruit pudding
die **Schokoladencreme** chocolate mousse
die **Zitronencreme** lemon mousse

Table setting

das **Besteck** flatware
der **Eierbecher** egg cup
der **(Eß)löffel** (table)spoon
die **Gabel** fork
das **Gedeck** table setting
die **Kaffeekanne/die Teekanne** coffee pot/teapot
das **Messer** knife
das **Milchkännchen** creamer
der **Pfefferstreuer** pepper shaker
der **Salzstreuer** salt shaker

die Schüssel   bowl
die Serviette   napkin
der Teelöffel   teaspoon
der Teller   plate
die Tortenplatte   cake plate
die Untertasse   saucer
die Zuckerdose   sugarbowl

chapter 13

Weather expressions

der Wetterbericht   weather report
die Wettervorhersage   weather prediction
die Warmfront   warm front
die Kaltfront   cold front
das Hoch   high
das Tief   low
der Niederschlag   precipitation
der Schneefall   snowfall
der Hagel   hail
der Landregen   all-day rain
das Schauer   shower
der Nieselregen (Sprühregen)   drizzle
der Luftdruck   air pressure
das Gewitter   thunderstorm
der Blitz/der Donner   lightning/thunder
die Windrichtung   wind direction
es gießt (in Strömen)   it's pouring
es regnet Bindfäden   it's raining cats and dogs
es ist naßkalt   it's damp and cold
neblig (der Nebel)   foggy (fog)
sonnig   sunny
schwül   humid
eisig   icy cold
wolkenlos   cloudless
heiter   fair
bedeckt   overcast

Geographical terms

die Anhöhe (der Hügel)   hill
der Atlantik   Atlantic
der Bach   brook
der Berg   mountain
das Bundesland   (federal) state
der Bundesstaat   (American) state
die Ebbe, die Flut   low tide, high tide
der Fluß   river

das Gebirge   mountain range
der Gipfel   peak
der Gletscher   glacier
die Hauptstadt   capital
die Insel   island
der Kanal   canal; channel
die Küste   coast
das Meer   sea
der Pazifik   Pacific
der See   lake
der Strand   beach
der Strom   river; current
das Tal   valley
der Teich   pond
das Ufer   shore
der Wald   woods
die Wiese   meadow

chapter 14

Modes of transportation

der Pferdewagen   horse-drawn wagon
die Kutsche   carriage
der Kombiwagen   station wagen
der LKW (= Lastkraftwagen)/der Laster   truck
der PKW (= Personenkraftwagen)   passenger car
der Anhänger   trailer
die Eisenbahn   train, railway
der Güterzug   freight train
die Bergbahn   mountain railway; cable car
die Fähre   ferry
der Schleppkahn   barge
das Boot   boat
das Ruderboot   rowboat
das Segelboot   sailboat
das Motorboot   motor boat
das Segelschiff   sailing ship
der Tanker   tanker
das Containerschiff   container ship
der Frachter   freighter
der Passagierdampfer   passenger ship
das Propellerflugzeug   propeller plane
der Jet   jet
der Hubschrauber   helicopter
das Segelflugzeug   glider plane

Parts of a bicycle

der **Fahrradhelm**   cyclists' helmet
der **Fahrradschlauch**   bicycle inner tube
die **Rücktrittbremse**   foot brake
die **Gangschaltung**   gears
die **Handbremse**   hand brake
die **Kette**   chain
die **Klingel (Glocke)**   bell
die **Lampe**   headlight
der **Lenker**   handlebar
die **Luftpumpe**   air pump
das **Pedal**   pedal
das **(Vorder-, Hinter-) Rad**   (front, back) wheel
der **Rahmen**   frame
der **Reifen**   tire
das **Rücklicht**   tail light
der **Sattel**   seat
das **Schloß**   lock
der **Schlüssel**   key

Parts of a car

das **Armaturenbrett**   dashboard
die **Batterie**   battery
der **Blinker**   turn signal
die **Bremse (das Bremspedal)**   brake (pedal)
das **Fernlicht**   high beam
das **Gas (das Gaspedal)**   gas (pedal)
die **Handbremse**   hand brake
das **Handschuhfach**   glove compartment
die **Hupe**   horn
der **Kofferraum**   trunk
der **Kotflügel**   fender
der **Kühler**   radiator
die **Kupplung (das Kupplungspedal)**   clutch
  (pedal)
das **Lenkrad**   steering wheel
die **Motorhaube**   hood
der **Nebelscheinwerfer**   fog lights
der **Rücksitz**   back seat
der **Rückspiegel**   rear-view mirror
der **Schalthebel**   gear shift
der **Scheibenwischer**   windshield wiper
der **Scheinwerfer**   headlight
der **Sicherheitsgurt**   seat belt
der **Sitz**   seat
die **Stoßstange**   bumper

die **Warnblinkanlage**   hazard signal
die **Wasserpumpe**   water pump
die **Windschutzscheibe**   windshield
die **Zündkerze**   spark plug

chapter 15

Landmarks

die **Autobahnauffahrt, die Autobahnausfahrt**
  expressway on-ramp, off-ramp
die **Autobahnraststätte**   expressway restaurant
das **Autobahnkreuz**   expressway interchange
die **Bahnlinie**   railroad (tracks)
der **Bauernhof**   farm
die **Brücke**   bridge
die **Bundesstraße**   federal highway
die **Burg**   fortress
das **Denkmal**   monument
das **Dorf**   village
die **Fabrik**   factory
der **Flugplatz**   airport
der **Friedhof**   cemetery
der **Funkturm**   radio and TV tower
der **Fußweg**   footpath
die **Kapelle**   chapel
das **Kloster**   monastery
die **Mühle**   mill
die **Ruine**   ruin
das **Schloß**   castle
der **Tunnel**   tunnel

Asking directions

Wo ist [der Bahnhof]?   Where is the [train
  station]?
**Wie weit ist es [zum Bahnhof]? nach
  [Stuttgart]?**   How far is it [to the train station]?
to [Stuttgart]?
Wie komme ich am schnellsten [zum Bahnhof]?
  What is the quickest way [to the train station]?
Wo ist hier in der Nähe [ein Café]?   Is there [a
  café] around here?
Wissen Sie den Weg nach [Oberndorf]?   Do you
  know the way to [Oberndorf]?
**Wir wollen nach [Stuttgart]. Wie fahren wir am
  besten?**   We're going to [Stuttgart]. What is the
  best route?

Wo geht's hier [zum Bahnhof]?   How do you get [to the train station] from here?

Wir wollen nach [München]. Müssen/Können wir über [Augsburg] fahren?   We're going to [Munich]. Must/can we go by way of [Augsburg]?

Was ist näher? Ist das näher?   What is closer? Is that closer?

Giving directions

Sind Sie zu Fuß oder mit dem Auto?   Are you walking or driving?

Da nehmen Sie am besten [ein Taxi, die Bahn].   It's best if you take [a taxi, the streetcar].

Da fahren Sie am besten mit [der U-Bahn].   It's best if you go by [subway].

Nehmen Sie die [Drei].   Take number [three].

[Dort/An der Ecke/An der Kreuzung] ist die Haltestelle.   The stop is [over there/on the corner/at the intersection].

[Zum Bahnhof] sind es [zehn Minuten].   It's [ten minutes] to the [train station].

An der [ersten/zweiten] Kreuzung gehen Sie [rechts].   At the [first/second] intersection turn [right].

Gehen Sie die [erste] Straße [rechts]!   Take the [first] street [to the right].

Gehen Sie [am See/an der Mauer] entlang!   Go along [the lake/the wall].

Fahren Sie um [die Kirche] herum!   Drive around [the church].

Lassen Sie [die Kirche] links liegen!   Keep [the church] on your left.

Supplementary Expressions

1. Expressing skepticism

rede keinen Unsinn/Stuß
ist das dein Ernst?
meinst du? wirklich? meinst du das wirklich?
das ist ja komisch/eigenartig
irgendetwas stimmt hier nicht
ist das wahr?
wer sagt das? wer hat das gesagt?
woher weißt du das? wo/von wem hast du das gehört?

2. Expressing insecurity or doubt

das ist unwahrscheinlich
es ist unwahrscheinlich, daß . . . [sie das gesagt hat]
das ist zweifelhaft
ich glaube nicht, daß . . . [er das gesagt hat]
ich glaube das nicht
das kann nicht sein

3. Expressing annoyance

Quatsch; Unsinn; Blödsinn
Blödmann; Dussel; Idiot
der hat/du hast wohl nicht alle Tassen im Schrank
bei der/bei dir ist wohl eine Schraube los/locker
hör mal
geh
also, wissen Sie; wirklich; tsk, tsk, tsk
(das ist doch) nicht zu glauben
(das ist) unerhört/unglaublich
(das ist eine) Schweinerei
das tut/sagt man nicht
das kannst du doch nicht machen/sagen

4. Stalling for time

also; na ja, ja nun
hmmmmmmm
laß mich mal nachdenken
darüber muß ich (erst mal) nachdenken
das kann ich so (auch) nicht sagen

5. Being noncommittal

(das ist ja) interessant
hmmmmmmm
wirklich?

6. Expressing good wishes

ich halte (dir/Ihnen) die Daumen
Gesundheit
(ich wünsche) guten Appetit/gesegnete Mahlzeit
Prost; auf Ihr/dein Wohl; zum Wohl
herzlichen Glückwunsch
ich wünsche dir/Ihnen gute Reise
       gute Besserung
       viel Glück
       viel Vergnügen/Spaß
       alles Gute

7. Courtesy expressions

bitte (sehr/schön)
danke (sehr/schön)

8. Saying "You're welcome"

bitte (sehr/schön)
gern geschehen
nichts zu danken

9. Expressing surprise

ach nein
(wie) ist das (nur) möglich?
das hätte ich nicht gedacht
das ist ja prima/toll/klasse
ich werd' verrückt
(das ist ja) nicht zu glauben
ich bin von den Socken
das ist ja das Schärfste

10. Expressing agreement (and disagreement)

natürlich (nicht); selbstverständlich (nicht)
warum denn nicht?
das kann (nicht) sein
(das) stimmt (nicht); richtig/falsch
das finde ich auch/nicht
genau; eben

11. Responding to requests

bitte; selbstverständlich; natürlich
gern; machen wir; mit Vergnügen
(es tut mir leid, aber) das geht nicht
ich kann (das) nicht . . . [reparieren]
das habe ich nicht
das ist zu schwer/groß/teuer

12. Expressing regret

das tut mir leid
es tut mir leid, daß . . . [ich nicht kommen kann]
leider . . . [kann ich morgen nicht]
es geht leider nicht
unglücklicherweise . . . [war ich gestern nicht zu
    Hause]
schade [,daß . . .]

13. Excusing oneself

Entschuldigung; Pardon; Verzeihung; entschuldigen
    Sie
entschuldigen Sie bitte, daß . . . [ich erst jetzt
    komme]
hier ist meine Entschuldigung
meine Mutter hat mir eine Entschuldigung
    geschrieben
das ist keine Entschuldigung

14. Expressing indifference

das ist mir egal
es ist mir egal, ob . . . [er kommt]
das macht mir nichts aus
es macht mir nichts aus, daß . . . [sie mehr verdient]
macht nichts
das ist mir wurscht
das kannst du machen, wie du willst
das kannst du halten wie der Dachdecker

so kann man das auch machen/sagen
ich habe nichts dagegen

15. Expressing admiration

ach, wie schön; klasse
erstklassig; ausgezeichnet
das ist aber nett (von dir, ihnen, *etc.*)
der/die ist nett
das sind nette Leute

16. Expressing joy and pleasure

wir freuen uns
wir freuen uns auf ihn/seinen Besuch/die Ferien
wir sind froh
wir sind froh (darüber), daß . . . [er wieder arbeitet]
es freut mich, daß . . . [sie gekommen ist]
das tun/kochen/essen wir gern
das macht mir/uns Spaß
das machen wir zum Vergnügen

17. Making requests

hätten Sie Lust . . . [mitzukommen]?
hätten Sie Zeit, . . . [uns zu besuchen]?
hätten Sie etwas [Zeit] für mich?
ich hätte gern . . . [ein Pfund Äpfel]
könnten Sie . . . [mein Auto reparieren]?
würden Sie bitte . . . [um zehn Uhr hier sein]?
hätten Sie etwas dagegen?
hätten Sie etwas dagegen, wenn . . . [ich mitkomme]?
dürfte ich . . . [ein Stück Kuchen haben]?
macht es Ihnen etwas aus?
macht es Ihnen etwas aus, wenn . . . [mein Bruder
    mitkommt]?
würden Sie so freundlich sein und . . . [den Brief
    schreiben]?
ich möchte fragen, ob [ich mitkommen] darf/kann?
könnte ich . . . [um neun Uhr zu Ihnen kommen]?

18. Asking for favors

könntest du mir einen Gefallen tun und . . . [mich
    mitnehmen]?
ich hätte eine Bitte: könntest/würdest du . . . [mich
    mitnehmen]?

19. Making surmises

ich denke ja; ich glaube schon
ich glaube (schon), daß . . . [sie das gesagt hat]
das dürfte/könnte wahr/richtig sein
wahrscheinlich; wahrscheinlich [stimmt das]
sicher; ich bin sicher; ich bin ziemlich sicher, daß . . .
  [er das gesagt hat]
ich nehme (das) an; ich nehme das (nur) an
ich nehme an, daß . . . [das stimmt]
das scheint . . . [nicht zu stimmen]

20. Expressing expectation

hoffentlich; hoffentlich . . . [kommt sie]
ich hoffe (es) (sehr)
ich hoffe, daß . . . [sie das Paket bekommen hat]
ich freue mich auf . . . [die Ferien]

21. Expressing fears

ich fürchte, daß . . . [sie nicht kommt]
ich habe Angst
ich habe Angst, . . . [nach Hause zu gehen]
davor habe ich Angst
ich habe Angst vor . . . [dem Hund]
[ich bleibe] lieber [hier]

22. Giving advice

ich schlage vor, daß . . . [wir um acht anfangen]
ich rate dir, . . . [zu Hause zu bleiben]
das würde ich dir (nicht) raten
das würde ich machen/sagen
das würde ich anders/so machen
das mußt du so machen
ich zeige dir, . . . [wie man das macht]

23. Correcting misunderstandings

das habe ich nicht so/ernst gemeint
das habe ich nur aus Spaß gesagt
das war doch nicht so gemeint
das war nicht mein Ernst

German-English Vocabulary

The German-English vocabulary contains the basic words and expressions listed in the chapter vocabularies, plus words that occur in headings, captions, cultural notes, and reading material. The symbol ~ signifies the key word (minus the definite article, if any) for that entry. For example, **guten ~!** under **Abend** means **guten Abend!** The numbers in italics following the definitions refer to the chapters in which the active words are introduced.

Nouns are listed with their plural forms: **der Abend, -e.** No plural entry is given if the plural is rarely used or non-existent. Both the accusative/dative and the plural endings are given for special **der**-nouns: **der Herr, -n, -en.**

Strong and irregular weak verbs are listed with their principal parts. Vowel changes in the present tense are noted in parentheses, followed by the past participle forms. All verbs take **haben** in the past participle unless indicated with **sein** — for example: **fahren (ä, ist gefahren).** Separable-prefix verbs are indicated with a raised dot: **auf·stehen.**

Adjectives and adverbs that take umlaut in the comparative are noted: **warm (ä).**

ab·biegen (ist abgebogen) to make a turn, *15*

der Abend, -e evening; **guten ~!** good evening! *1;* **zu ~ essen** to have supper, *12;* **am ~** in the evening

das Abendessen supper, *12;* **zum ~** for supper, *12*

abends evenings, in the evening, *4*

die Abendvorstellung evening performance

aber *flavoring word with the meaning of* really, certainly, *2; (coord. conj.)* but; however, *3*

ab·fahren (ä; ist abgefahren) to leave, to depart, *15*

ab·holen to call for, to pick up, *9*

ab·räumen to clear, to remove, *9*

ab·stauben to dust, *9*

das Abteil, -e (train) compartment

ab·trocknen to dry up, to wipe dry, *9*

ach oh, *2;* **~ so** oh, I see!, *2*

acht eight, *2*

achtzehn eighteen, *2*

achtzig eighty, *4*

adé good-by

adieu good-by

die Ahnung, -en idea, notion; **keine ~** no idea

aktiv active

alle all, everyone, *9;* **vor allem** above all

allein alone, *11*

alles all, everything, *7;* **~ Gute (zum Geburtstag)** all the best (on your birthday)

das Alphabet alphabet

als *(after a comparative)* than, *9; (sub. conj.)* as, *12; (sub. conj.)* when

also well, *7;* **~ gut** O.K. then

alt (ä) old, *2*

altmodisch old-fashioned, outdated, *5*

am (= an dem) in the; **~ Samstag** on Saturday, *4;* **~ Tag** in the daytime

(das) Amerika America

amerikanisch American, *13*

die Ampel, -n traffic signal, *15*

an (+ acc. or dat.) at, *7;* to, *14;* **schreiben ~ (+ acc.)** to write to

ander other; **etwas anderes** something different

ändern to change

anders different, *13*

an·fassen to handle, touch

an·kommen (ist angekommen) to arrive, to come, *15*

an·machen to switch on *(the light), 8*

an·rufen (angerufen) to call, to telephone, *10*

die Ansichtskarte, -n picture postcard, *8*

das Antonym, -e antonym

die Antwort, -en answer

antworten to answer

der Anzug, -̈e man's suit, *5*

der Apfel, -̈ apple, *11;* **der Apfelkuchen** cake topped with sliced apples

die Apotheke, -n pharmacy

der Apotheker, —/die Apothekerin,
—nen pharmacist, *4*
der Appetit: guten ~! enjoy your meal, *12*
der April April, *2*
die Arbeit, —en work; ~ machen to do work, *9;*
zur ~ to work, *14*
arbeiten to work, *4*
der Arbeiter, —/die Arbeiterin, —nen worker, *4*
der Arbeitsplan, ̈e work schedule, *9*
der Architekt, —en/die Architektin,
—nen architect
der Arzt, ̈e/die Ärztin, —nen doctor, physician,
4
der Atlantische Ozean Atlantic Ocean, *13*
auch also, too, *1*
auf (+ *acc. or dat.*) on; at, *14;* ~ eine Party
gehen to go to a party, *10*
auf·brauchen to use up
die Aufgabe, —n lesson; *(pl.)* homework, *6*
auf·hängen to hang up
auf·machen to open, *8*
auf·räumen to put in order, *9*
auf·schreiben (aufgeschrieben) to write down
auf·stehen (ist aufgestanden) to get up, *8*
das Auge, —n eye
der August August, *2*
aus (+ *dat.*) out of, from, *15*
der Ausdruck, ̈e expression
ausgezeichnet excellent, *12*
die Auskunft, ̈e information; bei der ~ at the
information desk
aus·machen to turn off *(the light), 8*
ausreichend sufficient
aus·sehen (ie; ausgesehen) to look, to appear
außer (+ *dat.*) besides, except for, *15*
die Aussprache pronunciation
aus·tragen (ä; ausgetragen) to distribute
der Ausverkauf clearance sale
ausverkauft sold out, *7*
das Auto, —s car, *8*
die Autobahn, —en expressway, *14*

das Baby, —s baby
backen (ä; gebacken) to bake, *9*
der Bäcker, —/die Bäckerin, —nen baker, *11;*
zum Bäcker to the baker; beim Bäcker at the
baker
die Bäckerei, —en bakery

die Badehose, —n bathing trunks, *13*
das Badezimmer, — bathroom, *9*
die Bahn, —en train, railway; track, *15*
der Bahnhof, ̈e train station, *15;* zum ~ to the
train station
bald soon, *4*
der Ball, ̈e ball
das Ballett ballet
die Banane, —n banana, *11*
die Band, —s band, *7*
die Bank, —en bank, *15;* auf der ~ at the bank;
zur ~ to the bank
der Bankangestellte, —n/die Bankangestellte,
—n bank employee
der Basketball, ̈e basketball, *3*
basteln to tinker (with), to work at a hobby, *9*
der Bauer, —n farmer
die Baustelle construction site
(das) Bayern Bavaria, *15*
bedeuten to mean
die Bedienung service
beeinflussen to influence
befriedigend satisfactory
beginnen (begonnen) to start, to begin, *7*
bei (+ *dat.*) at (place of business), *7;* with, at (the
home of), *9;* ~ Gerdas Eltern with Gerda's parents (at their home), *9*
beide both, *2*
das Beispiel, —e example, zum ~ *(abbr.* z.B.)
for example
bekannt well-known, famous
bekommen (bekommen) to get, to receive, *7;* ich
bekomme frei I'll get (the day) off, *7*
beliebt favorite, popular
benutzen to use
das Benzin gasoline, *14*
der Berg, —e mountain
bergsteigen gehen to go mountain-climbing, *10*
der Bericht, —e report, *13*
der Beruf, —e occupation, profession, *4*
beschreiben (beschrieben) to describe, *14*
besonder special; besonders particularly, especially, *13*
besser (*comp. of* gut) better, *13*
bestehen (bestanden): die Prüfung ~ to pass
the test, *14*
bestellen to order, *12*
bestimmt certain(ly)
der Besuch, —e visit, *15;* guest, company

besuchen to visit, *11*

bewölkt cloudy, overcast, *13*

bezahlen to pay, *11*

der Bierdeckel, — coaster *(used under a glass or mug), 8*

das Bild, —er picture, *4*

billig inexpensive, cheap, *5*

die Biologie biology, *6;* **die Bio** bio, *6*

bis till, until, *4;* **~ später** till later, see you later, *1;* **~ zu** up to, *15*

bitte please; you're welcome; **~ schön** please; you're very welcome; **~ sehr** certainly, *12*

blau blue, *5*

bleiben (ist geblieben) to remain, to stay, *3*

der Bleistift, —e *(abbr.* **der Stift)** pencil, *6*

der Blick, —e view

die Blume, —n flower

die Bluse, —n blouse, *5*

der Boden, — bottom

der Braten, — roast

brauchen to need, *5*

braun brown, *5;* **ein Mantel in Braun** a brown coat, *5*

die BRD *(abbr. for* **Bundesrepublik Deutschland)** Federal Republic of Germany

der Brei porridge

die Breite width

die Bremse, —n brake, *14*

der Brief, —e letter, *4*

der Brieffreund, —e/Brieffreundin, —nen pen pal, *4*

die Briefmarke, —n postage stamp, *8*

bringen (gebracht) to bring, *12*

das Brot, —e (loaf of) bread, *11;* sandwich, *12;* **das [Schinken] brot** [ham] sandwich, *12*

das Brötchen, — hard roll, *12*

der Bruder, — brother, *4*

der Brunnen, — fountain, well; spring, *15*

das Buch, —er book, *6;* **das Deutschbuch** German book

die Buchhandlung, —en bookstore

bummeln (ist gebummelt) to go for a stroll, to take a walk, *15*

die Bundesrepublik Deutschland Federal Republic of Germany

bunt colorful

der Bus, —se bus, *14*

die Bushaltestelle, —n bus stop

die Butter butter, *11*

das Café, —s café, coffee shop, *8*

das Camping camping, *10;* **ich war zum ~** I was camping

der Campingplatz, —e campsite

der CD-Spieler compact-disc player, *8*

Celsius Celsius

die Chemie chemistry, *6;* **die Chemieaufgabe —n** chemistry homework, *6*

der Club, —s club, *15*

cm *(abbrev. for* **der Zentimeter)** centimeter, *4*

die *(also* **das) Cola** cola drink, *12*

die Compact Disc, —s compact disc (CD)

die Corn-flakes *(pl.)* cornflakes

da here, there, *5;* then, *13*

das Dach, —er roof

daher therefore

die Dame, —n lady, woman, *5*

der Dank thanks; **vielen ~!** many thanks!, *12*

danke thanks, thank you, *1*

dann then, *7*

das that, the, *5*

daß *(sub. conj.)* that, *13*

der Daumen, — thumb; **halt mir die ~** cross your fingers for me *(literally:* hold your thumbs for me), *14*

die DDR *(abbr. for* **Deutsche Demokratische Republik)** German Democratic Republic

decken to set *(the table), 9*

das Defizit, —e deficit

dein your *(fam. sg.), 4*

denken (gedacht) to think, *13*

denn *flavoring word often used in questions, 1; (coord. conj.)* for, because, *11*

der the, *5*

(das) Deutsch German (language), *4*

deutsch German *(adj.)*

die Deutsche Demokratische Republik German Democratic Republic

(das) Deutschland Germany

der Deutschlehrer, —/die Deutschlehrerin, —nen German teacher

deutschsprachig German-speaking

der Dezember December, *2*

der Dialog, —e dialogue

dich *(acc. of* **du)** you, *10*

dick fat, thick, *6*

die the, *5*

der Dienstag Tuesday, *6*

dies (–er, –es, –e)   this, 6; ~ **und das**   this and that

das Ding, –e   thing

die Disco, –s   dance club, discothèque, 8; **in die ~**   to the dance club

die Diskussion, –en   discussion, debate, 14

doch   flavoring word used to persuade or to imply agreement, 8; yes *(in response to a negative statement or question)*, 9

der Donnerstag   Thursday, 4

doof   goofy, dumb, stupid, 4

das Dorf, ⸚er   village

dort   there, 11

drei   three, 2

dreißig   thirty, 4

dreizehn   thirteen, 2

du   you *(fam. sg.)*, 1

dumm (ü)   dumb, stupid, 7

dünn   thin, 4

durch (+ *acc.*)   divided by, 2; through, 11

durch·fallen (ä, ist durchgefallen)   to fail, to flunk, 14

dürfen (darf)   may, to be permitted to, 7; **was darf es sein?**   what would you like?, 11

der Durst   thirst, 12; ~ **haben**   to be thirsty, 12

echt   really, very *(colloq.)*, 5; genuine

die Ecke, –n   corner, 15

Ehrenwort!   honest! on my honor!, 9

das Ei, –er   egg, 11; **weichgekochtes ~**   soft-boiled egg

eifersüchtig   jealous, 14

eigentlich   really, actually, 8

der Eimer, –   pail, 9

ein   a, an, 4

einfach   simple, simply, 7

ein·fallen (ä, ist eingefallen)   to occur to; **da fällt mir gerade ein**   it just occurs to me, 15

einige   some

ein·kaufen   to shop, 8; ~ **gehen**   to go shopping, 8

der Einkäufer, –/die Einkäuferin, –nen   purchaser, buyer

die Einkaufsliste, –n   shopping-list

die Einkaufstasche, –n   shopping bag, 11

der Einkaufswagen, –   shopping-cart

ein·laden (ä; eingeladen)   to invite, 9

einmal   once, for once; **noch ~**   once again

ein·packen   to pack, 11

eins   one, 2

der Eintritt   admission

das Eis   ice cream; ice, 12

der Elektriker, –/die Elektrikerin, –nen   electrician, 4; **beim Elektriker**   at the appliance store; **zum Elektriker**   to the appliance store

elf   eleven, 2

die Eltern *(pl.)*   parents, 9

empfehlen (ie; empfohlen)   to recommend, 12

das Ende   end; **am ~**   at the end

endlich   finally, 13

(das) Englisch   English (language), 6

die Ente, –n   duck; **eine lahme ~**   a dull, boring person, 8

entlang   along; **die Straße ~**   along (down) the street, 15

die Entschuldigung, –en   excuse; **Entschuldigung!**   excuse me, sorry, 11

er   he, 1

die Erbse, –n   pea, 11

die Erdbeere, –n   strawberry, 11

die Erdkunde   geography, 6

Ernst: das ist doch nicht dein ~!   you can't be serious!, 9

erreichen   to reach

erst   only; first, 2; **ich bin ~ fünfzehn**   I'm only fifteen

erzählen   to tell, 14

es   it, 1

das Essen   meal, 12; food

essen (ißt; gegessen)   to eat, 10

etwas   something, 8

euch *(acc. of* **ihr**)   you, 10

euer   your *(fam. pl.)*, 4

(das) Europa   Europe, 5

das Fach, ⸚er   (school) subject, 6

fahren (ä; ist gefahren)   to drive, to go, 8

Fahrenheit   Fahrenheit

die Fahrkarte, –n   train ticket, 15

der Fahrlehrer, –   driving instructor, 14

der Fahrplan, ⸚e   (train) schedule

das Fahrrad, ⸚er   bicycle, 14

die Fahrschule, –n   driving school, 14

die Fahrstunde, –n   driving lesson, 14

der Fahrunterricht   driving instruction, 14

das Fahrzeug, –e   vehicle

fallen (ä; ist gefallen)   to fall, 10

falsch wrong, *2*
die Familie, –n family, *4*
die Farbe, –n color, *5;* **welche ~ hat dein Pulli?** what color is your sweater?, *5*
fast almost, *11*
faul lazy, *1*
der Februar February, *2*
das Fenster, – window, *8*
fern·sehen (ie; ferngesehen) to watch TV, *8*
der Fernseher, – television set, *8*
fertig ready, finished, *6*
die Fete, –n party, *10*
der Film, –e movie
finden (gefunden) to find, *4;* **wie findest du (Rock)?** how do you like (rock music)?, *4*
der Fisch, –e fish, *12*
flach flat
die Flasche, –n bottle, *11*
das Fleisch meat, *11*
fleißig industrious, diligent, *1*
fliegen (ist geflogen) to fly, *14*
fließen (ist geflossen) to flow
die Flöte, –n flute, *3*
das Flugzeug, –e airplane, *14*
das Flugzeugmodell, –e model airplane, *9*
der Fluß, –sse river
folgen (ist gefolgt) to follow
der Fortschritt, –e progress
das Fotoalbum (*pl.* **–alben)** photo album, *3*
der Fotograf, –en/die Fotografin, –nen photographer
fotografieren to photograph, *8*
die Frage, –n question, *7*
fragen to ask, *7;* **~ nach** to ask about
der Franken basic Swiss monetary unit
französisch French
die Frau, –en woman, wife; **~ X** Mrs. or Ms. X, *1*
das Fräulein young woman; Miss, *1;* term of address for waitress, *12*
frei free, not busy, *7;* **ich bekomme ~** I'll get (the day) off, *7*
der Freitag Friday, *4*
die Freizeit leisure time, *10*
der Freund, –e/die Freundin, –nen friend, *4*
frieren (gefroren) to freeze, to be very cold, *13*
frisch fresh, *11*
der Friseur, –e/die Friseurin, –nen hairdresser, *4*

froh glad, happy, *15*
früh early, *11*
der Frühling spring, *10*
das Frühstück breakfast, *9;* **zum ~** for breakfast, *12*
frühstücken to have breakfast, *12*
der Führerschein, –e driver's license, *14*
fünf five, *2*
fünfzehn fifteen, *2*
fünfzig fifty, *4*
für (+ ***acc.*)** for, *5;* **fürs = für das,** *9*
furchtbar terrible; terribly, *5*
der Fuß, ⁻e foot; **zu ~** on foot, *15*
der Fußball soccer, *3*
die Fußballmannschaft, –en soccer team
der Fußballplatz, ⁻e soccer field
das Fußballspiel, –e soccer game, *10*
die Fußgängerzone, –n pedestrian zone, *15*
füttern to feed, *9*

die Gabel, –n fork
die Gallone, –n gallon
ganz quite; complete(ly), *1;* **~ gut** OK, pretty well, *1*
gar: ~ nicht not at all, *1*
die Garage, –n garage, *9*
der Garten, ⁻ garden
die Gartenarbeit gardening, yard work, *9*
der Gast, ⁻e guest
die Gastfamilie, –n host family
das Gebäude, – building
geben (i; gegeben) to give, *7;* **es gibt (+ ***acc.***)** there is, there are, *7*
gebraucht used
der Geburtstag, –e birthday, *2;* **ich habe ~** it's my birthday, *2*
das Geburtstagskind birthday girl or boy
die Geburtstagsparty, –s birthday party
gegen (+ ***acc.*)** against, *10*
das Gegenteil, –e opposite; **im ~** on the contrary
der Gegenverkehr oncoming traffic
gehen (ist gegangen) to go, *3;* **wie geht's?** how are you? *1;* **es geht** OK, can't complain, *1;* it's possible, *7;* **das geht nicht** that doesn't work; that won't do, *10*
die Geige, –n violin, *3*
das Gelände ground; site
gelb yellow, *5*
das Geld money, *7*

gemeinsam communally

die Gemeinschaft, −en society

das Gemüse, − vegetable, *11*

genug enough

geöffnet open

die Geographie geography

gerade exactly, precisely; just, *8*

geradeaus: immer ~ straight ahead, *15*

gern (lieber) gladly, with pleasure, *3;* **~ haben** to like, to be fond of, *3;* **ich hätte ~ . . .** I would like . . . , *11*

das Geschäft, −e store, *8*

der Geschäftsmann, −̈er/die Geschäftsfrau, −en (*also pl.* **die Geschäftsleute**) businessman, businesswoman, *4*

das Geschenk, −e present; **Geburtstagsgeschenk** birthday present, *8*

die Geschichte, −n story, *9;* history, *6*

das Geschirr dishes, *9;* **~ spülen** to wash dishes, *9*

die Geschwindigkeitsbegrenzung speed limit

sich gesellen to associate with

das Gespräch, −e conversation

der Gesprächspartner, −/die Gesprächspartnerin, −nen conversation partner

gestern yesterday, *9;* **~ abend** last night; **~ nachmittag** yesterday afternoon

gesund healthy, well, *1*

das Getränk, −e beverage, *12*

gewinnen (gewonnen) to win, *10;* **wie hoch haben sie gewonnen?** by how much did they win?, *10*

gewöhnlich usually, *12*

die Gitarre, −n guitar, *3*

das Glas, −̈er glass, *11*

glatt slippery, *13*

glauben to believe, *7;* **ich glaube ja** I believe so, *7;* **das ist schwer zu ~** that's hard to believe

gleich like, similar; alike

gleichfalls likewise; same to you

das Glockenspiel carillon

das Glück luck

glücklich happy, *1*

das Gold gold

graben (ä; gegraben) to dig

der Grad degree, *13*

das Gramm gram, *11*

grammatisch: grammatische Übersicht grammatical summary

das Gras grass

gratulieren to congratulate

grau gray, *5*

der Groschen Austrian monetary unit (1/100 **Schilling**)

groß (ö) tall; big, *4;* **wie ~ bist du?** how tall are you?, *4*

die Größe, −n size, *5;* **welche ~ trägst du?** what size do you wear?, *5*

die Großeltern (*pl.*) grandparents, *9*

die Grube, −n hole

Grüetzi hello (*in Switzerland*)

grün green, *5*

die Gruppe, −n group, *7;* **die Lieblings ~** favorite group, *7*

Grüß dich hello, hi

Grüß Gott hello, *11*

der Gürtel, − belt, *5*

gut (besser) good, *1;* **gute Nacht!** good night! *1;* **guten Abend!** good evening! *1;* **guten Morgen!** good morning! *1;* **guten Tag!** hello! *1;* **es geht mir ~** I'm fine; **na ~** O.K. then

das Gymnasium, die Gymnasien college-prep secondary school

haben to have, *2;* **gern ~** to like, *3*

die Hafenstadt, −̈e port city

halb half; **um ~ neun** at 8:30, *6*

hallo hello, *1*

halten (ä; gehalten) to hold, *14;* to stop

die Haltestelle, −n (bus or streetcar) stop

die Hand, −̈e hand

der Handschuh, −e glove, *5*

häßlich ugly, *5*

hätte: ich ~ gern I would like, *11*

die Hauptstadt, −̈e capital city, *13*

das Haus, −̈er house, *9;* **nach Hause** home (*direction*), *3;* **zu Hause** (at) home, *3*

die Hausarbeit housework

die Hausaufgaben (*pl.*) homework, *3*

die Hausfrau housewife

der Hausmann house–husband

das Heft, −e notebook, *6*

heiß hot, *13*

heißen (geheißen) to be named, called, *4;* **ich heiße . . .** my name is . . . *1;* **wie heißt du?**

what's your name? *1;* **was heißt das?** what does that mean?, *9*

helfen (i; geholfen) to help, *9*

Helvetia *name for Switzerland used on official documents*

das Hemd, −en shirt, *5*

der Herbst autumn, fall, *10*

der Herr, −n, −en gentleman, *5;* **~ X** Mr. X, *1*

herum around

das Herz heart

herzlich cordial; **herzliche Grüße** best wishes, kind regards, sincerely *(closing in letters), 4;* **herzlichen Glückwunsch zum Geburtstag!** happy birthday!

heute today, *1;* **~ abend** tonight; this evening, *3;* **~ morgen** this morning, *3;* **~ nachmittag** this afternoon, *3*

hier here, *3*

hinaus out (to)

hinein in; into; **hinein·fallen** to fall in

hinten in the back, behind

das Hobby, −s hobby, *4*

hoch (höher) high, *10;* **wie ~ haben sie gewonnen?** by how much did they win?, *10*

das Hockey hockey; **das Eis ~** ice hockey

hoffentlich I hope, let's hope, *4*

höher *(comp. of* **hoch)** higher, *13*

hören to hear, *4;* **Musik ~** to listen to music, *4*

die Hose, −n pants, slacks, *5*

hübsch pretty, nice, *5*

das Huhn, −̈er chicken, *12*

der Hund, −e dog, *9*

hundert hundred, *4*

der Hunger hunger, *12;* **~ haben** to be hungry, *12*

ich I, *1*

ihn *(acc. of* **er)** him, *10*

ihr you *(fam. pl.),* 2; her, its; their, *4*

Ihr your *(formal), 4*

im = in dem in, *2*

immer always, *8;* **~ geradeaus** straight ahead, *15*

in in(to), *3*

die Information information

der Ingenieur, −e/die Ingenieurin, −nen engineer

ins to the; **~ Kino** to the movies, *7*

interessant interesting, *6*

ja yes, *1; flavoring word confirming that what is said is self-evident, 6;* **~, und wie!** sure, I do (I am), *7*

die Jacke, −n suit coat, jacket, *5*

das Jahr, −e year, *4*

die Jahreszeit, −en season, time of year, *13*

der Januar January, *2*

japanisch Japanese

je (weniger) . . . desto (mehr) the (less) . . . the (more)

die Jeans *(pl.)* jeans, *5*

jed (−er, −es, −e) *(sg.)* each; everyone, *9; pl.* **alle** all

jemand someone, *15*

jetzt now, *3*

der Job, −s job

joggen to jog, *10*

das Jogging jogging, *10*

das Jugendzentrum youth center, club, *7*

der Juli July, *2*

jung (ü) young, *2*

der Junge, −n, −n boy, *5*

der Juni June, *2*

der Kaffee coffee, *9;* **~ kochen** to make coffee, *9;* **~ trinken** to drink coffee *(with breakfast or with afternoon pastries), 9;* **zum ~ einladen** to invite for coffee and cake, *9*

die Kaffeestunde, −n (afternoon) coffee hour

der Kalender, − calendar

kalt (ä) cold, *13*

das Kapitel, − chapter

kaputt broken, out of order, exhausted, *1;* **~ machen** to break

die Karotte, −n carrot, *11*

die Karte, −n ticket, *7;* postcard, menu; *(pl.)* (playing) cards, *4;* **~ zu drei Mark** ticket at three marks, *7*

die Kartoffel, −n potato, *11*

der Kartoffelchip, −s potato chip, *12*

das Kartoffelpüree mashed potatoes, *12*

der Käse cheese, *11*

die Kasse box office, *7;* cashier

die Kassette, −n cassette, *8*

der Kassettenrecorder, − cassette recorder, *8*

die Katze, −n cat, *9*

der Kauf, −̈e purchase

kaufen to buy, *5*

der Käufer, −/die Käuferin, −nen buyer

das Kaufhaus, ⸚er department store, *15*
kein not a, not any, *5*
kennen (gekannt) to know, to be acquainted with, *10*
die Keramik ceramics, pottery, *8*
das Kilo(gramm) kilogram (= 2.2 American pounds), *11*
der Kilometer, – kilometer (= .062 miles), *3*
das Kind, –er child, *4*
das Kino, –s movie theater, *7;* im ~ in the movie theater; ins ~ to the movie theater
die Kinokarte, –n movie ticket
die Kirche, –n church, *15*
klar clear; ~! sure! of course!, *6*
die Klarinette, –n clarinet, *3*
klasse! terrific!, *5*
die Klasse, –n grade, class, *6*
die Klassenarbeit, –en test
die Klassenfahrt, –en class trip, *15*
der Klassenlehrer, –/die Klassenlehrerin, –nen homeroom teacher
das Klassenzimmer, – classroom, *6*
klassisch classical, *4*
das Klavier, –e piano, *3*
die Klavierstunde, –n piano lesson, *6*
das Kleid, –er dress, *5; (pl.)* clothes
die Kleidung clothing, *5*
das Kleidungsgeschäft clothing store; ins ~ to the clothing store
klein small, short, little, *4*
das Klima, –s climate
die Kneipe, –n pub, tavern
der Koch, ⸚e/die Köchin, –nen cook
kochen to cook, *4*
die Kohle, –n coal
kommen (ist gekommen) to come, *4*
kompliziert complicated, *8*
die Konditorei, –en shop serving pastries and coffee
die Konfektionsgröße, –n clothing size
der König, –e king
können (kann) can, to be able to, *7*
das Konzert, –e concert, *7;* ins ~ to the concert
kosten to cost, *5*
krank ill, sick, *1*
die Krawatte, –n necktie, *5*
kreuzen to cross
die Kreuzung, –en intersection, *15*

der Kuchen, – cake, *11*
der Kugelschreiber, – *(abbr.* der Kuli, –s) ball-point pen, *6*
kühl cool, *13*
die Kultur culture
der Kunde, –n, –n/die Kundin, –nen customer, client, *11*
die Kunst art, *6*
der Kurs, –e course, *14*
kurz (ü) short, *6*
die Kurzarbeit shortened work hours
die Kürze brevity

lachen to laugh
lahm lame; eine lahme Ente a dull, boring person, *9*
das Land, ⸚er country, land
die Landstraße, –n highway
lang (ä) long, *6*
lange *(adv.)* long; wie ~? how long?, *12*
die Langeweile boredom, *8;* ich habe ~ I am bored, *8*
langsam slow(ly), *14*
langweilig boring, *6*
(das) Latein Latin (language), *6*
laufen (äu; ist gelaufen) to run; to walk, *10*
laut loud
leben to live
die Lebensmittel *(pl.)* food, groceries, *11*
das Leder, – leather
der Lehrer, –/die Lehrerin, –nen teacher, *4*
leicht easy, light, *6*
leid: das tut mir ~ I'm sorry, *1*
leider unfortunately, *5*
lernen to learn; to study, *4*
lesen (ie; gelesen) to read, *8*
das Lesestück, –e reading selection
letzt last, *9*
die Leute *(pl.)* people
das Licht, –er light, *8*
lieber *(comp. of* gern) rather, *13;* ~ haben to like better, to prefer, *13;* ich esse ~ . . . I prefer to eat . . ., *12*
lieber/liebe dear *(opening in letters)*, *4*
das Lieblingsfach, ⸚er favorite subject, *6*
die Lieblingsgruppe, –n favorite group, *7*
liegen (gelegen) to lie; to be (situated), *13*
die Limo(nade) soft drink, *12*
links (to the) left, *15*

der Liter, – liter (= 1.056 quarts), *11;* **7 ~ pro 100 Kilometer** 100 kilometers to 7 liters, *14*

die Litfaßsäule, –n column to post ads

der Löffel, – spoon

logisch logical

das Lokal, –e place to eat, drink, dance; restaurant; *15*

los: was ist ~? What's the matter? *1;* **es ist viel ~** there is a lot going on, *15*

los·gehen (ist losgegangen) to go, to take off, *10;* **wann geht's los?** when does it start? *10*

die Lust pleasure, enjoyment; **~ haben** to feel like doing something, *7;* **er hat zu nichts ~** he doesn't feel like doing anything, *8*

machen to do; to make, *3;* **das macht Spaß** that's fun, *4;* **das macht zusammen 10 Mark** that comes to 10 marks, *7*

das Mädchen, – girl, *5*

der Mai May, *2*

das Mal time, occasion, *10;* **nächstes ~** next time, *10*

mal times, *2; flavoring word that leaves the time indefinite and softens a command, 7*

man *(indef. pronoun)* one, you, they, people, *11*

manch (–er, –es, –e) *(sg.)* many a, *12;* **manche** *(pl.)* some, several, *12*

manchmal sometimes, *12*

mangelhaft insufficient

der Mann, –er man, *5;* husband

die Mannschaft, –en team

der Mantel, – coat, *5*

die Mappe, –n briefcase, book bag, *6*

die Mark mark (basic German monetary unit) **(DM = Deutsche Mark = 100 Pfennig),** *5*

der Markt, –e market, *11;* **auf den ~** to the market, *11;* **auf dem ~** at the market

der Marktplatz, –e market place

die Marmelade jam, *12*

der März March, *2*

die Maschine, –n machine, engine

die Matheaufgaben *(pl.)* math homework

die Mathematik mathematics, *6;* **die Mathe** math, *6*

die Maus, –e mouse

das Mehl, –e flour

mehr more, *7*

die Meile, –n mile

mein my, *4*

meinen to think; to mean, *5*

die Meinung, –en opinion

meistens usually, mostly

der Mensch, –en, –en man, human being; **Mensch!** wow! brother! oh, boy! *6*

das Messer, – knife

der Meter, – meter (= 39.37 inches), *4*

der Metzger, –/die Metzgerin, –nen butcher, *11;* **zum ~** to the butcher; **beim ~** at the butcher's

mich *(acc. of ich)* me, *10*

die Milch milk, *11*

das Mineralwasser mineral water, *12*

die Minute, –n minute, *3*

mir *(dat. of ich)* me

mit *(+ dat.)* with; **~ dem Bus fahren** to go by bus, *14;* **~18** at the age of 18, *14*

mit·bringen (mitgebracht) to bring along, *13*

mit·fahren (ä; ist mitgefahren) to go (or drive) with someone

mit·kommen (ist mitgekommen) to come along, *8*

mit·nehmen (nimmt mit; mitgenommen) to take along, *13*

der Mitschüler, –/die Mitschülerin, –nen fellow student

der Mittag noon, *12;* **zu ~ essen** to have lunch, *12*

das Mittagessen warm noon meal, lunch, *12;* **zum ~** for the noon meal, *12*

mittags at noon, at lunch time, *12*

der Mittwoch Wednesday, *6*

die Möbel *(pl.)* furniture, *9*

möchte *(form of* **mögen***)* would like to, *7*

modisch stylish, *5*

das Mofa, –s moped, motorbike, *14*

mögen (mag) to like; **möchte** would like to, *7*

der Moment moment; **einen ~** just a moment, *11;* **~ mal** just a moment, *15*

der Monat, –e month, *2*

der Montag Monday, *4*

der Morgen, – morning; **guten ~!** good morning! *1*

morgen tomorrow, *6;* **~ abend** tomorrow evening, *7;* **~ früh** tomorrow morning

morgens in the morning

das Motorrad, –er motorcycle, *14*

müde tired, *1*

der Müll garbage, *9*

der Mülleimer   garbage pail, 9
das Museum (pl. Museen)   museum, 15
das Musical   musical
die Musik   music, 4; ~ machen   to play music, 4
musikalisch   musical, 4
das Musikinstrument, −e   musical instrument, 3
die Musikstunde, −n   music lesson
müssen (muß)   to have to, must, 7
der Mustersatz, −̈e   model sentence
die Mutter, −̈   mother, 4

na   well, 8; ~ gut   well, O.K., 8; ~ und?   so what?, 10
nach (+ dat.)   after, 6; Viertel ~ zwei   quarter past two, 6; to (with cities or countries), 8; ~ Hamburg   to Hamburg, 8; ~ Hause   home (direction), 3
das Nachbarland, −̈er   neighboring country
der Nachmittag, −e   afternoon; am ~   in the afternoon, 6
nachmittags   in the afternoon, 12
nächst   next, 10; nächstes Mal   next time, 10
die Nacht, −̈e   night; gute ~!   good night!, 1
der Nachtisch   dessert, 12
der Name, −n (acc. and dat. −n)   name, 4
nämlich   namely, you know, 11
naß   wet, 13
natürlich   naturally, of course, 3
nehmen (nimmt, genommen)   to take, 7
nein   no, 1
nennen (genannt)   to name, to call, 9
nett   nice, 11
neu   new, 5
neun   nine, 9
neunzehn   nineteen, 2
neunzig   ninety, 4
nicht   not, 1; nicht? = nicht wahr?   isn't that so? isn't that right? 1; ~ nur . . . sondern auch   not only . . . but also, 12
nichts   nothing, 7; ~ mehr   nothing left, 7
nie   never, 14
niemand   no one, 14
noch   still, yet, 4; ~ nicht   not yet, 8; ~ ein   another; ~ einmal   again; ~ schöner   even more beautiful, 13
der Norden   north, 13
nördlich (von)   northern, north (of), 13
die Note, −n   grade
der November   November, 2

null   zero, 2
nun   now, 8
nur   only, just, 1

ob (sub. conj.)   if, whether, 13
der Ober, −   waiter, 12; Herr Ober!   Waiter!
das Obst   fruit, 11
oder (coord. conj.)   or, 2; (at end of sentence) or not; isn't that right?, 2; Er geht doch, ~?   He's going, isn't he?
oft (ö)   often, 3
ohne (+ acc.)   without, 11
O.K.   O.K.
der Oktober   October, 2
das Olympiagelände   Olympic Park
die Operette, −n   operetta
die Orange, −n   orange, 11
der Osten   east, 13
(das) Österreich   Austria
östlich (von)   eastern, east (of)

paar: ein ~   a few, some, 7
packen   to pack, 11
das Papier, −e   paper, 6; (pl.) papers, documents
der Park, −s   park, 15
die Party, −s   party, 10
passen   to fit; to match, 5
die Pause, −n   break; intermission, 6; recess, 6
Pech: so ein ~   what bad luck, how unfortunate, 15
die Person, −en   person
der Pfannkuchen   pancake
der Pfennig, −e (abbr. Pf)   German monetary unit: 1 Pf = 1/100 Mark, 11
das Pfund (abbr. Pfd.)   pound (1 Pfd. = 500 g = 1.1 U.S. pounds), 11
die Physik   physics, 6
das Picknick, −s   picnic, 10
die Pille, −n   pill
die Pinte, −n   pub
die Pizza, −s   pizza
der Plan, −̈e   plan; schedule, 6
die Platte, −n   record, 8
der Plattenspieler, −   record player, turntable, 8
der Platz, −̈e   square, 15; seat
die Pommes frites (pl.)   French fries, 12
populär   popular
die Post   post office; mail, 15; zur ~   to the post office

das (also der) Poster, — poster, 8
die Postkarte, —n postcard
praktisch practical, 14
der Preis, —e price
preiswert worth the money, reasonably priced, 5
prima excellent, fine, great, 1
pro per, 14; ~ Stunde per hour; 10 Liter ~ 100 Kilometer 10 km to the liter
das Problem, —e problem
produzieren to produce
die Prüfung, —en exam, test, 14
der Pudding pudding, 12
der Pulli, —s pullover, 5
der Pullover pullover, 5
pünktlich punctual
putzen to clean, 9

Quatsch! nonsense! rubbish!, 10
das Quiz quiz

das Rad, ⁻er wheel; bicycle (short for das Fahrrad), 14
der Radfahrer bicyclist
der Radiergummi, —s (abbr. der Gummi) eraser, 6
das Radio, —s radio, 8
der Radioamateur, —e "ham" radio operator, 8
das Radiogeschäft, —e radio store
der Rappen Swiss monetary unit (1/100 Franken)
das Rathaus, ⁻er town hall, 15
raus·tragen (ä; rausgetragen) to carry out, 9
die Rechnung, —en bill, check, 12
recht: ~ haben to be right, 13
rechts (to the) right, 15
das Reden speaking
das Reformhaus health food store
der Regen rain, 13
der Regenmantel, ⁻ raincoat
der Regenschirm, —e umbrella, 13
regnen to rain, 13
die Reise, —n trip
reiten (ist geritten) to ride (horseback), 10
die Reklame, —n advertisement
reparieren to repair, 8
die Republik, —en republic
das Restaurant, —s restaurant
richtig correct, right, 2
der Rindsbraten roast beef, pot roast, 12
der Rock rock (music), 4

der Rock, ⁻e skirt, 5
rodeln (ist gerodelt) to toboggan; to go sledding, 13
die Rolle: eine ~ spielen to be important
das Rollenspiel, —e role-play
rot red, 5
das Rührei scrambled egg

die Sache, —n thing; (pl.) clothes, 5
der Saft, ⁻e juice, 11
sagen to say, to tell, 8; sag mal tell me, 8
die Sahne cream
der Salat, —e (head of) lettuce; salad, 12
Salut hello
das Salz salt
die Sammelfreude, —n joy of collecting
sammeln to gather, to collect, 8
die Sammlung, —en collection
der Samstag Saturday, 4; am ~ on Saturday, 4; samstags Saturdays
sarkastisch sarcastic, 9
der Satz, ⁻e sentence
sauer cross, annoyed; sour, 1
schade too bad, 5
die Schallplatte, —n record, 8
schauen to look. 15
der Schein, —e bill; der Zehnmark ~ 10 mark bill
scheinen (geschienen) to shine, 13; to seem, 15
der Scherz, —e joke
scheußlich horrible, hideous, 5
schick chic, stylish, 5
das Schiff, —e ship, 14
das Schild, —er sign, 15
der Schilling basic Austrian monetary unit
der Schinken ham, 11
das Schinkenbrot, —e ham sandwich, 12
der Schirm, —e umbrella
schlafen (ä; geschlafen) to sleep, 9
das Schlagzeug, —e drums, 3
schlank slender, slim, 4
schlecht bad, 1
schließlich after all, finally
schlimm bad, 6
der Schlittschuh, —e ice skate, 10
Schlittschuh laufen (äu) to ice-skate, 10
das Schloß, —sses, ⁻sser castle, palace, 15
schmecken to taste (good), 9
der Schnee snow, 13

schneien to snow, *13*

schnell fast, *14*

die Schokolade, –n chocolate, hot chocolate; bar of chocolate, *12*

schon already, *2;* **das ~** that's true, *7;* **ich habe ~ Lust** I do feel like it

schön beautiful, *5;* nice, *4;* **ganz ~ kalt** quite cold; **~ kühl** nice and cool

schreiben (geschrieben) to write, *4;* **~ an** (+ *acc.*) to write to

der Schuh, –e shoe, *5*

die Schuhgröße shoe size

die Schule, –n school, *6;* **in die ~** to school

der Schüler, –/die Schülerin, –nen student *(in high school)*, *4*

das Schulfach, –̈er subject *(at school)*

die Schulmappe, –n schoolbag

schwarz (ä) black, *5*

der Schwarzwald Black Forest

das Schweigen silence

das Schwein, –e pig; **~ haben** to be lucky, *14*

das Schweinskotelett, –s pork chop, *11*

die Schweiz Switzerland; **in die Schweiz** to Switzerland

schwer difficult; heavy, *6*

die Schwester, –n sister, *4*

schwimmen (ist geschwommen) to swim, *3*

(das) Schwyzerdütsch Swiss German (language)

sechs six, *2*

sechzehn sixteen, *2*

sechzig sixty, *4*

der See, –n lake, *14;* **an den ~** to the lake, *14*

segeln to sail, *10*

sehen (ie; gesehen) to see, to watch, to look, *8*

sehr very, *1*

sein his, its, *4*

sein (ist; ist gewesen) to be, *1*

seit (+ *dat.*) since, for, *15*

die Seite, –n side

selbst oneself, myself, *etc.*, *11*

der Senf mustard

der September September, *2*

Servus! hello *(in Austria)*

sicher sure, certain(ly), *7*

sie she, *1;* they, *2*

Sie you *(formal)*, *1*

sieben seven, *2*

siebzehn seventeen, *2*

siebzig seventy, *4*

das Silber silver

singen (gesungen) to sing, *4*

der Sinn, –e sense; mind

der Ski, –er *(pronounced* **Schi***)* ski, *10*

Ski laufen (äu; ist gelaufen) to ski, *7*

so so, *1;* **~ . . . wie** as . . . as, *11*

die Socke, –n sock, *5*

sogar even

solch (–er, –es, –e) *(sg.)* such a; **solche** *(pl.)* such, *12*

sollen (soll) should, to be supposed to, *7*

das Solo, –s solo

der Sommer summer, *10*

der Sommerschlußverkauf summer clearance sale

das Sonderangebot special offer (sale)

sondern *(coord. conj.)* but (on the contrary), *12*

die Sonne, –n sun, *13*

der Sonnenschirm sunshade, parasol

der Sonntag Sunday, *4*

sonst (noch) in addition; **was sonst?** what else?, *3;* **~ noch was?** anything else?, *11*

soviel so much

Spaß: das macht ~! that's fun!, *4*

spät late, *4;* **zu ~** too late, tardy, *4;* **wie ~ ist es?** what time is it?, *6;* **bis später** till later, see you later, *1*

der Spatz, –en sparrow

spazieren (ist spaziert) to walk, to stroll; **~ gehen** to go for a walk, *3*

der Spaziergang, –̈e walk, stroll; **einen ~ machen** to go for a walk, *9*

die Speise, –n food

die Speisekarte, –n menu, *12*

das Spiegelei, –er fried egg

das Spiel, –e game, *10*

der Spielautomat, –en slot machine, pinball machine

spielen to play, *3*

der Spieler, – player

die Spielsache, –n toy, plaything

der Spinat spinach, *11*

spinnen to spin; **du spinnst** you're crazy, *13*

der Sport sport, *6;* **~ treiben** to be active in sports, *4*

der Sportfreund, –e sports fan

der Sportverein, –e sports club

spottbillig dirt-cheap, *5*

sprechen (i; gesprochen) to speak, *13*

spülen to rinse, to wash; **Geschirr ~** to wash dishes, *9* der Staat, —en state

die Stadt, ⸚e city, *8;* **in die ~** to the city, to town

das Städtele, — *(dialect)* small town

der Stadtplan, ⸚e city map, *15*

der Stau, —s traffic jam

der Staub dust, *9;* **~ saugen** to vacuum, *9*

das Steak, —s steak

stehen (gestanden) to stand, *15*

die Stereoanlage, —n stereo system, *8*

der Stiefel, — boot, *15*

still still, quiet; calm

stimmen to be true, correct, *8;* **das stimmt** that's right, *8*

der Strandkorb, ⸚e (canopied) beach chair

die Straße, —n street, *3,* **auf der ~** on the street

die Straßenbahn, —en streetcar, *14*

stricken to knit

das Stück, —e piece, *11*

der Student, —en, —en/die Studentin, —nen student *(at a university),* *15*

das Studentenlokal, —e pub frequented by students, *15*

die Stufe, —n step

die Stunde, —n hour; class, *6;* **die [Klavier]stunde** [piano] lesson

der Stundenplan, ⸚e class schedule, *6*

suchen to look for, *15*

der Süden south, *13*

südlich (von) southern, south (of), *13*

super! great!, *10*

der Supermarkt, ⸚e supermarket, *11;* **in den ~** to the supermarket; **im ~** at the supermarket

die Suppe, —n soup, *12;* **die Tagessuppe** soup of the day

der Tag, —e day; **~!** hi, *1;* **guten ~!** hello! *1*

das Tagebuch, ⸚er diary

täglich daily

die Tankstelle, —n service station, gas station, *15;* **zur ~** to the service station, *15*

die Tante, —n aunt, *7*

tanzen to dance, *4*

die Tasche, —n bag; pocket; purse, *11*

das Taschengeld pocket money, allowance

die Tasse, —n cup, *12*

die Taube, —n dove; pigeon

tauchen to dive

tausend thousand, *4*

der Tee tea, *12*

der Teenager, — teenager

der Teig dough; batter, *12*

der Teil, —e part

das Telefon, —e telephone

telefonieren to telephone

der Teller, — plate

die Temperatur, —en temperature, *13*

das Tennis tennis, *3*

teuer expensive, *5*

das Theater, — theater, *7;* **ins ~** to the theater

die Theaterkarte, —n theater ticket

theoretisch theoretical

das Thermometer, — thermometer, *13*

der Thunfisch, —e tuna

tief deep

der Tisch, —e table, *9*

die Tischdecke, —n tablecloth

der Toast toast

toll great, fantastic, *1;* crazy

die Tomate, —n tomato, *11*

das Tor, —e gate, *15*

die Torte, —n (fancy layer) cake, *9*

die Tour, —en tour, trip, *14*

der Tourist, —en, —en/die Touristin, —nen tourist, *15*

tragen (ä, getragen) to wear, *5;* to carry, *10*

trainieren to practice a sport, to train, *10*

der Traum, ⸚e dream, *14*

treiben: treibst du Sport? are you active in sports? *4*

der Trimm-dich-Pfad *marked path for jogging and exercising*

trinken (getrunken) to drink, *9*

trocken dry, *13*

trotzdem nevertheless

tschüß! so long! *(informal),* *1*

das T-Shirt, —s T-shirt

tun (getan) to do, *8;* **tu nicht so!** don't put on an act!

die Tür, —en door, *8*

die Tüte, —n bag, sack, *11*

die U-Bahn, —en subway, *14*

über (+ *acc. or dat.*) about, above, over, *13*

überall everywhere

übermorgen the day after tomorrow, *7*

die Übersicht summary

die Übung, –en exercise
die Uhr, –en clock, watch, 6; um wieviel ~ ? at what time? 6; wieviel ~ ist es? what time is it? 6
um (+ acc.) at; around, 6; ~ ein Uhr at one o'clock, 6
unabhängig independent, 14
und (coord. conj.) and, 1
unentschieden undetermined; tied (in scoring), 10
ungenügend unsatisfactory
ungewöhnlich unusual
unglücklich unhappy, 1
die Universität, –en university; college, 15
uns (acc. of wir) us, 10
unser our, 4
unsicher dangerous; unsure, insecure, 14
Unsinn! nonsense! 1
unter (+ acc. or dat.) under
der Untertitel, – subtitle
der Unterricht lesson, instruction, 14

der Vater, – father, 4
das Verbot prohibition, ban
verboten forbidden
verderben (i; verdorben) to spoil
verdienen to earn
die Vergangenheit past
vergessen (i; vergessen) to forget, 15
der Verkauf, –e sale
verkaufen to sell
der Verkäufer, –/die Verkäuferin, –nen salesperson, 4
das Verkehrszeichen, – traffic sign
verlieren (verloren) to lose, 10; wir haben zwei zu drei verloren we lost 2–3, 10
verstehen (verstanden) to understand, 8
versuchen to try, 7
viel (mehr) much, many, a lot, 3; vielen Dank! thank you very much, 12
vielleicht maybe, perhaps, 7
vier four, 2
das Viertel, – quarter, 6
vierzehn fourteen, 2
vierzig forty, 4
die Vokabel, –n (vocabulary) word; (pl.) vocabulary
der Volleyball, –e volleyball, 3
von (+ dat.) from, 3; of, 4
vor (+ acc. or dat.) before, 6; in front of; Viertel ~ zwei quarter till two

vor·haben to plan, 8
vorne in the front
die Vorstellung, –en performance, 7
der VW (= Volkswagen) 14

wahrscheinlich probably, 13
wandern (ist gewandert) to hike, to go hiking, 3
das Wanderwetter hiking weather
wann when, 2
war (past tense of sein) was, 11
die Waren (pl.) goods, merchandise
warm (ä) warm, 5
warten to wait
warum why, 1
was what, 1; ~ ist (denn) los? (well,) what's the matter?, 1; ~ sonst? what else? 3; ~ für (ein) what kind of (a), 14
die Wäsche laundry, 9
waschen (ä; gewaschen) to wash, 9
das Wasser water, 10
weg away
weg·fahren (ä; ist weggefahren) to drive (go) away
das Weihnachten Christmas
weil (sub. conj.) because, 15
weiß white, 5
weit far (away), 3
weiter further, 13
welch (–er, –es, –e) which, 5
die Welt world
wem (dat. of wer) (to) whom, 14
wen (acc. of wer) whom, 10
weniger minus, less, 2
wenigstens at least, 9
wenn (sub. conj.) if, when, 13
wer who, 2
werden (wird; ist geworden) to become, 13
wertvoll valuable, 8
der Westen west, 13
westlich (von) western, west (of)
das Wetter weather, 13
der Wetterbericht, –e weather report, 13
wie how, 1; as, 9; ~ geht's? how are you (doing)? 1; ~ alt bist du? how old are you? 2; ~ (immer) as (always), 9; so . . . ~ as . . . as, 11; ~ lange? how long?, 12
wieder again, 1
wiederholen to repeat
die Wiederholung, –en review

Wiederhören: auf ~ good-by *(on the telephone)*
Wiederschauen: auf ~ good-by, *11*
Wiedersehen: auf ~ good-by, *1*
wieviel how much, *2; ~* **Uhr ist es?** what time is it? *6*
der Wind wind, *13*
windig windy, *13*
die Windjacke, —n windbreaker
windsurfen to go wind surfing, *10*
der Winter winter, *10*
der Winterschlußverkauf winter clearance sale
die Wintersonne winter sun
das Wintersportzentrum center for winter sports
wir we, *2*
wirklich really, *1*
wissen (weiß; gewußt) to know, *8*
wo where, *3*
die Woche, —n week, *4*
das Wochenende, —n weekend, *4; am ~* on the weekend
woher where (from)
wohin where (to), *8*
wohl indeed, probably, *11*
wohnen to live, *3*
die Wolle wool
wollen (will) to want, to intend to, to wish, *7*
worin in what, *6*
das Wort, ⁻er word; **du hast das ~** it's your turn
das Wörterbuch, ⁻er dictionary
die Wortschatzerweiterung vocabulary building
der Wunsch, ⁻e wish, desire, *11*
die Wurst, ⁻e sausage, cold cuts, *11*
das Wiener Würstchen, — frankfurter, *11*
die Würze spice; flavor

die Zahl, —en number, *2*
zahlen to pay, *12; ~* **bitte!** the check please! *12*
zart tender, delicate, *12*
zehn ten, *2*
die Zeit, —en time, *7*
die Zeitung, —en newspaper
zelten to camp, to pitch a tent, *10*
der Zentimeter, — centimeter, *4*
das Zentimetermaß measuring tape
das Zentrum, die Zentren center
das Zeugnis, —se report card; grades
ziemlich quite, *3*
das Zimmer, — room, *9*
zu (+ *dat.*) to; too, *3;* shut, closed, *15; ~* **Hause** (at) home, *3; ~* **Abend essen** to have supper, *12; ~* **Mittag essen** to have lunch, *12; ~* **Fuß** on foot, *15*
zuerst first; at first
zufrieden content, satisfied, *1*
der Zug, ⁻e train, *14*
zuletzt last
zum (= zu dem) to the, *8; ~* **Musikhaus** to the music store, *8; ~* **Frühstück** for breakfast, *12; ~* **Kaffee einladen** to invite for coffee and cake, *9*
zu·machen to shut, *8*
zur (= zu der) to the, *14; ~* **Arbeit** to work, *14*
zurück back, *11*
zusammen together, *11; das macht ~* **10 Mark** that comes to 10 marks, *11*
zuviel too much
zwanzig twenty, *4*
zwei two, *2; zweimal die Woche* twice a week
zwischen (+ *acc. or dat.*) between, *14*
zwölf twelve, *2*

The symbol ~ signifies the repetition of the key word in that entry.

a/an ein, eine
able: to be ~ to können
about über
above über
acquainted: to be ~ with kennen
addition: in ~ sonst
after nach
afternoon der Nachmittag, –e; **yesterday ~** gestern nachmittag; **this ~** heute nachmittag; **in the ~** am Nachmittag, nachmittags
again wieder
against gegen
ahead: straight ~ immer geradeaus
airplane das Flugzeug, –e
all alle, alles; **~ the best** alles Gute; **~ right** gut
almost fast
alone allein
along entlang; **~ the street** die Straße entlang; **to come ~** mit·kommen
already schon
also auch
always immer; **as ~** wie immer
am: I ~ ich bin
American (adj.) amerikanisch
and und (coord. conj.)
annoyed sauer
answer die Antwort, –en; **to ~** antworten
apple der Apfel, ¨
April April
are: you ~ du bist, ihr seid, Sie sind; **they ~** sie sind; **we ~** wir sind
around um
arrive an·kommen

art die Kunst
as als; wie; **~ . . . ~** so . . . wie
ask fragen; **to ~ about** fragen nach
at an; auf; bei; um; **~ one o'clock** um ein Uhr; **~ the age of eighteen** mit achtzehn
aunt die Tante, –n
autumn der Herbst

back zurück
bad schlecht; schlimm; **too ~** schade
bag die Tüte, –n; **shopping ~** die Einkaufstasche, –n
bake backen
baker der Bäcker, –/die Bäckerin, –nen
banana die Banane, –n
band die Band, –s
bank die Bank, –en
basketball der Basketball, ¨e
bathing trunks die Badehose, –n
bathroom das Badezimmer
be sein
beautiful schön
because denn (coord. conj.); weil (sub. conj.)
become werden
before vor
begin beginnen
believe glauben; **I ~ so** ich glaube ja; **that's hard to ~** das ist schwer zu glauben
belt der Gürtel, –
besides außer
better besser
between zwischen
beverage das Getränk, –e
bicycle das Fahrrad, ¨er; das Rad

big groß
bill die Rechnung, –en
biology die Biologie (die Bio)
birthday der Geburtstag, –e; **it's my ~** ich habe Geburtstag; **happy ~!** herzlichen Glückwunsch zum Geburtstag!
black schwarz
blouse die Bluse, –n
blue blau
book das Buch, ¨er; **~ bag** die Mappe, –n
bored: I am ~ ich habe Langeweile
boredom die Langeweile
boring langwilig; **a ~ person** eine lahme Ente
both beide
bottle die Flasche, –n
box office die Kasse
boy der Junge, –n, –n; **oh, ~!** Mensch!
brake die Bremse, –n
bread das Brot, –e
break die Pause, –n; **to ~** kaputt·machen
breakfast das Frühstück; **for ~** zum Frühstück; **to have ~** frühstücken
briefcase die Mappe, –n
bring bringen; **to ~ along** mit·bringen
broken kaputt
brother der Bruder, ¨; **~!** Mensch!
brown braun; **a ~ coat** ein Mantel in Braun
bus der Bus, –se
businessman der Geschäftsmann, ¨er (also pl. Geschäftsleute)

businesswoman die Geschäftsfrau, –en

but aber; sondern; **not only . . . ~ also** nicht nur . . . sondern auch

butcher der Metzger, –/die Metzgerin, –nen

butter die Butter

buy kaufen; **it's a good ~** es ist preiswert

by bei; **to go ~ bus** mit dem Bus fahren

café das Café, –s

cake der Kuchen, –; **layer ~** die Torte, –n

call an·rufen; nennen

camping das Camping; **to go ~** zelten, campen

can können

capital die Hauptstadt, ⁓e

car das Auto, –s; der Wagen, –

card die Karte, –n, **to play ~s** Karten spielen

carrot die Karotte, –n

carry tragen; **to ~ out** raus·tragen

cassette die Kassette, –n; **~ recorder** der Kassettenrecorder, –

castle das Schloß, –sses, ⁓sser

cat die Katze, –n

centimeter der Zentimeter, –

ceramics die Keramik

certain(ly) bestimmt; sicher; bitte sehr

cheap billig; **dirt– ~** spottbillig

check: the ~ please! zahlen bitte!

cheese der Käse

chemistry die Chemie; **~ homework** die Chemieaufgabe

chic schick

chicken das Huhn, ⁓er

child das Kind, –er

chocolate die Schokolade, –n

church die Kirche, –n

city die Stadt, ⁓e; **~ map** der Stadtplan, ⁓e

clarinet die Klarinette, –n

class die Klasse, –n; **~ trip** die Klassenfahrt, –en; **~room** das Klassenzimmer, –

classical klassisch

clean putzen, auf·räumen

clear ab·räumen

clock die Uhr, –en

close zu·machen; **~d** zu

clothes die Sachen (pl.), die Kleider (pl.)

cloudy bewölkt

club der Club, –s

coaster der Bierdeckel, –

coat der Mantel, ⁓

coffee der Kaffee; **~ shop** das Café, –s; **to make ~** Kaffee kochen; **to invite for ~ and cake** zum Kaffee einladen; **to have ~** Kaffee trinken

cola drink die (also das) Cola

cold kalt

collect sammeln

color die Farbe, –n; **what ~ is . . .** welche Farbe hat . . .

come kommen; **to ~ along** mit·kommen; **that comes to 10 marks** das macht zusammen 10 Mark

compact disc die Compact Disc, –s

compact-disc player der CD-Spieler, –

complete(ly) ganz

complicated kompliziert

concert das Konzert, –e

content zufrieden

cook kochen

cool kühl

corner die Ecke, –n

correct richtig; **to be ~** stimmen

cost kosten

course der Kurs, –e; **of ~!** klar! natürlich! doch!

crazy: you're ~! du spinnst!

cross sauer

cup die Tasse, –n

customer der Kunde, –n, –n/die Kundin, –nen

dance tanzen

dangerous unsicher, gefährlich

day der Tag, –e; **in the ~ time** am Tag

dear (in letters) lieber/liebe

degree der Grad

department store das Kaufhaus, ⁓er

describe beschreiben

dessert der Nachtisch

different anders

difficult schwer

diligent fleißig

dirt: ~-cheap spottbillig

disco die Disco

discussion die Diskussion, –en

dishes (pl.) das Geschirr; **to wash ~** Geschirr spülen

divided: ~ by durch

do machen, tun; **that won't ~** das geht nicht

doctor der Arzt, ⁓e/die Ärztin, –nen

dog der Hund, –e

door die Tür, –en

dream der Traum, ⁓e

dress das Kleid, –er

drink trinken

drive fahren

driving: ~ instructor der Fahrlehrer, –/die Fahrlehrerin, –nen; **~ school** die Fahrschule; –n; **~ lesson** die Fahrstunde, –n; **~ instruction** der Fahrunterricht

drums das Schlagzeug, –e

dry trocken; **to ~** ab·trocknen

dumb doof, dumm

dust der Staub; **to ~** ab·stauben

each jeder

early früh

east der Osten; **~ (of)** östlich (von)

eastern östlich
easy leicht
eat essen
egg das Ei, –er
eight acht
eighteen achtzehn
eighty achtzig
electrician der Elektriker, –/die Elektrikerin, –nen
else: what ~? was sonst?; **anything ~?** sonst noch was?
eraser der Radiergummi, –s
especially besonders
Europe (das) Europa
even (more) noch . . .
evening der Abend, –e; **good ~!** guten Abend!; **in the ~** abends; **this ~** heute abend
everyone alle, jeder
everything alles
exactly gerade
exam die Prüfung, –en
excellent ausgezeichnet, prima
except außer
excuse: ~ me Entschuldigung!
exhausted kaputt
expensive teuer
expressway die Autobahn, –en

fail durch·fallen
fall fallen
family die Familie, –n
fantastic toll
far weit
fast schnell
fat dick
father der Vater, ¨
favorite: ~ subject das Lieblingsfach, ¨er; **~ group** die Lieblingsgruppe, –n
feed füttern
feel: to ~ like doing something Lust haben; **he doesn't ~ like doing anything** er hat zu nichts Lust
few: a ~ ein paar
fifteen fünfzehn
film der Film, –e
finally endlich

find finden
fine gut
finished fertig
first erst
fish der Fisch, –e
fit passen
flute die Flöte, –n
fly fliegen
foot der Fuß, ¨e; **on ~** zu Fuß
for für; seit; denn
forget vergessen
fountain der Brunnen, –
four vier
frankfurter das Würstchen, –
free frei
freeze frieren
French fries die Pommes frites (pl.)
fresh frisch
Friday der Freitag
friend der Freund, –e/die Freundin, –nen
from aus; von
fruit das Obst
fun: that's ~ das macht Spaß
furniture die Möbel (pl.)
further weiter

game das Spiel, –e
garage die Garage, –n
garbage der Müll; **~ pail** der Mülleimer, –
gardening die Gartenarbeit
gas station die Tankstelle, –n
gasoline das Benzin
gate das Tor, –e
gentleman der Herr, –n, –en
genuine echt
geography die Erdkunde, die Geographie
get bekommen; **I'll ~ the day off** ich bekomme frei; **to ~ up** auf·stehen
girl das Mädchen, –
give geben
glad froh
gladly gern
glass das Glas, ¨er
glove der Handschuh, –e

go gehen; fahren
good gut; **~ night** gute Nacht; **~ evening** guten Abend; **~ morning** guten Morgen; **~ -by** auf Wiedersehen, tschüß
gram das Gramm
grandparents die Großeltern (pl.)
gray grau
great prima, toll, super
green grün
groceries die Lebensmittel (pl.)
group die Gruppe, –n
guest der Gast, ¨e
guitar die Gitarre, –n

hairdresser der Friseur, –e/die Friseurin, –nen
half halb; **at ~ past eight** um halb neun
ham der Schinken; **~ sandwich** das Schinkenbrot
handle an·fassen
happy glücklich, froh
have haben; **to ~ to** müssen
he er
healthy gesund
hear hören
heavy schwer
hello guten Tag; Grüß Gott
help helfen
her ihr (adj.); sie (pron.)
here da; hier
hi! Tag!
high hoch; **~er** höher
hike wandern
him ihn
his sein
history die Geschichte
hobby das Hobby, –s
hold halten
home: (at) ~ zu Hause; **~ (direction)** nach Hause
homework die Hausaufgaben (pl.)
honest! Ehrenwort!
hope: I ~, let's ~ hoffentlich
horrible scheußlich

hot heiß
hour die Stunde, –n
house das Haus, ⸚er
how wie; ~ are you? wie
geht's?; ~ long? wie lange?;
~ old are you?; wie alt bist
du?
however aber
hunger der Hunger
hungry: to be ~ Hunger haben
husband der Mann, ⸚er

I ich
ice cream das Eis
ice skate der Schlittschuh, –e;
to ~ Schlittschuh laufen
idea: to have no ~ keine Ahnung haben
if ob (sub. conj.); wenn
in(to) in; in what worin
indeed wohl
independent unabhängig
instruction der Unterricht
intend to wollen
interesting interessant
intermission die Pause, –n
intersection die Kreuzung, –en
invite ein·laden
is: he/she is er/sie ist
it es/er/sie
its ihr, sein

jacket die Jacke, –n
jam die Marmelade
jealous eifersüchtig
jeans die Jeans (pl.)
jog joggen
jogging das Jogging
juice der Saft, ⸚e
just gerade, nur

kilogram das Kilo(gramm)
kilometer der Kilometer, –
know kennen; wissen

lady die Dame, –n
lake der See, –n; to the ~ an
den See
last letzt

late spät; too ~ zu spät
later später; see you ~ bis
später
laundry die Wäsche; to do the
~ (die) Wäsche waschen
lazy faul
learn lernen
least: at ~ wenigstens
leave ab·fahren
left links; to the ~ links
leisure time die Freizeit
less weniger
lesson die Aufgabe, –n
letter der Brief, –e
lettuce der Salat, –e
license: driver's ~ der Führerschein
light leicht; das Licht, –er
like gern haben, mögen; I ~ to
play tennis ich spiele gern
Tennis; how do you ~ . . .?
wie findest du . . .?; what
would you ~? was darf es
sein?; I would ~ . . . ich
hätte gern . . .; he would ~
(to) er möchte . . .
listen: to ~ to music Musik
hören
liter der Liter, –; 10 kilometers to the ~ 10 Liter auf
100 Kilometer
live wohnen
long lang; how ~? wie lange?;
so ~! tschüß!
look schauen, sehen; to ~ for
suchen
lose verlieren
lot viel; there's a ~ going on
es ist viel los
luck: what bad ~ so ein Pech
lucky: to be ~ Schwein haben
lunch das Mittagessen; to
have ~ zu Mittag essen; for
~ zum Mittagessen; at ~
time mittags

make machen
man der Mann, ⸚er

many viele; ~ a manch (–er,
–es, –e); how ~ wie viele
market der Markt, ⸚e; at the
~ auf dem Markt
match passen
mathematics die Mathematik;
math die Mathe
matter: what's the ~? was ist
los?
may dürfen
maybe vielleicht
me mich
meal das Essen; enjoy your ~
guten Appetit!
mean meinen; what do you
~? was heißt das?
meat das Fleisch
menu die Speisekarte, –n
meter der Meter, –
milk die Milch
mineral water das Mineralwasser
minus weniger
minute die Minute, –n
Miss Fräulein
model airplane das Flugzeugmodell, –e
moment: just a ~ Moment
mal, einen Moment
Monday der Montag
money das Geld
month der Monat, –e
moped das Mofa, –s
more mehr
morning der Morgen, –; good
~! guten Morgen!; this ~
heute morgen; in the ~
morgens
mother die Mutter, ⸚
motorcycle das Motorrad, ⸚er
movie theater das Kino, –s
movie ticket die Kinokarte, –n
mountain-climbing: to go ~
bergsteigen gehen
Mr. Herr
Mrs. (or Ms.) Frau
much viel; thank you very ~
vielen Dank; how ~ wieviel;
so ~ soviel

museum das Museum (*pl.* Museen)

music die Musik

musical musikalisch; ~ **instrument** das Musikinstrument

must müssen

my mein

name der Name (*acc. & dat.* –n), –n; **my ~ is . . .** ich heiße . . .; **what's the ~ of . . . ?** wie heißt . . . ?; **what's your ~?**; wie heißt du?; **to ~** nennen

named: to be ~ heißen

namely nämlich

naturally natürlich

near bei

necktie die Krawatte, –n

need brauchen

never nie

new neu

next nächst; **~ time** nächstes Mal

nice nett, schön

night die Nacht, ̈e; **good ~!** gute Nacht!; **last ~** gestern abend

no nein; **~ one** niemand

nonsense! Quatsch!, Unsinn!

noon der Mittag; **at ~** mittags

north der Norden; **~ (of)** nördlich (von)

northern nördlich

not nicht; **~ at all** gar nicht; **~ a, ~ any** kein; **~ much** nicht viel; **~ yet** noch nicht

notebook das Heft, –e

nothing nichts; **~ left** nichts mehr

now jetzt, nun

number die Zahl, –en

occur: it just occurs to me da fällt mir gerade ein

o'clock: it's (one) ~ es ist (ein) Uhr

often oft

oh ach; **~, I see!** ach so!

OK ganz gut; es geht; na gut

old alt

old-fashioned altmodisch

on auf; an; **~ Saturday** am Samstag

one eins; man (*indef. pron.*)

oneself selbst

only nur; erst

open auf·machen

or oder (*coord. conj.*)

orange die Orange, –n

order bestellen

our unser

out: ~ of aus

pack ein·packen, packen

pail der Eimer, –

pants die Hose, –n

paper das Papier, –e

parents die Eltern (*pl.*)

park der Park, –s

party die Party, –s, die Fete, –n; **to go to a ~** auf eine Party gehen

pass: to ~ the test die Prüfung bestehen

pay bezahlen, zahlen

pea die Erbse, –n

pedestrian zone die Fußgängerzone, –n

pen: ballpoint ~ der Kugelschreiber, –; der Kuli, –s; **~ pal** der Brieffreund, –e/die Brieffreundin, –nen

pencil der Bleistift, –e

per pro

performance die Vorstellung, –en

permitted: to be ~ dürfen

pharmacist der Apotheker, –/die Apothekerin, –nen

photograph fotografieren

physics die Physik

piano das Klavier, –e

pick up ab·holen

picnic das Picknick, –s

picture das Bild, –er

piece das Stück, –e

plan der Plan, ̈e; **to ~** vor·haben

play spielen; **to play music** Musik machen

please bitte, bitte schön

pork chop das Schweinskotelett, –s

post office die Post

postcard: picture ~ die Ansichtskarte, –n

poster das (*also* der) Poster, –

potato die Kartoffel, –n; **mashed potatoes** das Kartoffelpüree; **~ chip** der Kartoffelchip, –s

pound das Pfund

practical praktisch

prefer lieber haben; **I ~ to eat . . .** ich esse lieber . . .

present das Geschenk, –e; **birthday ~** das Geburtstagsgeschenk

pretty hübsch

probably wahrscheinlich; wohl

pub frequented by students das Studentenlokal, –e

pudding der Pudding

pullover der Pulli, –s

quarter das Viertel; **~ to five** Viertel vor fünf; **~ after five** Viertel nach fünf

question die Frage, –n

quite ziemlich, ganz schön (*colloq.*)

radio das Radio, –s; **"ham" ~ operator** der Radioamateur, –e

railway die Bahn, –en

rain der Regen; **to ~** regnen

read lesen

ready fertig

really eigentlich; wirklich; echt

reasonably: ~ priced preiswert

recess die Pause, –n

recommend empfehlen

record die Schallplatte, –n, die Platte, –n; **~ player** der Plattenspieler, –
red rot
repair reparieren
report der Bericht, –e
restaurant das Restaurant, –s; das Lokal, –e
ride fahren; **to ~ horseback** reiten
right richtig; rechts; **to the ~** rechts; **to be ~** recht haben; **that's ~** das stimmt; **isn't that ~?** oder? *(at end of sentence)*
rinse spülen
roast: ~ beef, pot ~ der Rindsbraten
rock (music) (der) Rock
roll das Brötchen, –
room das Zimmer, –
run laufen

sail segeln
salad der Salat, –e
salesperson der Verkäufer, – /die Verkäuferin, –nen
sarcastic sarkastisch
satisfied zufrieden
Saturday der Samstag; **on ~** am Samstag
sausage die Wurst, ¨e
say sagen
schedule der Stundenplan, ¨e; der Plan, ¨e
school die Schule, –n
season die Jahreszeit, –en
see sehen
seem scheinen; **so it seems** so scheint's
serious: you can't be ~! das ist doch nicht dein Ernst!
set: to ~ the table den Tisch decken
she sie
shine scheinen
ship das Schiff, –e
shirt das Hemd, –en
shoe der Schuh, –e

shop das Geschäft, –e; **to ~** ein·kaufen
shopping: ~ bag die Einkaufstasche; **to go ~** einkaufen gehen
short klein; kurz
should sollen
sick krank
sign das Schild, –er
signal: traffic ~ die Ampel, –n
simple einfach
simply einfach
since seit
sincerely herzliche Grüße
sing singen
sister die Schwester, –n
situated: to be ~ liegen
size die Größe, –n; **what ~ do you wear?** welche Größe trägst du/tragen Sie?
ski der Ski, –er *(also* Schi*)*; **to ~** Ski laufen
skirt der Rock, ¨e
sleep schlafen
slim schlank
slippery glatt
slow(ly) langsam
small klein
snow der Schnee; **to ~** schneien
so so; **~ what?** na und?; **isn't that ~?** nicht? nicht wahr?
soccer der Fußball; **~ game** das Fußballspiel, –e
sock die Socke, –n
soft drink die Limo(nade)
sold: ~ out ausverkauft
some mancher; ein paar
someone jemand
something etwas
sometimes manchmal
soon bald
sorry: I'm ~ es tut mir leid; Entschuldigung!
soup die Suppe, –n
sour sauer
south der Süden; **~ (of)** südlich (von)
southern südlich

speak sprechen
spinach der Spinat
sports der Sport; **to be active in ~** Sport treiben
spring der Frühling
square der Platz, ¨e
stamp die Briefmarke, –n
stand stehen
start beginnen; los·gehen; **when does it ~?** wann geht's los?
stay bleiben
stereo system die Stereoanlage, –n
still noch
store das Geschäft, –e; **department ~** das Kaufhaus, ¨er
story die Geschichte, –n
strawberry die Erdbeere, –n
street die Straße, –n; **~ car** die Straßenbahn, –en
stroll der Spaziergang, ¨e; to ~ bummeln, spazieren
student der Schüler, –/die Schülerin, –nen *(in school);* der Student, –en/die Studentin, –nen *(in university);* **~ pub** das Studentenlokal, –e
study lernen
stupid doof, dumm
stylish modisch
subject das Fach, ¨er
subway die U-Bahn, –en
such solcher
suit der Anzug, ¨e *(for men);* das Kostüm, –e *(for women)*
summer der Sommer
sun die Sonne
Sunday der Sonntag
supermarket der Supermarkt, ¨e
supper das Abendessen; **to have ~** zu Abend essen; **for ~** zum Abendessen
supposed: to be ~ to sollen
sure sicher; **~!** klar!; **~, I do!** ja, und wie!
sweater der Pullover, –
swim schwimmen
switch on an·machen

table   der Tisch, –e
take   nehmen; **to ~ along**
   mit·nehmen
take off   los·gehen
tall   groß
taste (good)   schmecken
tea   der Tee
teacher   der Lehrer, –/die Lehrerin, –nen
telephone   an·rufen
television   der Fernseher, –; **to**
   watch ~   fern·sehen
tell   erzählen; sagen; **~ me**   sag
   mal
temperature   die Temperatur,
   –en
tender   zart
tennis   das Tennis
terrible, terribly   furchtbar
terrific!   klasse!
than   als
thanks   danke; **many ~**   vielen
   Dank!
that   das; daß *(sub. conj.)*
the   der, das, die
theater   das Theater, –; **movie**
   ~   das Kino, –s
their   ihr
them   sie
then   da, dann
there   da, dort; **~ is, ~ are**   es
   gibt
thermometer   das Thermometer, –
they   sie
thick   dick
thing   die Sache, –n
think   denken, meinen
thin   dünn, schlank
thirst   der Durst
thirsty: to be ~   Durst haben
this   dieser
through   durch
Thursday   der Donnerstag
ticket   die Karte, –n
tied   unentschieden
time   das Mal; die Zeit, –en;
   next ~   nächstes Mal;
   what ~ is it?   wie spät ist es?

wieviel Uhr ist es?; **at what**
   ~?   um wieviel Uhr?
times   mal
tinker   basteln
tired   müde
to   an; auf; nach; zu
toboggan   rodeln
today   heute
together   zusammen
tomato   die Tomate, –n
tomorrow   morgen; **~ evening**
   morgen abend; **the day after**
   ~   übermorgen
tonight   heute abend
too   auch; zu
tour   die Tour, –en
tourist   der Tourist, –en, –en/die
   Touristin, –nen
town   die Stadt, ⸚e; **~ hall**   das
   Rathaus, ⸚er
train   der Zug, ⸚e; **~ station**
   der Bahnhof, ⸚e; **~ ticket**   die
   Fahrkarte, –n; **to ~**   trainieren
true   richtig; **that's ~**   das
   stimmt
try   versuchen
Tuesday   der Dienstag
tuna   der Thunfisch, –e
turn   ab·biegen; **to ~ off**
   aus·machen
turntable   der Plattenspieler, –

ugly   häßlich
umbrella   der Regenschirm, –e
understand   verstehen
unfortunately   leider
unhappy   unglücklich
university   die Universität, –en
until   bis
up   auf; **~ to**   bis zu
us   uns
usually   gewöhnlich

vacuum   Staub saugen
valuable   wertvoll
vegetable   das Gemüse, –
very   sehr
violin   die Geige, –n

visit   der Besuch, –e; **to ~**
   besuchen
volleyball   der Volleyball, ⸚e

waiter   der Ober, –
walk   der Spaziergang, ⸚e; **to ~**
   spazieren, laufen, gehen; **to go**
   for a ~   spazieren, einen
   Spaziergang machen, spazieren
   gehen, bummeln
want   wollen
warm   warm
was   war *(past tense of sein)*
wash   waschen; **to ~ dishes**
   (Geschirr) spülen
watch   die Uhr, –en; **to ~**
   sehen; **to ~ TV**   fern·sehen
water   das Wasser
we   wir
wear   tragen
weather   das Wetter; **~ report**
   der Wetterbericht, –e
Wednesday   der Mittwoch
week   die Woche, –n; **~ end**
   das Wochenende, –n
welcome: you're ~   bitte, bitte
   schön
well   *(interj.)* also, na; *(adj.)* gut;
   gesund; *(adv.)* gut; **pretty ~**
   ganz gut
west   der Westen; **~ (of)**
   westlich (von)
western   westlich
wet   naß
what   was; **~ kind of (a)**   was
   für (ein); **~'s the matter?**
   was ist los?
when   wann; wenn; als
where   wo; **~ (to)**   wohin
whether   ob *(sub. conj.)*
which   welcher
white   weiß
who   wer
whom   wen, wem
why   warum
wife   die Frau, –en
win   gewinnen; **by how much**
   did they ~?   wie hoch haben
   sie gewonnen?

wind der Wind; **to go ~ surfing** windsurfen

window das Fenster, –

windy windig

winter der Winter

wish der Wunsch, ⁼e, **to ~** wollen

with mit; bei

without ohne

woman die Frau, –en; **young ~** das Fräulein

work die Arbeit, –en; **to ~** arbeiten, zur Arbeit; **to do ~** Arbeit machen; **to ~ at a hobby** basteln; **~ schedule** der Arbeitsplan, ⁼e

worker der Arbeiter, –/die Arbeiterin, –nen

wow! Mensch!

write schreiben; **to ~ to** schreiben an (+ *acc.*)

wrong falsch

year das Jahr, –e; **time of ~** die Jahreszeit, –en

yellow gelb

yes ja; doch

yesterday gestern

yet noch; **not ~** noch nicht

you du; ihr; Sie

young jung

your dein; euer; Ihr

youth center das Jugendzentrum

Useful Addresses

The following organizations may be of assistance in obtaining cultural information and materials for classroom use.

Austria

Austrian Institute
11 East 52nd Street
New York, NY 10022
(212) 759-5165

Austrian Press and Information
Service
31 East 69th Street
New York, NY 10021
(212) 737-6400 or 288-1727

Austrian National Tourist Office
500 Fifth Avenue, 20th Floor
New York, NY 10110
(800) 223-0284 or (212) 944-6880

Federal Republic of Germany

German Information Center
950 Third Avenue
New York, NY 10022
(212) 888-9840

German National Tourist Office
747 Third Avenue, 33rd Floor
New York, NY 10017
(212) 308-3300
and
444 South Flower Street, Suite 2230
Los Angeles, CA 90071
(213) 688-7332

Embassies of the Federal Republic of Germany

4645 Reservoir Road, N.W.
Washington, DC 20007
(202) 298-4000

P.O. Box 379, Postal Station A
Ottawa, Ontario, Canada K1N 8V4
(613) 232-1101

Consulates of the Federal Republic of Germany

Local consulates often have a cultural attaché who can provide information and publications on issues dealing with the Federal Republic; many consulates also maintain a free film and videotape lending library. Check with the consulate in your region to see which services and materials are available. In the United States, there are consulates in: Atlanta, GA; Boston, MA; Chicago, IL; Detroit, MI; Houston, TX; Los Angeles, CA; Miami, FL; New York, NY; San Francisco, CA; Seattle, WA.
In Canada: Edmonton, Alberta; Montréal, Québec; Toronto, Ontario; Vancouver, British Columbia.

Goethe Institutes

While the primary mission of the Goethe Institutes is to foster the study of the German language through course offerings and cultural events, the Institutes also have excellent lending libraries and instructors familiar with the German resources in the area. They are located in many major North American cities, as well as throughout West Germany and many major cities throughout the world.
In the United States: Ann Arbor, MI; Atlanta, GA; Beverly Hills, CA; Boston, MA; Chicago, IL; Cincinnati, OH; Houston, TX; New York, NY; San Francisco, CA;

Seattle, WA; St. Louis, MO.
In Canada: Montréal, Québec; Toronto, Ontario; Vancouver, British Columbia.

German Democratic Republic

Embassy of the German Democratic Republic
Office of the Cultural Attaché
1717 Massachusetts Avenue
Washington, DC 20036
(202) 232-3134

The Cultural Attaché of the GDR can arrange for free subscriptions to such magazines as *neue Heimat, Prisma, DDR-Sport,* and *Außenpolitische Korrespondenz,* and will send photographs, *Landeskunde* materials, and informational booklets from the series *Aus erster Hand* upon request.

Switzerland and Liechtenstein

Swiss National Tourist Office
608 Fifth Avenue
New York, NY 10020
(212) 757-5944

P.O. Box 215
Commerce Court
Toronto, Ontario, Canada M5L lE8
(416) 868-0584

The Swiss National Tourist Office represents both Switzerland and Liechtenstein.

Luxembourg

Luxembourg National Tourist Board
801 2nd Avenue
New York, NY 10017
(212) 370-9850

Index

aber (flavoring word) 23
accusative case 134–135
  definite article 127–128, 134
  dieser-words 284–286, 292
  direct object 127, 133
  ein and **kein** 128–129, 134
  personal pronouns 234–237, 240
  possessive adjectives 130–131, 135
  prepositions with 263–265, 268
  special **der**-nouns 262–263, 267
  time expressions 286–287, 292
  wer 233, 239
adjectives 121–122
  comparative with **als** 316
  comparative with **so . . . wie** 316
  comparison of equality 308
  comparison of inequality 308–310
  comparison of irregular forms 316
  comparison of regular forms 315–316
  comparison of umlaut forms 316
  descriptive 11–12
  possessive
    accusative case 130–131, 135
    dative case 337, 340
    nominative case 72–76, 79
adverbs
  comparative with **als** 316
  comparative with **so . . . wie** 316
  comparison of equality 308
  comparison of inequality 308–310
  comparison of irregular forms 316
  comparison of regular forms 315–316
  comparison of umlaut forms 316
alphabet 122
arithmetic problems 26
audio-visual equipment 177

capitalization
  du, dein/ihr, euer in letters 79
  nouns 18
chores 203
classroom objects 121
clauses
  dependent, word order in 317–318
  independent 293
clock time 124–127, 132–133
clothing 90
cognates x–xi
colors 94
commands 178, 185
  flavoring word **mal** in 179
comparison of adjectives and adverbs 308–311, 315–316
  of equality 308
  of inequality 308–310
  irregular 310, 316
conjunctions
  coordinating (**aber, denn, oder, sondern, und**) 288–291, 293–294
  subordinating (**daß, ob**) 312, 317
contractions
  accusative prepositional 265–266, 268
  dative prepositional 362–363, 365
conversational past
  with auxiliary **haben** 206–211, 213
  with auxiliary **sein** 259–261, 266–267
  of inseparable-prefix verbs 237–239, 240
  past participles 212–213, 214
  with separable-prefix verbs 212, 214
  of **werden** 312, 317
coordinating conjunctions (**aber, denn, oder, sondern, und**) 288–291, 293–294

currency 111

dative case
  definite articles and nouns 335–336, 340–341
  dieser-words 336–337
  ein-words 337–338
  indefinite articles 337–338
  prepositional contractions 362–363, 365
  prepositions with 355–361, 365
  special **der**-nouns 338, 341
  of **wer** 339, 341
days of the week 115
definite articles
  accusative case 127–128, 134
  dative case 335–336, 340–341
  plural **die** 99, 104
  as pronouns 131–132, 135–139
  singular **der, das, die** 97–98, 104
demonstrative pronouns 131
denn (flavoring word) 5
dependent clauses, word order in 317–318
dieser-words
  accusative case 284–286, 292
  dative case 336–337
  nominative case 284–286, 292
direct objects 127, 133
doch
  flavoring word 179
  as positive response 202–204

ein
  accusative case 128–129, 134
  dative case 337, 340
  nominative case 102, 107–108
  omission with nouns of profession 64
ein-words
  accusative case 130, 135
  dative case 337–338
  nominative case 72–75, 79
ess-tset 19

Art Credits

Illustrations

Penny Carter: p. 353; Chris L. Demarest: pp. x, xi, 13, 28, 46, 69, 95, 123, 150, 180, 206, 230, 259, 283, 306, 334 and 355; Anna Vojtech: pp. 6, 26, 67, 97, 121, 129, 153, 166, 177, 193, 201, 243, 255, 276, 280, 309, 343 and 366; Linda Wielblad: pp. 9, 11, 19, 39, 45, 50, 64, 80, 94, 109, 121 (spot art), 124, 125, 126, 136, 203, 215, 226, 270, 302, 304, 305 and 332; Map by James Loates: p. 349; Maps by Sanderson Associates: p. xiii, xiv and xv.

Photographs

Dennis Barnes: p. 42 bottom right; Fredrik D. Bodin: pp. 49, 76, 289, 322; David Brownell: p. 229; Stuart Cohen: pp. 111, 257, 351 right; Paul Conklin: p. 91; Peter Dreyer: pp. 254, 344; Focus On Sports: pp. 55, 228, 238, 244; Tony Freeman: pp. 43, 99, 189, 198, 329; Kevin Galvin: pp. 2, 5, 85 top left, 88, 142, 146, 174, 272, 292 bottom, 293 lower left and lower right, 300, 331; Jonathan George: p. 268; Beryl Goldberg: pp. 29, 40, 98, 101, 236, 262, 271, 285, 370, 372; J. Douglas Guy: p. 144; Cathy Hawkes: p. 35; Uta Hoffmann: pp. 62, 85 top right, 86–87, 93, 149, 176, 195, 247 bottom left, 250, 290, 357; Image Finders: p. 275 (Boulton-Wilson) The Image Source: p. 63 (Janis Miglavs); The Image Works: pp. xvi inset (Alan Carey), 8 bottom (Keystone), 217 (Alan Carey), 248 inset (Alan Carey) 281 (Alan Carey); Inter Nationes: p. 163 top (IN-Press/Sven Simon), bottom (IN-Press/Presse-Agentur Kövesdi); Bob Joyce: p. 330; Duncan Kretovich: p. 86 inset; Light Images: pp. xvi–1 (Helfand); Magnum Photos: p. 247 top (Erich Hartmann); Gordon Müller-Fuchs: pp. 42 middle left, 140; Landeshauptstadt München Fremdenverkehrsamt: pp. 347, 351 left; Suzanne Murphy: p. 130; Palmer & Brilliant Photography: pp. 84, 204, 252, 265; The Picture Cube: p. 42 top left (Schaefer); Judy Poe: pp. 42 top right, 170, 196; Todd Powell: pp. 31, 36, 42 middle center, 278; San Francisco Photo Network: pp. 209 (Michael Jacobs), 321 (Brent Lindstrom), 361 (Marie Ueda); Eric Shambroom: p. 297; Kathy Squires: pp. 10, 15, 22, 42 bottom right and middle right, 53, 65, 67, 74, 75, 85 bottom, 89, 90, 162, 164, 167, 178, 194, 211, 225, 246, 256, 277, 306, 315, 324, 326, 352, 360; Erika Stone: p. 78; Swiss National Tourist Office: p. 222; Taurus Photos: pp. 156 (Julius Fekete), 218 (Sid & Nancy Nolan); Jim Umhoefer: p. 345; Susan Van Etten: pp. 114, 117, 118; Visum: pp. 216 (Dirk Reinartz) 242 (Michael Wolf), 248–249 (Michael Wolf), 323 (Jo Röttger), 371 right (Rudi Meisel); Manfred Vollmer: pp. 60, 120, 125, 137, 172, 220, 291, 371 left; Ulrike Welsch: pp. 4, 7, 17, 27, 33, 38, 71, 233, 247 bottom right, 303, 363; ZEFA: pp. 8 top (Damm), 25 (Benser KL), 44 (Damm), 126 (Damm); Marcel Zuercher: p. 153.

Realia

Chapter 1: p. 2, Grundig Elektrogeräte GmbH, Fürth/Bayern; p. 20, Harlekin Geschenke, Wiesbaden. *Chapter 2:* p. 23, Verkehrsverein Hameln; p. 24, Horn; p. 37, PANORAMA DDR – Redaktion „Prisma"; *Chapter 3:* p. 41, Offizielles Verkehrsbüro, Bern; p. 47,

Steinway & Sons Pianoforte Fabrikanten, Hamburg; p. 48, Günther Poehling, Hamburger Tennisschule, Hamburg; p. 51, © DSB/Sport-Billy Productions, 1987; p. 57, Musikhaus Bastian, Kehl. *Chapter 4:* p. 72, BURDA / Mein schöner Garten, Offenburg; p. 81, Damensalon Günter Hönes, Münchingen. *Noch einmal:* p. 84 top, SCALA, Frankfurter Societäts Druckerei GmbH, Frankfurt am Main; p. 84 bottom, Goethe-Institut, Munich; p. 85, Goethe-Institut, Boston. *Chapter 5:* p. 100, Karstadt Boutick, Düsseldorf; p. 103, *Brigitte,* Gruner und Jahr AG, Hamburg; p. 105, Pinkstar, Berlin; p. 106, Meloni, Korntal; p. 107, *Brigitte,* Gruner und Jahr AG, Hamburg; p. 112, Bundespressedienst, Vienna. *Chapter 6:* p. 118, Schroedel Verlag, Hannover; p. 122 top, Tourist Information, Bonn; p. 122 bottom far left, Internationales Zelt-Musik-Festival, Freiburg; p. 122 bottom left, Bayerische Motoren Werke AG, Munich; p. 122 bottom right, Deutscher Paket Dienst GmbH, Unna; p. 129, Geha Werke GmbH, Hannover; p. 135, Lexica Verlag, Munich; p. 138, Günther Poehling, Hamburger Tennisschule, Hamburg. *Chapter 7:* p. 145, Internationales Zelt-Musik-Festival, Freiburg; p. 147, Bill Graham Associates, New York; p. 148 top, Der Wolladen am Nollendorfplatz, Berlin; p. 151 top, St. Jacobi-Kirche, Berlin; p. 151 bottom, Bauhaus-archiv museum für gestaltung, Berlin; p. 154, Leipzig-Information, Leipzig; p. 156, Courtesy of Du darfst; p. 158 Graffiti, filmbühne, Berlin. *Chapter 8:* p. 171, Dütt & Datt, Lübeck; p. 175, MetaCafé, Berlin; p. 182, Cadillac Discothek, Munich; p. 184, Radio Lau, Darmstadt; p. 187, Karstadt Boutick, Düsseldorf. *Chapter 9:* p. 204, Oetker Haushaltsgeräte Gesellschaft, Bielefeld; p. 208 top, TCHIBO, Frisch-Röst-Kaffee AG, Werbeabteilung, Hamburg; p. 208 bottom, Heatwave, Hamburg; p. 212, Hertie Wertheim, Steglitz; p. 216, Herder, Freiburg. *Chapter 10:* p. 223, *Kicker Sport Magazin,* Olympia-Verlag, Nürnberg; p. 227, Foto Fleurop, Berlin; p. 238, *Sport Illustrierte,* Deutscher Sportverlag, Cologne; p. 242, Sport Gebhart, Landsberg/Lech. *Noch einmal:* p. 246, *Fußball Magazin,* Olympia-Verlag, Nürnberg; p. 247, *Brigitte,* Gruner und Jahr AG, Hamburg. *Chapter 11:* p. 253, Fritz Bässler Bäckerei, Korntal-Münchingen; p. 260, "Fit mit Freizeit und Sport", Herausgeber: Deutscher Sportbund, Frankfurt/Main; p. 263 top, *Hobby,* Hamburg; p. 263 bottom, nf Music, Musikhandel/Musikschule, Kaufering; p. 267, Metzgerei Altmann, Munich; p. 269, SPAR Handels-Aktien-Gesellschaft, Osterbrooksweg, Schenefeld. *Chapter 12:* p. 279, Courtesy of Herr Altvater, Teekanne GmbH, Düsseldorf; p. 280, Interhotel "Astoria", Leipzig; p. 281, Courtesy of Jazz in Berlin; p. 282, *Musik in Stuttgarter Kirchen,* Kirchenmusikalische Veranstaltung, Stuttgart; p. 292, Eis-Café Cortina, Tübingen; p. 294, Pizzeria Ristorante "La Stanza"; p. 295 top, Courtesy of Bali Fashion; p. 295 bottom, Courtesy of Alno; p. 296, Restaurant Gottfried, Vienna; p. 298, Dallmayr, Munich. *Chapter 13:* p. 301, Rosner & Seidl, Munich; p. 310, Ramee GmbH, Kempton/Allgäu; p. 311, Berliner Verkehrs-Betriebe, Berlin; p. 316, Autohaus Breisgau, Freiburg; p. 317, Courtesy of Milkana; p. 325, *Tagesanzeiger,* Zurich. *Chapter 14:* p. 328, Wössneer Fahrschule, Trossingen; p. 335, A. Timm, N. Rolshoven, Alles für das Fahrrad, Hamburg; p. 340, Technikus GmbH, Berlin. *Chapter 15:* p. 348, Münchner Verkehrsamt, Munich; pp. 349, Fremdenverkehrsamt des Landes-hauptstadt München, Munich; p. 357, Spar Handels-Aktien-Gesellschaft, Osterbrooksweg, Schenefeld; p. 359, Städtische Galerie im Lenbachhaus, Munich; p. 362, Wuerttembergische Metallwarenfabrik AG, Geislingen; p. 364, *Bravo,* Bauer Verlag, Munich; p. 368, Kulturamt der Stadt Wien, Vienna; *Noch einmal:* p. 370, *Brigitte,* Gruner und Jahr AG, Hamburg; p. 372 far left, bottom left, bottom right, SCALA, Frankfurter Societäts Druckerei GmbH, Frankfurt am Main.